THIS EFFING LADY

CORAL BROWNE

'THIS EFFING LADY'

A BIOGRAPHY BY ROSE COLLIS

OBERON BOOKS
LONDON

First published in 2007 by Oberon Books Ltd.

521 Caledonian Road, London N7 9RH

tel 020 7607 3637 / fax 020 7607 3629

info@oberonbooks.com / www.oberonbooks.com

A catalogue record for this book is available from the British Library.

ISBN: 1 84002 764 9 / 978-1-84002-764-8

Printed in Great Britain by Antony Rowe Ltd, Chippenham

For Sally McMahon,
Happy Anniversary
Ten years and counting

And for my friend
Paul Boyd (1947–2006)
'No wire hangers!'

Contents

*Photographs appear on plates between pages 128 and 129
and between pages 192 and 193.*

Acknowledgements

My first thanks go to the organisation which supported this book in its very early stages by giving me the Michael Meyer Award in 2004 – the Society of Authors, and the panel of judges, Simon Brett, Mark Bostridge, Jane Gardam, Paula Johnson and Christina Patterson.

I am most grateful to the following archives for their assistance: Laura Kells and the staff of the Library of Congress Manuscripts Division; Harry Ransom Humanities Center at the University of Austin, Texas; Julia Bell, BFI Special Collections Assistant; Sean Delaney and all the staff of the BFI Library; Kathleen Dickson, Research Viewings, BFI; Janine Stanford, National Theatre Archive; The British Library and The British Newspaper Library, London; Susan Scott, Savoy Archives; Doreen Dean, BAFTA; The Theatre Museum Archive and Library; Jubilee Library and Brighton History Centre, Brighton & Hove; Linda McInnes and Sylvia Carr, The National Library of Australia; State Library, Melbourne, Victoria; the volunteers of the Footscray Historical Society, Melbourne; and my special thanks go to Patricia Convery, Access Co-ordinator of the Performing Arts Museum, Melbourne, for granting me extended access outside normal public opening hours.

Acknowledgement is made of quotations from articles, interviews and reviews in the following publications: *Age (Melbourne)*, *Daily Mail*, *Daily Telegraph*, *Times*, *Guardian*, *Independent*, *Independent on Sunday*, *Spectator*, *Sydney Morning Herald*, *Woman's Journal*, *LA Times*, *New York Times*, *Sunday Telegraph*, *Plays and Players*, *Theatre World*, *Herald (Melbourne)*, *Time*, *Table Talk*, *Christian Science Monitor*, *Evening Standard*, *Dallas Morning News*, *Observer*, *Tatler*, *Illustrated London News*, *Sunday Express*, *Daily Express*, *Daily Mirror*, *News Chronicle*, *Northern Echo*, *Glasgow Herald*, *Birmingham Post*, *People*, *News of the World*, *Financial Times*, *ABC Film Review*, *Morning News*, *New York Post*, *Sun*, *Life*, *Women's Wear Daily*, *Playbill*, *Washington Star*, *Diva*, *Gay News*, *Varsity*, *Varsity Weekly*, *Photoplay Film Monthly*, *Variety*, *Sunday Mirror*, *Evening News*, *Evening Argus*, *Stage & Television Today*, *Punch*, *What's On*, *Daily Express*, *Daily Sketch*, *People*, *Bay Area Reporter*, *St Louis–Globe Democrat*, *Chicago Sun Times*, *San Francisco Chronicle*, *New Yorker*, *USA Weekend*, *Vanity Fair*, *Pink Paper*, *Advocate*, *Brighton & Hove Gazette*, *Pittsburgh Press*, *Radio Times*, *Boston Globe*, *San Francisco Examiner*, *TV Times*, *Parade Magazine*, *Footscray Advertiser*, *Sun-Herald (Sydney)*, *The Bulletin*, *Australian Women's Weekly*, *LA Herald-Examiner*, *The Sketch*.

My thanks go to the following people who have been so generous with their time, contacts, memories, memorabilia, professional assistance, advice, support and encouragement: Jonathan Altaras, Robin Anderson, Dame Eileen Atkins, Sarah Badel, Michael Baldwin, David Ball, Frith Banbury MBE, Terence Bayler, Alan Bennett, Thea Bennett, Gyles Brandreth, Michele Browne, Mark Bunyan, Peter Burton, Jonathan Cecil, Richard Compton-Miller, Ric Cooper, Caroline Cornish-Trestrail, Eleanor Fazan, Pam Gems, Arch Garland of Flyleaf, New York, Garry Gillard and his website, www.garrygillard.net, Liza Goddard, Matthew Guinness, Barrie and Tarne Ingham, Michael Jensen and his website www.coralbrowne.com, Ruth Leon, Bruce Martin, Jill Melford, Gavin Millar, the late Sheridan Morley, Patrick Newley, Eden Phillips, Victoria Price, Peter Quilter, Prunella Scales CBE, Kevin Scullin, Peter Stenson, Alan Strachan, Ned Sherrin CBE, Hugo Vickers, Sarah Vernon and the Rogues & Vagabonds website, www.roguesandvagabonds.co.uk.

I am grateful for the generosity of Caroline Cornish-Trestrail, for copies of her letters from Coral; Kevin Scullin, for copies of Coral's letters to Arnold Weissberger; and Peter Burton, for the excerpt from his unpublished manuscript, *Another Little Drink*. Extract of a private letter by James Agate (© James Agate 1946) is reproduced by permission of PFD (www.pfd.co.uk) on behalf of the Estate of James Agate. My special thanks go to Alan Bennett, for permission to quote from his unpublished letters to Coral and for the copies of Guy Burgess's letters to Coral; to Barry Humphries, for permission to reproduce the full version of his *Chorale For Coral*; to Matthew Guinness, for copies of Coral's letters to his father, Sir Alec Guinness, and for permission to quote from them; and to Victoria Price, for permission to quote from letters by her father, Vincent Price, for her assistance and her honesty.

I gratefully acknowledge The Arts Centre, Performing Arts Collection, Melbourne for permission to reproduce the accredited photographs, and the Picture Collection, National Library of Australia for permission to reproduce the accredited photograph of Gregan McMahon. For permission to use photographs from their private collections, my thanks go to Robin Anderson, Garry Gillard, Bruce Martin, Victoria Price and Kevin Scullin. Unless otherwise stated, all other photographs are from my own collection.

Though every care has been taken, if, through oversight or failure to trace the present owners, copyright material has been included without acknowledgement or permission, apologies are offered to all concerned and appropriate acknowledgment will be included in all future editions.

I would like to thank everyone at Oberon Books for their outstanding work and support: especially Dan Steward, James Stephens, David Miller, Charles Glanville, Will Hammond and Jo Dyer. My biggest thanks go to James Hogan, for his courage and vision in saying 'yes', when bigger but less perfectly-formed publishing companies said 'no'.

On a personal note, my love and thanks go to Vicky Blake, Sally Blann, Sharon Boyd, Mark Bunyan, Peter Burton, Helen Dady, Robert Devcic, Debra Doherty, Rosie Garland, Claire Goodall, Stevie Knowles, Gaby Kompalik, Maureen McEvoy, Margaret Porokhnya, Peter Quilter and Kate Rouse, who have all been especially supportive during the development of this book. To Sally McMahon: *intelligenti pauca*.

Introduction

'Many a woman has a past, but I am told that she has at least a dozen and that they all fit'

Oscar Wilde, *Lady Windermere's Fan*

Coral Browne once told a reporter, 'I disapprove of most biographies. The books are not a success unless you have been to bed with 82 people in the first three chapters.'[1] Sadly, despite my best efforts – and hers – the first three chapters of this biography don't quite meet that target.

But the story of Coral Browne (and the 'Coral Browne stories') contains more than enough to satisfy even the most salacious – and the most studious. It's a heady brew: a stage, film and television career, played out on three continents over six decades, and a private life – including her marriage to the 'King of Horror', Vincent Price – which fuelled enough gossip to last throughout those decades, and endure beyond her death. Elegant, acerbic and memorable, Coral Brown was born in an industrial suburb of Melbourne, and went on to become Coral Browne, a glamorous star who graced the West End and Broadway, Hollywood and television while spawning some of the bawdiest, best-loved and oft-quoted anecdotes in stage and screen history. The *Evening Standard* once described her as 'that Australian man-eating tigress, almost certainly the wittiest woman alive and trenchant with it'.[2] When she played the title role in Somerset Maugham's *Lady Frederick*, *The Tatler* said, 'Coral Browne…is never so good as when playing a quick-witted coquette, gay in her perversity, keenly delighting in her power over men, capable of quixotic generosity, a fury in her nerve-storms and then, by a sudden word of kindness, dissolved in happy tears.'[3] Of all her roles, then, it appeared that there was little to choose between Coral and Lady Frederick Berolles.

She could inspire awe, affection and anger in man, woman, child and beast in equal measure. Her friend, Joan Rivers – no wilting violet herself – recalled the first time she saw Coral: 'I thought, who is that incredibly beautiful woman in the grey Halston dress? Little did I know just what a full package was standing there – so full of glamour, so compassionate, so caring of her friends once she committed to them.'[4] She even kept the likes of 'No More Mr Nice Guy', Alice Cooper, on his toes: 'She is SO sharp! She can cut you to pieces in a second if you step out of line. But if you are her friend, she is so fun and generous and nice.'[5] The author and critic Ruth Leon said, 'She was what one wanted to be when one grew up. You'd look at her and think, "I want to be beautiful like you, I want to be quick and funny like you."'[6]

Coral Browne's career took her from melodrama to drama, to farce to the classics to comedy – and back again. She had what one critic described as 'A talent which combined the impact of an Ethel Merman with the intensity of a Judith Anderson'.[7] Her stage career in Britain spanned more than 40 years, during which she played Shakespeare, Joe Orton, Edward Bond, Jean Anouilh, Maugham, Wilde, Lillian Hellman, Christopher Marlowe and George Bernard Shaw. Sheridan Morley said, 'One tends to underestimate her as an actress because of all the jokes. In fact, if you remember her towards the end of her career, she did everything from Shakespeare to Alan Bennett. She was amazingly versatile. Her quality was for picking up the familiar and making it unfamiliar.'[8] And yet, for all the critical and public acclaim, here's an incongruity: Coral Browne never won a British theatre award. The only British awards she won were for two performances in film and television, both given within the last decade of her life when her theatre career had effectively ended.

Her film and television roles were frustratingly few in number, given her professional longevity. In many of them, the parts were virtually interchangeable: she was usually seen playing a vamp – *Let George Do It*; a sex-starved wife – *Dr Crippen*; a murder victim – *Theater of Blood*; or somebody's mother – *American Dreamer*. As Lady Claire Gurney in *The Ruling Class*, she actually managed to be all four. But, as her friend and co-star Alan Bates observed, 'If we have not had as much of Coral Browne the actress as we could, and would have liked to have had, it is for a very particular reason. She worked at her *life*; her relationships, her friendships and her marriages were *successful*. She was not *only* ambitious as an actress – she was a superb one and did quite enough work to establish that – but living her life was important too. She loved travel, art, fashion, people and was totally curious about the world around her.'[9]

As one who endured a classic love-hate relationship with her mother Vicky – who almost managed to outlive her own daughter – Coral wasn't big on family ties. Instead, she had an enormous appetite and capacity for friendship, and demonstrated unswerving loyalty and generosity. It's regrettable that, since her death, some of those on whom she lavished both – as well as legacies – look back in rancour. Of course, to be a friend of Coral Browne was to be in the firing line as much as her enemies, even if the 'bullets' went behind your back: for instance, she would extend the hand of friendship to Ralph Richardson, Laurence Olivier and Joan Plowright – then turn two fingers up at them by dubbing them, respectively, 'Sir Turnip', 'Lord Puddleduck' and 'Lady Blowright'. She would remonstrate with one friend about another's lack of letters, phone calls or visits. Her cut-glass voice was stained with enough 'strine' which rendered her put-downs, come-ons and *bons mots* deadlier than the average female's. One of her co-stars, Paul Rogers, said that 'to be the subject of one of Coral's stories is to be the subject of a master'.[10] Alan Bates commented, 'I think the reason why we all loved her was perhaps because we all sensed that underneath her wicked sense of humour was this vulnerability, and it made all her outrageousness wonderfully acceptable.'[11] In later life, Coral would rue the fact that theatre and film practitioners spent more time and imagination in repeating or embellishing these 'Coral Browne stories' than they did on creating new parts for her. One of the challenges presented when researching her life has been sorting out the accurate from the apocryphal – including a number of printed 'true stories' which, on investigation, turned out to be nothing of the sort. But they were no great loss, as there were more than enough stories that did check out.

Coral Brown was a frumpy Australian girl who became Coral Browne, one of the most desirable West End stars of the Forties and Fifties, an untrained actress who turned herself into a leading lady. Her zest for work, life and love remained unimpaired through all her decades, even when battling cancer during her final years. She liked life to be 'jolly'. For a woman who became renowned for her style, elegance and beauty, photographs of the young Coral Brown show a surprisingly moon-faced, rather plain girl in need of some cosmetic dentistry. It was an image she worked hard to change, by all and any means available – cosmetic or otherwise. And it worked, to great effect: no one, it seemed, could resist Coral Browne's seductive charms – even so-called 'confirmed homosexuals'. The actor and theatre historian Richard Bebb was spot-on when he observed, 'She was blessed with great good looks rather than outstanding beauty, and it is to be doubted that any other actress in the long history of British theatre had the art of making more of the gifts she was given by God.'[12] As well as refining her looks and image, Coral laboured her lifelong against an underlying, undermining sense of social inferiority, stemming from her suburban, Antipodean origins – and, once she put it behind her, she remained ostensibly derogatory towards her home country. Yet she was, for all the refinement, fundamentally Australian, both in her forthrightness and her sense of fun.

Friends and colleagues have testified to Coral's generosity and kindness – yet in the last years of her life, when she was a good deal more than 'comfortably off', she developed a parsimonious streak in certain circumstances that went well beyond the call of prudence. It's a tiresome trait that often manifests itself in those with considerable wealth.

But then Coral Browne was nothing if not a bundle of contradictions. She was an obsessive weight-watcher who tried out every faddish new diet, but loved to chow down on the richest, finest cuisine. A childless woman, not known for her fondness for children, she was also 'Ma Browne', a caring mother figure to her friends and to some of the younger actresses she worked with; the most Catholic of Catholic converts who could commit most of the seven deadly sins on a daily basis; a much-feared figure who could reduce grown men to mush with a well-placed glance or remark, yet who, for most of her career, suffered nightly terrors before going on stage.

Rupert Everett has observed that, 'A real diva is split between utter conviction of her brilliance and secret crashing panic.'[13] If this is true, then it is doubtful there was a bigger diva than Coral Browne. And, perhaps most puzzling of all, she was a *grande dame* of the theatre who was never made a Dame, nor even granted a lesser honour. British theatre is littered with grand Dames whose careers criss-crossed Coral's: Edith Evans, Sybil Thorndike, Flora Robson, Wendy Hiller, Peggy Ashcroft and Maggie Smith. Even fellow Australian Judith Anderson got in on the act. Why Coral should have missed out remains a mystery.

Tarne Ingham – whose husband Barrie witnessed first-hand some of Coral's most memorable and oft-repeated utterances – made one of the most perceptive observations about her: 'She made life interesting.' Well, she certainly made this author's life interesting: in pursuit of Coral Browne's story, I've travelled close to 40,000 miles, in Northern and Southern hemispheres. Who would have thought she'd play so hard to get? Despite periodic 'clearouts' of personal documents, Coral left a remarkable paper trail behind her in the three continents in which she lived and worked – Australasia, Europe and America. Coral didn't confine her razor-sharp comments and observations to the spoken word. She was a prodigious correspondent, whose letters and cards to friends and colleagues brimmed over with gossip, goodwill (though not to all men) and advice, all peppered with her idiosyncratic punctuation and emphases (preserved here). It's been my supreme good fortune that so many of her letters survived, not only in public archives, but in private collections – much-treasured mementoes of, and testimony to, her wit and wisdom. Through them, Coral's 'voice' comes through loud and clear. My journey began, subconsciously, in 1983 – several years before I even became a journalist, let alone an author. With my very first (rented) colour TV and video, I watched a recording of *An Englishman Abroad* – tape number three in my eventual collection of over 1000. Only then did I realise it was the same 'wonderful actress' from *Auntie Mame* and *The Killing of Sister George*, and that she'd married Vincent Price, her 'murderer' in the gory *Theater of Blood*. Like every other subject I've written about, Coral Browne imbued herself on me over the years, even when I was immersed in some other fascinating life story. Her obscure films would pop up on afternoon television – and be added to the video collection. Theatre programmes and magazines in which she featured would mysteriously find their way into my hands in charity and second-hand bookshops. A tidy number of friends and acquaintances all had 'Coral Browne stories', including personal encounters. And all this, even before the internet marketplace saw a healthy trade in Coral Browne ephemera. She wouldn't go away; she demanded my attention. It would have been churlish to refuse – and I would have missed out on a lot of fun.

Of course, given her views on the subject, it's highly unlikely that any biographer would have met with Coral's approval – and I'm not convinced I would have passed muster. On paper, we don't make a natural 'Collis Browne compound'. I'm sure she would have preferred someone who was, well…a bit *thinner*, and, certainly, more glamorous and fashion-conscious – someone who knew the difference between an outfit by Jean Muir and an outfit by Frank Muir.

But, as someone with such a propensity for truncating the tiresome with a few well-aimed words, I hope she might have appreciated my own efforts, such as when I politely suggested that a crashing bore who had hijacked a dinner party might like to give his arse a rest and try talking out of his mouth for a change. There's obviously a bit of Coral Browne in all us working-class suburban girls.

For this one, it's been a privilege, a challenge and an entertainment getting to know this effing lady. As her friend, the critic Sheridan Morley observed, 'Unlike most actresses, the older she got, the better she got – she grew into her own skin. In a curious way, she was awkward when she first came from Australia – a colt. By the end, she was a great racehorse. She had somehow discovered how to be Coral Browne. And it was as though she had invented this part and learned how to rehearse and rehearse it, and play it – not just on the stage but on screen and in conversation. She had become Coral – and all of us benefited from knowing her.'[14]

Rose Collis
West Sussex, September 2007

Prologue

On the afternoon of 5 September 1991, just before 1pm, a stellar cast from stage and screen gathers in Mayfair, at the Church of the Immaculate Conception, to celebrate one of their own, who died three months ago in Los Angeles. 'Farm Street' is a particularly beautiful Gothic church, with dangerously well-polished pews and a high altar designed by Augustus Pugin – a Protestant-turned-Catholic. Here, the actress Coral Browne – surely one of the most incongruous of Catholic converts – spent many hours in the confessional box. It was not her only place of worship: she often attended services at the rather grander, more theatrical Brompton Oratory. But even that piece of hallowed ground produced what became one of the most infamous 'Coral Browne stories'. Depending on the version, the 'leading man' in this comic scene is sometimes Charles Gray, in others it's Peter Woodthorpe. One morning, after Mass, as Coral was coming down the steps of the Oratory, she was spotted by a queeny actor friend, who started to regale her with a juicy piece of gossip. She stopped him mid-dish and said, 'I don't want to hear such filth, not with me standing here in a state of fucking grace...'

A glance round the 'cast' assembled today reveals a litany of famous names who represent all eras and facets of the life and career of Coral Browne. Reading one of the lessons is her great friend, Sir Alec Guinness, another devout Catholic convert. The bidding prayers will be given by Jean Marsh, the actress and creator of *Upstairs, Downstairs*. Marsh was an extra in one of Coral's films, *The Roman Spring of Mrs Stone*, lurking in the background during a party scene which featured the assorted egos and neuroses of Vivien Leigh, Lotte Lenya and Warren Beatty. In the 1970s, she worked with Coral in two stage productions in Los Angeles, and often stayed in the tiny guest house in the garden of the home Coral shared with her second husband, Vincent Price.

The West End of the elegant era in which Coral made her name is represented by other actresses who did the same: Nora Swinburne, Margaret

Courteney, Elspeth March, Margaret Rawlings and Margaretta Scott. They are joined by Paul Rogers, one of Coral's leading men when she switched to the classics in the 1950s and surprised everyone with her depth and range. Many of Coral's co-stars became her closest friends: they include Adrienne Corri, who met Coral when they performed in *The Rehearsal* on Broadway and Charles Gray, who starred with her in the New York productions of *Troilus and Cressida* and *The Right Honourable Gentleman*. One of Coral's closest female friends, Jill Melford, met her when they appeared together in the London production of this show. Coral was godmother to her son, Alexander Standing, whose godfather, Dirk Bogarde, is accompanying Melford today. They are sitting with the singer Marti Stevens, a friend and neighbour to Coral in London, LA and New York, and Robin Anderson, the interior designer who came into her life when he was commissioned to give her Eaton Place home a controversial make-over in the early 1970s. Dressmaker Jean Muir, whose whiter-than-white home inspired Coral's 'changing rooms' moment, is also present, as is Robert Flemyng, who appeared in *Ardèle*, the play they performed together in 1975, directed by Coral's good friend Frith Banbury. Penelope Wilton and Celia Bannerman have come to remember the actress with whom they appeared in television versions of the plays in which she gave two of her best-loved performances – *Mrs Warren's Profession* and *The Importance of Being Earnest*. It's also fitting that Verity Lambert is here, producer of *Dreamchild* – the film which almost made Coral into a major movie star in her seventies.

Today's memorial service has been arranged by two of her friends. One is the man who, when Coral first met him, had spiky hennaed hair – and so she dubbed Jonathan Altaras her 'punk agent'. Acting as ushers at the service are four extremely good-looking men, all friends of Altaras; none of them knew Coral, but he had thought it appropriate that she should have such attractive attendants. The other is Noel Davis, casting director and close friend of John Schlesinger, and a permanent fixture at the director's London home, where Coral was a regular and much-welcome guest. Schlesinger first saw her on the stage during the Second World War, as Maggie Cutler in *The Man Who Came to Dinner*, the show that established her as a West End star. Davis and Schlesinger didn't have a chance to work with Coral until 1983, when she returned to the BBC after a lengthy absence and made a television drama that won hearts, scooped awards and stayed long in the memory: *An Englishman Abroad*. It's appropriate, then, that Alan Bennett, its writer, is also reading a lesson today, and Alan Bates, her leading man who played exiled spy Guy Burgess, is delivering the eulogy.

But today, Bates is a worried man. First, he's been politely asked by Vincent Price not to tell any 'Coral Browne stories'. Now, he's been told that John Schlesinger is to read out a tribute from Price – *before* he gives his eulogy. Bates thinks, with some justification, that this is going to be a tough act to follow. Then someone reminds him: 'Alan, darling, it's a *eulogy* you're giving – not a performance.'[1]

After the lessons are read, John Schlesinger mounts the podium and reads out a letter from Vincent Price, too ill to make the journey to London to pay tribute to his late wife in person. He says, 'I find I miss every hour of Coral's life – I miss her morning cloudiness, noon mellowness, evening brightness. I miss her in every corner of our house, every crevice of my life. In missing her, I feel I'm missing much of life itself. Over her long illness, as I held her hand or stroked her brow, or just lay still beside her, it was not the affectionate contact we'd known as we wandered down the glamorous paths we'd been privileged to share in our few years together; we were marching towards the end of our time and we both knew it. But, in our looks, our smiles, the private, few, soft-spoken words, there was hope of other places, other ways, perhaps, to meet again.'[2] Later, Jean Marsh writes to Vincent and tells him his letter stunned the congregation into breathless silence.

Now Alan Bates is 'on'. First, he makes a self-deprecating reference to his understandable trepidation: 'I can hear Coral now saying, "So you got stuck with the address, did you, darling, good luck; and don't think I won't be listening...".' He continues: 'We all knew the Coral Browne that she presented to us socially, a great personality, mischievous, alarming, unpredictable, outrageous. It could be said that this "Coral Browne" was one of her great performances, one she certainly relished, and revelled in. She was kind, she was generous, she was loyal, she was extremely sensitive to other people's condition, their bereavements, and their vulnerability. She loved people – she could see right through us all, of course, and we loved her because she dared to say what she saw. Above all, she was brave, fearless in her defence of those she loved and cared for, and totally courageous in the period of her illness. I first knew her as the wife of my first agent, a lovely man, Philip Pearman, who she adored... In later life she met and married Vincent Price; this is one of the great love affairs that we have witnessed, two witty, compassionate, intelligent, handsome people in late life showing us all how to do it, how to share a life. The eloquence with which Vincent expressed his love for Coral in the letter to John we've just heard is unforgettable.'[3] And so, in its own way, is Bates's tribute. It's a fitting way to bring the curtain down on this 'matinee performance'.

Jonathan Altaras and his companion, together with Dirk Bogarde, Jill Melford and Marti Stevens, head off to a grand lunch at the Connaught. As the rest of the cast disperse to their separate destinations, they can now ditch the decorum and start swapping their favourite 'Coral Browne stories'. And, as they clamber into their taxis, one in particular springs to a few minds:

Once, Coral was in Piccadilly, and hailed a taxi. But then, as the cab drew up, a man on the other side of the road, who hadn't seen Coral standing by the kerb, ran up and jumped in.

The driver told him politely, 'I'm sorry, sir – I think you'll find this lady was first.'

'Which lady?,' said the hapless chap.

Coral climbed in, sat down and snapped, '*This* fucking lady!'

'Coral Brown Is An Australian...'

1913–1939

'Australians, unlike Americans, have never felt like they had a Mission or a message for a fallen world...the truth is that Australians tend to be natural pagans...'

Robert Hughes, *Time*, 11 September 2000

In a purely pagan sense, there was no one more naturally Australian than Coral Browne. She once said, 'I don't think I've ever felt anything but Australian.'[1] But, in her private life and public career, her 'mission' was to be, simply, 'Coral Browne' – even if it meant appearing to be anything *but* Australian.

She was hardly alone in this conviction: as Clive James observed, 'Up until the late 1960s, Australia undervalued itself as a country, or anyway its intelligentsia thought it did, giving this alleged Cinderella complex the unlovely journalistic title "the cultural cringe".'[2] The playwright Pam Gems recalled, 'When I wrote *Piaf*...we'd established that Edith slept with anything. And at one point, after she's come back from America, she says, "Oh, there was this chap I fancied on the plane – but he was Australian..." And that always got a big laugh, back in the Seventies. Australians were totally and unacceptably naff. And Coral Browne was one of the people who broke through that, with her wit, her style and her guts.' But Ned Sherrin always felt that, despite those qualities so abundant in Coral, 'Almost to the end, coming from Australia, there was something of that "I'm from Australia, I've got to show them I'm smarter" attitude about her.'[3]

Such social inferiority could only come from one source – home. And Coral Browne was made in Melbourne.

Unlike Sydney, Melbourne had not been a dumping ground for white English convicts: a New South Wales businessman, John Batman, 'bought' land on the western side of Port Philip, Victoria from the local Aboriginal people in 1835. Batman and his colonists founded a village on the banks of the Yarra River and, like all good colonists, quickly displaced the indigenous people who had lived there for thousands of years. In 1851, Melbourne's development accelerated with the discovery of gold in nearby Ballarat – £100 million worth was extracted in the 1850s alone: 'Here everywhere one can see gold, the basis for the licence and luxury of the Melbourne populace.'[4] By 1888, more than a million people had emigrated to Australia, mostly from England, Scotland and Ireland. Victoria's first parliament consisted mostly of land-owners, merchants, lawyers and affluent businessmen and, from its more affluent, less penal origins came the aspirational, more refined qualities of Melbourne's population. In 1880, a visiting British journalist covering the Melbourne International Exhibition, dubbed it 'Marvellous Melbourne'.[5]

But considered somewhat less than 'marvellous' were some of the city's industrial suburbs. Footscray was one of them: in the 1850s, it was a village comprised of no more than 50 dwellings. By the end of the century, an economic boom resulted in it becoming home to a thriving assortment of noisy and smelly industries, including brick-making, quarrying, fat-boiling, meat-canning and candle-making. In 1870, it was noted that, 'There are few suburbs going on faster than Footscray. Property, land, or houses quote 30 per cent advance; tall chimneys keep rising; factory artisans throng the stations and the streets; every place that can by nails, by saw and hammer be tortured into a house is let, and many go to the near city. Here are troops of bullocks, there a mob of sheep, en route for England, passage paid in tin cans, by the first ship… Nor that Footscray air gets purer. Oh no! But sir…that is better, some say, than empty pockets, empty houses, and no employment.'[6] The Maribyrnong (or 'Saltwater River') was essential to Footscray's industries, as the river had the enforced task of carring away all their pollutant by-products. From such a blue-collar neighbourhood came the girl who was Coral Brown – who became the entirely different creature called 'Coral Browne', and turned her collars from blue to mink. And, as far back as she could remember, Footscray's most famous 'by-product' yearned to be carried away: 'It was a bit on the grim side… I remember always wanting to leave – that was the height of my ambition…'[7] She would not, of course, be the first or last famous Australian desperate to broaden her horizons: her friend Patrick White, said, 'I don't think I have learnt to *accept* Australia, but to *endure* it.'[8] Germaine Greer claimed she planned her escape at the age of 12: 'It was like being under a bell jar, with no indication that anything was happening anywhere... I used to stand on the quay and watch all the boats leave for Europe.'[9]

Under the bit of the bell jar that covered Footscray were the Bennetts and the Browns. From Scotland and the North of England they had come, to mine and to build. Subsequent generations would down tools and don suits, to buy and sell, home and away. Depressions came and went, but the Bennetts and the Browns always managed to stay in work. They prospered – not on a grand scale, but on one that was sloping gently upwards. Though the prosperity of Footscray was founded on heavy industry, its citizens still aspired to some of the simple pleasures available to any good English suburban Edwardians. They demanded their own botanical gardens and, to this end, the Footscray Park Beautification Committee, supported by local businesses, was given responsibility for the park's development. Footscray Park opened in 1911 – the second largest botanical garden in Victoria. Many of its plants were native Australian, but it was created the English way: much of the initial landscaping and planting work was carried out by local volunteers, including the local Boy Scouts.

According to Phillip Adams, producer of the ultra-Australian film *The Adventures of Barry McKenzie*, this 'Englishness' permeated and dominated the country well beyond the Edwardian era: 'We were all brought up on a diet of A A Milne...and we thought of ourselves absolutely as part of the great Imperial British adventure – a parallel universe stuck right down the wrong end of the globe.'[10] Until after the Second World War, Australian families celebrated Christmas in traditional English fashion – roast turkey or goose, figgy pudding and all – despite the 90°F-plus summer temperatures. And everywhere, there were, as Barry Humphries recalled, the 'hamlets with evocative names...all with their picturesque Devonshire tearooms in the Tudor style, named Devon Dell, Dew Drop Inn or Clovelly.'[11]

Coral's maternal great-grandfather, Henry Bennett, was a miner who emigrated from York, and became part of Victoria's thriving industrial community with his wife, Christina Patterson, who hailed from Stirling, Scotland. Her paternal great-grandfather, George Brown, came to Australia from Isley, Berkshire in 1857, with his wife, the former Elizabeth Stephenson. Coral's ancestors nurtured large families: the Browns had seven daughters and one son, the Bennetts six sons and four daughters.

Leslie Clarence Brown was born in Kaniva, a small country town near the Victoria border, on 19 March 1890; his father, George, was Kaniva's first station master. On 7 November 1912, Leslie had married Victoria ('Vicky') Elizabeth Bennett, daughter of William and Edith Bennett, born 9 April 1890, in Footscray. Coral said, 'On my mother's side, my grandfather [William Bennett] was a commercial traveller for H V McKay who made farming implements, tractors and things like that. And he travelled a great deal and went to far away places: Africa, and all sorts of places. I used to be brought back little dolls and funnies from my grandfather's trips.'[12]

Leslie and Victoria Brown were rather out of step with their respective families' tradition of prodigious reproduction: their only child, Coral Edith Brown, was born on 23 July 1913, at 36 Gordon Street, Footscray. The baby was named after one of Leslie's sisters and Vicky's mother; she was also known affectionately as 'Coralie' or 'Coralin'.

Coral remembered 'running across to see the [Western] Bulldogs play before the family shifted to Hocking St near the Western Oval.'[13] The Hocking Street house was a one-storey, detached abode (now demolished); and, following another quaint English suburban tradition, the Browns combined their first names and gave the house its own: 'Lesvic'. Leslie worked as a Provedore for the Victorian Railways, in charge of supplying refreshments for stations and trains; in his spare time, he helped run the 5th Footscray Scout Group. 'We lived in Footscray, I think, mainly because my mother's mother lived there,' Coral said. 'Footscray was nearer to Sunshine which was where the big works of H V McKay was.'[14] In 1906, H V McKay had moved his Harvester Works factory from Ballarat to Braybrook Junction near Footscray which, at its peak, employed 3000 workers. The factory and its environs were renamed 'Sunshine', after McKay's world-famous combine harvester. McKay created an entire infrastructure for his workers, including houses, parks, a school and a library. But it wasn't all 'sunshine': in 1907, the low wages and poor working conditions of the McKay employees were used in a test case to determine a national 'basic wage'. The high noise levels in the metal shop made many of the men deaf and there was a running 'joke' on the shop floor that, if you hadn't lost at least a couple of fingertips in the unguarded machines, you weren't considered experienced.

Coral observed, 'Naturally, in those days, the women did nothing. Both my grandmothers were just very good housewives…I don't really think my mother did anything. [After I was born] I think she sort of took to her bed or something...'[15] But this didn't stop Vicky ruling the roost and being the dominant presence in the Brown household: as Patrick White observed, 'Australian women generally appear stronger than their men. Alas, the feminine element in the men is not strong enough to make them more interesting.'[16] Coral once suggested that Vicky might have missed her calling: 'If she had chosen the stage instead of a family when she was young, Ma would have been a success.'[17] But it appeared that she was extremely successful in one thing: criticising her only child. And the cavilling didn't stop with childhood, as Jill Melford confirmed: 'She was evil to Coral, *evil* – vitriolic about everything. She didn't understand why Coral had become an actress – none of that. Nothing was right – nothing that Coral wore was right, no performance she ever gave was right.'[18]

However, despite her mother's constant hectoring, little Coral did not grow into a wilting violet: she told her friend John Schlesinger that, even at the age of four, she was the boss of everyone. Childhood friend Jean Kizer, who lived opposite the Browns, said that Coral 'used to have us dressing up as brides and things'.[19] She had the right physique to be bossy: 'I was very big, buxom, heavier than I am now – oh, a big girl!'[20] Jill Melford said, 'She was much more beautiful when she got older – she was *not* a pretty girl! She had a great moon face.'[21]

The Browns sent their daughter to be educated at Claremont Ladies College, Pickett Street, a private establishment run by the Misses Maude, Joan and Elsie Watkins, where there were never more than a couple of dozen pupils in total (it closed down in 1945). The girls were tutored in music, singing, elocution, maths and French. Anna Littlejohn was one of Coral's teachers: she recalled the seven-year-old sitting 'in the back row with Wilma Gooding and Jean Perkins and Jean Bolwell. I remember [her] as a very clever well-behaved and good looking little girl.'[22] 'I was awfully bad at algebra,' said Coral. 'I thought I was rather good at French until I once tried to say three words to a Frenchman and I think I said, "Avez vous un mouchoir?" in a most ghastly Australian accent. He laughed like mad and I never had the nerve to ever say another word in French.'[23]

In September 1922, Coral made her first stage appearance during a concert staged by Claremont's students for parents and teachers: she played a maid in a sketch called *The Doll's House Party*. Sometimes, the young ladies of

Claremont were taken to the Princess Theatre to see Allan Wilkie's Shakespeare Company – and, occasionally, something more daring and 'contemporary': 'I remember vividly seeing *The Last of Mrs Cheyney* with an actor called George Barrord,' said Coral. 'He inflamed me a lot and I dropped my box of chockies in the second act. The bedroom scene…'[24] Inflammation aside, Wilkie's shows staged Shakespeare in a way that she approved of throughout her career: 'He didn't have very much money – he had a lot of black velvet curtains, very tacky they were. And people came on and did the Shakespeare plays in front of these curtains. And I'm absolutely convinced that the best way to see Shakespeare is that way. You hear the words, the rhythm, the music, you look at the acting.'[25]

Vicky nurtured social aspirations for her daughter: 'I was very keen for Coral to take up elocution,' she claimed later.[26] But sending a little girl for elocution wasn't unusual – after all, it was the English thing to do. Coral was taught to *en-un-ci-ate* by teacher Ruth Conabere, and then Dulcie Bland: 'She entered me for competitions,' said Coral. 'I used to do dreadful things… I think a lot of *Hiawatha* got in there somewhere.'[27]

For all its shortcomings, Longfellow's epic did the trick: in 1927, Coral won her first elocution competition in the under-16 category. A year later, it was reported that 'Misses Coral Brown, Hocking St, and Roma Forge, Paisley St, both pupils of Miss Ruth Conabere were successful in gaining their diploma of ALCM for elocution at the London College of Music examinations.'[28] Coral's winning recitations included passages from *Cymbeline*, 'The Jackdaw', 'On a Spanish Cathedral' – and *Hiawatha's Wooing*. In 1929, she won an under-18 championship held in Ballarat, where her delivery of 'The Dancer' 'gained praiseworthy comment from the judge'.[29]

Her progress was watched by her favourite great-aunt, Christina 'Aunt Teen' Robertson, who began to keep a scrapbook of cuttings about her great-niece's achievements.

But, while the Browns were undoubtedly proud of the way their daughter spoke, they were becoming increasingly concerned by what she was actually saying. 'Her tongue was inclined to run away and she upset people,' said Frith Banbury. 'And even when she was growing up, she told me, her parents were worried about this.'[30] Apparently, the Browns were so concerned by what might be termed Coral's 'anti-social behaviour', they considered seeking medical advice. Years later, the writer Christopher Buckley, who met Coral in her dotage, described how this mixture of earthy vocabulary and perfect pronunciation made her speak like 'a grand duchess who has spent some time in East End pubs'.[31]

Coral blamed society – *and* 'the parents': 'To make any form of emphasis – I know this happened in my father's case, and I caught it from him – instead of saying, "It's a lovely day today," they would say, "It's a *bloody* lovely day!" It's a form of emphasis, pointing to the operative word...'[32] Their propensity for profanities sometimes came back to haunt Australians: Barry Humphries recalled the horror caused in 1946, when debates from the House of Representatives were broadcast on national radio for the first time. 'Initially, this was thought to be a radio hoax programme...to frighten listeners into thinking their country was run by yahoos and guttersnipes, but slowly the truth dawned... *This was us.*'[33]*

Profanities notwithstanding, Coral's achievements in elocution brought her to the attention of the Melbourne Repertory Company and its director Frank Clewlow, who had come from England in 1928 to take charge of the ensemble. At 15, she made her semi-professional stage debut in a production of Molière's *The Rogueries of Scapin*, followed by an appearance in Shaw's *You Never Can Tell* at the Garrick Theatre, for which she received her first favourable review: 'As the self-repressed aloof Gloria, who disdains love and marriage, Coral Brown is admirable.'[34] However, Clewlow was not the director of *You Never Can Tell*: it was a man who was a devotee of Shaw's work, who could (and often did) boast of his close professional relationship with the playwright. More significantly, he was, Coral said, 'the man who had more influence on my career than anyone else'.[35] It is no exaggeration to say that, without him there would have been no Coral Browne. Summing up his achievements, one commentator said, 'His guiding rule was "only the best plays". In 27 years, he produced at least 350 plays, taught hundreds of Australians to act and kept the serious-minded section of theatre-goers abreast of all that was significant on the stage.'[36]

Gregan McMahon was born in Sydney on 2 March 1874. He was educated at Sydney Grammar School and then studied law at the University

---

* In March 2007, Tourism Australia was told in no uncertain terms that it had to take down its posters in the UK – because they featured the slogan, 'So where the bloody hell are you?' Stating the (bloody) obvious, a TA spokesman said, 'The campaign adopted the "irreverent" Australian tone...' [37]

of Sydney. McMahon trained as a solicitor, but the young lawyer nurtured a secret passion for theatre, and became involved in amateur dramatics. In June 1900, he abandoned the law and made his professional acting debut in Brisbane in Robert Brough's company, before embarking on a 15-month tour of Australia, India and China. In 1906, McMahon considered leaving for England to further his career but ultimately decided to stay, and joined the giant commercial theatrical company J C Williamson, known as 'The Firm' – as a producer. In the meantime, he kept his eye on plays performed abroad, that had been written, he said, 'to illustrate an idea, social, moral, poetic or fantastic or even utilitarian', and in which characters were 'true to life instead of to the idiosyncrasies of individual actors'.[38]

In 1911, McMahon founded the Melbourne Repertory Theatre, Australia's first full-time repertory company. He aimed to cater for a more intelligent, refined audience than 'The Firm' and other producers, such as actor-manager William Anderson, who resolutely specialised in melodramas and 'Australian plays for Australian audiences'.[39] Anderson's productions included *The Squatter's Daughter* which, in case there was any doubt that it was *thoroughly* Australian, had a cast that included two kookaburras, a wallaby and a kangaroo.

In contrast, the Melbourne Rep's early plays included works by Ibsen and, most notably, George Bernard Shaw, a particular favourite of McMahon's. The feeling was mutual – Shaw said of McMahon, 'I know of only two worthwhile products of Australia – sheep and Gregan McMahon!'[40] Shaw gave McMahon *carte blanche* to produce his plays in Australia, starting with *Arms and the Man* in 1911. Over the next five years, McMahon produced seven Shaw plays, including *Pygmalion* and the first English language production of *The Millionairess*. Writer Allan Ashbolt said, 'In argument Mac flaunted his intimacy with Shaw in the manner of an Old Testament soothsayer. Instead of pronouncing, "Thus saith the Lord," Mac merely stated: "But my boy, Shaw once wrote to me…".'[41]

The Melbourne Rep closed down for the duration of the First World War and McMahon went back to work as a director for J C Williamson. Then, in 1918, he established the Sydney Repertory Company, which staged matinees of Shaw, Ibsen and Galsworthy, and, in 1929, set up his own semi-professional company in Melbourne, the Gregan McMahon Players. The audience consisted of nearly 2000 subscribers – mostly of a class who needed their theatre seats adorned with antimacassars and who wanted to see more cultured fare than J C Williamson served up. In just 11 years, the Gregan McMahon Players presented nearly 100 plays. McMahon's friend, R W Beetham, said he 'was a little old-fashioned. Broadly speaking, he was conservative... His was the "picked and fit" audience – the intellectual nucleus of the greater audience of the future... He had a strong partiality for Galsworthy, and the conservative Galsworthy was a rebel in the Theatre...'[42]

Offstage, McMahon's private life was less conservative than it looked on paper. Since 1917, he had lived apart from his wife Mary 'Molly' Hungerford, whom he had married in October 1899; the couple had two children, Gregan Thomas and Patricia Rebecca. Mary's father, Thomas Hungerford, was a wealthy farmer; at its peak, his estate comprised more than 3000 square miles of land in New South Wales and Queensland. In the 1870s and 80s, Hungerford was a member of the the New South Wales Legislative Assembly. Ashbolt observed, 'Mac had married a Protestant lady in the sense that her husband, with his background of what the upper crust of English society calls "common Irish", was not a gentleman. Molly suffered a fairly rough fate at the hands of her husband, but she bore him two children and, before she retired to live alone in her own country house outside Sydney, imparted to the first Melbourne Repertory Company a polish and politeness which it otherwise would have lacked. Molly was a snob, but with her charm and superficial accomplishments, acquired for Gregan several wealthy patrons.'[43]

Having reached an 'understanding' with his wife, McMahon engaged in a series of affairs with some of his leading ladies. He was an unlikely looking ladykiller. Allan Ashbolt again: 'His habits were sober and his conversation unexciting. He never used an unusual word, a loud tone or a flourishing gesture. Except that his blue eyes twinkled elfishly, he had a face like Humpty Dumpty. In middle age, his high-domed head went bald and his skin wrinkled and yellowish as faded parchment.'[44] Despite his wife's family wealth, McMahon regularly sent money back to Mary and financed a trip to Europe for their daughter, even though his productions never made great fortunes for him. 'He never had any money – I don't know if he wanted money,' said Coral. 'But he never looked broke, he never thought broke. I never heard him complain in my life. He looked rather like a school master and I suppose he was more than anything else. A marvellous teacher, with impeccable taste in choosing plays and people to play in them. He wanted to educate his audience, his subscribers. He never wanted to give them *muck*.'[45]

But it was a lack of leading ladies *onstage* that was McMahon's major problem. According to Ashbolt, McMahon had trouble finding good actresses – 'a condition which reflected male dominance among the bourgeoisie and also revealed threads of puritan resistance to theatrical display in their womenfolk'.[46] The mostly non-professional status of theatre didn't help, either. Actress Zoe Caldwell – who, like Coral, would depart Australia to pursue an acting career in England – observed, 'All local Melbourne theatre was amateur. Only the commercial management firms of J C Williamson and Garnet H Carroll brought people from London and New York and surrounded them with good Australian actors.'[47] But Gregan McMahon's next, and most famous, leading lady, was just waiting in the wings.

By 1931, the Browns had ascended the suburban social ladder; they had moved from Footscray to Kew, an area of Melbourne as leafy and desirable as its British namesake, graced by ornate Victorian Italianate villas with verandas and balustrades. One of these houses – 'Fernhurst' at 13 Fernhurst Grove – had been left to Leslie by a wealthy aunt. Kew was a world away from Footscray – it was 'a prettily situated township...a very favourite place of residence for the merchants and well-to-do tradesmen of the city...dotted with their elegant houses, cottages and villas, and trim and well-kept gardens.'[48] As befitted its populace, Kew had the highest concentration of private schools in Melbourne.

But Coral had no need of them: by the time she was 15, she had left school and begun a five-year Art course, incorporating everything from painting to costume design, at the Melbourne Working Men's College (now the Royal Melbourne Institute of Technology), at 124 La Trobe Street. 'I had intended to be a painter,' she said. 'That was the way my career was going...I used to go to the Melbourne Art Gallery and draw birds and butterflies. It was a very good course and I had to learn lettering, fashion, drawing...all the bits of it.'[49] 'I had no ambition at all to go on the stage until the stage designer at the Melbourne rep died and they sent round to the art school to see if there was anyone who could take over. ...[I] started acting quite by mistake. I went in to do the sets of a play, and the young girl who was in it was suddenly taken ill with appendicitis.'[50] The Comedy Theatre production was Galsworthy's *The Roof*, which looked liked it was about to fall in – until Coral was asked to prop it up by taking the part of Nell. 'The director asked me if I thought I could do it and I said, "I don't know," but I did it. And very successfully, too. On opening night, I was offered a five-year contract as an actress. My parents had no idea what it was all about, so they couldn't object.'[51] Her parents had enough idea of what she was doing to start keeping a cuttings' scrapbook about their daughter's unfathomable new career.

Coral's contract was with J C Williamson's – 'The Firm': 'I was going to get £10 a week, rising at the end of five years, by I think three pounds a week for about 40-odd weeks… And I liked that, I liked the idea of the independence that it would give me, rather than go on in the art bit for four years, taking money from the family. I didn't like taking money from anybody. It was obvious then that I was not going to be an artist in the true sense, a painter, but I continued with costume design… I did a lot of my own things. Acting seemed to me to be well-paid, design seemed to be badly paid.'[52] In the future, this first-hand experience and expertise would make Coral one of the actresses most feared by stage and film designers. She would say, 'I *know* when a set isn't quite right or when a costume isn't ideal. And I can't give a performance unless I feel comfortable with what I'm wearing.'[53] John Schlesinger later observed, 'Wig and Wardrobe departments [*sic*] have good reason to worry before a fitting, as she has an uncanny knowledge of what suits her best and is totally exacting about the way she or the character she is playing should look.'[54] But Michael Baldwin, one designer who worked with her, backed Coral's judgement: 'She never dressed either too young or too old – she was always spot on.'[55]

In her first role under the Williamson contract, Coral took a giant leap from last-minute stand-in to juvenile lead, playing Margaret Orme, 'A Society Girl', in another Galsworthy play, *Loyalties*, which opened at the Comedy Theatre on 2 May 1931. The magazine *Table Talk* made her a cover girl, and enthused that she had 'shown unusual promise…and her future will be watched with particular interest. Talented and possessed of piquant beauty…there are many who believe this clever play will give her the opportunity to scale the heights of success.'[56] But flappers like Margaret Orme would be few and far between in this early phase of her career: her tall physique and dark looks – one critic noted 'one of her striking features is a pair of topaz coloured eyes flecked with brown'[57] – ensured she was usually cast as women who were much older and bigger drama queens. Commenting on Coral's early roles, Gertrude P

Lancaster made the wry observation that, 'When a girl is five feet nine inches in heels, with statuesque bearing and a voice both deep and powerful, it is obvious that her prowess as an actress will not come through ingenue parts.'[58] *The Bulletin* observed, 'She is a very neat-looking lady, apparently doomed by matters of nature to be a stage villainess.'[59] Coral herself said, 'When I first started acting, it wasn't fashionable to be so tall... I was much bigger than I am now – statuesque, I suppose you'd call it. I was never built to be a maid. I was made to sin.'[60]

And sin she did: in *The Calendar*, a drama about the world of horse-racing, 'The honours...go to Miss Coral Brown whose 17 summers one would regard as a definite handicap for the worldly role – the black-hearted Wenda, who manages to conceal beneath her very attractive physical charms the soul of a lying, rapacious Jezebel... Miss Brown is to be congratulated upon her efficient grasp and delineation of the part.'[61] For Edward Knoblock's *My Lady's Dress*, Coral learned the part of 'Lize the London workgirl in the Whitechapel shop' in just 20 hours, and 'impersonated that highly distinctive product of London with startling lifelikeness'.[62] In *A Warm Corner*, the Melbourne critics enjoyed 'Coral Brown as the blackmailing married lady...sinuous and vampish in her striking costumes [including a sports trouser suit and a white flannel lounge pyjama suit].'[63] But it wasn't just Melbourne's critics and audiences who were getting excited by this striking new leading lady: Coral's contract took her to theatres in Adelaide, Sydney and Brisbane, with shows including *Hay Fever*, *The First Mrs Fraser* and the quaintly titled *Let Us Be Gay*. This comedy caused Coral to be noticed for something other than her acting: 'Coral Brown and her theatre pyjamas caused a few gasps – not that the pyjamas were so noticeable with their wide and flowing legs but there were such perfect fitting undies beneath them that they suggested tights.'[64] She went down a storm in Brisbane: 'Whenever Coral Brown of *Let Us Be Gay* walks through the streets both masculine and feminine eyes get into focus. This striking young actress belongs to a very smart crowd in Melbourne. She has a real Hollywood walk, and the gift for wearing bizarre clothes and getting away with it... Leslie Victor, who follows her around on the stage, keeps up the good work offstage. Some of Brisbane's smart young men are not averse to doing the same.'[65] One of those who saw her was a stage-struck 12-year-old boy called Loudon Sainthill, destined to enjoy a glittering career in the West End and on Broadway as a designer for theatre and ballet shows, including *The Right*

Honourable Gentleman, where his leading lady was…Coral Browne. His death in 1969, aged just 50, shocked her: 'He was a dear, dear friend. He only lived around the corner and when I wasn't well he used to put soup in the lift and things like that. I miss him terribly.'[66]

Coral, free from Vicky's watchful and critical eye, was revelling in the freedom offered by life away from home, especially when she reached Sydney: 'Ooh that was lovely, living on one's own. I was away from Melbourne…played poker until 11 o'clock at night on a Sunday…it was beautiful then. I used to get on the ferry at night and go to a place called Mosman.'[67] However, in Brisbane, someone overplayed their hand: 'I had a little trouble with the night porter, who decided to come into my room in the middle of the night uninvited. He got booted out…'[68]

Coral's first two seasons with 'The Firm' had, it appeared, been successful in every respect; she had even won praise from Lewis Casson who, with his wife Sybil Thorndike, toured several productions to Australia in 1932. In Melbourne, Coral was introduced to Thorndike, who even encouraged her to try her luck in England. But one man wasn't happy with her progress: Gregan McMahon. 'I was going to be with J C Williamson for five years. McMahon…watched me all the time – I really didn't know him very well then – and he used to watch me doing *Hay Fever* and all this, and it made him as mad as it was possible to be (he was a very even-tempered man). He saw it as a tremendous waste, that I was put into play after play which was not doing anything to make me grow. And it was McMahon who went to Williamson's and asked for my release [from the contract], which was quite remarkable. I don't think they cared one way or another.'[69]

Coral duly joined The Gregan McMahon Players where, under McMahon's direction, she was given what Allan Ashbolt described as 'the sort of training no longer obtainable in Australia. As a producer, he could mould an actor and blend a cast to his own desired shape.'[70] Nearly 50 years later, Coral had no hesitation in acknowledging her debt to McMahon: 'He was a very, very, very exceptional man; dedicated to the theatre. He taught me more than I ever learned in my whole life, from anybody else. He took my theatrical education very seriously; he was quite determined that I would know how to judge a play. He used to give me homework of that kind; four or five plays a week, and I had to go home and read them and come back and discuss them with him. He gave me…various technical books on how to write plays. All the plays that I did which had long runs were due to the fact that I could read a play and not read my own part, and McMahon taught me that. He always discussed things with me; we were very close. There was always a sort of tender discussion we had. I don't know what he did with other people.'[71]

The local press had no doubts: 'Despite the croakings of Dame Sybil Thorndike and other imported stars who have flopped in this country, mainly because they refused to give the public what it wants, there is always hope for the Australian stage, so long as we have men like Gregan McMahon in the theatre... If only she gets the chance she deserves, Coral Brown should prove as fine an actress as Judith Anderson. It is to be sincerely hoped that she will be provided with such a chance and so persuaded to stay in Australia.'[72] And, within months of joining the McMahon Players, a headline trumpeted the claim, 'Youngest Leading Lady in the World is Melbourne Girl'.[73]

Later, the 'youngest leading lady' would blithely claim that life then was all work and no play: 'There was no going out with boys. I didn't have time to get into the backs of cars. I was in a grown-up world.'[74] *Extremely* grown-up. For it wasn't only Coral's dramatic endowments McMahon was nurturing: despite their age difference and his obvious lack of physical charms, they had become lovers. Typically, Coral would put it more bluntly: 'Gregan taught me everything I knew about acting – and a great deal about fucking, too.'[75]

Coral made steady progress under McMahon (in all senses): with his company, her diverse appearances would include *Autumn Crocus*, *The Command to Love*, Shaw's *The Apple Cart*, Mrs Dearth in J M Barrie's *Dear Brutus* and Fraulein von Benberg in two productions of *Children in Uniform* (the stage version of the classic film, *Maidens in Uniform*). Among her busy schedule, she managed to squeeze in her first film appearance – an uncredited part in Pat Hanna's farce, *Waltzing Matilda*, made in Melbourne by Frank Thring's Eftee Studios. Coral couldn't recall much about her role, except that 'I had to wear a farmhand's dress which I wasn't too keen on'.[76]

Then, in the spring of 1933, came a brief news item: 'Miss Coral Brown... is seriously ill. She is a patient at Chelmer Private Hospital, St Kilda Road, where she recently underwent an operation.'[77] It was later reported that, 'She had just gone to the country to recuperate after a long illness, during which she had almost given up the idea of a stage career... [and had spent a] long period in hospital...'[78] Naturally, in those days, the press showed more discretion and respect for privacy when it came to revealing details of surgery undergone by celebrities. Coral's illness or operation may merely have been an appendectomy or an ovarian cyst. At worst, given her sexual relationship with Gregan McMahon, it could have been a miscarriage or even a botched abortion, requiring more radical surgery. Coral never disclosed the reason – but it was serious enough to prevent her from working for several months that year.

Her return to the stage wasn't ideal: she appeared as Diane – 'a Parisian actress' – in the musical play *The Quaker Girl*. It was, she said, 'my first and last experience with musical comedy. It nearly drove me out of my mind – everybody running up and down stairs, and they'd all be limbering up their voices. I found the whole thing very unrestful.'[79] She was much happier with her 'heavier' roles, including Fraulein von Bernberg in *Children in Uniform*, with Gregan McMahon directing an all-female cast of 27. Coral said, 'I was about 30 years too young, like all the parts. It was the part of a teacher, about 35; a younger pupil fell in love with her; I know that it was very tight-lipped and severe but very tender underneath.'[80] The critics were more than tender: *The Graphic of Australia* gushed, 'Coral Brown shares the highest honours of the play...she played it with supreme artistry and amply deserved the tribute she received from the audience at the final curtain,'[81] while another reviewer declared, 'The play is undoubtedly Coral Brown's and her best work to date.'[82] But this was before they had seen her as Hedda Gabler, when 'A dull evening was retrieved by Miss Coral Brown who, even at this early stage of her career, made the rest of the cast look like amateurs.'[83] And so it continued into 1934, with *Musical Chairs* and Don Marquis' *Out of the Sea*, a drama set in Cornwall, featuring a character called Tregesal, who was stabbed to death with that most unusual of weapons, a bodkin.

It was now increasingly clear that, having become a big frog in the small pond that was the Melbourne theatrical establishment, there was only one route for Coral to take: across the sea to London and the West End. But there was more to it than that: Australian journalist Frank Doherty, in an article called 'Don't Put Your Daughter on the Australian Stage, Please, Mrs Worthington', revealed an ugly truth about his country: 'For some unfathomable reason we in this country who laud our jockeys, footballers and cricketers treat our actors, actresses and playwrights with all the acclamation and enthusiasm we show lepers. Our theatricals are the perfect prophets without honor.'[84] And, 70 years later, some commentators believed this attitude still prevailed: 'Australia has never honoured its artists as fully as its sports figures; there is always an undertow of resentment, of the lowbrows' residual suspicion that the highbrow is conning them.'[85]

Although Coral would claim that 'The decision to go to London was made by McMahon. Entirely,'[86] she was hardly a passive party. Shortly after recovering from her mystery surgery, she told a reporter, 'I am afraid I shall not have much chance of going much further here. I am "typed" and that is fatal. Because I am tall and dark I am supposed only to be able to play adventuress parts. I would love to play comedy roles.'[87] And she was adamant that she wanted to play those roles on stage, *not* films: 'What in the theatre is called a good carrying voice becomes a shout when it is addressed to the microphone. My real ambitions are for the legitimate theatre. An actress should be able to interpret every type of human being. Of course, I want to study abroad. Opportunities are limited here for local girls until they have a chance to make their names abroad.'[88] As late as 1965, according to Liza Goddard, Australian actors who wanted to further their careers had a clear-cut choice: 'You could go to Hollywood and have a film career, or you could head for London and the West End and have a stage career. You couldn't do both.'[89]*

It was, of course, nonsense that the decision had been Gregan McMahon's alone: the matter was discussed at length with the Browns: 'After I'd done 28 plays in Australia, Gregan went to my parents and said, "She can't learn any more here and she's miles from everything that's happening." So instead of a car or whatever, I got a ticket to England for my 21st birthday, and £50 to live on – with orders to come back when that ran out.'[90]

It says much for both McMahon and Leslie Brown, at that time the two most important men in Coral's life, that although they must have been bereft

* Not for Coral, then, a career like that enjoyed by Lotus Thompson. At 15, this Sydney girl won a beauty contest, largely by dint of her luscious legs, deemed by one judge as 'the sort of limbs a Diana or Venus must have had'. [91] Lotus's mother needed no further encouragement; after some experience with a repertory company, Mrs Thompson whisked her daughter off to Hollywood, where she was signed up by Paramount Pictures in 1921. But instead of being offered dramatic roles in the silent movies, Lotus's legs became stars in their own right, doubling for actresses with less pleasing pins. By 1925, Lotus's resentment had blossomed and she decided to take drastic action: she poured an acidic solution down her legs. Incredibly, the day after this self-mutilation, she received a telegram from Rudolph Valentino, promising her a part in his next film. Other offers duly followed and, thereafter, Lotus Thompson worked steadily, if unspectacularly, in feature films until 1949.

at the thought of her losing her, both supported her decision to deracinate. And it also says a good deal about the depth of Coral's ambition, and her desire to get away from Australia and 'Mother', that she had no hesitation in doing so. However, in one respect, Coral's escape plans were thwarted: as a concession, it was agreed that Vicky would accompany her daughter to London and stay long enough to see her settled. In the weeks prior to her departure, the two men in Coral's life busied themselves by writing letters of introduction to every contact in Britain in their respective address books, from producers and agents to manager of provisions' companies with whom Leslie Brown did business. McMahon himself wrote letters addressed to his theatrical contacts in Britain, including the producer Alfred Waring; he told him that Coral 'has all the mental and physical attributes of the best class of leading lady. Would you be so good as to spare time to have a chat with her, and give her some guidance.'[92]

Coral's final performances in Australia were in a revival of *Children in Uniform* featuring the British vaudevillian Ada Reeve, then touring the country. 'In 1934, I had an offer to play the mad German dancing teacher,' said Reeve. 'It was then that I met Coral Brown, who was playing the part of Fraulein von Bernberg – the young mistress to whom the child Manuela is so passionately devoted. And what a magnificent performance she gave! She had such dignity, such repose, such charm – and she was so young. In real life Coral was as unlike Fraulein von Bernberg as one could imagine: she was brimming over with restlessness and *joie de vivre*.'[93] Knowing of Coral's plans to decamp to London, Reeve gave her a letter of introduction to the agent and producer Barry O'Brien, which she deliberately left unsealed. It read: 'The bearer of this letter has great dignity – *on the stage*; a lot of repose – *on the stage*; a beautiful speaking voice – *on the stage*; and tremendous charm – *on the stage*.'[94]

On the evening of Monday 29 May 1934, Coral was given a farewell party at the Occidental by Nancy Ford, Kathleen Howell and the cast of *Children in Uniform*. The next day, accompanied by 'Mother', she left Australia on the Orient liner Ormonde. Among the crowd waving her off were Leslie Brown and Ada Reeve: 'I met her father when I came to the boat to see her off,' said

Reeve. 'He was very young-looking – in fact, he looked like her brother, and a young brother at that.'[95]

None of them could have predicted that the departing actress would return to her homeland just twice in the next 50 years. Allan Ashbolt summed up what Gregan McMahon – and Australian theatre – was losing with her departure: 'The finest actress he [McMahon] ever nurtured was undoubtedly Coral Browne.'[96]

Among Coral's sheaf of letters was one from Gregan McMahon, expressing the private agonies he had endured prior to her departure: 'Dearest in the world. Please forgive my horrible selfish behaviour but I am losing all control… I am troubled and appalled at the prospect ahead.'[97] Publicly, he predicted that his protégé and lover '…cannot escape success. She has everything – beauty, presence, intelligence…'[98]

In the years to come, there would be stories in the press that Coral was to return to the Australian stage – a production of the Alan Melville comedy, *Simon and Laura*; an invitation by Hugh Hunt to play Cleopatra in Sydney – but there was to be no going back. Coral Brown had given her last performance in Australia – now, she was on her way to a new role: 'Coral Browne'.

But, in Britain, Coral Brown was just another Australian. She said, 'It was once very important to me to try and conceal it and I don't think anyone could tell I was Australian. Of course, one can't get straight off a boat from Australia and hope to play a duchess the next day…'[99] She wasn't fooling anyone: John Gliddon, her first agent, later recalled how, when he first met her within days of her arrival in London, '…your accent was very much Australian.'[100] And, as Liza Goddard observed, that accent could be useful: 'It came out mostly when she was being rude – she could get away with it more…'[101] Sheridan Morley observed, 'England was a very snobbish society in the theatre – particularly class-ridden – Coral, because she was Australian, cut through all that; she had no respect, no loyalty and that gave her this lifelong ability to say the wrong thing. The warning light that flashes when you say the wrong thing didn't work for Coral at all. I think her being Australian was very important – it gave her a kind of outsider quality. She was like a Martian.'[102]

She had certainly landed in an alien theatrical kingdom – a West End ruled by the likes of Edith Evans and Sybil Thorndike, Gwen Ffrangcon-Davies and Flora Robson, Diana Wynyard, Fay Compton, Peggy Ashcroft and Marie Tempest, Gertrude Lawrence and Martita Hunt, where blunt-speaking young female Australians were not readily embraced into the fold – even if they had been 'the world's youngest leading lady'. Charles Landstone, Drama Director at the Arts Council, observed: 'In the between the wars years, we had a predominantly playwright's theatre. At the end of the 1930s, change was in the air. It came in this case from the Old Vic where, during the 1920s and 1930s, a great school of classical acting was coming into being. In the forefront of this movement were John Gielgud, Sybil Thorndike, Edith Evans, Olivier, Richardson, Wolfit, Peggy Ashcroft...'[103] Up against this cast of heavyweight drama divas, it seemed that comedy and Coral were made for each other: 'When I first came over from Australia, I had had very little experience of playing comedy. With my height, dark colouring and deep voice I felt that I was singled out to play the more serious heroines. London thought otherwise and directed my career along comedy channels from the start. I soon had to take stock of my ambitions and think about perfecting the technique of making audiences laugh if I hoped to make my mark. By way of compensation, my London roles have at least sharpened my sense of humour, which is worth more than all the allure of an enchantress.'[104]

And another factor came into play: for this was the era of producer-power. As director Eleanor Fazan pointed out, 'You used to be a producer's choice; directors were merely hired hands. Donald Albery, Binkie Beaumont, Val Parnell, Bernard Delfont – they were the big showmen of the day. The producer wasn't interested in self-aggrandisement, unlike directors today. It was the box office that interested them.'[105] And the biggest showman of them all was Hugh 'Binkie' Beaumont, who had become managing director of H M Tennent Ltd in 1941. His style was to use 'the greatest stars in gorgeous classic revivals amidst the most sumptuous settings which taste and money could devise'.[106] Accordingly, his roster of stars included Noël Coward, John Gielgud, Peggy Ashcroft, Ralph Richardson, Vivien Leigh and Diana Wynyard, while his 'house playwright' was Terence Rattigan. Beaumont paid his stars well and lavished the finest Parisian fashions on his leading ladies. Richard Huggett explained, 'The whole of the Tennent structure was based on the stars...they were the crown jewels of his empire and the centrepiece of his theatrical philosophy.'[107] His stars rewarded him with their loyalty: Edith Evans often rejected offers from other producers to keep herself available if Beaumont needed her for a role. But, as Jonathan Cecil commented, 'If you fell out with Tennent's you were in a very bad way: you were back into rep, back into the provincial theatre, no matter how much you'd been heralded… He was very powerful. But he was also a man of the theatre, he understood it thoroughly. It was nothing but the best, whether it was costumes, scenery, everything…and actors, down to the smallest understudies.'[108]

Armed with her letters of introduction and dressed to impress, Coral immediately set about doing the rounds. First, she went to see the actor Edmund Gwenn, who had been Shaw's leading man in *Man and Superman* in 1902, and was then in a show called *Laburnum Grove*. He advised Coral to hire a theatre, with full cast and crew, for one night, put on a show and invite managers to attend; this would have cost, at that time, somewhere in the region of £1000. He also advised her to go back to Australia as soon as possible. Next, she went to see Dame Sybil Thorndike, who, when they had met in Melbourne, had had nothing but words of encouragement for Coral. Gregan McMahon had written to her, 'Your always helpful enthusiasms suggest my presuming on our short Melbourne acquaintance to ask your interest in a young actress of quite extraordinary gifts who is proceeding to London to try her luck.'[109] But now, on her own territory, the grand dame struggled even to remember who the young actress was. She told Coral, 'But my child, 250 girls from Australia are here: some say they have been leading ladies with J C Williamson's for ten years. I'm telling them all the same – Go home at once.'[110] It was advice quickly given – and just as quickly forgotten.

Coral had a letter of introduction addressed to another grand dame, Marie Tempest, with whom Gregan McMahon had once worked, and still kept up a correspondence. In a letter to her husband, Graham Browne, he said Coral 'is really unusually gifted and brings distinction to any class of good work. Would you and Miss Tempest be so good as to give her a little guidance if you yourselves cannot place her.'[111] James Agate said of Tempest, 'She had a small, exquisite talent and was generally recognised as an actress of the first rank. New movements passed her by – or rather she passed them by… Her technique was flawless, and her comedy had everything that comedy should have, except the gift of tears. She had unsurpassable elegance, exquisite poise, and a sense of proportion which enabled her to give her effects their exact value and no more… Her best role was that of Marie Tempest. In this she was superb.'[112] And she was equally superb with Coral: she sent the young actress to see 'Binkie' Beaumont, who put her up for an audition for an Ivor Novello show, *Murder in Mayfair*, directed by Leontine Sagan. Two other young actresses auditioning that day were Sally Gray and Vivien Leigh – who, apparently, were not even given a second look. Coral was offered a role in the play, but boldly turned it down: she didn't think it was good enough. It would turn out to be the correct decision – within 24 hours, she cabled her father: 'Got job as understudy. We leave on August 18 for Southsea, Eastbourne, Nottingham, Glasgow and Edinburgh, then London.'[113] The day after Coral turned down the Novello play, Binkie Beaumont sent her a cabled instruction to, 'Be at my office 10.30 tomorrow.' There, she met Owen Nares, then one of London's most popular leading men, who was about to star in *Lover's Leap* with Nora Swinburne and Isabel Jeans. Nares was more impressed with Coral's CV and cuttings than Sybil Thorndike and agreed that she should understudy his two leading ladies — and so, after just three days in London, Coral had landed her first job, for the modest salary of £5 a week.[114] She recalled, 'I had bed and breakfast for £3 a week in Gloucester Place [96 Gloucester Place, Portman Square], and I knew a man who owned a restaurant so I ate the leftovers for free.'[115] This was El Patio, a fashionable Spanish eaterie run by former actor Edward Ashley-Cooper, who became Nora Swinburne's second husband on 3 December 1934; Coral was one of the wedding guests.

Born in 1902, Nora Swinburne was one of the West End's biggest female light comedy stars, a great beauty and a generous soul. She trained at RADA but her career had started while she was still at school, touring in *Where the Rainbow Ends*; by the age of 16, she had already appeared in four West End shows. Eric Shorter said, 'Here was a profile of striking beauty… Her gracious presence brought dignity and a dry wit to scores of forgotten farces.'[116] When she met her new understudy for the first time, she needed that grace and dignity: 'Her language was – well, *really*…I'd never heard so many words. Half of them, I didn't know what the meant – and I'd been in the chorus at the Gaiety, where the language was not exactly proper…'[117] As actor Peter Stenson observed, 'In those days, women didn't swear – nor did most men, certainly not at that sort of level, so it was terribly shocking.'[118] Frith Banbury said, 'Nora was always amused by, and appreciated, Coral. I remember Nora telling me that she took Coral down to her parents in the country – and Coral's use of swear words was renowned. So she told Coral that she was not to use any; and Coral behaved wonderfully. Nora was very amused that Coral could be persuaded *not* to use all the four-letter words possible.'[119]

In *Lover's Leap*, Swinburne was playing opposite another popular star, Owen Nares; she was Helen Storer, the estranged wife of an Egyptologist who returns to England after seven years, seeking a divorce. The couple agree to play happy families, to demonstrate the joys of marriage to her sister and fiancé, who are getting cold feet about their imminent wedding. The first-night critics enjoyed it: the *Guardian* reported that, 'Almost from the rise of the curtain, there were ripples of laughter, and the ripples soon rose to waves which drowned the dialogue,'[120] and even *The Times* conceded that, 'An entertainment which even its well-wishers might describe as a waste of time wastes an evening with disarming good humour.'[121]

With those notices in the bag, Coral resigned herself to spending many long afternoons and evenings in her dressing room, improving her needlework skills. The critic Eric Johns described the life of the 1930s understudy: 'One in a thousand has the good fortune to play in London and to seize success with both hands. The other 999 understudies lead a pathetic existence… Their life, as well as their day's work, simply consists of waiting…the understudy has to be at the theatre at the same time as the star every evening, and cannot leave until after the star has made her last entrance. For three hours every night she is faced with the problem of killing time. She gossips in various dressing rooms, with her ears open for a job; she drinks tea; she knits; and occasionally finds someone to try her in her lines… The mornings are not her own, for she is called two or three times a week down to the theatre to rehearse on the stage, so that she will know the right moves and "business"…'[122]

But then, on the second night, came the understudy's dream – or nightmare, depending on the ambition of the understudy: Swinburne succumbed to a bad bout of influenza. The show had to go on – and so did Coral. She cabled Gregan McMahon immediately: 'Now leading lady Nora off second night Influenza Success Continuing until Nora recovers Love Coral.'[123] That night, the audience were duly informed, via an insert in their programmes, that 'Owing to the indisposition of Nora Swinburne, the part of Helen Storer will be played at this performance by Coral Brown.'[124] As luck would have it, the second night press reviewers, including the Sunday papers, were in attendance for Coral's West End debut; they were not disappointed: Coral 'gave a brilliant portrayal…to play such a part so well at short notice was a real tour de force.'[125] Others concurred: 'I was gratified to find in Miss Swinburne's role an alternative actress…in a style so assured and polished as to suggest that her services will be of value to London in future. She is an actress with unusual carriage and deportment.'[126] And, even though one critic thought that 'Coral Brown…is not an ideal comedian; she is too intense,' they said, 'She performed her frightening task so unfalteringly that she proved herself an excellent actress.'[127] Eric Johns once observed, 'The understudy cannot give an original interpretation of the part he is taking over. It must be something of a carbon copy of the star's performance because it has to fit into the pattern of the existing production.'[128] However, with her performance, Coral had showed it was possible to be both original *and* fitting. Philip Johnson, the author of *Lover's Leap*, expressed his gratitude for her efforts: 'I simply dare not let myself think what would have happened if anyone less competent had been in your shoes on Friday night.'[129] Of course, Leslie Brown was delighted by his daughter's early success – but, as he admitted to Coral's first leading man, Owen Nares: 'It was with some trepidation that I permitted her to settle down so far from home…she is very young and will no doubt need some friendly guidance in her activities in a strange country. She is an only child and I am perhaps unduly anxious…'[130]

Coral had joined a list of eminent performers – including Jessie Matthews, Jack Buchanan and Beatrix Lehmann (who understudied Tallulah Bankhead in *Green Hat*) – who got their first big break stepping in for a star. It was heady stuff: she moved from her Portman Square flat into a suite at 140 Piccadilly, a few doors away from the Duke and Duchess of York's town house at number 145 – but it was an address befitting star status she hadn't yet achieved, despite her success as a stand-in. Then, in May 1935, she changed address again: her new flat in Eccleston Square boasted black floors, beige sheepskin rugs, pink curtains, cushions and divans; on the wall hung a portrait of her in oils. That Christmas, she sent friends and family in Australia seasonal greetings on personalised cards etched with her new address. However, the reality was that Coral was not yet being offered the weight of roles that 'overnight stardom' promised. She told Gregan, 'While everyone is talking salaries of £100 a week to me, I am living on nuts and apples.'[131] One man who was trying to get her off this frugal diet was John Gliddon, a former actor and journalist who had set up his own agency with the express aim of nurturing British screen actors. In this capacity, his most famous discovery was Vivien Leigh, who was introduced to him by his friend Beryl Samson when she had but one small film role to her name. Gliddon put her on his books, and helped create her new stage name. He signed up Coral and set about finding parts in the British film industry suitable for a tall, dark, outspoken young Australian woman. He had already received offers of film work for her from Fox, Universal and British Lion; RKO wanted her do a screen test for them, tempting her with the offer of a seven-year contract.

Soon, she was able to send Leslie a cable with good news: 'Half finished film British Lion forty pounds weekly Commence Arts Seventh Paul Robesons Leading Lady No Salary Inform Gregan All Love Coral.'[132]

After *Lover's Leap*, she featured in what were called 'Sunday try-outs' – plays staged in the West End for short runs – sometimes a single performance – in small venues, usually club theatres such as the Arts, where, as Patrick White explains, 'a group of small-part actors and actresses…sat around in the lounge…waiting for the roles which eluded them, worrying about their health, their rent, their liaisons, their abortions'.[133] She knew why: 'I'm not exactly easy to cast. I was never a juvenile lead. When I arrived here, I got involved in mostly arty productions.'[134] The first of these 'arty productions' was *Mated*, a drama by Christopher Sandeman, about a young Italian widow (played by Coral) which had a brief run at the Arts Theatre in February 1935. Once again, she impressed the critics: the *Daily Mail* said 'The fine performance of Miss Coral Brown was the outstanding feature of the evening.'[135] Another commented that she '…is a young actress of distinction who should find her place on the London stage. She has a striking personality, a good voice and apparently considerable emotional power.'[136] And – as would often be the case – the critics thought more of her performance than the play she was in: 'Of all the cast she succeeded most in helping me forget the play.'[137]

Within weeks, she was rehearsing another 'arty production', *Basalik*, at the Arts Theatre. The experimental play, set in the fictitious African kingdom of Albatuland, had been written especially for Paul Robeson by Norma Leslie Munro, under the pseudonym 'Peter Garland'. Coral played Lady Amerdine, wife of the governor of the bordering British protectorate who has been taken hostage by the chief Balu (Robeson), to persuade the colonial domain to leave his people in peace. She was excited that the play had once been banned by the Lord Chamberlain: 'I was dying to do it because I knew it would be a sensation.'[138]

Robeson, of course, was a legendary figure, for his achievements as a singer, actor and activist. His *Othello* at the Savoy Theatre in 1930, with Peggy

44

Ashcroft as Desdemona, had been welcomed by some, shunned by others, for having a black actor perform in the title role (as a black man, Robeson was not allowed inside the adjoining Savoy Hotel). His role as Balu marked his return to the dramatic stage, after an absence filled with recording, films and singing tours. Robeson and his wife, Essie, had been in London since January 1935; he began a concert tour of Britain at the Royal Albert Hall, performing spirituals, popular songs and European folk songs, including some in Russian and Hebrew. By 2 April, Robeson was back in London to attend the gala premiere of his latest film, *Sanders of the River* at London's Leicester Square Theatre, and to begin rehearsing *Basalik* for a three-day 'try-out' run.* Although the presence of Robeson ensured it was a sell-out, *Basalik* did not hit the right note with the critics. Coral was praised for her 'cool and stylish' performance[139] and, while 'Robeson was enthusiastically received, [and] Coral Brown and Wyndham Goldie both were excellent,'[140], the *Daily Telegraph* called the play 'thin and unsatisfying'[141] and plans for a six-month regional tour of the show were cancelled.

The demise of the short-lived show didn't mean the end for Coral and her leading man. Despite his marriage, Robeson's numerous affairs were an open secret among his colleagues (including Peggy Ashcroft in 1930) and, during *Basalik*, he and Coral began a passionate liaison. Their assignations were arranged with great degree discretion: both were aware of the double taboo of an inter-racial, adulterous relationship. Coral was not oblivious to the prejudice faced by the great man she was now involved with: 'I remember that somebody took Paul to the Savoy for lunch and they refused to serve him.'[142] And, after reading one review which said she failed to express fully the emotions of her character in *Basalik*, she wrote on the cutting, 'Done on purpose – as showing & feeling sexual desire for a black – bad for career – so did not play it with great sincerity. Am I right???'[143]

After *Basalik* closed, Robeson remained in London and agreed to star in *Chillun*, an American play about black workers who stand up to their oppressive white bosses. During the play's month-long rehearsals, and its two-week run at the Embassy Theatre, Coral and Robeson continued to meet in secret –

---

* Robeson was a regular face at theatrical parties held in Ivor Novello's flat above the Strand Theatre, which usually began with a midnight supper at the Savoy. Sometimes, Robeson would sit in the middle of the floor and sing spirituals for the assembled guests, who often included Jack Buchanan.

though, evidently, not as often as they wanted, if his letters were anything to go by. At first, they were formal: 'Dear Miss Brown, Am furiously rehearsing at Embassy. I would so like to see you again. We usually finish rehearsal about 4.30 every day. May I come by on the way into town some afternoon. I could arrive about 4.45. I am sending this by messenger and am asking him to wait for a message in case you are free this afternoon. If not, perhaps sometime this week. Every good wish and lots of luck. Sincerely, Paul Robeson.'[144]

Then, as the affair progressed, they became more affectionate and impassioned: 'Darling. Simply couldn't get away to-day without complications. Terribly sorry, I do miss you. Please save Monday evening, will call about 8';[145] and then: 'I do miss you so, darling. I am so happy you wanted me to write. You are a dear. We will see soon if these terrible gaps can't be bridged. This is simply silly, seeing you every 3 or 4 days. Quite impossible. Lots and lots of love, Paul.'[146]

Liaisons became even more difficult to arrange when, in late June, Robeson embarked on another concert tour – and, by the end of September, he and Essie had returned to the States. Coral would later say that Robeson was instrumental in persuading her to persevere with her acting ambitions in England – but, in reality, it was unlikely she every seriously considered returning to Australia. In any case, at that stage, she was still confident enough to reject work if it didn't cut the mustard. She told Gregan McMahon, 'I had an offer to play all of [Alice] Delysia's matinees for her in an all-star cast [*Accidentally Yours*]. George Robey was instrumental in getting me the offer from Firth S. But I preferred to be top dog in *Desirable Residence*. Saw PR's show, *Stevedore*, last night. Flora Robson took me to PR's show.'[147] As she told her father in a cable, the 'top dog' role was in a 'Marvellous Play Commence Eighty Years Finish Twenty.'[148]

In *This Desirable Residence*, Coral had to portray the character of Mary Penshott, a young woman in love with her architect father's clerk, first in her youth and then in old age. The critics were more than convinced: the *Daily Mail* wrote, 'Miss Coral Brown's interesting personality is displayed to advantage both as a young girl and an old spinster.'[149] Her performance prompted another critic to predict, 'I have another tip for the future. Watch Miss Coral Brown who has dignity as well a tall, imperious flawless beauty, a moving rich contralto, speaking voice and great intelligence. She has no stage mannerisms.'[150]

That November, cinema audiences got their first sample of the beauty and the voice with the release of Coral's first film, a vapid murder-melodrama, *Line Engaged* – 'the most unusual drama ever screened', according to its producers.[151] Novelist David Morland (Bramwell Fletcher), the son of a Scotland Yard detective, is in love with a married woman, Eva Rutland (Jane Baxter) whose gambling, philandering cad of a husband, Gordon (Leslie Perrins), is murdered. When Morland becomes a suspect, his detective dad perverts the course of justice away from his son and in the direction of anyone who stands still long enough to have an accusing finger pointed at them. Coral played Doreen – the first in a succession of cinematic vamps – whose affections veer between Gordon Rutland and his rival in both love and luck. The press were informed that 'Until her comparatively recent arrival in this country, Coral Brown was a well-known society debutante in Sydney [*sic*]. Not long after crashing into the London theatrical world, she made her name in a colour problem play featuring Paul Robeson. Miss Brown's appearance (she has been described as the talkie prototype of the famous Nita Naldi [the silent movie vamp who starred with Valentino in *Blood and Sand*]) and her polished diction, ensure her a successful career on the British screen.'[152]

In every respect, 1935 was turning out to be something of a watershed year for Coral – including a development in her personal life that wouldn't feature in any cable or press cutting sent back to her parents. It was something she revealed to her step-daughter, Victoria Price, more than 50 years, two marriages and what must have felt like several lifetimes later: 'Not long after moving to England, she had a five-year relationship with a woman. I got the sense that the woman was also an actress, or at the very least in the theatre. They lived together or were together for five years, but then this woman, whoever she was, asked Coral to be more public about the relationship. Essentially, Coral chose her career over the woman, and she said it was the hardest decision she had ever had to make. And what hurt the most was that the woman began another relationship not too long thereafter.'[153] When Coral made this revelation, she was past the stage when anyone would have been surprised to hear she had, in sexual terms, covered the waterfront. Ruth Leon said, 'The thing not to be underestimated was that she was *absolutely* beautiful. Women and men were *mad* about her – with very good reason.'[154] And, prior to her memorial service, when Vincent Price was asked if Coral had any favourite hymns, he replied: 'Yes – and quite a few hers.'[155] There was no shortage of contenders for the identity of Coral's favourite 'her' among London's theatrical community. But there were two actresses who could easily have fitted the part. They were both women who, like Coral, were of unconventional looks and sexuality, and notable personalities within the London theatrical world of the 1930s.

One was Beatrix Lehmann, sister to literary siblings, Rosamond and John Lehmann. Adrian Wright, John Lehmann's biographer, said, 'In the theatre, such intelligence was too often unwelcome, and Beatrix could be a forbidding and arresting presence.'[156] According to Wright, 'Rosamond had a Queen Victoria-like attitude to Beatrix's sexuality, simply believing it did not exist.'[157] Christopher Isherwood's biographer, Peter Parker, said the bisexual 'Peggy' Lehmann was 'no great beauty, but she was certainly striking in appearance. Fiercely left-wing, funny, a gifted actress and mimic...she represented for Isherwood "woman in an acceptable form".'[158] In the 1920s, Lehmann had had a relationship with Henrietta Bingham, daughter of the American Ambassador to Britain and one-time lover of Bloomsbury artist, Dora Carrington. One of her secretaries fell in love with her; when the affection was not returned, the woman attempted to kill herself. For the last 15 years of her life, Lehmann had a relationship with fellow actor Shelagh Fraser, who she met when they appeared together in the play, *Igloo*, at the 1965 Edinburgh Festival. In 1980, Trader Faulkner was approached by John Lehmann to write Beatrix's biography but, after Rosamond vetoed any mention of her sister's sexuality, Faulkner withdrew from the project.

One of those expunged from any sanitised Lehmann biography would have been an equally unorthodox actress who, during her time as Beatrix's understudy, had fallen in love with her: Mary Morris. Born in Fiji in 1915, Morris had two ambitions: to be an actress or a painter – preferably both. She studied at RADA and started her theatre career in London as Lysistrata at the Old Gate Theatre and then set up her own repertory company, The Stranger Players, who performed at the Barn Theatre in Oxted from September 1936 to March 1939. She spent six months in Hollywood under contract to MGM, who failed to supply a single role. On her return to England, Alexander Korda gave her a contract with London Films; in her first film, *Prison Without Bars* (1938), she played 'a lesbian reform school inmate.'[159] Peter Noble said, 'Like all great theatre personalities she is unique, and added to this she is independent, highly intelligent, sometimes arrogant...she is distinctive, sometimes aggressive... She is an Orson Welles fan, a chain smoker, likes wearing slacks and staying in bed until lunch'[160] By 1946, Morris was living in an artist's studio in Notting Hill Gate with Cecilie Krog, daughter of the Norwegian playwright, Helge Krog. Her last public appearance was in London in May 1988, when the 72-year-old actress arrived for a screening of one of her films, on a motorbike, dressed in full black leathers.

Lehmann or Morris: if Coral's female lover was either of these, it's unlikely the split came down to a simple choice of career over partner. Both had powerful personalities, and enough eccentricities and ambitions of their own, to ensure that the course of love with Coral would not, in the long run, have run smoothly – especially as her sexual tastes were mostly on a steady trajectory towards men.

For the time being, her professional path led her to more theatrical comedies throughout 1936: *The Golden Gander* was set in a goldmine in the Australian desert 'where men are men and women mere incitements to lawlessness',[161] while in *The Happy Medium*, staged by The Repertory Players, Coral was 'imposing as a lovely lady crook'.[162] Another member of the Repertory Players was Andrea Troubridge, the daughter of Una, Lady Troubridge, the longtime consort of infamous writer Radclyffe Hall. Andrea joined the Players and had a number of small roles in shows such as *Family Hold Back* (1936). Troubridge and Hall did anything but 'hold back': they attended Andrea's rehearsals, her opening night in Wimbledon, her matinees and even theatrical parties, where they were at home with the likes of John Gielgud and Noël Coward's designer, Gladys Calthrop.

Then came the real deal: in June, Coral was cast opposite Rex Harrison in the Margot Neville hit comedy, *Heroes Don't Care*, at St Martin's Theatre. In the souvenir programme, theatre-goers were informed – in a phrase that sounded more like a warning than an introduction – 'Coral Brown Is An Australian'.

She played a Kate Hepburn-like, trouser-clad pilot and explorer, Connie Crawford, who wants to join a polar expedition being organised by Sir Edward Pakenham (Felix Aylmer) and 'will use anything from blackmail to a sharing of sleeping bags in order to join the party and be the first woman at the Pole'.[163]

The play was a critical smash, with both Harrison and Coral scooping plaudits: *Empire News* said, 'The cast is about as perfect as any judge of acting could wish,'[164] while Coral 'sacrifices charm to give a horrific impersonation of ruthless efficiency as the airwoman'.[165] According to one reporter, 'Half the cause of her rapid success, she told me frankly, is the lack of tall dark young women on the London stage at the moment.'[166] News trickled back to Australia via a London correspondent, who reported that, 'Coral Brown, clad in mannish clothes, makes the airwoman a devastatingly efficient and disturbing person.'[167] And, according to Patrick Garland, Coral was causing disturbances off stage: Harrison told him that, during one performance, he looked towards the wings, and saw Coral lift up her pullover and display two of her best assets. Not surprisingly, Harrison said the rest of his scene was a blur. Opinions remain divided as to whether Harrison and Coral actually had an affair; she claimed to have turned down Harrison's advances, and is credited with giving him the ironic sobriquet, 'Sexy Rexy'.

Harrison and the rest of the cast got a shock when, on 22 September, the assertive airwoman collapsed on stage at the end of the first act. A doctor was summoned and she was escorted home. But Coral was back on her feet and in her trousers a few days later: she told a reporter that she thought her indisposition was caused by 'inoculations against colds'.[168] It would, perhaps, be too facetious to suppose that it was in any way linked to a recent visit by 'Mother'.

Meanwhile, John Gliddon was pressing on with his efforts to develop Coral's film career: in 1936 and 1937, she had supporting roles in a number of British-made films, including Nils Asther's *Guilty Melody*; *Charing Cross Road*, a drama starring John Mills, about a group of out-of-work actors who share the same digs; and, more significantly, the Regency period drama, *The Amateur Gentleman*, opposite the dashing Douglas Fairbanks Jr. It was a swashbuckling tale of an 18th century publican's son, Barnabas Barty, who makes his way into 'proper' society and unmasks a jewel thief in the process. Filmed at British International Pictures Studios, Borehamwood, it was Fairbanks's first venture as an independent producer, having formed his own company, Criterion Film Productions Ltd, to try to carve out a career away from Hollywood and the shadow of Fairbanks *père*. Coral played Pauline Darville, mistress of the thief, Louis Chichester (Basil Sydney) – Mona Maris was due to take the part but, when illness intervened, Coral stepped in at short notice. This role was the first, but by no means the last, time her character ended up being murdered. Coral and Fairbanks were two of four stars invited to perform at a midnight charity showing of *Broadway Melody of 1936* at the Empire Leicester Square on December 4. In a section called 'Films in the Making', they re-enacted a scene from *The Amateur Gentleman* on a stage set depicting a film studio.

Though ostensibly enamoured of his leading lady, the intense and serious Elissa Landi, Fairbanks soon bored of her and found Coral more alluring: 'She was not only a beauty but the possessor of a wicked and frequently bawdy wit,' he said. 'She struck out at anyone...she was so bright that it was sometimes difficult to accept the challenge of her very presence.'[169] But accept he did – though he kept his affair with Coral a secret from the volcanic Miss Landi.

The Amateur Gentleman enjoyed the accolade of a royal premiere but only modest reviews: *The Times* said it was 'primarily a film of action and of atmosphere... Mr Fairbanks plays with assurance',[170] while elsewhere it was dismissed as 'well in the top class of England's more unimportant pictures... agreeably wholesome, superior in workmanship, and uniformly uninspired'.[171] The film had a strange claim to fame: it became the subject of a minor court case, when Akos Tolnay and James Williams claimed that Criterion Film Productions Ltd had failed to pay them for writing an early version of the script.

But *The Amateur Gentleman* was responsible for something more significant: Douglas Fairbanks had suggested that 'Coral Brown' wasn't really a film star's name. He suggested that she change it to 'Coral Brune'; then they discovered there was a German actress with the same name. Instead, Coral underwent her first piece of cosmetic surgery, and grafted an 'e' onto her surname. Later, she gave a slightly different version of events to the press:

'Recently an American, who is interested in numerology, said that there was something wrong with the number of letters in my name. So I added the 'e' for luck on his advice and it really does seem to be bringing me better fortune.'[172] However it came about, one thing was certain: Coral Browne had arrived.

Her new moniker made its debut on the credits of her first show of 1937, *The Great Romancer*, starring Robert Morley at the New Theatre. The play was based on the life of author Alexandre Dumas *père*, and memorably opened with the author cooking a rabbit still in its skin. In its try-out for the Repertory Players at the Strand Theatre on 9 May, Coral played Dumas's great love, Adah Isaacs Menken; but when the show opened in the West End at the New Theatre on 15 June, she had switched to the role of Ida Ferrier (later Madame Dumas). The production was hailed as 'a masterpiece in which humour, pathos and top-speed charm are brilliantly blended'.[173] – while Coral won the admiration of its producer, Charles Lefaux, who told her: 'You're God's gift to a producer, because you take direction so quietly.'[174] She was always astute enough to know when and how to sharpen her skills: in March 1937, she appeared as the Widow in a production of *The Taming of the Shrew* starring Alec Clunes and Edith Evans, an actress she greatly admired. Coral admitted later, 'I volunteered to understudy her so I could learn.'[175] But she was about to learn another, harsher lesson – don't go near a man who fires blanks.

She was cast opposite Alastair Sim in *The Gusher*, a melodrama about – once again – a group of gold-hunters. The show comprised 17 scenes, a cast of 70, and settings including a prison kitchen, a coroner's court, a luxury liner, an East End dance hall and a Panama City resort. As *The Times* observed, 'Those who pay for their seats will at any rate have no cause to complain that they are not given quantity for their money.'[176] *The Tatler* concurred: '*The Gusher* is colossal, if not epic.'[177] Once again, Coral was playing a villainess: 'Jacqueline', the manageress of Barney's Club, who ends up being shot by fellow villain Robert Rutherford (Ivan Samson). Apart from its large cast, this show was memorable for two other things: first, it brought Coral to the attention of the show's co-producer, Firth Shephard, at a crucial point in her career. And second, it almost brought the curtain down on that career.

During one performance in August, Coral and Samson were in the throes of their scene in which, after a struggle with a pistol (loaded with a blank cartridge), he 'shoots' Jacqueline dead. That evening, life nearly imitated art: the unfortunate Samson fired the gun too early, and the 'blank' exploded against Coral's forehead. She collapsed, her temple bleeding. The only piece of luck was that the wound hit an existing scar she'd had since she was a baby. All actresses worried about being fired – but few ever had to worry about being shot.

But the management were adamant: the show had to go on: 'They rang me up the next day and asked if I could possibly carry on,' said Coral. 'I felt all right, so I said yes. I carried on for a week until I began forgetting my lines, so they took me off to a nursing home and found I had delayed concussion. The specialist's bill for my heart was £200 and for my head £120, and I lost six weeks' salary.'[178] She was ordered by her doctor to rest for three months, but took less time than prescribed. And, when she returned to the stage, she discovered she had developed a new 'scar' that would never heal: for the rest of her career, she would suffer from crippling stage fright. At least she was in good company: Laurence Olivier, Antony Sher, Derek Jacobi, Ellen Terry, Ian Holm and Alec Guinness are all on the roll-call of revered theatre practitioners who suffered from what Sher dubbed 'The Fear'. Peter Finch gave up stage work entirely in favour of films because of the condition.

Even 40 years later, Coral admitted, 'I have perpetual stage fright, and it gets worse as the years go on. The first nights are dreadful, really, absolutely dreadful. It takes three weeks to get into stride.'[179] She tried to calm her nerves by endless activity at home and in her dressing room: making jam and pickles, knitting, embroidery – anything to occupy her hands and her mind. Jill Melford said, 'She was the most frightened performer I think I've ever worked with. Terror – I mean, she would have mini-heart attacks. I was very surprised. The shakes, and sick, hyperventilation. Terrified. She worked well with it, but she did suffer.'[180] And, even after nearly 40 years on stage, she said, 'I love going to the theatre, working in the theatre. I love talking to my fellow beings. This is my life. But I doubt whether in ten years' time I'll want to be going to the theatre to work and suffer all these agonies.'[181]

The stage fright was also the reason she steered clear of television during the years when everything was broadcast live. Her one foray into live television was a guest appearance on the satirical series, *That Was the Week That Was*, on 30 March 1963. 'We'd already had guests like Michael Redgrave, Sybil Thorndike and Edith Evans,' said Ned Sherrin. 'When we asked her, she said, "Well, I've got to do that – it's like a Royal Command."'[182] As usual, the thought of doing the show terrified her, so she wrote her first line on her immaculately manicured nails. According to Sherrin, 'She entered with her head held up and her fingers stretched out. Her hand shook so much that she was quite unable to read the blur.'[183] Coral later said, 'I could not understand why anyone would want to go through opening night jitters to do a live performance with practically no rehearsal in a space the size of a postage stamp, in front of a rather cumbersome one-eyed box with no film in it.'[184]

Later, when the acting jobs had dried up and been replaced by social engagements, the stage fright still emerged. In 1984, she told fellow stage fright sufferer Alec Guinness, 'I've eight for dinner on Tuesday and as it's a year since anyone, except Santa, got a foot in I'm highly nervous & "rehearsing" the glasses, plates, silver, etc, so I won't have a complete collapse when the dreaded guests appear.'[185]

But at least while Coral was recovering from her physical wounds in 1937, she had something to take her mind off the trauma: a fling with Maurice Chevalier. From late August 1937, the French star was at Pinewood, starring in the René Claire musical comedy *Break the News*; his co-star – and fellow 'chorus boy' – was one Jack Buchanan. In Paris, Chevalier lived with the actress Nita Raya; in London, he played away with Coral. After her accident, he told her, 'You deserve the best because you are a brave girl and a fine example of "take it on the chin and smile".'[186] When he had to return to France to star in Julien Duvivier's *L'Homme du Jour*, he told Coral, 'Leaving tomorrow for Paris. Just want to say goodbye and wish you very sincerely to get absolutely well and happy in your life and in your work. You are alright by me and a fine person.'[187] And, from Paris, he wrote: 'Your letter was welcome and reminded me of some really delicious moments and be sure that I'll go directly to your theatre as soon as I am in London… So here is hoping – may I kiss you?'[188]

Meanwhile, Coral had been busy in front of the cameras herself – first, there was the mild murder-mystery *Black Limelight*, in which she appeared as Raymond Massey's mistress Lily James, a victim of the film's killer. It was adapted from a stage play which had run for over a year in the West End with Margaret Rawlings. Apparently happy family man and salesman Peter Charrington (Massey) flees after Lily is found dead at the Dorset holiday home he's been renting for their assignations. In her few scenes, Coral got a chance to show off her elegant figure, first in a bathing suit, then – daringly for the time – stripping it off in front of her lover before slipping into an even sexier silk dressing gown. Before she's bumped off, Lily reveals to Peter that she's pregnant (though the word itself isn't actually said, the implication is clear). Lily's killing is linked to a series in the area, attributed to the 'Dorset murderer'. Amid much talk of 'moon madness', (some of the murders take place during the full moon), Massey's loyal and questioning wife Mary (Joan Marion) solves the case for the police and snares the real culprit – not bad for someone they previously dismissed as 'just an hysterical woman'. The film's premise was, according to an unknown critic, 'quite logical if we accept the theory that a man can suffer from an affliction of the eyes which prevents him from seeing perfectly except in the dark.'[189] If you couldn't, it looked suspiciously like pure hokum. *The Times*' critic was not impressed either: 'In the film Miss Joan Marion has only a half of Miss Rawlings's work to do but that half is made extremely difficult by the refusal of the director to realize that suspense on the stage cannot be reproduced on the screen unless the camera is allowed to exclude what is not natural to it and is given a licence to explore what is. There is throughout the film a lack of nervous tension.'[190]

The same year, Coral appeared as another femme fatale in the cinematic curio, *Yellow Sands*. The film's opening credits declared: 'The film you are about to see has been produced in response to the wishes of that large public which calls for British films about Britain.' The public may have wished it kept its calls to itself after seeing this ludicrous offering, scripted by a misfiring Rodney Ackland. Set in a fictional West Country seaside village, the 'story' starred Robert Newton as fisherman Joe, a rabid proselytising Bolshevik, whose worst curse is to call someone – almost everyone, in fact – 'a blasted capitalist'. Dame Marie Tempest was his elderly aunt, contemplating her imminent demise and her dysfunctional family, who suffered the indignity of having to tell one of her fussy relatives to 'please move away from the sun – it's much nicer to look at than your bosom'. Coral played barmaid Emma Copplestone, the only vamp in the village, who's simply too worldly and sophisticated to have credibly ended up pulling pints and punters in such a rural pub. The red-haired Emma is wooed by both Joe and his cousin Arthur (Patrick Barr) who, Joe warns Emma, is a 'confirmed polygamist'.

Coral got a chance for a brief reunion with Maurice Chevalier when she went to Paris to make an uncredited appearance in *Alert in the Mediterranean*, a melodramatic action film where the captains of French, German and English ships attempt to rescue passengers on another boat about to be overcome by poisonous smoke. Saved from the foreign fumes, she returned to Blighty to appear in *We're Going to Be Rich*, a '…Gracie Fields vehicle about music hall singer Kitty Dobson who becomes embroiled in the get-rich-quick schemes of her doting but dopey husband, Dobbie (Victor McLaglen). After leaving Melbourne, the pair end up in South Africa during the 1880s gold rush, where Kitty lands a job as the singer at Yankee Gordon's saloon and wows the customers with one of her best-known songs, 'Walter, Walter (Take Me to the Altar)'. However, she has unwittingly usurped the previous warbler – Coral at her most vampish, as the vengeful Pearl, all boas, feathers and dropped aitches, especially in her bar-room rendition of 'Don't 'Ang My 'Arry'. And when Pearl takes her revenge by pretending to spend the night with Dobbie, he gets his own back by dumping her in a horse trough. That year, Coral told a reporter, 'I think that an actress of my type must use her young years to create for herself a position in the minds of the public in a series of amusing and modern parts.'[191] Being doused in a trough full of cold water while Gracie Fields trilled away to 'Walter' wasn't quite what she had in mind.

But her position was about to change — and, even though it would mean her lying down in some strange places, her days with her nose in the trough would soon be over.

Firth is my Shephard

1939–1950

T hough Coral wasn't short of good reviews to send to her parents for their scrapbook, it was a notice published in the summer of 1939, unrelated to any specific performance, which then gave her the most satisfaction:

> The dignified Garrick Club spent a frivolous evening lately choosing by ballot London's three most attractive actresses…
>
> 1) Gwen Ffrangcon-Davies
> 2) Margaret Rawlings
> 3) Coral Brown [1]

Coral sent the cutting to her father, with the comment, 'I wish you could get that in the Aussie press. It's the <u>biggest</u> compliment paid to me since I got here. Garrick Club – Gawd, and I don't even know anyone rich enough to be a member. My shares seem to be going up.'[2] She was right: and soon she would have an address which would impress any member of the 'dignified Garrick' – *and* the affections of another older man who would, as Gregan McMahon had done, take her into the next stage of her career ascent.

Frederick Edward Shephard – known as 'Firth'– was a successful producer of musical revues, including *Shephard's Pie*, featuring Bobby Howes and Richard Hearne. Born in East London on 27 April 1891, Shephard had spent most of his adult life in the theatre. He began his career in music hall, writing revues and sketches with, among others, Fred Karno. His first full-length musical comedy was the 1919 *His Little Widows*, later adapted into his first major success, *Lady Luck* (1927), which ran for more than 300 performances at the Carlton Theatre. The show's co-producer and leading man, Leslie Henson, set up a management company with Shephard in 1928 and, over the next six years, they staged a string of successful comedies, musicals and farces. In

1934, Shephard struck out on his own and continued to produce a stream of shows firmly in a light theatrical vein. He had married Constance Evans in August 1911 and their only child, Phyllis, was born the following spring. Phyllis was widowed in her twenties after just a year of marriage; her second husband was Leslie Mitchell, BBC Television's first commentator. The couple were introduced in 1937 by Nora Swinburne on the opening night of a Firth Shephard production, *Wise Tomorrow.*

Coral had first come to Shephard's attention in 1935, when she turned down the chance to understudy Alice Delysia in *Accidentally Yours*. He made her a provisional offer to appear in his next show that August, but instead she opted to take up *This Desirable Residence* and it was to be another two years before she signed up for a Shephard show, *The Gusher* – the play that nearly ended her career. As John Gliddon recalled, 'I arranged for you to meet Firth Shephard – that was the end for me.'[3]

Una Troubridge had warned her actress daughter, Andrea, during her time with Coral's former employers, The Repertory Theatre, that 'Even better class theatrical managers would fight shy of any girl who suggested obvious immorality'.[4] It appeared that Firth Shephard preferred a touch of immorality *and* a touch of class – and he got both with Coral.

He had an apartment at 36 Curzon Street in London's smart Mayfair district (his offices were at 19 Charing Cross Road) and Coral moved in with him. It was not a *ménage à trois*: Mrs Shephard lived outside of her husband's theatrical circle. After Phyllis's marriage to Leslie Mitchell, Constance went to live in Cannes. When war broke out, she escaped on one of the last boats to leave the Riviera, and went to live with her daughter and son-in-law in the cottage they rented at Harefield, close to Denham Film Studios. Coral was accepted socially as Shephard's mistress: in August 1943, she became godmother to Gillian, the daughter of Firth's manager, Stanley French, and his wife, Paddy; within the profession, she became known as 'Shephard's Bush'. And for the best part of the next decade, the 'Bush' was a perennial at the Savoy Theatre, flourishing with one hit show after another. Coral was always blithe about her position – in all senses: 'Firth is my Shephard, I shall not want. His rod and staff comfort me. Though he makes me lie down in strange places...'[5] In fact, this 'debt' was acknowledged in almost identical language, by the cast of one of his shows who gave his a first-night present: a plaque which read 'The Firth is our Shephard. We shall not want!'[6]

However, according to Frith Banbury, Coral herself provided Shephard with her own kind of comfort: 'His background was really revue and musicals, and she vetted any straight plays or ideas for straight plays that came along.'[7] In allowing his mistress to give him professional advice, Shephard was breaking his own 'house rules': he was resistant to suggestions from anyone, but especially his friends and family. At one time, he let his daughter Phyllis pick plays for him but, after he rejected the sure-fire hit, *Edward, My Son*, she gave up. Coral persuaded Shephard to produce a number of hit shows which he had initially turned down, including *Arsenic and Old Lace*, directed by Marcel Varnel. This opened in London in 1942 and clocked up 1332 performances, making it then the longest-running US show ever in the West End. Such was Shephard's success during the war with American imports that there was a joke in the profession: 'What's Firth Shephard looking so unhappy about? – Oh, someone's given him an English play to read.'[8]

But it was another American play that would give Shephard one of his biggest successes – and make Coral Browne a star, in the most inauspicious of circumstances.

Even before Britain declared war on Germany, London's tourist population was dwindling because of the worsening political situation, and those who had arrived in the capital were becoming eager to leave. When Neville Chamberlain formally declared war on 3 September 1939, any business that was deemed by the government as not 'essential to national life' was ordered to close – and theatres fell into this category. George Bernard Shaw declared this decision to be 'a masterstroke of unimaginative stupidity'.[9]

However, as weeks passed and no air raids came, the rules were slightly relaxed and theatres were allowed to go on with the show: by 28 October, 20 had reopened, though their doors had to be closed by 11.15pm, so 'curtain-up' was brought forward by at least an hour for the duration of the war. Defiantly, West End theatres enjoyed a period of almost unprecedented prosperity. Norman Lebrecht observed, 'the closer the threat, the more urgent was the public demand for spiritual catharsis - not in the old remedies of religion, ideology and alcohol but in the distilled products of artistic imagination'.[10] Audiences flocked to see shows that took them as far as possible from the realities of war - even if it didn't meet with the approval of some of their elected representatives. Beverly Baxter MP, who (in the best parliamentary tradition) had a second job as theatre critic of the *Evening Standard*, berated producers and theatregoers alike for their preference for revivals, revues – like Alan Melville's hugely successful *Sweet and Low* – and imported American comedies. In another parliamentary tradition, Baxter badly misjudged the mood of the people: 'Our people are still able to find laughter and refreshment of mind to fortify them against the spiritual deprivations of war.'[11] By the summer of 1940, 18 shows were running in the West End, many playing to capacity houses. John Gielgud, whose production of *The Importance of Being Earnest*, opened at the Globe Theatre just before hostilities broke out, took the show on a long tour around the provinces. Robert Atkins continued staging Shakespeare at the Regent's Park Open Air Theatre for most of the war; in July 1941, he built an Elizabethan platform in Southwark Park and staged *The Taming of the Shrew* with the American actress Claire Luce. Later in the war, Donald Wolfit staged a popular series of 'lunchtime Shakespeares' at the Strand Theatre.

It was gas attacks, rather than bombs, which were feared the most during the early days of the war. Thus, West End stars like Gielgud and his *Earnest* co-stars Edith Evans and Peggy Ashcroft took to arriving at the Globe with gas-masks in tow. Stars of their magnitude were also encouraged by the Home Morale Emergency Committee to help keep the public's collective chin up, leading community singing and other cheery activities in their theatres. According to Robert Morley, this wasn't entirely welcome: 'What the public didn't like was that, after the performance was over, if a raid was going on, the company tried to entertain them and prevent them going out…so we used to recite 'If' and things like that, and do sketches. And pretty soon, they decided that the bombs were preferable to the home-made entertainment, and they staggered out into the street.'[12]

Apart from the triple horrors of imminent bombings, gassings and enforced sing-songs, Londoners had other hardships to endure. A black-out was imposed: no street lighting or external building lights and thick curtains became the order of the day. Petrol and oil was rationed from the first day of hostilities, and no one, not even the biggest stars, would be immune to the impositions.*

---

* In 1944, Ivor Novello – a hero from the First World War for penning the anthemic 'Keep the Home Fires Burning' – fell foul of the rationing laws and served four weeks in Wormwood Scrubs for misuse of petrol coupons. In his defence, Novello said that he needed the petrol to

Food rationing was introduced in January 1940; meals eaten away from home were 'off ration' (during the war, Coral's grandfather's old firm, H V McKay Massey Harris, sold 20,000 Sunshine Drills, Disc Harrows and Binders to England to help step up food production). West End restaurants still offered a sumptuous bill-of-fare, although prices were rocketing and most customers were in uniform. In 1942, the government prohibited restaurants from charging more than five shillings a meal. Clubs like Quaglino's, the Embassy and the Café de Paris, closed for the first few weeks at the beginning of the war, were soon jam-packed every night with servicemen and women.

Inevitably, when the full-scale bombing of London ensued, some theatres, including the Little Theatre in the Adelphi, the Queen's, the Shaftesbury and the Holborn Empire, did not survive the onslaught. The Piccadilly Theatre was badly bomb-damaged, but in 1941 Noël Coward was still able to open his new comedy *Blithe Spirit* there. RADA's Vanbrugh Theatre in Malet Street was completely destroyed by a bomb in April the same year. And there were casualties among the West End's most popular entertainers: band leader and dancer Ken 'Snakehips' Johnson, whose band had a residency at the Café de Paris, was one of 30 people killed when a bomb hit the packed nightclub on 8 March 1941. A few weeks later, on the evening of 17 April, singer Al Bowlly was killed when a German Luftwaffe parachute mine exploded outside his Jermyn Street flat.

For the first time since she had left, going back to Australia might have seemed like a tempting proposition to Coral – especially, as one commentator noted, 'While war in Britain has decimated theatre there, Australian audiences are enjoying a boom in productions…producers have found a market for straight plays…in Melbourne, Gregan McMahon's Repertory Players have enjoyed an excellent season… Australian artists have returned in large numbers from London.'[13]

Of course, she stayed – and offered to 'do her bit' for the war effort. Like many of her acting contemporaries, Coral was interviewed by the War Office to establish her suitability for active service in one of the armed forces. 'There

drive himself (in his gas-guzzling Rolls-Royce) between the West End and 'Redroofs', his house near Maidenhead, and that his appearances in *The Dancing Years* at the Adelphi, constituted 'very important work for morale'.[14] Novello's misguided attitude – coupled with the fact that he had tried to bribe the officer of the court who had served the summons on him – sealed his fate.

was a committee who said whether you could act in the theatre or not, or whether you had to go and be a WAC or answer the telephone in Stonehenge or somewhere like that... I don't think I'd have been any good on a telephone exchange, and I think they thought that, too... I did a first aid course, like Judy Kelly. But they said it was more important to go back to our jobs in the theatre, so we did.'[15] Others in the profession also found their way back to the stage. Frith Banbury had registered as a conscientious objector. At a tribunal, he was asked if he was prepared to do farm work: he answered, 'Prepared – but not equipped.' The tribunal decided he should continue acting.[16]*

Being rather handy with the needle, Coral could have joined one of the numerous women's 'Make Do And Mend' groups that sprang up. Instead, she kept her ever-nervous hands busy making what were described as 'surrealistic toys' from wool oddments, for sick children.[17] And, like many performers during those years, she was only too willing to donate her services to help a good cause – when it was permitted. In November 1942, Coral – who remained largely apolitical all her life – added her name to a star-studded letter to *The Times*, complaining that 'owing to the persistent action taken by the Lord's Day Observance Society in upholding the law passed in 1677...we, the undersigned, wish to state with regret that we are not allowed to give stage performances for any charity, or performance to which money is subscribed, on any Sunday. We take pleasure in the thought that we are still at liberty to give our services for the free entertainment of his Majesty's forces.'[18] Even Coral's style became part of the war-effort: increasing numbers of women were working in factories, but they refusing to wear safety caps that prevented them from catching their long hair in the machinery. So the War Office prevailed upon Audrey Withers, editor of *Vogue*, to promote to her readers the virtues and attractions of having shorter hair. Withers duly obliged, and ran a feature, highlighting the trim cuts favoured by Deborah Kerr – and Coral Browne.

Coral's first wartime play, in January 1940, was the successful but unremarkable Alec Coppel comedy, *Believe It or Not*, co-starring fellow Australian (and qualified first-aider) Judy Kelly. The plot revolved around the

---

* Howard Goorney, one of the founders of Theatre Workshop, was serving in a tank regiment when he received a letter from Joan Littlewood, with whom he was then working with the Theatre Union: 'It instructed him to get demobbed – and get back. Some fervent praying to a single candle did the trick. Classified an "A2 psychopathic personality of the artistic type", he was given an honourable discharge.' [19]

havoc wreaked by a butler who blackmailed his young employers, with the action taking place in a Paris hotel and on a luxury liner. It duly received positive but unremarkable reviews: 'Mr Griffith Jones and Miss Coral Browne make quite an amusing thing of this Parisian adventure.'[20]

She augmented her regular West End employment throughout the war years with a succession of small film roles. In 1939, she appeared in the crime drama *The Nursemaid who Disappeared*, about a man's quest to solve the kidnapping of his sister's baby in America. Coral played Mabel Barnes, friend of Janet Murch, the said disappearing nursemaid. The following year, she had two uncredited parts, also in crime sagas: first, in *The First and the Last*, aka *21 Days* (scripted by Graham Greene from a John Galsworthy tale), starring Laurence Olivier and Vivien Leigh; and *They Came by Night*, starring Phyllis Calvert.

But her most famous film during this era was the George Formby vehicle-cum-wartime propaganda exercise, *Let George Do It*, directed by Marcel Varnel. By 1940, Formby was enjoying his third successive year atop the list of Britain's biggest money-making film stars, ahead of the likes of Gracie Fields and Charles Laughton.

The film's plot stretched the suspension of belief to snapping point. Formby – as ukulele player George Hepplewhite – misses his rendezvous with the Dinky Doo Concert Party and ends up in Norway, where he is mistaken for a British agent before finally exposing band leader Mark Mendes as a Nazi agent. It featured a dream sequence, which culminated in the heroic George descending on a Nazi rally in a balloon and landing a punch on Hitler. Coral played the vampish Iris, Mendes's accomplice, and the woman who had to pretend she couldn't keep her hands off Formby, as she attempted to find his passport and ascertain his real identity. As usual, Formby's ever-present and jealous wife and business manager, Beryl (a former champion clog dancer) put paid to any possibility of Iris and George kissing (it was another Australian, Googie Withers, who gave him his first screen kiss, in *Trouble Brewing*).

Coral's first scene in *Let George Do It* featured an elaborate dance which ended with the splits, 'Oh Don't the Wind Blow Cold': 'I was supposed to be a ballet dancer tapping out the code with my feet,' said Coral. 'Only I couldn't dance and my dancing was "dubbed".'[21] The routine was actually performed by the ballerina Diana Gould, later second wife of Yehudi Menuhin. Apart from getting to grips with Formby, Coral also had to spend a scene pretending to enjoy his rendition of 'Mr Wu's A Window Cleaner Now'. It was no surprise when she later admitted she had done the film 'for the money'.[22]

Money was also important to Formby – but to a ridiculous degree. According to Phyllis Calvert, Britain's highest-paid film star spent most of his time off set tinkering with old watches which he'd bought from junk shops for a few shillings. 'He'd sit in his dressing room, restoring watches, which he would then go round the studio trying to sell. He was like a man with dirty postcards, coming up to you and saying, "Like to see a pretty watch?"'[23]

Under the title *Dinky Doo*, a dubbed version of *Let George Do It* was released in Russia, where it played in one Moscow cinema alone for over a year. Phyllis Calvert received Russian fan mail and Reginald Bishop, editor of *Russia Today*, declared: 'Next to Joseph Stalin and one or two military men, George Formby is probably the most popular single figure in the Soviet Union.'[24]

By the time *Let George Do It* was released in Britain, Firth Shephard had taken over as manager of the Savoy Theatre, so he and Coral took up residence in a corner suite on the adjoining hotel's fifth floor. Other long-term residents included Beatrice Lillie and – after his Belgravia home was bombed – Noël Coward. Shephard maintained the Curzon Street flat, but the Savoy would be their base for the duration of the war. However, their luxurious new home would not escape unscathed: 70 members of the Savoy's staff trained as ARP wardens and most of the hotel's valuables were put into storage in cellars under Waterloo Station. On 16 April 1941, a landmine fell outside the hotel's Embankment entrance, shattering every river-facing window and putting the restaurant, kitchen and more than 60 suites out of commission – Coral later recalled that having windows in her suite became something of a novelty during one winter: 'I had no panes in the window for more than 24 hours at a time.'[25] In 1941, Latry, the Savoy's head chef, invented a 'war dish' – a pie made from vegetables and fatless pastry. But, despite the daily dangers and discomforts, the war years would be some of Coral's best, providing her with commercial success, stardom – and love in some *very* unexpected places.

The first of her 'Savoy' plays reunited her with her *Great Romancer* co-star, Robert Morley who, unlike many of his British stage contemporaries, had resisted any attempts to lure him to Hollywood; in 1939, he turned down the leading role in *The Hunchback of Notre Dame* before it was offered to Charles Laughton. Morley displayed a refreshingly realistic attitude towards the temptations of fame and fortune in America: 'All that sitting around in overheated Californian swimming pools, just waiting to be insulted by producers…'[26]

Like Coral, Morley was content with what British stage and cinema could offer him – and had similarly been officially permitted to continue working in the theatre. In 1941, they were cast as the leads in the Moss Hart/George Kaufman comedy *The Man Who Came to Dinner* – one of those American imports so disdained by Beverly Baxter. It was a show which Firth Shephard had initially rejected, but which canny Coral finally persuaded him to produce as a tax-loss. Hart and Kaufman based the central character, Sheridan Whiteside, on their friend, the corpulent, acerbic and much-quoted critic and columnist, Alexander Woollcott, doyen of the Algonquin Hotel Round Table literary set. He had once described Los Angeles as 'seven suburbs in search of a city', and declared, 'All the things I really like to do are either immoral, illegal, or fattening' – a claim that was more apt for Coral than the sexually-confused (and probably celibate) Woollcott.

With raw material of this calibre to work with, Hart and Kaufman would have been hard-pushed to produce a play that was anything other than witty and entertaining. The premise of the play was that Sheridan Whiteside, a famous radio lecturer, is travelling through Ohio when he injures his leg outside the home of the Stanley family, who have invited him to dinner. Confined to a wheelchair temporarily, Whiteside imposes his Christmas presence on the Stanleys, inflicting his own brand of injurious insults to anyone within range, as his New York literary world wreaks havoc in their mid-Western home. The play had already been a major success on Broadway and a hit film, both starring Monty Woolley. For London, director Marcel Varnel cast Morley as Whiteside, with Coral as his wisecracking secretary and general factotum, Maggie Cutler. The play was given a provincial try-out in Birmingham and Manchester, to favourable reviews, before opening at the Savoy, where it would come in after the closure of Noël Coward's hugely successful *Design for Living*. And for Morley, the role would be memorable for more than just establishing him as a leading man.

On 4 December 1941, the opening night in London, Morley was almost upstaged by domestic events: he barely made curtain-up and, huffing and puffing, explained to a disgruntled Coral that his wife had gone into labour, and he'd just rushed from his home near Ascot. The Morleys first child was duly born a few hours after the first-night curtain came down, on 5 December.

The baby boy was named Sheridan and, in another twist that couldn't have been scripted, Alexander Woollcott agreed to be the infant's godfather – fitting for a future theatre critic and writer.

Morley *père* and his leading lady wet the baby's head by making their show the toast of the West End. *The Times* called it 'a bright, light, genially American, slightly farcical and thoroughly enjoyable comedy'.[27] *Theatre World* gushed, 'Not in years has London enjoyed a comedy like this…war-time London is certainly grateful that Mr Shephard's faith and courage have brought such abundant wit and good fun to cheer us in these days… Miss Browne plays a none too easy role with admirable restraint and conviction.'[28] Richard Bebb later said, 'In a way, this was a quintessential part for [Coral] – immaculately dressed, she emanated a cool command over the rackety situations of the play, distancing herself from the chaos with wit and charm'.[29] As a tax-loss, *The Man Who Came to Dinner* was a massive failure – it had a run of over 700 performances.

During that time, one 'rackety situation' Coral had to deal with was her leading man's onstage japes: 'To annoy her, Robert used to put the brakes on and then she would be wheeling this leaden figure across the stage,' said Sheridan Morley. 'He loved her very much and she loved him. I think her being Australian appealed to him, because you didn't see many Australians then – they were a rare sight in London – and I think her feistiness appealed to him. They made a very good pair, because they both gave as good as they got.'[30] Not to mention her courage: as the bombing of London intensified, Morley said, 'Coral didn't take any notice; she wasn't going to let it interfere with her performance – *I* was the one who was so nervous I screamed, and the first to hide under the table.'[31]

Nothing – not even a Blitz – was going to stop Coral savouring every moment of the show. For, after several false starts, *The Man Who Came to Dinner* had well and truly established her as a West End star – a role she revelled in playing.

The Austrian actress and director, Leontine Sagan (the first in London to audition Coral) was once asked by the theatre journalist Eric Johns for her advice to young performers. She told him, 'Always work to become a star, but never be a star.'[32] Coral was always willing to put in the work to become a star – and always ready to act like one. Johns wrote: 'Stardom is a full-time job… Like the traditional housewife's duties, the star's work is never finished. The star is ever conscious of her reputation... Maintaining a reputation hampers one's activities and drains one's purse. You expect a star, even in her private life, to live up to certain standards. You demand that she eats at the most exclusive restaurants where the house charges are far more costly than the meal. A goodly portion of her astronomical income must be devoted to the acquisition of an exclusive address with a Mayfair, Sloane or Grosvenor telephone number. She could live just as comfortably in Tooting, Acton or Islington, but her prestige could never hope to survive in so remote a district. *She might just as well choose the Australian Bush.* You expect your star to be a leader of fashion. No badly dressed woman has touched even the fringe of stardom. She must dress well at all costs, even if her last penny goes on her back. You expect new photographs of her to appear at frequent intervals. Constant visits to the photographer mean constant changes of hair style. In rare cases, stardom may be won overnight, but in every case the price of maintaining it, once the artist's debut has ceased to be news value, is an expensive and exhausting business.'[33] [*author emphasis*]

In every respect, Coral excelled in playing the part of 'Coral Browne, West End star'. For the next 30 years, she would only live at addresses in the exclusive and affluent Mayfair and Belgravia districts. She dined at the Caprice and the Ivy, often accompanied by her French poodle Blossom, the first of a succession of toy dogs. According to Mario Gallati, owner of the Caprice, Coral was just one of a number of actresses, including Hermione Gingold and Dulcie Gray, who brought their dogs to his elegant restaurant and ordered special dishes for their pets. However, she waged a lifelong battle to 'fight the flab': she said, 'When I came to England I was 12 stone, I'm now nine. I make a great effort to keep slim. Lunch is something that's gone out of my life completely, and I never eat breakfast...I go on a different diet every week... I've been on a diet all my life. I'm ruled by my stomach...'[34] She weighed herself every morning; even when she was in her seventies, she would take a set of bathroom scales with her on holiday, to check she wasn't piling on the pounds. She would try whatever diet was in fashion, and then avidly recommend it to everyone she knew. It was all part of her perverse make-up, then, that the two men she married were both gourmet cooks.

But it was worth keeping in shape to fit into the clothes that now filled her wardrobe – outfits from the finest couturiers, including Balenciaga, Molyneux, Chanel and Balmain. To go with the bespoke couture were diamonds, pearls and mink coats. According to actor Peter Stenson, 'She always insisted on having a fur for the plays – which she then took home at the end of the run.'[35] Frith Banbury observed, 'She was always conscious of what she looked like, and she had wonderful taste in clothes. It was natural to her, and you wouldn't necessarily have thought that of a girl who came from Melbourne at that time, who was lower-to-middle class.'[36] Designer Norman Hartnell was reported to have called her 'the most beautifully dressed woman on the London stage'.[37]

Liza Goddard reflected, 'It's very different if you've got a family, but actresses like Coral didn't: they devoted themselves to their careers. A lot of them used to meet for lunch at the Ivy. In those days, when they were working in the West End, they didn't get up 'til about midday. And they usually had a maid who looked after them, and they'd get dressed very carefully and go to the Ivy, where they'd bitch about each other across the table. And it was incredibly amusing. Then they'd go home and have a rest, and then they'd go to the show. After the show, they'd go out. They lived fantastic lives.'[38]

Coral began to build up a serious art collection: by the 1950s, it included a Picasso and a Graham Sutherland, as well as works by Australian artists, including Edgar Pritchard (also a friend). In 1942, Augustus John asked if he could draw her. She also had collections: her set of fans included a Victorian one given by Jack Buchanan to mark her fourth consecutive year at the Savoy. There was also an impressive assortment of sphinxes – in all shapes, sizes and media. 'She had dozens and dozens of them in her flat,' recalled Michael Baldwin, 'Bronze, china, pewter, paintings, everything…but she wouldn't talk about them at all.' The reason for the fascination was fairly obvious to Jill Melford: 'Well, if you look at her, she looks likes a Sphinx – especially in profile.'[39]

As the writer Hal Porter observed, 'Flexibility of talent and power of attack were not the only traits she had in common with actresses of an earlier day. She had also their grand manner. Coral Browne had a presence on and off stage. She dressed the part. The public could see where its money went.'[40] And it was going to Coral: by the end of the 1940s, she was, along with Edith Evans and Diana Wynyard, one of the West End's three highest paid actresses.

Coral added the last touch of star quality by becoming a regular client, and valued friend, of *the* top theatrical photographer Angus McBean; his studios at 8 Grafton Street, and later, 53 Endell Street were, handily, just a few minutes' walk from the West End's theatres, and the watering holes and eateries favoured by his starry clientele. McBean became renowned for his stylish portraits and surrealistic compositions of thespians (his favourite client was Vivien Leigh): Hermione Gingold hoisted through the air by party balloons; a tiny Beatrice Lillie atop a piano keyboard; and the iconic 1956 image of a bare-shouldered young Audrey Hepburn rising out of sand, flanked by Grecian pillars.

In 1942, Coral proved, not for the last time, her unswerving loyalty to a friend during their time of trial – quite literally, in McBean's case. In November 1941, at his house in Bath, he was arrested on suspicion of 'homosexual offences'. He had taken in a teenage male acquaintance who had run away with a young woman. Ostensibly, the police were looking for another teenage runaway, a petty thief, but it soon became apparent that McBean and his social circle had been targetted. The police case was that McBean ran a 'homosexual ring' from his house; many of his friends believed he had been set up. McBean was charged with three counts of buggery and gross indecency with two men and the trial began at Winchester Assizes in March 1942. Hoping for some semblance of leniency, McBean pleaded guilty to one charge of buggery and one of indecency. There was no leniency: he was sentenced to four years' hard labour for the first charge, and 12 months for the second, to run concurrently – 'twice as long as Oscar Wilde', he later observed.[41]

While McBean adapted to the rigours of life in Lincoln prison, comprising a dawn to dusk, six days a week regime labouring in the neighbouring fields, many of McBean's friends and clients couldn't be seen for dust as they rushed to put distance between him and themselves. Others, however, including James Agate, Laurence Olivier and Vivien Leigh, remained loyal – and so did Coral. According to McBean's longtime partner, David Ball, Coral was 'one of the better people...she sent him Christmas cards and occasional letters during his prison term, through his mother'.[42]

McBean wasn't the only gay man with whom Coral forged deep bonds during her years in *The Man Who Came to Dinner*. While she was rehearsing the show in the autumn of 1941, Cecil Beaton (who had, unlike Coral, done a stint of night-shifts at the telephone exchange near his home in Wiltshire) had been commissioned to photograph her in her dressing room – one picture of her hands was captioned, 'Hands of An Actress' – and the professional assignment led to an assignation: 'He asked me to lunch, then to dinner. But I really was extremely surprised when the "great leap" took place.'[43] This 'great leap' signalled the beginning of an affair that, in order not to jeopardise the professional and personal benefits she was enjoying through being 'Shephard's Bush', Coral kept strictly clandestine.

On many subsequent afternoons, Coral and Beaton would meet at his home in Pelham Place, Kensington. She would use air raids to explain her frequent and lengthy daytime absences from the Savoy to Firth Shephard. There was no doubt in her mind that, whatever the risk, it was worth it: 'I have been in love with three men in my life,' she would later say. 'Two I married, and the third was Cecil…he was a great enthusiast, tremendously interested in everything he did. We were very compatible and I was tremendously happy.'[44] According to Sir John Gielgud, Coral told him Beaton was 'the best lay she ever had'.[45] Sometimes, amidst the passion, the lovers would find time to discuss more artistic matters: 'I used to listen to the play he'd written about the Viceroy of India', said Coral. 'It was amateur time when it came to playwriting, but we had the same interests at heart.'[46] But, according to her, one moot subject never came up in conversation: 'We never discussed homosexuality.'[47]

The affair lasted until March 1942, when Beaton left London to fulfil a lengthy assignment in the Middle East as photographer for the Ministry of Information. It's entirely possible that, but for this posting, the relationship would have continued – a possibility that Coral alluded to more than two decades later when, in 1966, she starred in the Beaton-designed production of *Lady Windermere's Fan*. She admitted that, 'I was just as attracted to him as when I first met him.'[48]

In the meantime, matters were further complicated when Beaton's secretary, Maud Nelson – who herself had an unrequited crush on her boss – took a keen an interest in his affair with Coral and spread gossip about it, knowing that this would eventually get back to Firth Shephard. Although still married himself, Shephard was reportedly devastated by Coral's infidelity and attempted suicide. Later, Coral would talk about the possibility of doing a play based on this real-life melodrama. Wisely, perhaps, the idea was taken no further – but Beaton was never far from her mind, even after her two happy marriages: some forty years later, Coral revealed, 'I've got a very nasty black book, which isn't a book, it's a great big suitcase, and in it I keep my life, a sort of diary, I suppose…all the things that mean something to me… Cecil's photographs of me…'[49] She also kept an obituary of Beaton from the *Guardian*'s international edition in the case, after his death in 1980.

At that time, Coral's attitude towards fidelity and jealousy was refreshingly relaxed. Once, the actress Betty Marsden went to visit her at the Savoy, with the purpose of getting some career advice. During the conversation, Coral casually remarked that if Marsden wanted to sleep with Firth Shephard to gain some advantage, she would have no objection: 'After all, darling, what's a fuck between friends?'[50] Coral knew that anything was possible between two consenting adults, regardless of their hidden or declared proclivities and inclinations. Late in life, irritated by the screams of disbelief and mockery that greeted Beaton's revelations of his sexual relationships with women, she went public about her affair with him: 'I get rather bored with people laughing about him and Garbo, and saying he was effete. Cecil was very passionate and I should know – I've been under the bridges in my time…'[51] Indeed she had. On one level, she was a good old-fashioned 'fag-hag': working in the theatre, there was no shortage of gay male acquaintances to gossip and bitch with. And Coral could dish with the best of them. But she also forged some of her deepest personal and professional relationships with gay men, including Charles Gray, Angus McBean, Frith Banbury, Milton Goldman, Noel Davis, John Schlesinger, Roddy McDowall and Alan Melville. Prunella Scales recalled a story which summed it up nicely: 'She caught sight of a photo outside the Old Vic of her and somebody else in the cast curtsying to the King and Queen – and she said, "There's another photo of me going down to some old queen, dear."'[52] Throughout her life, Coral's attraction to, and for, gay men traversed the perceived physical boundaries. She said, 'Women feel very comfortable with homosexuals. There's a certain delicacy. We don't want to be pounced on every 30 seconds by some hairy ape.'[53] She once told Tyrone Guthrie, 'I like all my men scented up, perfumed and put into the water and taken out and absolutely lovely.' Guthrie's response was all-man: 'You're the most degenerate woman I ever met in my life.'[54]

Two of the three (admitted) great male loves of her life were with men previously known as being, at the very least, primarily homosexual. And she was not averse to rising to what she saw as a sexual challenge – or making others rise to it. In 1945, she turned her charms on James Agate, the openly homosexual drama critic of the *Sunday Times*. Ivor Brown said of him, 'He was a hedonist in the best sense, seeking pleasure of the senses to the end; but his hedonism was mitigated by discernment'.[55] Apparently not on this occasion: in return for Coral's unexpected attentions, he wrote to thank her: 'For years you have intoxicated me with your beauty, and at Christmas you sought to do the same thing on a lower plane, which was very naughty on your part and as successful as it was nice.'[56]

Coral's affair with Beaton wasn't the only memorable event to occur during the rehearsals for *The Man Who Came to Dinner*. After Coral's departure for England, Gregan McMahon had kept abreast of his former protégée and lover's progress through her parents, with whom he had remained in contact. Coral admitted, 'I didn't write, as I should have done. And I think my father must have felt that someone should be in touch with Gregan and tell him how things were going for me. I also think he felt that Gregan might have needed a good meal from time to time. I think my father often gave him lunch. Mainly, I suppose, to talk about me. Because my father was very devoted to me.'[57] On 30 August 1941, McMahon was due at the Browns for lunch. When he failed to turn up, a concerned Leslie went to his home at 50 Jolimont Road, East Melbourne (he'd been able, at last, to move out of his makeshift digs at the Garrick) and found him dead.

McMahon had ended his days a somewhat disenchanted figure who, according to producer and broadcaster Allan Ashbolt, 'had lost faith in the stage, prophesying that the cinema would at length oust it from the pickings of popular favour'.[58] A requiem mass was held for him at St Patrick's Cathedral on 1 September and he was buried in the Catholic section (RC NA 407) of Melbourne General Cemetery, near the gate house. The meagre funeral was attended by a mere 20 mourners; Coral was not among them. The bleak scene led Ashbolt to write, 'Where were his friends and supporters now, the hundreds he had trained, the thousands whose minds he had opened? McMahon was buried like a soldier in battle, hurriedly, cursorily, unsung.'[59] And uncommemorated: no headstone or any other marker was ever placed on the grave.

Tragically, McMahon was even denied the satisfaction of seeing his best, and much-loved, protégé became the West End star he'd always envisaged.

After nearly two triumphant years, the curtain came down on *The Man Who Came to Dinner*. But Coral would stay at the Savoy throughout the war years, capitalising on its success by starring in hit show after hit show. The first of these was another American comedy, *My Sister Eileen*, written by Joseph Fields and Jerome Chodorov (Rosalind Russell starred in the film version). She played Ruth Sherwood, sister of the heroine who, after decamping from the country to New York, soon has most of the male population of New York's Greenwich Village beating a path to her door. In a tragic twist, shortly before the play had opened on Broadway, Eileen McKenney, the inspiration for the play's title character, was killed in a car accident, with her husband, novelist and screenwriter Nathanael West, on 22 December 1940.

Sally Gray was playing sister Eileen.* Predictably, Coral's reputation went before her, leaving her fellow leading lady in a state of some trepidation. During one scene, the Sherwood sisters, alarmed by noises in the night, huddle in bed together – and theatre archivist Joe Mitchenson remembered that Sally Gray was 'terrified' by the prospect of being under the sheets with Coral, albeit for the briefest moment.[60] When it opened at the Savoy on 22 September 1943, the *Tatler* declared that 'such hilarity…has rarely shaken the stolid sides of London audiences in wartime'. Other critics praised the 'delicious performances' of Sally Gray and Coral – 'Miss Browne, whose coolness under every sort of provocation is something to be wondered at',[61] while one notice declared, 'For relaxation and a brief reprieve from the worries of the everyday world…a crazy, lighthearted comedy to be enjoyed, laughed at – and not forgotten.'[62]

Coral continued her series of successful wartime comedies with one set in the Edwardian era: *The Last of Mrs Cheyney*, 'a comedy of the day before yesterday',[63] in which she would be playing opposite one of Britain's most popular stars of the '20s and '30s, Jack Buchanan.

The Scots-born musical comedy star had recently returned to the West End after an absence of six years. Known as 'the British Fred Astaire', he was

---

* Like Coral, Gray enjoyed the patronage of an older, married lover/mentor: Stanley Lupino – father of actress and director Ida. He was regarded as something of a national hero by Londoners – he had braved the hazards of the Blitz, serving as an ARP Warden. He and Gray starred in the musical *Lady Behave* at Her Majesty's; on its opening night in July 1941, Lupino – then already ill with cancer – found himself borne on the shoulders of audience members and paraded through the theatre's aisles. The show closed a month later because of his illness, and he died on 10 June 1942, leaving Gray as the beneficiary of a £10,000 insurance policy. Grief-stricken, she suffered a breakdown and was absent from stage and screen for some time as a result; *My Sister Eileen* marked her return.

a true star on both sides of the Atlantic. As one critic said, 'The tall figure, the elegant gestures, the friendly drawling voice, the general air of having a good time, cheered up the most languid house from stalls to gallery.'[64] Arthur Marshall observed that Buchanan '...danced in a lissom manner that was called "lazy", sang rather nasally and not very well, and acted hardly at all but in the theatre his presence was magical'.[65]

Buchanan made his name in André Charlot's 1921 revue *A to Z* with Gertrude Lawrence, which featured the duo's trademark songs, 'A Cup of Coffee', 'Limehouse Blues' and 'And Her Mother Came Too'. Lawrence gave Buchanan his nickname – 'Johnny B' – and he responded by dubbing her 'Annie'. They worked together in the Charlot revues for over five years, during which they formed an offstage relationship to which Lawrence was more committed than her leading man. He appeared in a number of musical comedy films, including alongside Maurice Chevalier in the 1938 film *Break the News*, co-produced by his own company and made at Pinewood. During the 1930s, he had become acquainted with Coral, as they often attended the same showbiz parties.

Alan Melville said, 'Mr Buchanan toured in style. The Rolls, the chauffeur the best hotels. He also worked in a grand manner.'[66] Buchanan was rarely seen without a carnation in his button-hole and a pearl grey trilby on his head. Commercially astute, his business ventures included the Garrick, King's and Leicester Square theatres and owned, with old school friend John Logie Baird, Television Limited, a manufacturing and rental company. He regularly wrote articles about fashion for men and women and his endorsements appeared on many clothing and accessory advertisements and in shop fronts – including one in a New York men's outfitters, where a waistcoat was displayed with a slightly misleading sign claiming that 'Jack Buchanan wears nothing else'.[67] He advised one of his leading ladies: 'If you want to wear old woollies and slacks, go home. But you must always dress up both to go out on the town and when going to and from the theatre.'[68] It was advice that Coral certainly didn't need.

A man of charm, sophistication and wit, Buchanan was, naturally, enormously attractive to women. The 'gallery girls' queued for hours outside theatres where he played. Anna Neagle said, 'Every girl who worked within fifty feet of Jack Buchanan was madly in love with him.'[69] Ruth Leon commented,

'I think he was a man who could only relate to women sexually. All of his female friends he either did have affairs with or wanted to.'[70]

In Frederick Lonsdale's comedy, Fay Cheyney is believed to be a wealthy widow from Australia, and much fawned on by Edwardian society. In fact, she's actually a former shop girl turned jewel thief, and her servants are her accomplices. She attracts the attention of the dashing Lord Arthur Dilling (Buchanan), who eventually discovers the truth about her. It was Coral who chose the play's director, and many questioned her judgement when she plumped for Tyrone Guthrie, then director of the Old Vic company which featured Ralph Richardson, Laurence Olivier and Sybil Thorndike among its ranks. To ask Guthrie was, Coral said, 'sort of unheard-of, because Tony was not a man who was ever likely to do anything like *The Last of Mrs Cheyney*, which wasn't in his sphere at all. To my amazement he said he would be delighted to do it… We found out that the reason that he did it was that he needed money desperately, not for himself – he needed it for the Old Vic. He did it for a percentage of the gross, two and a half per cent. All of that money, I understand, he put back into the Old Vic.'[71] The cast themselves weren't in it for the money: all actors were all on reduced salaries, as part of the 'war effort' – even Coral's was a relatively modest £10 per week.

As they worked on *Mrs Cheyney*, Coral forged a great friendship with 'Tony' Guthrie. She became a regular visitor to the home he shared with his devoted wife, Judy – but was less than impressed with their standards of housekeeping: 'I went to dinner one night, and I swear that that dinner was a tin of Kit-e-kat. I swear it was. I know it was. Judy bustled it up in the frying-pan and put some peanuts on it. On another night, I went there to dinner. It was a room filled with books and kittens – kittens everywhere. There was the eternal frying-pan, and the most extraordinary things among his books, which he absolutely adored, like old socks. Old socks hanging down – stiff and everything.'[72]

During 1944 and 1945 Coral and the Savoy, along with the rest of London, faced a new danger: the V1 and V2 rocket bombs. They were most egregiously effective: within a few weeks of the first assault by these deadly weapons, only ten West End theatres remained open. '1944 was a year of which the West End theatres might well be proud,' declared *Theatre World*. 'It contained the biggest testing time for London…we shall not forget the few shows that bravely withstood the onslaught and remained open throughout.'[73]

Martita Hunt – an actress with a regal deportment and wit to match Coral's – spent the war years living in a top floor flat in Wimpole Street. In 1945, when she was filming *Great Expectations* with her friend and former drama pupil, Alec Guinness, he observed her ritual of mid-morning 'tea' – actually a pot of whisky – and blamed the habit on the terrors of countless air raids. The relentless bombing didn't drive Coral to drink, but at one point, according to Victoria Price, it did send her west: 'One day, she couldn't bear the Blitz any longer, and she got in a cab and essentially said, "Take me as far away from London as possible" – which, of course, was Land's End. And I got the sense that there was just this one pub there, and that's where everybody congregated.'[74] But even here, Coral was unable to get away from everything that reminded her of London and its horrors: as luck would have it, one of the regulars who 'congregated' at the village pub was the woman she called 'the dreaded Una Troubridge'. Suddenly, the bombing didn't seem quite so bad.

The Last of Mrs Cheyney opened at the Savoy on 15 June 1944; after the first performance (marked by Jack Buchanan's first night present to Coral, a music box with miniature bird and a note that read, 'I'm giving you the bird'[75]), Coral and Buchanan were having dinner with Firth Shephard in the Savoy Grill when, as she recalled, 'there was an awful crunch'. They didn't find out what the 'crunch' was until the morning: 'We didn't realise at the time what had happened but it was the arrival of the first doodlebug,' said Coral. 'We picked up the papers the next day to read what we expected would be marvellous notices to find there was nothing at all. Well, there was hardly anything because the papers were full of this thing that arrived from outer space.'[76] When King George came to see the play in October, he congratulated the cast afterwards for continuing with the performance despite a doodlebug attack.

Despite the continuing crunches from 'outer space', *The Last of Mrs Cheyney* was another success for Coral. *The Sunday Express* called it a 'play of exquisite elegance, superbly acted';[77] *The Times* concurred: 'All the acting may be called good…Coral Browne carries off the elegant thief with a languorous flourish.'[78] The play settled in at the Savoy for a long run – and so, apparently, did Coral and Buchanan. Firth Shephard remained devoted to her, but their relationship had reached an impasse and, though she still lived with him, the on and offstage couple of Buchanan and Browne became the talk of the West End, with rumours flying that they would marry. 'I was very much in love with him. He was very wonderful with women. Very kind, very generous. He knew how to live and live well.'[79] Apart from their fondness for the finer things in life and fashion, Coral and Buchanan had something else in common: chronic stage fright. Although they made a glamorous couple, Coral's friendships with so many gay men might eventually have posed a problem: according to Alexander Walker, Buchanan was 'homophobic' and 'notorious for his refusal to hire any chorus boy with what he thought were effeminate traits'.[80]

The Last of Mrs Cheyney closed at the Savoy in February 1945; the war was starting to end. In April, the blackout was abolished and, symbolically, the Savoy switched every light on and left every curtain open. *Theatre World* predicted a healthy future for the West End: 'These are halcyon days for theatre managements, when money is plentiful and goods scarce.'[81] Right on cue, Laurence Olivier and Ralph Richardson opened a memorable season at the Old Vic, including *Oedipus Rex*. But Coral continued in comic vein: in 1946, she scored another success with a revival of Somerset Maugham's *Lady Frederick*, which had been the author's first major stage success in 1907. James Agate had suggested that she do a revival of another Maugham play, *Our Betters*, but a revival of any sort was not her first choice: 'I was more than anxious for a modern play after the run of *The Last of Mrs Cheyney*,' she explained. 'For a whole year I read five new plays a week...but for one reason or another they happened to be unsuitable. Too often they were photographic pictures of the times – housing problems facing newly-weds. They are all burning questions of the day, but surely the playgoer does not want to pay to hear the pros and cons all over again. Then I heard that Ethel Irving scored the triumph of her career in 1907 with a play by young [Somerset] Maugham... I read it and did not need much persuasion to play the part...as a dramatist, Maugham is such a magnificent constructionalist.'[82] As usual, her preparation for the part was thorough and dedicated: 'I went away from the telephone, and my friends, and stayed at a seaside hotel. For three weeks I learnt solidly for hours at a time, then relaxed to work at my tapestry before going on once again.'[83]

When the production opened at the Savoy on 21 November, critics praised its 'elegance and suavity...the superb settings and costumes' – a minor miracle, given that clothing coupons were still in effect. Coral explained, 'My first act dress was made out of a pair of curtains discovered in a Chelsea antique shop and my second act dress was built up out of lengths of wide ribbon, left to a friend of mine by her grandmother.'[84] But most of the praise was for 'the discovery of a new and entrancing Lady Frederick... Coral Browne dominates the play with the best performance of her career.'[85] The *Tatler* declared, 'Coral Browne is a tower of Edwardian strength through joy.'[86] James Agate rang her up and read her the gist of his review for the *Sunday Times* – something, he said, he'd never done before: 'Delightful play. Endlessly non-boring. Coral Browne superb.'[87]

It was during the regional tour of *Lady Frederick* that one of Coral's traits became legendary. An unknown critic observed that 'Miss Browne, as she made her superb entrance in Maugham's *Lady Frederick*, even went so far as to acknowledge the applause as to raise her left eyebrow; but since Miss Browne possesses the most expressive left eyebrow on the English stage, the effect satisfied every admirer from the stalls to the gallery.'[88] As her future leading man Paul Rogers observed, 'Just like certain film actresses have a love affair with the camera, there is no question that Coral had a love affair with a live audience.'[89]

Despite her continuing affection for, and loyalty to, Firth Shephard, Coral was not oblivious to the fact that she was now in a position to renegotiate a better financial deal for herself. In December 1946, she and Shephard drew up a new contract: 'You are to continue your part in *Lady Frederick* and you grant me the sole and exclusive option on your services for five further plays. Your salary is to be for *Lady Frederick* and the next two plays: 6% of the box office with a guarantee of £75 per week for eight performances. For the next two plays 7% with a guarantee of £100 per week. For the sixth play 10% with a guarantee of £125 per week. I am entitled to your sole and exclusive services. I undertake to continue to use the same care and attention in casting you as I have always done in the past and if at any time I produce *The Second Mrs Tanqueray* by Arthur Pinero you agree to play the part of Paula. If at any time I find myself without a suitable play for you I am to be entitled to sub-let your services to any other first-class management for the run of a play. I confirm that you are to be entitled to receive all salary from the film which you are at present making for Herbert Wilcox [*The Courtneys of Curzon Street*].'[90]

Before *Lady Frederick* opened, Coral made one of her occasional forays into cinema, tagging onto the elegant coat-tails of Britain's favourite cinematic couple of the time, Anna Neagle and Michael Wilding. She had small roles in two consecutive Neagle/Wilding films which were replete with trademark ballroom dancing, Neagle's singing, and champagne bottles being popped on the slightest pretext. *Piccadilly Incident*, the first outing for the Neagle/Wilding team, was a romantic melodrama about a WREN (Neagle) who meets and quickly marries marine captain Wilding before she's shipped off to serve in Singapore. When the city is evacuated, she boards a ship back to Blighty, which is torpedoed by a Japanese U-boat. She is reported as missing, believed drowned, but in fact spends the next three years shipwrecked on an island, during which she and her fellow survivors have to endure an array of hardships – including warding off advances from smitten sailors and jolly Jack Tar Leslie Dwyer's harmonica-playing.

Coral played Wilding's older, bolder ambulance-driver sister; her biggest challenge was to utter, straight-faced, the line, 'I must go – I've been invited to a bottle party with some FANYs.' Eventually, Neagle and her marooned mariners escape the island and return to England, where she discovers Wilding has remarried and fathered a son – who, as her former father-in-law, a judge, reminds her, is technically 'illegitimate', because the second marriage is bigamous. The film ends with a messy mix of reconciliation, death and rough justice; its producers asked critics not to spoil the film for audiences by revealing its final denouement, causing one to comment that he couldn't do so, even if he tried. Despite its peculiarities, *Piccadilly Incident* was the year's second biggest hit at the British box office.

Coral had a bigger part in *The Courtneys of Curzon Street*, a family saga set right in her own neighbourhood, which traversed 45 years, three wars and a seemingly endless succession of Teddy Courtneys who invariably joined the Army and died in action, leaving a male heir behind to follow in their footsteps. Wilding played the first Teddy, son and heir of a titled family, who causes a society scandal by marrying Kathy, his mother's 'Oirish' maid (Neagle). Coral played the bitchy Valerie Lindsay, an ex-beau of Teddy Courtney, and one of a gaggle of gowned grand dames who scrutinise the out-of-sorts young bride at a recital attended by Queen Victoria. She is delighted to fire a disapproving glance (complete with elevated left eyebrow) when Neagle commits a faux pas by letting her over-wafted fan shoot off into the lap of a lady – an obvious sign of her social unsuitability. As venomous Valerie – whose 'bad' dark looks, clothes and fan contrasted sharply with the blonde, all-white 'good' Kathy – Coral had an eventful time: within a few scenes, she landed on her rear-end after slipping on a floor newly-polished by the still housemaidly Kathy; got married and went to live in India; and was kissed by Wilding, before he slapped her soundly round the face for her witchy bitchery. Her role was small but effective: one critic said it gave her '...the chance to give a polished exhibition of all-in cattiness'.[91]*

After her appearances in these successful Wilding/Neagle vehicles, Jack Buchanan had high hopes for Coral's film career. He told her, 'Ah, old girl, just wait till you get to Hollywood.' When Coral said, 'What – with a face this size?,' Jack replied, 'The screen was big enough to take Marie Dressler's face and she, too, went into movies late in life!'[92] Coral didn't share her beau's confidence: as Peggy Ashcroft believed of herself, she sensed that film was not her medium. Early in her career, Ashcroft had been told by a cameraman that 'she could be a great star if she had her nose adjusted or shortened with surgery. She also needed her teeth fixed.'[93] Of course, Coral was more than willing to make such physical adjustments – but no amount of surgery could fix her belief that her film career would come a poor second to her stage work. 'The femme fatale went out as I came in,' she observed.[94]

After six years living mainly at the Savoy, Coral and Firth Shephard were able to return permanently to Curzon Street. But her romance with Jack Buchanan continued to blossom, and the glamorous couple were also keen to keep their successful professional partnership on track. In November 1947, they co-starred in another Frederick Lonsdale comedy, *Canaries Sometimes Sing*, a four-hander with Austin Trevor and Heather Thatcher about two married couples swapping their affections. Although the play itself was disdained by critics and audiences alike – '...there is a faint aroma of Coward about the whole thing, but never for one moment his wicked wit,' said *Theatre World*[95] – this did nothing to stint their increasing affection for the leading lady: 'Miss Coral Browne...is formidably mischievous as the wife whose chorus girl manners fret her husband's sense of decorum.'[96]

However, her leading man found himself upstaged by the canary which was supposed to symbolise the narrow and selfish lives of the play's four characters. Coral recalled, 'That canary did not utter a cheep all through

---

* This rather tame, protracted film was at the centre of a curious political controversy when the self-appointed and anointed Sons of Liberty, 'an anti-British organisation', threatened to picket the Elysee, a small New York cinema where it was running and forced it to be withdrawn after just two days. The *Daily Mirror* reported that 'the Sons of Liberty are mainly Jews but some Irish Americans who don't like Britain have joined them. They say they mean to picket any cinema which shows a film which might bring profit to Britain.'[97]

rehearsals. On the opening night, it took one look at Jack and sang its guts out every time he tried to say a line.'[98] The menagerie expanded when a rat decided to come and watch every performance, usually under the footlights, unseen by the audience, but in full view of the leading ladies.

After *Canaries Sometimes Sing* enjoyed a month's tour in the provinces, Coral and Jack made more plans to work together – but not before she took some rare time out to see her family. In April 1948, she returned to Australia for the first time in 14 years: her maternal grandmother, Edith, was remarrying and so Coral decided to take the opportunity to spend a month with her parents. By now, Leslie had resigned from the Victorian Railways and become Provedore of the James Richardson chain of hotels. In May 1946, he and Vicky had moved from Fernhurst to a smaller house a few minutes walk away, at 22A Pakington Street. Edith Bennett remained at her Footscray home, 52 Victoria Street.

Coral left for Melbourne by flying boat on 23 March. When she arrived on 2 April, she was dressed to impress: her parents and grandmother were there to greet their Coral Brown. Instead, it was 'Coral Browne', resplendent in a mink coat, and a frock by Molyneux, who arrived, complete with 68lb of luggage containing nearly £3500 worth of clothes, including a chinchilla coat which alone was worth £3000. She divided her time between her grandmother's house, her parents' home in Pakington Street and the more salubrious Menzies Hotel in Melbourne's Bourke Street. While there, she entertained five of her former classmates from Claremont College and former headmistress, Joan Watkins.

The Australian press – not known for giving warm welcomes to their homecoming artistic ex-patriots – greeted Coral enthusiastically and chronicled every event in her itinerary.* Coral told Australian reporters that she didn't think Footscray had changed much – no one seemed to notice that she didn't

---

* In contrast, Peter Finch – actually an Englishman by birth – returned to Australia in 1957 to make the films *The Shiralee* and *Robbery Under Arms*, and was met with hostile indifference; he never went back again. Finch's friend and biographer, the Australian actor Trader Faulkner observed: 'Australia has a reputation for cutting down tall poppies.' [99] Amusingly, when Merle Oberon visited Tasmania in 1978 (supposedly as a 'returning daughter'), she was accorded a heroine's welcome – even though it was, in fact, the first time she'd ever been near the place. The story that she was born in Hobart had been fabricated by director Alexander Korda in the 1930s to hide the actress's mixed race Indian heritage.

mean it as a compliment. She warned other Australian actresses against going to London without proper funding or training, and revealed that she hoped to return to Australia within a few months to tour in either *The Last of Mrs Cheyney* or *Lady Frederick* with Jack Buchanan. During her visit, Laurence Olivier and Vivien Leigh were touring Australia with the Old Vic Company – a trip which, according to Sheridan Morley, was 'a kind of thespian reward to Australia for her help in the Second World War'.[100] Barry Humphries recalled that, 'All Melbourne was talking about "Sir Oliver Leigh".'[101] The British Council held a reception for the Oliviers and their company on 21 April, and Coral joined the party; the day before, she had been to see the couple in *The School for Scandal* at the Princess Theatre. The Oliviers' tour soon produced its own scandal: Vivien Leigh suffered a bad episode of manic depression and became besotted with…Peter Finch.

On 1 May, Coral headed back to London, where she had a new show to rehearse. After the huge success of his wartime revues, Coral had encouraged Alan Melville to try his hand at straight drama, and his first pitch for mainstream success was *Jonathan*, a curious reworking of the Old Testament tale about the relationship between the eponymous hero and his beloved friend, David. But it was to prove a disaster of biblical proportions. As Melville admitted, 'I don't think it helped much in 1948 to suggest that David was kinky for Jonathan. Perfectly true, of course. But in 1948 that sort of thing just Wasn't Done.'[102] Melville recalled that, at the first dress rehearsal in Leeds, eight people watched: 'Mr Firth Shephard, the director, the designer and one of those publicity men, one or two hangers on and myself. And for some extraordinary reason, a local vicar.'[103] Coral, playing Bathsheba, Jonathan's competitor for David's affections, made a memorable first entrance, through the legs of the figure of an Assyrian warrior. Melville said, 'Miss Browne was wearing not a great deal of pure white butter-muslin and had her hair put up and topped with a small veil of tulle. There was a quiet religious hush…The hush was abruptly shattered when Miss Browne's veil caught in the apex of the Assyrian's triangle and she was yanked smartly back almost into the wings. In a voice which echoed round the West Riding, she said, "If anyone thinks I'm coming through this ***** crutch, they're ***** well mistaken." Nor did she; after that she came down the stairs.'[104] Sadly, there's no record of what the vicar thought of it all.

When *Jonathan* opened at the Aldwych on 29 July 1948, no man of God could save it from the critics. In some of the kinder notices, Coral's portrayal of Bathsheba was deemed 'seductive in a vaguely eastern way, and she has little chance to be anything else...it is an evening of uneasy entertainment'.[105] It lasted just 12 performances.

Alan Melville later maintained, 'I still consider it the best play I have ever written.' The problem lay, he felt, in some of the casting: 'Although I love her dearly, if Miss Browne, with not a stitch on, had been about to take a bath on the rooftop of her house right opposite David's Palace, she'd have asked *him* over. Which would have ruined the plot.'[106] Coral had a different theory: 'I finally decided that the notices would have been better had the author been someone other than Alan Melville,' she observed. 'It was not the sort of play expected from the witty revue writer...only with rare exceptions have Biblical plays enjoyed a long run on the English stage, so poor *Jonathan* started against terrific odds.'[107]

But the show's failure was soon put into perspective: the two most important relationships in Coral's life were both about to come to cruel and abrupt endings.

The end of the war had signalled the start of a bleak period for Firth Shephard. On 9 April 1945, his wife Constance died in University College Hospital, London, three months after being diagnosed with a brain tumour. Son-in-law Leslie Mitchell said, 'It was an overwhelming blow for Phyl as she and her mother had been drawn even closer by the war and my frequent absences elsewhere.'[108] And, no doubt, a long-absent husband and father. Then, in the winter of 1946/7, his famed Midas touch failed; suddenly, everything he put his name to turned to fool's gold. He decided to invest his own money in three shows within a few months of each other: *The Shephard Show*, *Peace Comes to Peckham* and *Fifty-Fifty*. Unfortunately, forces beyond his control would condemn the shows to commercial failure: still recovering from the ravages of war, Britain was in the grip of an economic and climatic crisis. Fuel shortages were leading to four-day weeks and lay-offs for millions of workers. This worsened when, in January 1947, temperatures plummeted to −16°F, and coal trains couldn't make their way through 20-foot snowdrifts. Food shortages were made worse when shipping across the Channel was stopped. Homes were without light and heat for long periods – even Buckingham Palace was candlelit. And, naturally, theatres were hit, with many shows forced to close

– including Firth Shephard's. As an independent producer, without the benefit of being part of an organisation large enough to withstand such losses, he was in trouble. According to Leslie Mitchell, 'Firth personally paid all the artists and the theatres involved. All his accumulated savings had gone after a long and outstanding series of successes... He had seen the fruits of a lifetime's work disappear by a trick of fate.'[109] It taught Coral a salutary lesson: invest wisely – and it was a lesson she only needed teaching once. For the rest of her life, she put her money in solid, low-risk stocks, shares and savings accounts, and kept the true amount of her wealth a secret – even from her nearest and dearest.

It all took its toll: in late 1948, Shephard suffered a serious heart attack and was sent to recuperate in Cornwall, accompanied by his daughter. 'He returned to London somewhat improved in health if not in spirits,' said Leslie Mitchell.[110]

On Monday 3 January 1949, he spent the day at his offices, working with Stanley French, before returning home at 5pm. That evening, while reading in bed at home in Curzon Street, he suffered another, fatal heart attack; he was 57. His devotion to Coral had remained undiminished: in his will (signed just four days before he died), he left the bulk of what was left of his estate to her. Though not the fortune many imagined (approximately £2500 cash and roughly the same amount again in shares) it still provided her with a measure of financial security. With her newly-acquired funds, Coral was able to buy her own home for the first time: from the Grosvenor Estate, she purchased the leasehold of 17 Wilton Row, a mews cottage tucked behind St Paul's Church in Knightsbridge.

A memorial service for Firth Shephard was held at St Martin-in-the-Fields on 13 January; those present included Leslie and Phyllis Mitchell and most of Shephard's fellow theatrical producers. Leslie Banks gave a reading, Marie Burke sang and Jack Hawkins read Revelation 21: 1–7. A collection was made for The Actors' Orphanage and The Actors' Church Union.

Discreetly, the press kept Coral's name out of the proceedings. She was always aware of the gossip surrounding her relationship with Shephard – but, of course, that never stopped her casting aspersions on anyone else's. The 1948–9 Stratford season included a production of *Macbeth*, starring Godfrey Tearle and Diana Wynyard. Also in the cast, playing Fleance, was a young Jill Bennett, fresh out of RADA. Bennett was also Tearle's lover – an unlikely but apparently genuine 'May to December' romance, which prompted Coral's oft-quoted sally, 'I could never understand what Godfrey Tearle saw in Jill Bennett until I saw her eating corn-on-the-cob at the Caprice.'[111] In 1983, Bennett published a ghosted memoir about her relationship with Tearle, called *Godfrey: A Special Time Remembered*, with plenty of references to lunches at the Caprice – but strangely without any to corn or cobs.

One of Firth Shephard's last productions, *The Human Touch*, starring Alec Guinness, was running at the Savoy. Coral went to see it and, impressed by Guinness's performance, visited him backstage. The pair formed a lifelong, devoted and affectionate friendship; Coral was equally devoted to Guinness's long-suffering and much-loved wife, Merula. Their friendship even survived those moments when Coral tested Guinness's patience with her unruly tongue. In 1960, when he was portraying T E Lawrence in the Terence Rattigan play, *Ross*, Coral made a passing remark to his friend Richard Leech that Guinness 'had been cottaging again' – a remark which Leech duly reported back to a dismayed and angry Guinness. After going to confession, Guinness had lunch with Binkie Beaumont and his agent Dennis van Thal, after which the three men, like the Spanish inquisition, descended on Coral in her dressing room at the Haymarket (she was appearing in *The Pleasure of his Company*). When Guinness threatened her with legal action, Coral claimed it had all been a misunderstanding – she said her comment was that Guinness had been 'doing up a *cottage* in Ennismore Garden Mews'.[112] Homosexuality was a touchy subject for the great actor, as emerged in a conversation he had, late in life, with Simon Callow: 'When I told him a few things about [Charles] Laughton's sex life, he quite casually told me that he, too, had engaged in sexual relations with men, "but then one married and gave up all that sort of thing". He liked to talk about people's sex lives, not in a salacious way, but more in a spirit of gossip… There were probably lapses, and his feelings found other forms of expression: supper *à deux* as a substitute for, or a sublimation of, sex. It is the readily recognisable situation of a repressed gay man of a certain epoch.'[113] Garry O'Connor, one of Guinness's biographers, was told by his solicitor that the secret of Guinness's friendship with Coral was because she regarded him as 'another woman'.[114] Professionally, their friendship was never put to the test – they never worked together.

Meanwhile, Coral and Jack Buchanan were keen to continue their onstage partnership, but their brand of light and frothy comedies was increasingly being overshadowed by a more heavyweight acting couple: the Old Vic Company's 1949 season featured a series of plays, including *Antigone*, *Richard III* and *The School for Scandal*, in which Laurence Olivier and Vivien Leigh were making their first West End appearances together. Coral and Buchanan pressed on regardless and, in 1949, found another vehicle – an Alan Melville play, *Castle in the Air*. Despite the failure of *Jonathan*, Melville had written it especially for them at Coral's request: she had often complained to him how difficult it was to find an existing play with good parts for her and her leading man. Melville's play centred on the attempts by an impoverished Scottish laird, The Earl of Locharne (Buchanan), to sell his castle to a rich American instead of the National Coal Board, who want to requisition it and turn it into a holiday home for miners. Coral played the Earl's secretary, Boss Trent (clad in tartan skirt). Jack's understudy was a very tall, dark and handsome actor called Philip Pearman.

As soon as rehearsals began, there were signs that all was not well, as Alan Melville recalled: '[Coral] was playing the impoverished Earl's even more impoverished housekeeper who had not been paid any wages for several weeks if not months. The gown [from Norman Hartnell] had a very wide flared skirt with a large centre panel which was completely encrusted with sequins and embroidery; it was the sort of thing the Queen Mother wears superbly but it really wasn't totally right for a financially harassed housekeeper in the Highlands. She made her entrance in it coming down the stairs, looking a million dollars; she was absolutely mad about it. Jack was discussing golf with Bill Kendall. He half-turned to Coral, said, "By the way, old girl, get rid of that frock," and then went on talking to Bill. Miss Browne was red-eyed for weeks. Jack told her she could have the dress as a present. Miss Browne, still smouldering, said she never wished to see the bloody thing again in her life and it went back to the wardrobe. Coral went off and bought a simple little black number more befitting her role; I think it only cost around 120 guineas.'[115]

Having committed himself to the play, Buchanan took a break from rehearsals to travel to America and make another pledge: to marry a young American, Susan (Suzzie) Bassett. He had met Suzzie at a cocktail party in Nassau in January 1947 – she was then still married to Theodore Bassett, a leading amateur golfer, and had a young daughter. According to Suzzie, she and Jack had discussed marrying as early as March 1948. Despite his frequent trips to New York to see Suzzie – ostensibly, 'on business' – Coral had no idea that she was not fated to be Buchanan's 'leading lady'. He and Suzzie were married on 14 January 1949 at a friend's house in Connecticut.* Coral was having lunch with Alan Melville when news of Jack and Suzzie's marriage came through: 'Eternal Bachelor Jack Weds American Society Girl.'[116] According to Melville, Coral 'was besotted about the man; she pushed her plate to one side and said she couldn't think why, but she had absolutely no appetite.'[117]

It seemed that for once, Jack the Gentleman had behaved like a cad. But, incredibly, the show went on: displaying an unbelievable generosity of spirit, Coral not only continued with the play, but readily embraced the new Mrs Buchanan. Suzzie had been wary of her husband working with the woman he had come close to marrying but, after being introduced in Coral's dressing room, they became instant and lifelong friends. Coral even introduced Suzzie to the joys of needlepoint.

After a short regional tour, *Castle in the Air* opened on 10 December at the Adelphi Theatre, where its cast received the best of the reviews: 'Whatever the nature of the jokes, Mr Jack Buchanan, Miss Coral Browne and Miss Irene Manning can be trusted to turn them to excellent account. It is a pleasure to hear dialogue timed so exquisitely...'[118] But not everyone who saw it was so delighted: possibly tipped off about their dishonourable mention, two Coal Board representatives, legal adviser R S S Allen and PR man F Pullin, were present at a preview on 7 December. They subsequently demanded a meeting to express their displeasure at the misrepresentation of their powers to requisition the castle, and made it clear that the Coal Board had no such powers. Buchanan's co-producer, Stanley French, said, 'They refused to leave the theatre unless I went to see them after the show. They wanted an undertaking that all references to the Coal Board would be removed before the performance tomorrow night, otherwise they would report the matter to the Coal Board, who would consider referring it to the courts, with a view to having the show closed down.'[119] No such undertaking was given and Buchanan smoothly observed, 'I cannot believe we can possibly be that important.'[120] Nonetheless, on the principle that no publicity is bad publicity, the Coal Board's decision to kick up some dust created more interest in a show that was, according to one

---

* In fact, it was Jack's second marriage – he was briefly wed to the Russian opera singer Saffo Arnau, known as Drageva, in 1915. It may have been a marriage of convenience to enable Arnau to get British citizenship, and was annulled in 1920.

critic, 'lightly and continuously entertaining, and there is little more to be said about it'.[121]

It was the last time Coral and Jack Buchanan worked together on stage. But, despite his rather duplicitous behaviour, they remained good friends and often saw each other in London and Brighton, where they both had second homes: Coral's was in the Seven Dials area, at 2A Alexandra Villas, while Buchanan and Suzzie had a rather grander flat at 19 Lewes Crescent, Kemp Town. Buchanan would die of spinal cancer just seven years later. Coral reflected, 'It was terrible that such a lovely man had to suffer so much.'[122]*

The curtain had fallen on this act of Coral's life: now it was time for her to get a new leading man.

* After Jack's death, Suzzie married twice more – first, to DeWitt Sage and then, in 1983, to C Douglas Dillon, who served as Treasury Secretary in the Kennedy administration.

The Englishman, the Irishman and the Gentleman

1950–1958

In true theatrical tradition, having lost her leading man, Coral turned to his understudy instead. Philip Westrope Pearman was not born into a theatrical family: his father, Albert, ran a large farm and corn mill in the Hertfordshire village of Walkern, like his father before him. Born on 7 May 1911, Philip was the youngest of three children of Albert and his wife, Lillian; there was a brother, Albert John, known as Jack, and a sister, Joan. As an undergraduate at Jesus College, Cambridge, he began acting with the University Amateur Dramatic Club. Some of Philip's other Cambridge contemporaries who became involved in dramas (on and off stage) included Michael Redgrave and, when not busying himself recruiting graduates to the cause of Communism, Guy Burgess. In an exceptional series of coincidences, the lives of all three men would eventually converge with Coral's.

One of the guests at Philip's 21st birthday party, held at his rooms in Maid's Causeway with Lillian co-hosting, was a former Cambridge graduate, actor Dennis Arundell, who made his West End debut in 1926. And, according to the college paper, it seemed that Philip was all set to follow his friend onto the boards: 'It was whispered afterwards that he was destined to become a matinee idol. He certainly does make-up like one, when on the stage.'[1]

But, while amateur dramatics were part of the enjoyment of university life, a stage career was not at that time on the list approved for most Cambridge graduates. When Philip's friend, Ronnie Hill, a gifted writer and musician who had served as president of the Footlights Revue, left Cambridge (by mutual consent), the 'Undergraduate's Diary' columnist sniffed: 'Now he will be able to gratify his life's desire – to go into the theatre. And after twenty years at five pounds a week, he will retire to finish his life as a country gentleman, married to a sweet but simple ballet girl.'[2]

No such bland fate awaited Hill or, for that matter, Philip Pearman. After graduating, Philip was a member of the touring Brandon-Thomas Repertory Company for three seasons, until 1936. Thereafter, he enjoyed a steady, if unremarkable career, as a supporting player in productions such as *The Happy Hypocrite* (1936), starring Ivor Novello and Vivien Leigh; *The Constant Sinner* (1937); *Cage Me a Peacock* (1948) and *Mrs Inspector Jones* (1950). He was also in the 1937 Ben Lyon film, *Stardust*. He was, briefly, on John Gliddon's books, but the agent found there was limited interest in his client.

During the Second World War, Pearman served in North Africa with the 12th Lancers Armoured Division, where he formed a close and intimate friendship with a fellow Lancer and actor who, like other men in Philip's life, would one day cross paths with Coral. Peter Willes had returned to England in 1940 from Hollywood where he had forged a fairly successful film career. The two men served together in the Desert and North African campaigns, seeing action in Egypt, Tunisia and Libya. Early in 1943, the 12th Lancers narrowly missed a chance to capture Rommel – overcoming a German armoured unit which, they were told, the 'Desert Fox' had been visiting [the troops] a mere 20 minutes earlier. That same year, Willes was badly wounded and taken prisoner. However, he was quickly repatriated, due to the seriousness of his wounds: his legs had been shattered and he was left with a permanent limp. By the early 1960s, he had, by various twists and turns, become head of drama at Associated Rediffusion, before taking up the same post at Yorkshire Television. At both companies, Willes brought the works of Harold Pinter, John Osborne and Joe Orton to a wider audience via the small screen.*

Philip Pearman had had to wait for 207 performances before he was granted a chance to step in for Jack Buchanan on stage; the opportunity came

---

* For all his success within theatrical circles, Willes' name was inextricably linked to an unexplained tragedy that made the headlines in March 1937. His companion at the time was the actor and writer Frank Vosper; they were aboard the liner *Paris*, en route to Plymouth from New York, where Willes had been assisting on the production of Vosper's new play *Love from a Stranger*. On 6 March, one of their fellow passengers, Muriel Oxford – a former 'Miss Europe' who had gone to Hollywood for screen tests – threw an 'end of voyage' party in the cabin and invited Vosper and Willes. The champagne flowed and all was going well; Vosper was last seen by Muriel Oxford on a veranda outside her cabin, looking out of its porthole. A few minutes later, she and Willes noticed Vosper had disappeared. The alarm was raised and Willes noticed footprints around the porthole. Vosper's body was found washed up on 21 March at the foot of the Seven Sisters cliffs near Beachy Head.

in 1950 when Buchanan decided to go on holiday to France for a month. The understudy didn't have to wait nearly as long for a chance to take his place in Coral's life. During the few weeks he stood in for Buchanan, Philip's relationship with the leading lady became intimate and impassioned – and within weeks, they announced that they were to marry.

To put it mildly, this came as a complete surprise to many friends and colleagues, as it was common knowledge that Philip was homosexual. Noel Davis said, 'I don't think it would be indiscreet to say, his feet had not touched the ground in a very long time.'[3]

But there seemed to be little doubt about the depth or authenticity of Philip's feelings for Coral: during their courtship, he wrote passionate notes to her: 'How much more do I love you before you believe me please? ...Oh my lover, and my love always, be happy always because I love you.'[4] As Victoria Price observed, 'She married a gay man who was going to dote on her – she married into her constituency.'[5]

Whatever reservations they may have had about the relationship, Coral and Philip's friends and family gathered for their wedding at St Mary's Church, Letchworth on 26 June 1950, where Jack Pearman, now the Vicar of St John's, Ryde was officiating at his brother's wedding. Simon Jack was best man, Alan Melville gave the bride away and Suzzie Buchanan (Coral's matrimonial 'usurper') was matron of honour. Other guests included Jack Buchanan, fellow cast members Ewan Roberts, William Kendall and Irene Manning, Lillian and Joan Pearman, Michael Redgrave and his mother, Daisy Scudamore, and

The more fanciful elements of the press tried to bolster a rumour that Vosper had killed himself because Miss Oxford spurned his proposal of marriage. Vosper's father pooh-poohed the idea: 'If a passenger heard a man's voice saying that if a woman would not marry him he would throw himself overboard it was certainly not my son. To me it is nonsense.' [The Times, March 8 1937]. Quite. Willes later said it was he who asked Muriel to marry him for a joke – which it must have been, as Willes was definitely not the marrying kind. At the inquest, it was speculated that the rather short-sighted Vosper had merely wished to leave the party without a fuss and thought he could get back to his cabin via a non-existent walkway. The jury reached an open verdict, but rumours persisted for years about exactly how Vosper ended up in the sea. For decades after, a new adage circulated around the acting fraternity: 'Never get on a ship with Peter Willes.' [6]

Regardless of the gossip, Philip and Willes remained devoted lifelong friends – even after Philip's marriage to Coral, which would have been both surprising and baffling to his old comrade.

Emlyn and Molly Williams. Like Philip, Redgrave and Williams were men whose sexual relationships with men had not precluded marriage – or, indeed, having children.

For her wedding outfit, Coral plumped for a stone-coloured romaine Molyneux outfit, with matching hat. Later that evening, the new Mr and Mrs Pearman held a reception backstage at the Savoy Theatre for other cast members, dressers and stage management. During the party, Jack Buchanan told Philip, 'Well ol' boy, you've got the girl and now you've got the part. You can go on for me tonight!'[7]

The bride and groom spent a brief honeymoon at the Letchworth Hall Hotel (paid for by Coral) before settling into their unorthodox married life at Wilton Row.

Coral was certainly devoted to Philip, who adored and doted on her: he arranged for roses to be delivered to her every Tuesday, and they gave each other campy, ironic nicknames: she was 'Mouse', while he was 'Tycoon'. But this didn't mean she made a miraculous overnight conversation to physical monogamy. While she embraced being Mrs Pearman, of course that didn't mean she would, or could, stop being Coral Browne. However, as Eleanor Fazan observed, 'A very surprising side of her character was that she was a loving wife – incredibly loving – to her husband. She was a very *adoring* wife. You didn't quite expect it, to the extent that she was, in her type of character.'[8] Coral could be loving *and* forthright to her husband – during one of her overseas trips, she left him some unusual bedtime reading: 'It's a little worrying to find the Kinsey Report by the bed with a pansy bookmark in it at "Masturbation", I must say.'[9]

After their wedding, Philip briefly continued his theatrical career: he played a variety of non-speaking 'spear-carrier' roles in the 1951 Peter Brook production of *A Winter's Tale*, starring John Gielgud. He also appeared with Godfrey Tearle in *Hanging Judge* at the New Theatre in 1952, and opposite Alec Clunes in *Carrington VC* at the Westminster Theatre a year later. But it soon became clear that he would never emulate his wife's distinguished stage career – especially when she was inclined to put a dampener on his hopes. In bed one night, Coral was reading *King Lear* when Philip casually asked if there were any suitable roles for him. Flicking over a few pages, she announced, 'I've found the perfect part for you. Look, it says, "Act Four, Scene Three. A Camp near Dover."'[10]

Eventually, Philip decamped from acting and found the perfect role for himself – as a highly successful agent. 'He was a dear, very fey and elegant, very camp,' said Jill Melford. 'But sweet and jolly and quite witty himself – he needed to be! In the agency business, he was as successful as Coral was as an actress.'[11] Philip later joined MCA England Ltd (later London Artists) whose partners included Laurence Evans, the legendary Olive Harding and Ronnie Waters. As Ronald Waterall, Waters had been a classmate of Patrick White at Cheltenham College and, like Philip, had abandoned a disappointing stage career to become an agent. This came as no surprise to White, who remembered his first encounter with Waters: 'He made his entrance camping down the sweat-room stairs, singing "California, here I come..."'[12] Philip soon proved he was a worthy partner, whose diligence was greatly appreciated – Coral said Philip 'would never let a client do a thing he hadn't studied'.[13] Within a few years, he had discovered and represented the likes of Albert Finney and Julie Christie. John Gliddon recalled: 'He never ceased to go out and about in search of star material...'[14] His 'star material' also included Michael York: after graduating from Oxford, where he had performed well in student productions, York wrote to a number of agents and Philip took him on. He advised the young actor to audition for the Birmingham Rep and the Royal Shakespeare Company. When York was offered a spear-carrying role with the RSC, his agent counselled caution: 'On the face of it, it looks rather tempting, but I think you might get terribly depressed coming down from Oxford where you have been, let's face it, something of a local star and finding yourself plunged into a crowd. Unless you are very anxious to do this, I would have thought it better to wait and go to Stratford later on a higher level.'[15] York heeded the advice, passed up the RSC's offer and immediately landed a job with the Dundee Repertory Company, where the young actor got a chance to develop his skills in a greater variety of roles on a trajectory that would soon take him from Dundee to Hollywood.

Some of Philip's other clients, including Alan Bates, Peter Bowles and Sarah Badel, would end up working with Coral. 'I'd left RADA, and my first job [in January 1963] was with the Bristol Old Vic, on a projected tour of India for the British Council,' recalled Badel. 'I was Ophelia in *Hamlet*; we'd had a run-through before we left and Philip came to see it. He wrote me a very sweet letter, saying: "I thought your mad scene was very good, because you didn't nibble the carpet."'[16] However, by his own admission, Philip's judgement wasn't infallible. In 1960, Alan Bates was offered two jobs: one was to appear as Hotspur in a BBC production of *Henry IV Part I*, the other was to play Mick in Harold Pinter's *The Caretaker* at the Arts Theatre, for a modest £6 a week. As far as Philip was concerned, the choice was obvious: it had to be Hotspur. But his client disagreed: he wanted to do the Pinter play. 'Over my dead body,' said Philip. 'In a play which I find completely incomprehensible?' Bates stuck to his guns: 'Philip…looked at me with an expression that seemed to suggest I would shortly be dropped from the MCA client list.'[17] However, after he saw the play on its opening night on 27 April, Philip went backstage to see Bates and said, 'Never listen to me again. The play is brilliant.'[18]

Philip was a good match for Coral in all respects – even after she became one of his clients. 'It was an ideal marriage,' she would recall. 'He understood what my career entailed. Added to which he was a wonderful cook.'[19] According to Coral, life at Wilton Row had an air of 'Box and Cox' about it, because of their incompatible hours: 'We have three dogs and a mad Spanish maid, and we do our entertaining at home…my husband has to get to the office by 8.30AM and when he comes home in the evening, I'm leaving for the theatre…'[20]

Their three poodles, Alexander, Blossom and Ada, took it in turns to go with Coral to the theatre and wait in her dressing room. Her customary stage fright-soothing needlework now included making knitwear and embroidering initialled slippers for her husband – although eventually that gave way to carpets and cushion covers, as reporter Norman Holbrook revealed: "'I've given up knitting," she said, "My husband's got all the socks and scarves he can ever use and, now that he's my agent and sits in an office in Piccadilly all day he doesn't wear cardigans." I forbore to ask whether he took the usual ten per cent…'[21]

When *Castle in the Air* finished its run at the Savoy in August 1950, Coral – for the first time in nearly a decade – was at a loose end. She did agree to feature in *Yesterday and Today*, an 'All-Star Matinee' in aid of the Irene Vanbrugh Memorial Fund to rebuild the still-damaged Theatre at RADA. The matinee took place at the Theatre Royal, Drury Lane on Monday 6 November, with Queen Elizabeth in attendance. Most of the gala was compéred by Coral's former co-star Robert Morley and featured a Masque devised by Tyrone Guthrie, incorporating the first scene of *Carousel*, with Epilogue written and spoken by Noël Coward. Stars appearing in this Masque included Coral, Jack Buchanan, Tyrone Power, Rachel Kempson and Alec Guinness.

A few months later, Guthrie wrote and asked her to play Emilia and Goneril in his forthcoming productions of *Othello* and *King Lear* for the Old Vic. Though the salary on offer was considerably less than one of the former top-three earning actresses in the West End was used to (£25 per week in London plus £5 extra in the provinces), Coral had no hesitation in accepting the first decent Shakespearean parts offered her since she arrived in England.

Guthrie's production of *Othello* clashed with another at the St James's Theatre, starring and directed by Orson Welles, with Peter Finch as Iago. Guthrie had cast Paul Rogers as his Iago, with Desdemona being played by the American-born star, Irene Worth – around whom, according to Sarah Badel, Coral appeared none-too-comfortable: 'I think Irene gave her a slight inferiority complex – about acting. "Hatty Abrams from Omaha", Coral always called her. And somehow, I don't think she surrendered to Coral's wit…"[22]

Perhaps the women had a bit too much in common: one critic said that Worth 'combined an eloquent voice, which could rise from a purr to a cry of passion, with a striking physical presence'.[23] It was her humour that stuck in fellow actor Peter Eyre's memory: 'In Melbourne, in the middle of rehearsal, she suddenly said, "Have you ever seen a kangaroo? I saw one yesterday. He was eating a piece of cake, and playing with himself at the same time." Irene, aged 80, leapt and hopped across the room. She was the kangaroo; she was improvising.'[24]

Despite – or possibly because of – their alleged rivalry, the two actresses triumphed in their respective roles. *Theatre World*, comparing the Guthrie and Olivier productions, said, 'It was generally agreed that the Old Vic scored particularly on the production side, while Irene Worth and Coral Browne earned special praise for their outstanding performances.'[25] Others agreed: 'It is curious to have to remember *Othello* solely for the performances of the women, yet that is how we shall remember the present production…'[26]

Coral had other reasons to remember the production: it was during this show that she began considering converting to Catholicism. Alec Guinness said Coral's decision was influenced in large part by her friendship with the American-born, Jewish-turned-Catholic actor Ernest Milton, who was playing Lodovico 'with his characteristic decorations'.*[27] Alec Guinness said Milton

---

* Milton had performed with Guinness in the latter's 1946 adaptation of *The Brothers Karamazov*. Of this performance, James Agate remarked that 'Ernest Milton's Father Zossima is twin

'was eccentric but he was one of the two or three best actors I have ever seen. [Coral] became fascinated by him.'[28] Perhaps she also recognised something in Milton that he had long battled to hide: his latent homosexuality. Devoted to his wife, Naomi Royde Smith – in the same way that Philip was devoted to Coral – Milton once waxed lyrical to Guinness about the 'beauty' of Richard Burton and that the only woman he had ever found sexually arousing was, incongruously, Lilian Baylis. Of course, Coral's first mentor, Gregan McMahon, had also been born, raised and buried a Catholic, so she was aware that it was indeed a broad church that would readily embrace those who, in their personal lives, couldn't *quite* put into practice what was preached.

Milton put Coral in touch with his priest, Father Francis O'Malley, at St Etheldreda's at 14 Ely Place, close to Hatton Garden, London's diamond, gold and silver trades' district.[†]

Even more than her decision to marry an obviously gay man, Coral's fervent new faith was surprising to many friends. 'I never understood it, and we never really discussed it,' said Jill Melford. 'I've known several Catholic converts and she was the most *Catholic* Catholic that ever happened. But it bore no relation to the way she lived. I think it was something to hang on to – and also it's a very theatrical thing – all that purse-swinging and that…it was kind of a bizarre thing for Coral to be. But it suited her.'[29] According to Frith Banbury, 'It meant a lot to her. And I think one of the reasons why…you see, her tongue was inclined to run away, and she upset people. She didn't seem able to draw the line between something that was really hurtful and was better not said, and something that was said in criticism but was funny. I think

---

brother to Hermione Gingold's King Lear.'[30] As for his *King John* in 1941, Agate observed, 'Milton wore a wonderful wig made out of what looked like a discarded tea-cosy…he got all the poetry out of the part, and I suspected him of putting some of it in.'[31]

† Britain's oldest Catholic church, it was steeped in theatrical history: the chapel was part of the Ely Palace comples, occupied by John of Gaunt in the late 14th century. His former residence – the Savoy Palace – was burnt down during the 1381 Peasants' Revolt. In *Richard II* (Act II, Scene 1), Shakespeare gave John probably the most quoted deathbed speech in English literature: 'This royal throne of kings, this sceptred isle…' The strawberries grown in the church's gardens also got a mention in *Richard III*, Act III, Scene 4. And in its crypt lie the remains of 18 Catholics who, along with some 300 others, crammed into a nearby building in 1623 to attend a clandestine mass and perished when it collapsed. This building, the Gatehouse, was once owned by Shakespeare.

– and this is my feeling – that her joining the Catholic Church was to try and counteract this.'[32] It almost goes without saying that the order to 'go and sin no more' wasn't adhered to for much longer than the time it took to leave the church.

After a lengthy instruction, Coral was baptised into the Catholic Church (with her name recorded as 'Coralia Pearlman') by Father O'Malley at St Etheldreda's on 6 February 1953. In the future, her usual place of worship would be the Church of the Immaculate Conception, Mount Street – more commonly known as 'Farm Street'. In the 1920s, Tallulah Bankhead once owned a house across the street from the church, and gave callers plenty to confess by greeting them at the door stark naked. Eventually, Farm Street gave way to Brompton Oratory.

Coral's Catholicism would bind her closer to Alec Guinness: he converted to the faith in 1956, a year after he had portrayed the Cardinal in *The Prisoner*, directed by Peter Glenville, who was his Catholic sponsor. Guinness turned to the faith partly to counter his bouts of severe depression. He and fellow convert Coral would fill their prodigious correspondence with irreverent tales of the unexpurgated: their letters became a type of 'confessional', where the two Catholics could freely discuss all manner of sin – including other people's.

In September 1951, the production of *Othello* went to Berlin, to form part of an arts festival, which also featured a 'day of sensations' at the city's Olympic Stadium. At the Hebbel Theatre, the company gave five performances (with three dress rehearsals) in three days, 'so gruelling that they "nearly killed" even [Paul] Rogers'.[33]

Rogers and the company survived and returned to London in November, where the production enjoyed a short run at the Old Vic. 'I've made a great success in the play – considered by the experts to be the best Emilia the living can remember,' Coral told her mother.[34]

Soon, she had more to write home about: buoyed by the success of her first classical role, she agreed to play Regan in Hugh Hunt's production of *King Lear*, opposite Stephen Murray – there was even a part for Philip, playing the King of France. In January 1952, the Old Vic Company took the show on a taxing 35-performance tour of Holland, Belgium, West Germany, Denmark, Sweden and Finland. The company found themselves performing in a challenging variety of venues: 'Lighting effects and stage machinery differed in each of the theatres they visited. One night the thunder claps would be on the left, the next on the right, which meant that the actors could never relax with any degree of confidence.'[35] And when the production returned to England and opened at the Old Vic on 3 March, prior to a provincial tour, one critic observed that 'the company…appear to have forgotten the acoustic properties of their own theatre. It is hard to recall an Old Vic performance in which the tails of so many sentences were bitten off and swallowed.'[36] But there was nothing truncated about Coral's performance: Kenneth Tynan said, '…very few members of this cast seem vocally capable of competing with the continuous roar of the Old Vic's ventilation system…the clearest, as well as the most audible, performance is Miss Coral Browne's flamboyant Regan, which is played in this actress's best "Scarlet Empress" vein…'[37]

The tours of *King Lear* gave Coral a chance to indulge her passion for shopping – for herself and her new home. According to Jean Soward, 'Every time she goes off on tour, some picture, or piece of furniture or china ornament is bound to catch her eye. Miss Browne admits that she buys 20 pairs of shoes and at least 20 hats a season. They are her "extravagance".'[38]

In 1952, Coral and Philip bought the leasehold of 46 Chester Row, a four-floor house which was 'as narrow as a slice of cake, with almost as many stairs as the Eiffel Tower'.[39] As before, the leaseholders were the Grovesnor Estate, landlords of most of Belgravia. The house was decorated in Coral's favourite white and shades of green: white cupboards, white fireplace, white Venetian blinds, olive green and white willow-pattern wallpaper. The bathroom had some unusual features: a shaggy bearskin rug and pots of roses on top of the lavatory cistern. Its most unusual feature, however, was a poltergeist which, according to Coral, was particularly fond of wreaking havoc at dinner parties.

A more welcome visitor to the new house was Thelma Scott, a former colleague from Coral's years with the Gregan McMahon Players who had moved to London in 1951. A friend of Louisa Humphries, mother of Australia's most famous cultural export Barry, Scott appeared with Coral in the McMahon productions *Take Two from One* and *Dear Brutus*. In the intervening years, Scott had become one of Australia's biggest radio stars, a mainstay of popular drama series including *Big Sister* and *Crossroads of Life*. Scott had to wait more than three years for her big break: it came when Beatrice Lillie chose her to replace Constance Carpenter, one of her 'assistants' in her hit show at the Globe, *An Evening with Beatrice Lillie*. Eighteen months after her arrival, Scott was joined by her longtime companion, Gwen Plumb, and the couple became part of Coral's regular social circle. After the pair returned in 1957 to Australia, where both enjoyed successful television careers, they kept in touch with Coral until her death.

In 1952, Coral starred with Wilfred Hyde-White and Hugh Williams in another successful but unremarkable comedy, Louis Verneuil's *Affairs of State*, about the marital complications of a Washington politician seeking to avoid a public scandal about his private life. According to one critic, 'In a more comfortable age…[it] might have been called a good after-dinner play.'[40] Once again, Coral's performance was rated more highly than the play itself: 'Miss Coral Browne's scheming lady is…precisely calculated and exquisitely timed, to the least flicker of an eyelid or the last little humorous grimace of defeat.'[41] *Affairs of State* ran at Cambridge Theatre until February 1954, clocking up more than 600 performances.

That summer, Coral and Philip took their first holiday for nearly two years. 'We think it's delicious to go to Spain and take a month off,' she said.[42] It was also around this time that Coral (who by now had turned 40) decided to give her face a 'holiday': according to Peter Willes, she had a facelift – the first in a long series of facial enhancements. She later admitted, 'I've had it lifted everywhere.'[43] She made other physical adjustments during these years: in 1957, she spent a couple of weeks in the London Clinic where, she assured Arnold Weissberger, 'There hasn't been anything more sordid than the removal of some odd beauty spots – I've now lost every one, except the one that doesn't show & that ceased to be irresistible years ago.'[44]

With her face, body and mind refreshed, she turned her attention to a new Alan Melville comedy, *Simon and Laura*. Steering well clear of Biblical subjects for his plays, Melville switched to the modern religion of television. Coral and Roland Culver played a bickering husband and wife acting team, the Fosters, who are given the challenge of appearing on a TV series as a happily married couple, broadcast daily from their home. Dora Bryan, who played Janet Honeyman, said she 'found Coral positively frightening at the outset… In those days you had a dress parade on stage before the show to see if your clothes were right. Coral just looked at me and said, "She's deformed." That was her idea of being amusing. She used to say terribly hurtful things and we were supposed to laugh, but I didn't think it funny.'[45]

Coral's ill-concealed animosity may have been stirred by Bryan's other commitments: 'I don't think she liked me filming during the run of the play.

[Bryan was making *Mad About Men.*] I suppose she thought it made me too tired to work in the evenings. One night I was standing in the wings next to her, waiting to go on, when she suddenly said accusingly, in that chillingly clear voice, "You've been filming again." "Not today, Coral," I replied. "Yes you have," she argued. "You can't fool me. Your eyes are like great pools of blood on the stage."[46] Coral later made her attitude towards this 'doubling-up' quite clear: 'I've made very few pictures. Each I've done has been contingent on my activity in the theatre. If I'm busy in a play, I won't try a picture. Much too tiring. I learned that the hard way, trying to balance a London play by night and roaring off daytimes to the studio.'[47]

There was enough to keep her occupied in *Simon and Laura*: the elderly actor Ernest Thesiger was playing Wilson, the butler. During one scene, Coral became aware of some distraction going on behind her and realised the audience's attention was on Thesiger, who had decided to improvise some background business during her speeches. After the show, she invited Thesiger round to her dressing-room for a drink. She solemnly informed him that she had to 'have a bit of medical surgery next week' and that he might have to work with her understudy. Alarmed by the prospect, Thesiger enquired as to the nature of the surgery, and Coral reassured him, 'Oh, it's nothing very much – I'm just having eyes sewn into the back of my fucking head!'[48] *Simon and Laura* was not a huge hit, running only three months in the West End; one critic said, 'The performance is curiously like the play, full of amusing things but unsatisfactory as a whole.'[49]

By the end of 1954, Kenneth Tynan revealed his wish for the theatre of 1955: 'Better plays, better acting, better productions.'[50] Decrying the state of British playwriting, he declared that, 'We need plays about cabmen and demi-gods, plays about warriors, politicians and grocers – I care not, so Loamshire be invaded and subdued.'[51] And Tynan knew who should be acting in these new works: 'All plays should contain parts fit to be turned down by Gladys Cooper, Coral Browne, Hugh Williams and Robert Flemyng,' he asserted.[52]

Sadly, Coral was not about to help grant his wish: in 1955, she would accept a part that was not only fit to be turned down – but, in hindsight, certainly should have been. For once, her usually unerring judgement was swayed by her loyalty to an old friend.

Under the direction of Rex Harrison, Edith Evans had been due to play the lead in André Roussin's comedy, *Nina* – 'a farce built on the Gallic axiom that there are three sides to every story, *Nina* has the husband decided in the first act to kill the lover, in the next act to kill the wife, in the last act to kill himself'.[53] The omens for the play were never good: a 1951 Broadway production starring David Niven and Gloria Swanson had lasted just 45 performances at the Royale Theater. In England, Charles Goldner, Harrison's leading man, was taken ill at the first reading. He died ten days later, aged just 55, and was replaced by David Hutcheson. Then during rehearsal one afternoon Edith Evans was overheard saying, 'I suppose it comes to every actress in time; this is the end of my career.'[54] According to Rex Harrison, the fault lay with the supporting players – specifically James Hayter and David Hutcheson who, he claimed, didn't have 'the experience and the extraordinary fine intelligence' of their leading lady. 'She was always playing a scene with one or the other, and she became more and more unhappy.'[55] To help Evans cope with her increasing misery, Harrison resorted to offering her one of his time-release Phenobarbital capsules – possibly the first, and last, pill the devout Christian Scientist actress ever took. But the drugs didn't work. On the Sunday before the play was due to open at the Royal Court Theatre, Liverpool, its producer Binkie Beaumont informed Harrison that Evans had suffered some sort of breakdown and couldn't go on. The press were told her disposition was due to a severe influenza attack, but the critic Harold Hobson suspected she found 'this delightful comedy of a *ménage à trois*…morally impermissible. She knew no peace until she had been released from her contract.'[56] Michael Hordern, who took over from David Hutcheson for the West End run, later said, 'Perhaps she just realised she was much too old for the part…a month or two later, she was back on the boards playing in something much more suitable.'[57] Evans was temporarily replaced by her understudy, Billie Hall who, according to Hordern, 'had omitted to learn her lines and had to go on with the script'.[58] This sorry scene greeted André Roussin on his arrival from Paris.

Meanwhile, Coral, always an admirer of Evans, was holidaying with Philip in Majorca and had reminded him to book their seats for the first night of *Nina* in London. Before he could make the call, they took one from an old friend who'd tracked Coral down to ask a huge favour. 'Binkie Beaumont begged her to take on the part; she didn't want to do it but eventually agreed,' said Frith Banbury. 'But Binkie didn't allow her enough time to rehearse it.'[59] 'I'm what they call a slow study,' Coral said. 'I like to take a script away to some remote spot and steep myself in it for three weeks before I even begin rehearsing. This time I've had to read it and rehearsed it all in one month. But it's been as good as a slimming diet. I lost eight pounds in six days.'[60] Soon, everyone involved in the show was losing weight – and queuing up behind Edith Evans to have the next breakdown. Michael Hordern described the cast as 'a depressing sight; a more unhappy bunch of thespians it would be hard to imagine',[61] and the collective mood was not improved by the insensitivity of their director. After seeing one of their performances in Eastbourne, he declared, 'What I have seen tonight is fit only for the end of the pier.'[62] Harrison would later admit: 'My inexperience as a director, my six-day-week commitment to *Bell, Book and Candle* conspired with the preoccupation of my own life to produce a failure on my part.'[63]

With optimism prevailing over honesty, Binkie Beaumont wrote Coral a letter for the first night, sent 'With my love, gratitude, and great admiration for a glorious *Nina*. Great success.'[64] But there was to be no glory – especially for Coral. When it opened at the Haymarket on 25 July, the critics savaged all aspects of the production – and Coral's performance in particular. In the *News Chronicle*, Alan Dent wrote, 'We come away from André Roussin's play, not so much regretting that Dame Edith Evans' indisposition has prevented her appearing in it, as wondering why she ever had the notion that it would suit her.'[65] The *Observer* said of the show, 'Everything is wrong about it…it has been badly translated…the dialogue is feeble…it was too obvious to cast the strapping Coral Browne for the indomitable domesticated Messalina…the direction of Rex Harrison was absolutely no help at all…'[66] The *Financial Times* considered it a simple case of physical miscasting: 'We require a dumpy, bustling little body of certain middle age, rather plain and endearingly ludicrous. Instead, we get Miss Coral Browne looking very young, very glamorous, very slender and very beautiful.'[67] But the review which, according to Coral, stung the most was that by Milton Schulman. Headlined 'Miss Browne's Soufflé Doesn't Rise to the Occasion', he opined that '…this should be a play about a frivolous, madcap dominating woman called Nina…but Miss CB strides rather than flouts, bullies rather than tantalises, pontificates rather than charms. She is a soufflé that never rises and the play nestles stubbornly into a soggy lump because of it… *Nina* remains a fairly trying evening.'[68]

Though it wasn't all brickbats – *Theatre World* said Coral played Nina 'with tremendous aplomb'[69] – collectively, the reviews amounted to her worst. No copies of the negative ones found their way into her scrapbook.

The play closed five weeks later, after 45 performances – just like its Broadway predecessor – and Michael Hordern was in no doubt who was responsible: 'It was a disaster because of Rex Harrison.'[70] However, as far as he was concerned, 'meeting Coral made up for a good deal of the nightmare of *Nina*. She was terribly attractive, with a marvellous dry sense of humour which got us through many tricky moments.'[71] The attraction was apparently mutual, but the pair controlled themselves until one evening when, as was customary after a show, Hordern popped into her dressing room to have a drink and a chat: 'She was standing in front of the mirror in her dressing gown. When she saw me she let it slip to the floor. She was beautiful naked and I was finished. I fell in love with her and she became terribly important to me. Too important: my marriage and family life were threatened.'[72] Their affair continued much longer than the ill-fated *Nina* – but when Hordern's wife Eve found out about the relationship, he ended it.

Amatory success was the only kind that *Nina* brought Coral. The irony of all the criticism was that, before she agreed to play the part, she had been considering an offer from Hugh Hunt to return to Australia to play Cleopatra for him at the Australian Elizabethan Theatre Trust in Sydney. Naturally, the prospect of returning 'home' didn't hold much appeal; but after *Nina*, the temptation to flee to the other side of the world must have been strong. 'I couldn't stand the barrage of lousy notices,' she said later. 'I thought, "Well, the place for me is not the theatre. Get out of this job. You'll never be able to do it again".'[73] Her fragile confidence, slowly built up over 20 years, had, indeed, collapsed like a failed soufflé.

She believed then that she would never act again.

***

It was the Irishman labelled a 'giant gadfly, the inspired puppet-master' by Kenneth Tynan who would persuade Coral back to the stage.[74]

Tyrone 'Tony' Guthrie was, according to Alec Guinness, 'I suppose, our own, original home-grown "enfant terrible" of the theatre; galvanising, delighting and shocking a whole generation of performers and spectators…'[75] The six-foot-four director was 'a genie who can change into many forms and is always an exacting taskmaster. At one moment he may burst into song to simulate an orchestra. The next he may bound about the stage in a pair of carpet slippers to show how he wants a battle scene done…and he gets the results he wants by dipping into an apparently bottomless well of patience and good humour.'[76] Frith Banbury said, 'It was such fun to work for him. The atmosphere of concentration, combined with enjoyment.'[77] Guthrie had always felt Coral was squandering her talent on commercial West End productions – something he told her as far back as 1944, when he directed her in *The Last of Mrs Cheyney*: 'At that time he said to me, "You know, it's so ridiculous. You're wasting your time in these plays *My Sister Eileen*, etc, when you should be in the classical theatre."'[78]

Her performances in *Othello* and *King Lear* bolstered his conviction and, some months after the *Nina* debacle, Guthrie persuaded Coral to leave England and join his Shakespeare Festival Theatre in Stratford, Ontario, where he would be staging four of Shakespeare's tragedies, including *Macbeth* and *Troilus and Cressida*, before touring them in Canada and the US. After spells as Director of the Old Vic and Sadler's Wells, Guthrie, believing London theatres to be over-commercialised and provincial theatre woefully neglected, had established the Stratford Company in 1953. He told Coral, 'If you're away from all the dreadful horrors of the press that you're so afraid of, then come with me where it won't be like that.'[79]

The first play Coral was to appear in was *Tamburlaine the Great*; she had marvelled at Guthrie's 1951 production with Donald Wolfit at the Old Vic: 'I don't think I've ever seen anything that excited me more. All the arrows, the cruelty, the costumes, the extraordinary settings.'[80]

But now, away from home, husband and friends, and with the harsh appraisals for *Nina* still echoing, there was no excitement for Coral – only fear. 'I felt nervous being in a strange country. They were marvellous actors, and they had all come from universities…they were very dedicated people who had made up their minds to go into the theatre, like Bill Shatner and Lloyd Bochner. I thought, "Why have I been brought over? What am I doing here? Oh, I'm terrible."'[81] Her co-star, Paul Rogers, observed, 'She was really quite sort of timid inside about tackling this specific type of job.'[82]

And when rehearsal started, her fears threatened to overwhelm her: 'I said to Guthrie at rehearsal one morning, "I feel like a fish out of water. I don't know what I'm doing." And he said, "Aren't you funny? I always thought you were a man, and now I find you a mouse."' During the lunch break, he took her to one side, methodically explaining her role and how it should be played: 'He took me over it word by word, line by line, like a child. And he did it *absolutely* for me.'[83] This was typical of Guthrie, who was famous for knowing 'every part and direct[ing] every part, however minor, as if it were the star role...'[84] It did the trick for Coral: after a successful run in Stratford, *Tamburlaine the Great* headed for the Winter Garden on Broadway in January 1956. There, it would feature a cast of 100 – and a new leading man, Anthony Quayle. Coral subsequently told her friend and fellow Ocker, Myles Eason (and anyone else within earshot), that acting with Quayle was 'like acting with two tons of condemned veal' – a put-down that she accorded any leading man she felt was not up to scratch.[85] The unfortunate Quayle – who, for all his perceived shortcomings, Coral would agree to co-star with for more than one show – was given another Brownesque nickname: deciding that his eyes were a bit close together, she dubbed him 'Old One Eye'.

Unfortunately, there's no record of the nickname Coral reserved for another member of the company: 'They had a very strange wardrobe mistress. She had decided, for the opening in New York, that she would wash my wig and do it all herself. At the half I was about to get into my wig, struggling like Cinderella and the glass slipper. And then the tears started to come because I couldn't get this thing on. It had shrunk into a peanut and there was no gum. Tony...ran to a drugstore somewhere, got some gum, and I got the wig on. He cut it up the back with scissors; he did it himself.'[86]

Thanks to Guthrie's Heath Robinson skills, 'Cinderella' didn't miss the ball that was her Broadway debut. The first night audience – which included Anthony Asquith and Terence Rattigan – accorded the show a standing ovation, and the critics burst forth with fulsome praise: 'Mr Tyrone Guthrie's production might best be described as a collector's piece...[it] shows a scope and vitality to match Marlowe's gigantic and flamboyant thrashings,'[87] while Brooks Atkinson singled out Coral's performance: 'As the wife of the defeated Emperor, Miss Browne makes a deep impression...'[88] However, despite its good reviews, the play was withdrawn after a mere 20 performances. There was some consolation for Quayle and Guthrie, who both received Tony nominations. There was also some consolation for Coral: according to Frith Banbury, she had a brief affair with the show's American producer, Robert Whitehead (later husband of fellow Australian emigrant, Zoe Caldwell).

Professionally, it was a case of 'mission accomplished': Coral had put the nightmare that was *Nina* behind her – and, as Tony Guthrie had always envisaged, proved to herself and everyone else that she had the chops to tackle any part, be it high comedy or high drama. She never forgot what Guthrie had done for her: 'There's never been anybody who has made it the fun that he did. I'd have done anything in the world that he wanted me to do. I would have walked over broken bottles to be with him.'[89]

She was to continue her run of Shakespeare roles when she returned to England: she replaced Ann Todd in *Macbeth* at the Old Vic, and seized the opportunity to announce her new credentials as a classical actress. But she was taking nothing for granted: 'Learning the verse wasn't easy,' she admitted. 'I slogged away at it for weeks and I'd walk around London talking to myself. I did a lot of the memorizing in cabs and on the buses…Lady M is a ruthless woman; she's a lot of the women I've known, but she isn't a friend…When I get to the sleepwalking scene I go at it as if I were really asleep…'[90]

The preparation paid off: the critics who had given her such a kicking for *Nina* were now at her feet. She was 'an exceptionally good Lady Macbeth; strong and baleful,'[91] playing '…this glorified gangster's moll with a fierce ashen beauty…and a majestic air of evil.'[92] Others were not oblivious to another quality she brought to the production: 'She is the first actress of recent years to put sex into the part.'[93]

It wasn't long after this triumph that Tyrone Guthrie called on her services again – without the inconvenience of her having to crawl across broken bottles. In the autumn, she returned to New York to reprise her Lady Macbeth and also to play Helen of Troy in 14 performances of *Troilus and Cressida* at the Winter Garden, as part of an eight-week Old Vic repertory season that also included productions of *Richard II* and *Romeo and Juliet* by a company which included John Neville, Paul Rogers and Claire Bloom. It was the Old Vic's first visit to the city since 1946, when Laurence Olivier and Ralph Richardson starred in *Henry IV Part I*.

According to Coral, the New York production of *Macbeth* engendered some unexpected drama: 'I had such trouble with Macbeth [Paul Rogers], he was so jealous,' she claimed. 'I got all the notices, you see. It's the baby. That's the crux of the matter. I wanted to play her with a baby at her tit in the first scene. He wouldn't hear of it. Afraid I'd get the pathos, you see.'[94]

There was nothing pathetic about the show's reception on opening night: the company took ten curtain calls while the audience applauded for a full five minutes. And, when the reviews appeared, there was no doubt who the star of the show was: Brooks Atkinson enthused, 'Coral Browne's Lady Macbeth is an extraordinary piece of acting. On her first entrance…a sensual baleful woman of grace and authority who sends a shudder through the whole play. By the time of the sleep-walking scene, Lady Macbeth is a worn, dishevelled, glassy-eye creature who has tumbled over the brink into madness…this Lady Macbeth is the triumph of the performance.'[95] John Chapman of the *New York Daily News* raved, 'I've seen better Macbeths but never a better Lady Macbeth,'[96] and his paper gave Coral a headline to treasure: 'Callas a Success in Met Debut: Old Vic's Exciting Lady Macbeth'.[97]

Little wonder, then, that Coral later described playing Lady Macbeth as 'the most rewarding thing I ever did in my life'.[98] Playing the part on both sides of the Atlantic meant she had plenty of sage advice to pass onto other actresses who tackled the part. In 1967, she asked Vivien Merchant (then about to start a long run in the role), 'What are you going to do with the fucking candle? I wouldn't bring it on. I left it in a sconce offstage.'[99] And she warned Maggie Smith, 'It's a fucker, darling, and all I can say is keep your eyes open in the sleepwalking scene. For some reason, it rivets the fuckers.'[100]

'The fuckers' in New York were similarly riveted by *Troilus and Cressida*. Of course, Guthrie being Guthrie, there was nothing traditional about this production. 'He set it during the First War, with the soldiers all dressed up as Tommies and Huns,' said Coral. 'His idea was that Helen was not the loveliest siren of all time…so there I was, in a pound of platinum false curls, spilling out of my gown, biting my pearls and holding forth form the top of a piano with Paris passed out underneath it.'[101]

'The whole point of the play was the futility of fighting over a woman not beautiful any more – a woman who for 17 years had been drinking steadily, with big tits and the hair all dyed blonde. It all took place in this mad summer house… There was this drunken lady singing on the piano with Pandarus playing and an atmosphere of champagne in everybody's shoe. She was a wild sort of Mae West…they saw that I was dressed in coral-velvet everywhere, with the breasts coming out – one or the other was always coming out.'[102] The critics were divided over what Roger Dettmer called 'Tyrone Guthrie's bold, brilliant, faultlessly fanciful production,'[103] which was greeted with 12 curtain calls on opening night. But they had no reservations about Coral's 'sketch of Helen of Troy as a night club hussy.'[104] Walter Kerr enjoyed the portrayal of 'Helen of Troy…as a beerhall prima donna, her blonde hair piled high of her arrogant head...audacious and absolutely defined'.[105] She was 'a Helen who combines some of the best qualities of Tallulah Bankhead and Mae West'.[106] After they closed in New York, the company went on tour to Boston, Philadelphia, Washington and Chicago, grossing more than a million dollars in box office sales in the process.

Despite being separated from Philip (who visited briefly in December), Coral's six months in America were a joy and a triumph. In New York, she amused herself with daily visits to Manhattan's famous stores – including one to Saks on Fifth Avenue, where she bought three strings of beads in the dogs' department for her poodles. And these weren't the only unusual accessories in her luggage: in Washington, she was presented with an eight inch-long golden key to the city. Its home wouldn't be Chester Row, but the Old Vic's foyer. As well as developing a lifelong affection for New York, Coral forged a close friendship with top agent Milton Goldman (later Vice-President of ICM) and his longtime partner, showbiz lawyer and photographer Arnold Weissberger. This popular couple had client lists that featured some of the biggest names in entertainment on both sides of the Atlantic, from Helen Hayes and Douglas Fairbanks Jr to Laurence Olivier and John Gielgud, and held memorably star-studded 'July 4' parties at the Savoy Hotel when they were in London.

Inevitably, she still found something to moan about: on the company's return to England, John Neville told a reporter he found 'most of the theatres in America quite ghastly' and both he and Coral berated the large number of people arriving late to performances. She said, 'I don't think it was bad manners. Americans have dinner later than we do and they drive to the theatre.'[107]

The Old Vic Company was returning to a theatrical establishment that, on 8 May 1956, had been rocked by, of all things, the appearance of an ironing board on a London stage. The Royal Court's production of John Osborne's *Look Back in Anger* had initiated a falling out of fashion for playwrights like Coward, Rattigan *et al*, and middle-class dramas set in country houses, Mayfair salons and holiday resorts in the south of France and the South Seas. Popular theatre was starting to be flushed out of the well-heeled drawing rooms and into the kitchen sinks by a wave of Osbornes, Pinters and Weskers. Naturally, the theatrical establishment put up considerable resistance to this – and none more so than the producer who had the most to lose, Binkie Beaumont, whose H M Tennent organisation still controlled 21 West End theatres. Osborne's biographer, John Heilpern, said: 'The West End Theatre that fed the rest of the country its contented Loamshire diet was ruled absolutely by the Machiavellian Hugh Beaumont.'[108] Peter Hall, who at 27, had just been put in charge of the Shakespeare Memorial Company, said, 'Binkie's West End, which was a year's run with a great star who signed for the whole year, was going. The arrival of commercial television had given actors as well as audiences new opportunities.'[109] Binkie Beaumont kept an eye on the new competition: he attended the first night of *Look Back in Anger*, but left at the first interval.

The world was changing: but, for the time being, Coral eschewed reality and settled for the relative rigour of a nine-month season at the Old Vic, opening in September 1957; she had been offered roles in *A Midsummer Night's Dream*, *King Lear* and *Hamlet*. It was the company's fifth and final season in a five-year plan to present all 36 plays in the First Folio of Shakespeare. The director of *Hamlet* was to be Michael Benthall, artistic director of the Old Vic, and initiator of the 'First Folio' plan. Benthall knew the challenges of the play inside out: he had assisted Tyrone Guthrie, his predecessor at the Old Vic, with his 1944 production and staged it himself at Stratford in 1948 with a cast that included Paul Scofield and Benthall's lifelong partner, Robert Helpmann, alternating in the title role.

For this production, the cast featured John Neville as the Prince, with Coral as Gertrude, Jack Gwillim as Claudius and John Humphry as Laertes. Two other actors in the cast, David Dodimead – usually known as 'Dodders' – and Harold Innocent, became members of Coral's queeny coterie. Also among the ranks was a future dame: in her first major role, Ophelia was being played by Judi Dench. The company included another young actor, also then at the beginning of his long and varied career – Barrie Ingham. Before being promoted to play Fortinbras, Ingham was originally cast in the small role of Military ADC. During a rehearsal of Act IV, Scene 5 with Coral and Stanley Meadows (Guildenstern), he received his Browne 'baptism': 'I decided I was going to learn my line – I only had one couplet. It was about Ophelia: 'She is importunate, indeed distract. Her mood will needs be pitied.' Coral had to come on from the back and say something like, "What is the message?," and I had to say this to her. But I couldn't remember the second line – and Coral said out of the side of her mouth: "Not half as fucking distract as you are, darling."' To a young actor, she was scary: you really thought, "Don't put a step wrong with this one" – and that's why I dried.

'At that same rehearsal, during the break, Stanley bought an orange, and came back peeling it on stage. Now there are two things you don't do on stage – one is to drink in case you spill it, and the other is, you don't eat fruit. And he walked up behind Coral – and he swears to this day that he thought it was somebody else – and slapped her on the bum. Not a thing to do on a Monday morning at rehearsal. And she turned round and faced him, and said, "Mr Meadows, I don't mind being slapped on the arse, but I can't stand the smell of oranges."'[110]

Remembering Alan Wilkie's setting for the play from her childhood, Coral suggested the 'black velvet curtain' approach to his *Hamlet*: 'We set it in the Winterhalter period... But it was curtains, curtains, curtains, and there were just faces and costumes – vague costumes of sort of no period at all. And the play came out much better.'[111] Kenneth Tynan, for one, agreed: 'Textually and conceptually it is as near to a definitive *Hamlet* as anything I have ever seen' and enjoyed Coral's portrayal of Gertrude as a 'maternally voluptuous queen'.[112] Coral's performance was singled out for plaudits: 'Coral Browne gave one of her best performances of the season as Gertrude. She has vigor [*sic*] and intelligence; her voice and appearance have richness and authority as well as beauty.'[113] Judi Dench later said, 'Coral was never to be forgotten as Gertrude.'[114] That autumn, her performance was committed to posterity, with the release of a box-set LP recording of *Hamlet*, released by HMV, with John Gielgud as the Prince. It lost nothing in translation: 'The acid in her voice perfectly matches the bitter fear that is eating away at her heart.'[115]

During the production, Coral displayed the kindness and somewhat surprising maternal instinct that she would often bestow on younger cast members. When Judi Dench became allergic to the soap powder used to wash the bed clothes in her digs, Coral invited her to move into the top floor of Chester Row for the duration. According to many, Coral was not averse to 'mothering' younger actresses and, in some cases, even passing on some of her expensive clothes to them. 'She would become a company's Mother Hen,' said Sheridan Morley. Eileen Atkins agreed: 'She was a wonderful mixture – there could be this amazing bitchy streak, and then she could be very maternal.'[116] But Coral would rarely lavish such affection on children – the psychology is obvious: if a woman has a combative, love-hate relationship with her mother, she is less likely to develop strong maternal feelings herself.

Coral and Judi Dench appeared – respectively, as Helena and First Fairy – in Michael Benthall's second production of the season, *A Midsummer Night's Dream*. Tyrone Guthrie had warned Coral never to play Helena but, for once, she ignored his advice. The production was also notable for the surprise casting of Frankie Howerd as Bottom in the Shakespeare play referred to by many actors as 'the Tit and Bum Show'. Howerd's sexual proclivities were common knowledge, so the announcement caused much backstage tittering. According to Barrie Ingham, 'Terry-Thomas came up to him in the green room and said, "Hello Frankie, when's your Bottom opening?" So he said, "Next Tuesday – and the free list is entirely suspended!"' *Theatre World* kept the in-joke running, by declaring Howerd 'a deliciously cocksure Bottom',[117] while another critic observed, 'Michael Benthall must know there is nothing we find more exhilarating than a little bit of unconventional casting…there may perhaps have been more Widow Twankey than Bully Bottom about Mr Howerd's Old Vic creation.'[118] Howerd struggled to learn his lines and find the correct rhythm for the verse, and occasionally clashed with director Benthall. Judi Dench said Howerd was often 'hysterically funny, though he just made it up a lot of the time'.[119]

Ultimately, however, Howerd became one of the surprise hits of the 'Tit and Bum' show – 22 years after the young Francis Howard had auditioned for RADA and been rejected. Coral was also '…an unexpected success. She plays with a fine precision and restraint.'[120] One critic mused, '…would one have expected so light a touch from Coral Browne, whose Helena is both lively and amusing'.[121]

But at least one member of the cast could have testified to the wonders of Coral's unexpectedly light touch. It's an oft-told tale – probably *the* most famous 'Coral Browne story' – which has, over the years, been inflated by Chinese whispers as it passed into theatrical legend. No two versions are the same, but it's a story that bears repeating – and the honour of doing so goes to Barrie Ingham, who witnessed the entire incident: 'David Dodimead and Coral were standing in the wings stage left, and I was there. It was the scene where the lovers had to go and lie down together and fall asleep. John Humphry was a gorgeous looking fellow, about six feet two – he had to lie down and Coral had to lie down next to him. He had a little short Greek skirt on him, and Dodders said to Coral, "I bet you can't give him a hard-on." So she said, "I bet you a quid [20 shillings] I can." So on she went. And we could see a very slight movement of the hand…and John was starting to twitch a little bit. At the end of the scene, she came back into the wings and said to Dodders, "I owe you ten shillings.'"[122]

Coral abandoned her light touch to play Goneril in the next Folio season play, Douglas Seale's production of *King Lear* – and to create another much-repeated and altered 'Coral Browne story'. At the dress rehearsal, Coral came on stage – or, at least, it appeared to be Coral: her face could barely be seen by her colleagues in the stalls, including Seale, Barrie Ingham and Stanley Meadows. 'This wig covered her completely,' recalled Ingham. 'And Dougie said to her, "Hmmm – not too sure about the wig, darling…" And Coral slowly parted the wig and said, "Dougie, what am I going to do? I feel as if I'm looking out of a *yak's ass!*'"[123]

Coral's portrayal of Goneril was 'properly presented as the more obviously spiteful and dangerous of the two sisters'.[124] And she and her stage sister, Barbara Jefford, were the talk of the production: one critic enthused, 'Coral Browne is a magnificently sensual Goneril, Barbara Jefford a cruel Regan.'[125] Barrie Ingham recalled that 'Barbara Jefford and Coral were the sexiest women you've ever seen on a stage – they played them like that.'[126]

After the season ended, many of the company members embarked on an extensive tour of America and Canada, with *Hamlet, Twelfth Night* and *Henry V.* Coral did not go with them – she had her own appointment way out west.

Apart from a small role in 1954's *Beautiful Stranger*, a forgettable melodrama starring Ginger Rogers, Coral had stuck to her self-imposed policy of not juggling film roles with up to eight theatre performances a week. But she was about to start work on her biggest movie to date, in her biggest role to date – and it was all thanks to Helen of Troy.

During rehearsals at the Old Vic, Coral received a call from film director and producer Morton De Costa – he had seen her in New York in *Troilus and Cressida*. The image of Coral's Helen of Troy – with her blonde hair, cigarette holder and louche living – bore an uncanny resemblance to a film character that De Costa was trying to cast: the blonde, louche-living Vera Charles, bosom buddy of *Auntie Mame*. He subsequently met Coral at a party in New York that ex-pat actor Maurice Evans gave for the show's cast – after which, De Costa reminded her, he had to carry her home. This display of alcoholic over-indulgence convinced him he had his Vera, and he arranged for Coral to do a screen test: Vera's first 'hangover' scene, in which she is introduced as 'a star and one of the great actresses in the theatre...the First Lady of the American Theatre...she doesn't live here – she drinks here and does her passing out here.'

Having passed the passing-out the test – on and off screen – Coral would be playing opposite Rosalind Russell, who was to repeat on film her barnstorming performance as Mame Dennis, the 'crazy sister' of Edward Dennis, to whom he entrusts the care of his son Patrick. The role of Vera – Mame's fellow wise-cracking, lotus-eating clothes horse – required an actress who could simultaneously handle the full-throttle, comedy dialogue; resist being swept off the screen by Russell; wear Orry-Kelly's costumes as if to the mannequin born; portray an elegant lush – *and* be credible as the 'first Lady of the American stage'. Coral would bring all of this to the part – *plus* her effective left eyebrow into the bargain. She told Arnold Weissberger, 'I'm absolutely delighted that I'm going into the movies at last. The same thing happened to Marie Dressler when she was my age!!!'[127] It all seemed too perfect – and it was, for there was trouble waiting in the wigs, and a 'yak's ass' would have been only too welcome.

Apparently, it was all the fault of royalty: 'I got out to Hollywood late for the film because Her Majesty had a laid a stone at the Old Vic [The Queen unveiled a plaque on 18 March, to mark the building of a new annexe] and I had to stay around to do my bits of a Shakespeare evening, so by the time I arrived at Warner Brothers it was all a rush,' Coral explained. 'They took one look at me and died, "Oh God! You've got black hair! But it was blonde in the test!" and I said I thought everyone knew it was a wig. *They* didn't, and didn't seem to have one anywhere in the studios [Rosalind Russell's role required no fewer than 12 wigs] so they sent me to have my hair dyed not just blonde – pla-ti-num! I knew my hair was almost impossible to dye, but that's Hollywood. They put on ten volumes, then twenty then thirty...there were tears absolutely streaming down my face and they told me, "Don't be silly, it's because you're not used to it." AGONY! The next morning I woke up bald, not a hair on my head, not one. They were all on the pillow. My scalp was running. I was immediately bandaged, doctor sent for, all that. They had to run up a turban with nauseating little kiss curls down here on my cheekbones. Roz Russell lent me all sorts of feathery hats and helmets with wonderful bunches of wisteria on them, but they looked rather daft with bathing suits.'[128] During one of their scenes together, referring to Vera's blonde hair, Mame correctly observes, 'If I kept my hair natural the way you do, I'd be bald.'

Betty Comden and Adolph Green's unconventional screenplay managed to include the words 'heterosexual' and 'libido' and the immortal phrase, 'How bleak was my puberty.' The story of ex-actress Mame's adventures in gay abandon incorporated taboo social issues, such as unmarried motherhood and anti-Semitism. The opening party scene featured a man playing the piano upside down, a monkey, a Buddha caviar dish made of ice and, lurking in the background, two Radclyffe Hall lookalikes with tweed suits and men's hats – all evidence of Auntie Mame's 'decadence'.

Mame and Vera's best moments together came when Mame makes a return to the stage in a two-line role in Vera's new show *Midsummer Madness*. It's Coral at her best – and her most natural. In character, Vera is resplendently elegant; when she's being upstaged by Mame, she shoots barbed asides at her.

After the movie was completed, Coral returned to London, with follicular activity fully restored – and a new chum added to her collection: Robert Hanley, designer of the film's set. And she would need all the friends she could get now: she was flying back to a nightmarish situation – one which, for the next 30 years, would make her want to pull her hair out.

A few years previously, lamenting the loss of her own mother, Mother had written to Coral: 'It's a lonely feeling dear to realise I have only three bloody relations left…if Dad goes, who is going to do anything for me?'[129] Coral had not seen 'Mother' or 'Dad' since her 1948 visit. She once said, 'As I am an only child, I often have a conscience and think I ought to spend more time at home.'[130]

Now it was too late: Leslie Brown died at home, of heart disease, aged 67, on 13 October 1957. His funeral took place two days later at Spring Vale Crematorium and his ashes were placed in a wall niche in Kew Cemetery (now Boroondara General Cemetery). Vicky reserved the plot next to him for her own future remains. Coral rarely spoke about her father – as a child, he had doted on his 'Coralin'. But once the decision had been taken to leave Australia, 'Coralin' was gone – for good. Once she became 'Coral Browne', there was no room in her life for looking back in sorrow or sentimentality – one single visit back to see her parents demonstrated that beyond any doubt. For Coral, Australia, and her family, represented the past and she had no desire to live there again: they did things differently. But now the past was about to come and plonk itself centre-stage in the present.

'When Mother found herself a widow and all her friends were dying off, she said, "I must go and be with my dear little Coral,"' said Frith Banbury. 'And she announced she was coming over, much to Coral's horror. So Mother came over here and was the bane of Coral's life.'[131] Coral was flying to America on April 1 to begin work on *Auntie Mame* and, as she told Arnold Weissberger, '…my mother arrives from Australia a week after I go so my poor husband is going to have a nasty "cope".'[132] And, according to everyone who met Mother, she devoted the rest of her life to uttering nothing but discouraging words towards her only child. The endless criticism and cavilling was payback for Coral's decision to put family and Australia behind her more than 20 years earlier – lacking her daughter's quick wit and riddled with self-pity and jealousy. For the rest of their lives – in Vicky's case, an exceptionally long one – mother and daughter were bound together by complex bonds forged from a mixture of love and loathing.

Coral set Vicky up as a permanent resident at the Suncourt Hotel in 59–63 Peckham Gardens, Kensington – close enough to home, but without being on her doorstep. Though it was Vicky's decision to move to England, she always disliked London – and, as one letter to her cousin, Mary Gillard, showed, a penchant for watching the pennies may have been her most lasting legacy to her daughter:

'One never makes friends in England. Even in the Hotel it is only, "Good morning", no more. How I miss my beloved Australia, and my pals. London these days… It is full of blacks, and queer drug addicts. Its all terribly expensive. If Coral and self go out to lunch it is never under £3.15 for one course. Soho is much cheaper to dine in, and good food but of course one must be prepared for shooting at any old time. This Hotel is the most reasonable, by that I mean of a standard where one can live. It is £16 gns weekly – Sterling. Food not the best but one no longer finds good food in London.'[133] Coral was careful to keep Mother away from most of her friends, but Jill Melford had an encounter with Vicky that left no room for ambivalence: 'I did say to Coral, "I'll do anything in the world for you, darling, but don't ask me to cope with your mother…"'[134] Frith Banbury was prevented from having any close encounters with Vicky, but was left in no doubt that she 'was a pain in the arse. Coral complained about her mother from dusk to dawn. I was only allowed to see the back of her head once. I went to the flat one day and Mother was there; she wasn't going to introduce me to Mother…'[135]

Faced with the prospect of spending the winter of 1958 suffering the slings and arrows fired at her by 'Mother', Coral decided to accept an offer from the Shakespeare Memorial Company to play Gertrude opposite Michael Redgrave in *Hamlet*, as part of an historic British Council-sponsored visit to Russia. And historic it was – for the Company, and for Coral. An episode from the past was about to determine one in her future.

On Saturday 11 February 1956, the Moscow correspondents from the *Sunday Times*, Reuters, the Tass Agency and *Pravda* had been summoned to attend a press conference being held at – in a nice Cold War touch – Room 101 at the National Hotel. The assembled reporters found themselves face to face with the much-sought 'missing diplomats', Guy Burgess and Donald Maclean, who had absconded from England in 1951. The press were issued with a statement from both men, explaining their reasons for defecting to the Soviet Union, and denying that they had been spies. Burgess subsequently sold his story to one newspaper and, in a gesture borne of his innumerable encounters with seamen, donated his fee to the Royal National Lifeboat Institution.[136] Journalist and ex-MP Tom Driberg (no stranger to Communism, or sailors, himself) had become friends with Burgess during World War Two, when the latter worked on the radio programme *The Week in Westminster*. Driberg wrote an article in *Reynolds News*, speculating that Burgess and Maclean might have helped to ease East-West relations – a view that earned him condemnation from fellow fourth-estaters in the *Daily Express* and *Daily Herald*. Driberg contacted his old acquaintance, and asked Burgess to meet him in Moscow. He agreed – 'I should like to go round Moscow with an English Socialist'[137] – and the two men rendezvoused at the Moskva Hotel, then Burgess's place of residence. Over the next few weeks, the two men met many times, as Burgess sought to give his side of the story. The conversations formed the basis of Driberg's book published that year, *Guy Burgess: A Portrait with Background*.

Since his arrival in Moscow, Burgess had done some work for the Foreign Literature Publishing House, which produced translations of English books, suggesting possible authors, including Graham Greene and E M Forster. He claimed to have 'a large circle of friends in all the departments, including the Foreign Ministry, and at all levels, and from time to time I am consulted…it might be anything from Somerset Maugham to British policy in Trinidad. You might call me an expert Englishman with a roving commission.'[138]

By 1958, the circle of friends had diminished and the 'expert Englishman' had lost his commission. Unlike fellow traveller Maclean, who had become assimilated into Russian life, Burgess cut a lonely figure: press interest in him had diminished to the point that, when he offered his services to *Reynolds News* as their Moscow correspondent, they politely declined. His Soviet 'comrades' no longer seemed to know what to do with him, he could only speak enough Russian to give instructions to the housekeeper at his *dacha* – and (probably worse from his point of view) he was starved of opportunities for gossip and casual sexual pick-ups. He had admitted to Driberg, 'Sometimes, yes, I am lonely. I'd like to have a good gossip with some old friends. But here I'm lonely for the unimportant things. In London, I was lonely for the important things – I was lonely for Socialism.'[139]

Now, the unimportant things had become increasingly important. He took solace in drink and chain-smoked; one of the few advantages of living in Moscow was that both alcohol and cigarettes cost less than they did in London. In the summer of 1958, he tried to arrange a meeting with Driberg and the Labour Party leader, Hugh Gaitskell, when they holidayed with their wives in the Black Sea resort of Sochi.

The days of living in the Moskva Hotel were long gone: Burgess's home was a flat in vast, characterless complex and he had to wait for a phone call from 'his people' before he was permitted to leave. When he did, he often visited the Orthodox church close to his home to listen to its choir, an experience which often moved him to tears. He'd been hoping to be housed in rooms in one of Moscow's older houses, but his relocation to such a dreary dwelling was symbolic of his diminishing status in the eyes of the Soviet authorities. His loneliness was partially alleviated by the company of Tolya, a young electrician he'd picked up while 'cottaging' in the gent's underground lavatory behind the Hotel Metropole – a venue discovered and recommended by Tom Driberg. He was not alone in suspecting that Tolya had been 'assigned' to him.

So, when he learned that a company of English actors, including an old chum, Michael Redgrave, would be visiting the Soviet Union that year to perform Shakespeare, he was offered a brief respite from his cultural 'Siberian' exile – and an opportunity to improve his worsening sartorial situation.

﹏

The Shakespeare Memorial Company's visit to Leningrad and Moscow in 1958 was arranged by the British Council and the Russian Ministry of Culture, after the Director of Moscow Art Theatre had visited Stratford in June. It wouldn't be the first time since the Revolution that English would be spoken on a Moscow stage: that honour had gone, two years previously, to Peter Brook's production of *Hamlet*, starring Paul Scofield. A million Muscovites watched its television broadcast.

It was announced that the company, comprising 70 actors, stage managers, technicians and musicians, would give 11 performances in Leningrad and 15 in Moscow. The plays would be *Romeo and Juliet* (opening the season in Leningrad on 12 December) and *Hamlet* (both directed by Glen Byam Shaw), and Peter Hall's production of *Twelfth Night*.

The company, which included Richard Johnson, Dorothy Tutin, Zoe Caldwell and Geraldine McEwan, also boasted no less than five married couples. Incongruously, the diminutive Ian Holm (5 feet 6) was understudying Michael Redgrave (6 feet 3) in *Hamlet*, so they had separate outfits made.* At Stratford, Googie Withers had played Gertrude, but would not be joining the company in Russia 'because she has already arranged to meet her husband in Australia for Christmas'.[140] Since Coral had played the part so recently, and with considerable success, she was first choice to take over from her fellow Australian.

---

* Michael Redgrave's mother, Margaret 'Daisy' Scudamore, had died on 5 October, aged 73. Coral, Philip and Vicky attended Daisy's memorial service on 18 October, at St Paul's, the actors' church in Covent Garden. Like Coral, Redgrave had had a difficult relationship with his mother – something Coral had been aware of for many years. She and Daisy, an erstwhile actress, had become friends after Coral became involved with Firth Shephard. An increasingly unhappy Daisy took out her professional and personal frustrations on her more successful son – and sought refuge in the bottle. Redgrave paid for Daisy to go on several of what were discreetly referred to as 'rest-cures' and, after one serious bout in 1948, Coral had kindly offered to accompany her while she went for a 'rest' in Brighton.

This job hadn't been her first choice: she complained to Arnold Weissberger, 'I've been diddled out of the Roger Stevens Giradoux play [*Duel of Angels*].'[141] Instead, Binkie Beaumont had chosen one of his stalwarts, Vivien Leigh, to play the role of Paola. This clearly rankled with Coral who, despite her affection for Leigh, appeared to take some pleasure when the troubled actress began to show symptoms of the manic depression which plagued her: 'Your friend Lady O is MUCH worse & sent for a doctor AND an ambulance – when same arrived at the theatre Lady O sent them to collect ANN TODD!!!!!!!'[142] Resigned to spending a winter of some discontent, she told Arnold Weissberger, 'I am taking over Dirty Gertie for Russia...if you have any chums in Moscow I'd love to meet same – I would prefer it if they were in the fur trade!'[143]

The company prepared for the practical challenges posed by the forthcoming tour. Redgrave's wife, Rachel Kempson, recalled that, 'Paddy Donnell, the company manager, gave us a long talk about the sort of food we would get, the allowance we would be given in roubles and the kind of clothes we would need to buy for the extreme cold of Russia in the winter.'[144] Meanwhile, Geraldine McEwan practised her Russian on the telephone to a *Daily Express* reporter: the phrases were 'I love you', 'I don't love you' and 'How dare you!', which covered most eventualities.[145] Coral, of course, was used to performing in cold climes: 'Miss Browne is no stranger to northern latitudes. She was with the Old Vic when they played in seven countries in seven weeks. Helsinki was one of the stops. "I was a lot colder when I got back to Britain," she said, "Over there you prepare for the cold. Here we take it as a nuisance which shouldn't happen to us."'[146]

Former prime minister Sir Anthony Eden sent the actors a message of good luck, while the Air Ministry donated a consignment of overcoats. Coral stuck with her customary furs. Thus, well wrapped up, the company departed on a specially-chartered BOAC DC-7 from London Airport on 8 December. Ahead of them, 28 tonnes of scenery and 350 costumes had been shipped to Russia 'eight days after the last date on which ice-free sea passage is guaranteed'.[147] The sea might have been ice free, but the land wasn't: 'The temperature was 30 degrees below zero,' said Rachel Kempson. 'We gasped as we got out of the plane, and poor Angela Baddeley had a bad attack of asthma... My first impression of Russia as we drove through the streets was that everything looked grey and depressing.'[148]

As they boarded a night train for the 12-hour journey from Moscow to Leningrad, the company was joined by four interpreters: Natasha, Maya, Olga and Svetlana. Reporter John Goodwin, covering the tour for the *Daily Telegraph*, wrote: 'Driving across the capital to board the night express for Leningrad, we sang carols to keep warm…samovars steamed and stubby middle-aged women dispensed vodka and thick clots of caviar on hunks of bread, if one cared to pay the price.' They reached Leningrad the next morning and were taken to their accommodation, the Astoria Hotel, where they were given 'breakfast, Russian-style: yoghurt, salami, cheese, toast and jam'.[149] Diversions included a guided tour of the city, via Peter the Great's fortress and the Rembrandts in the Hermitage, and a trip to the Kirov Ballet at the Opera House.

Reunited with their scenery and costumes, the company got down to business: 'The Stratford Shakespeare Company tonight became the first English actors to play Leningrad since the Revolution – and took the city by storm. A capacity audience of 2100 Russians saw *Romeo and Juliet*. It was the first of 11 performances for which all tickets were sold 36 hours after the box office opened. Thousands of Russians stood for hours in snow and ice to buy tickets. "No, I don't speak English," one was heard to say, "but fancy hearing Shakespeare by a company from his birthplace!" Many in the audience did not understand English but they clapped enthusiastically and responded to both the tragic and light moments.'[150] After two successful weeks in Leningrad (the final performance of *Hamlet* received 14 curtain calls), the actors returned to the ornate rooms of Moscow's Hotel Metropole: 'a lot of red plush, hermetically-sealed double windows and white lace bedspreads'.[151]

Eileen Atkins recalled: 'On the first night, we all had to go to the circus, and we were asked not to all sit together, so I was sitting somewhere else apart from Coral. And we became aware that, all around us, there was obviously wild excitement and chattering – and people were gazing at Coral. There was this American student there, who spoke Russian and he explained, "They are all saying she must be royalty – a princess or a queen."'[152]

The trip was full of unexpected 'delights'. Angela Baddeley and Rachel Kempson discovered a popular kiosk in Red Square where, at the press of a button, customers could get a squirt of foul-smelling perfume, appropriately named 'Stalin's Breath'. Most of the cast picked up what Kempson called the 'Moscow tummy', and the food was hardly inspiring: 'There was a distinct lack of fresh vegetables; the meat was a grey stew; the bread was heavy and black;

and we never even glimpsed the famous caviar.'[153] Dorothy Tutin, performing in all three plays, reportedly lived on virtually nothing but Guinness.

But the abiding memory was of the weather: Zoe Caldwell remembered Moscow as a city that was 'so cold that my nose bled'[154] and Eileen Atkins witnessed the effects of the cold on Coral's regal appearance: 'We were in the foyer of the hotel. Coral decided to redo her mascara and she used Spit Black [little cakes of solid mascara, applied with brush and water or saliva]. And as we came out of the foyer, Coral said, "My God! My fucking eyelashes have dropped off!" And they had – they'd frozen straight away.'[155]

However, there was one person in Moscow keen to give the visitors a warm welcome. Michael Redgrave recalled: 'When our plane landed in Moscow, an English journalist took me aside and said he had a message for me: "Guy Burgess wants to know if you would agree to meet him."'[156] The two men had been contemporaries at Cambridge; Burgess designed the sets for a student production of *Captain Brassbound's Conversion* in which Redgrave appeared.

Redgrave had little time to consider the request. On the first night of *Hamlet*, the dressing room ambience was shattered by the clamour of English journalists who had gathered outside his door – through which lurched a tired and emotional Guy Burgess. 'He was very, *very* drunk,' recalled Eileen Atkins. 'He tried to get into Michael Redgrave's room but Michael utterly refused to see him then. Somehow, Burgess got into Coral's dressing room, which is where he was sick in the sink. And she looked after him.'[157]

Redgrave wrote a sanitised version of the encounter in an article for the *Observer* on 'Theatre in Russia': 'I remember the face of Guy Burgess, his eyes red with tears and his voice only just in control. He had come in to my dressing room after a performance. "I suppose it's partly because I haven't heard this glorious stuff in English for years but, believe me, this is the most wonderful thing that could have happened."'[158]

Once (relatively) sober, Burgess met several members of the cast, including Mark Dignam, who Burgess thought was 'an angel'[159], and found time to cast an appreciative eye over his old friend's understudy: Coral told Ian Holm, 'Darling, you've got an admirer...'[160]

Burgess arranged for Redgrave to have lunch with him at his flat, Apartment 68, 53/55 Bolshaya Pirogoboskaya Witza, where his housekeeper served them pâté de foie gras, followed by a main course of roast hare. However, the hare had been cooked with its gall-bladder intact, rendering the rest of its carcass bitter and inedible. Burgess rarely ate, preferring a cigarette to sustenance, and spent most mealtimes pacing up and down. After this 'meal', Burgess took Redgrave to hear the singing at the basilica, during which Redgrave noticed that Burgess's suit 'was well worn and a bit shiny'.[161] Another guest was soon to be treated to Burgess's unique brand of hospitality – Coral.

Had she ever cast an eye over Tom Driberg's account of his meetings with Burgess, Coral would have noticed some clues as to the ulterior motive behind the invite. There was a reference to Burgess dropping cigarette ash 'on his rumpled dark-grey suit';[162] in its breast pocket (along with his wallet and Soviet identity document) he kept a tailor's label: Messrs Tom Brown of 1 High Street, Eaton and Mayfair. The gentleman wanted some new clothes.

Coral duly made her way to Burgess's flat where she was served the usual disastrous fare at the luncheon table. 'It was pretty foul,' she said. 'Actually we ate small withered oranges which cost a pound a time. Guy did eat whole cloves [of garlic].'[163] He complained to Coral about Russian false teeth and Russian clothes: 'It was terrible sitting there. He was ill. His teeth didn't fit. I mean, you don't wish anyone dentures that don't fit.'[164] He grilled her for gossip about his old friends, but since Coral didn't know most of them, she had little to give him. 'Guy started to talk bitterly about his exile. He thought what he had done was nothing. Then I did speak out. I did explain he was a traitor. I made it clear what I thought of him.'[165]

Not all of their conversation was about politics: 'Burgess was asking after this and that "pretty boy" he had known at Cambridge. It was sad. By then they were all unattractive middle-aged men.'[166] Coral met Tolya, Burgess's companion: 'I assume, as part of the deal they provided him with a lover to stop him corrupting someone round the corner. I think the Soviet punishment for that sort of thing is death... The Ballet is obviously as gay as goats and Burgess's lover was an electrician from the Bolshoi.'[167] 'I felt tremendous sympathy for the man. If you betray your country, that's about as low as anybody can get. And then, to find at the end of it, that you're left with a pair of pants that has no knees left in it, except darns and you've got a lousy apartment, a lover you didn't choose and no job.'[168]

To break the monotony, Burgess offered to play Coral a record – he only had the one, he said, which he had brought with him when he defected. He wound up the gramophone and played the record: it was Jack Buchanan, singing 'Who (Stole My Heart Away)?' Coral would later say, 'There I was, two days before Christmas, it was snowing and one couldn't have felt more miserable to be away from home. What made it all the more poignant was sitting there in the most unlikely place in the world listening to Jack's voice forever perpetuating a lighthearted and carefree land of make believe.'[169]*

Finally, after a lunch that lasted until 4.30pm, Burgess's 'people' called and he was allowed to leave the flat, and accompany Coral back to her hotel. The shopping list he gave her was for several suits, including a single breasted chalk-stripe suit in grey; a flannel summer suit and another in dark blue flannel and terrylene – for Tolya – and two Homburg hats (with turned up brims) green and blue, 7 and 3/8, from Locke's in St James Street or Scott's in Piccadilly.

She didn't take his measurements during lunch – he sent them round to her hotel room, together with a cheque for £6 for her to have lunch at the Caprice with Mark Dignam. Burgess later sent his housekeeper round with 100 roubles and another note, requesting – for her purposes, not his – a pound of white wool and a pound of green wool, enclosing a sample strand. Bidding Coral farewell, he wrote: 'It was a great pleasure to gossip with you all. The Comrades, tho' splendid in every way of course, don't gossip in quite the same way about quite the same people and subjects.'[170]

On Boxing Day, the British Ambassador and his wife, Sir Patrick and Lady Reilly, invited the entire Stratford company to a black tie dinner and dance at the British Embassy. Lady Reilly casually informed her guests that all the tables were bugged but since, as Rachel Kempson said, 'we were only talking of the ballets we had seen and our families at home whom we all

---

* Coincidentally, Coral's ex-lover and mentor Paul Robeson was also in Moscow that winter, staying at the Metropole (following eight years without a US passport after he refused to sign a document stating he was not a Communist). Once in Moscow, Robeson and his wife Essie had both fallen ill and ended up in the Kremlin Hospital. In February, Robeson went for a month's convalescence at the Barveekha Sanatorium, a rest home for government officials and honoured guests. Coral suggested that Burgess try and meet Robeson during his visit. More than a decade earlier, when still in the British Foreign Office, Burgess had been warned by Deputy Foreign Minister Hector McNeil to avoid becoming involved with anyone connected with left-wing or racial politics – and any homosexual scandals. Burgess summed up the order: 'In other words, Hector, you mean I mustn't make a pass at Paul Robeson.'[171] Burgess later told Coral, 'I found myself too shy to call on him... I always am with great men and artists. Not so much shy as frightened...tho' I know that he is as nice as can be and that because of you it would have been OK.'[172]

missed',[173] it didn't halt the flow of conversation. Of course, no one mentioned their respective encounters with Guy Burgess. On New Year's Eve, a group of Moscow actors threw a party for their British counterparts at a club on Gorky Street, where the entertainment included some puppeteers and an octet from the Soviet Army Choir, who sang 'It's a Long Way to Tipperary' in English. At midnight, all the guests sang 'Old Lang Syne'.

A new year had begun, and the tour was nearly over. On 5 January, the final performance of *Hamlet* was relayed live on television to five million viewers on Moscow's Channel 1. At the end, Zoe Caldwell recalled, 'They clapped, they cheered, they stood. They threw flowers, watches, and eventually jewels, which they stripped from their own bodies. We clapped them, blew kisses, until it looked like we might be there all night. I didn't think we were that good but perhaps their apartments were very cold. We never had the same effect on British audiences.'[174] So, armed with supplies of vodka and caviar and a mixed bag of memories, the company departed for England on 6 January. At London Airport, they were greeted with a champagne reception; glasses were raised, speeches were made and quotes given to the massed reporters. Then the company dispersed to the comforts of their respective homes – and that, it appeared, was that.

But Coral had some shopping to do for her Englishman abroad. As good as her word, she visited bespoke tailors, Turnbull & Asser, at 71–72 Jermyn Street, and ordered a new gentleman's wardrobe for Guy Burgess. 'The various clothing shops played ball and it never got out,' she said. 'It had to be very old and established firms to make it work…you might have got an assistant who would have immediately phoned a newspaper. But they were so establishment, it was almost like a gentleman's club.'[175] 'I never paid for any of the clothes. That was arranged through Burgess's account at the Bank of Canada.'[176] That Easter Sunday – his birthday, 16 April – Burgess wrote to Coral, to report that everything 'except the wool' had arrived,[177] and to thank her for 'all your trouble (which must have been great) and even more for your wise and happy choices. Everything fits.'[178]

As he rightly observed, 'There was no reason, let's face it, why you should take so much trouble, no backing of personal obligation between us – so it was just sheer niceness and kindness on your part. Why you should do all this I simply can't think – perhaps the kindness that always comes from the Commonwealth to mangier London.'[179] Burgess didn't hesitate when Coral offered to buy a few more items for him: this time, it was four pairs of pyjamas – two white or off-white, two navy blue, in silk or nylon or terrylene – 'not crepe de Chine'[180] He recommended she purchase them from Savile Row outfitters Gieves (who had been supplying items to royal households since George III's reign) or A Sulka & Co.

Coral told no one except Philip Pearman about her shopping expeditions: 'Well, it wasn't going to look very good for me if anyone found out: "Leading lady buys clothes for Russian spy."'[181] When she sent the last consignment of clothes off to Burgess, that was her last contact with him.

In October 1960, with his health failing, Burgess told Western reporters at a party that he wanted to return to England for a holiday: 'It comes to everybody to feel he has made a mistake.' He repeated the assertion that he was neither a spy nor a Communist. A reporter noted that Burgess was 'wearing an Old Etonian tie'.[182] The Old Etonian died less than three years later, on 30 August 1963, at the Botin Hospital, where he had spent the previous ten days undergoing what little treatment there was for a patient in the final stages of heart disease. It was enigmatically reported that 'an Englishman was with him when he died'.[183] He was cremated in Moscow, with the coffin borne aloft by Donald Maclean, Burgess's brother Nigel, three Russians and an unnamed British journalist. Only 15 people attended the funeral; its finale was a brass band thumping out 'The Internationale'. On 5 October, his ashes were interred in the churchyard of St John the Evangelist in West Meon, Hampshire, where his family had once lived. The Englishman had returned home at last.

'Dying was his only way out,' observed Coral.[184] And, tucked away in her big black suitcase, she kept her letters from Burgess – and his uncashed cheque for £6. Thanks to him, Coral's final Shakespearean outing had provided her with memories – which would, one day, provide her most memorable role.

Drama Queen

1959–1968

*A*untie Mame was released in the UK in early January 1959, within days of its American premiere. The film garnered six Oscar nominations, including Best Picture, Best Actress for Rosalind Russell (who won the Golden Globe for her performance) and Best Supporting Actress for Peggy Cass. But most of the British press did not greet it so enthusiastically: one critic said, 'It is kindest to conclude that *Auntie Mame* is a private American joke that does not take kindly to transplanting',[1] while another cheekily warned, 'Don't take the children unless you want them to learn how to mix a dry martini.'[2] Coral's performance did not go unnoticed next to Russell's ostentatious act: 'In a strong cast, I salute especially Coral Browne's original Vera Charles.'[3]

After her classical adventures in the Communist bloc, Coral returned to the West End, pitching up in more familiar (and more commercial) comic territory with a long run in *The Pleasure of his Company*, an American comedy by Samuel Taylor and Cornelia Otis Skinner. Nigel Patrick starred as the preposterously-named Biddeford 'Pogo' Poole, an ageing playboy and mostly absent father, who returns to San Francisco for the wedding of his debutante daughter. Coral was Pogo's ex-wife, Katherine – and, when it opened at the Haymarket on 23 April, her notices were better than the play's: she was 'elegant, colourful and interesting as always, and extremely funny in the cable-opening episode…'[4] *The Sketch* said, 'In her best performance yet, CB sophisticated and witty, superbly matched Mr P's charm.'[5] One crusty critic, reacting against the new wave of 'reality' drama, opined, 'The play deserves to repeat its Broadway hit if only because it gets us away from angry adolescents pouring their slops down sleazy kitchen sinks.'[6] Coral was also a hit with its audiences: when the show moved to the Liverpool Royal Court on 23 March, her first entrance was greeted with a chorus of wolf-whistles, as they showed their appreciation of her Balmain outfit, a 'black-fringed nasturtium-red tailored suit with a black straw hat the size of a cart wheel'.[7] Decades later, Penelope Keith could still remember the first appearance of the stylish actress who was of her heroines: 'I think of her entrance in *Pleasure*…she was wearing some fabulous creation and said, "I've just put on a *rag*."'[8] Coral's performance – and appearance – kept the play running for the best part of a year.

That same year, the Browne-Pearman household acquired another new guest. Writer and broadcaster Arthur Marshall had begun working for Binkie Beaumont as a script-reader for Tennent's; the company had recently struck a deal with ATV to provide plays for television in which Beaumont's clique of stage stars could feature. The Cambridge-based Marshall had no permanent London home and had been staying in John Gielgud's Cowley Street house while the actor was in America for six months. Writer and musician Ronnie Hill, one of Philip's Cambridge contemporaries and a friend of Marshall's, brokered a favour from the Pearmans. So, when Gielgud returned to London, Arthur Marshall moved into the top floor of 46 Chester Row, where he remained happily ensconced for the next four years. He said, 'It cannot be easy having a paying guest in the house…having to listen to assorted noises overhead, but the Pearmans were saints of kindness and goodness…they never registered even so much as a half-frown.'[9]

Having had her fill of *Pleasure*, Coral entered the steamy world of the Southern belle, in Lillian Hellman's *Toys in the Attic*. Setting the play in New Orleans – Hellman's birthplace – the writer explained that she 'wanted to say that not all kinds of love are noble and good, that there's much in love that's destructive… I started out with a man, who interested me, his two unmarried sisters who raised him, and his wife. All these women love him and seem to want him to be successful but once he is, they find they don't want him that way.'[10] Coral was cast as one of those sisters, Albertine Prine, 'a rich woman who has cut herself off from society to carry on a liaison with a black chauffeur…her function appears to be to comment coolly and precisely on what is wrong with the rest of the characters'.[11] In New York, the play, starring Maureen Stapleton and Irene 'Hatty Abrams' Worth, had won the New York Critics' Award for Best Drama, and was still running on Broadway when the British production opened with a strong female-led cast which included Wendy Hiller and Diana Wynyard. Success in London seemed assured.

Nevertheless, the production soon ran into problems – on and off stage. According to Peter Stenson, Coral was worried about the size of the dressing rooms in the diminutive Piccadilly: 'They offered her dressing room number two – so she told them, "Don't worry, darling, just knock down the wall between that and the one next door and I'll have them both…" So they did. She came to inspect the work, and of course, she was wearing a fur coat…the door jamb was still wet with paint – and some of this paint got stuck to the fur. And she said, "Well, *that's* the most fucking expensive door jamb in London…"'[12] The play proved equally costly: the critical reception for it was, at best, lukewarm; one critic spoke for many others by wondering if 'it was perhaps a mistake to attempt a London production with an all-English company'.[13] T C Worsley believed the play fell victim to forces beyond its control: 'This play belongs to the old well-made tradition and that alone was almost enough to damn it in the eyes of the younger critics and those who follow them. Of course, we don't share the obsessional love of our playwrights and audiences for the psychotic South; and a very English cast couldn't, skilful though each of them was, carry us into that bizarre region.'[14] The production closed after just three months.

However, there was one positive: during its provincial try-out, Lillian Hellman had cabled Coral, saying, 'I am sure you know by this time, how much I appreciate that hard work you have done and the wonderful performance that you will give. You have been a real pleasure.'[15] Their warm friendship endured the production's failure and lasted until Hellman's death in 1984. Coral tried to see the writer whenever they were both in New York, and occasionally stayed in Hellman's apartment on East 82nd Street.

During the run of *Toys in the Attic*, Coral broke her strict rule about not doing a West End show and a film simultaneously – and, typically, it was to help an old friend. Coral accepted the small role of Meg in the 1961 adaptation of Tennessee Williams's *The Roman Spring of Mrs Stone*, starring Vivien Leigh. She did so 'as a favour to Vivien who was frankly frail and needed all the support I could give'.[16] Coral was playing Meg, the savvy best friend of beautiful, recently-widowed actress Karen Stone, who gives up on her fading career and her friends, and becomes embroiled in a seedy Roman underworld of greed and deception. Meg introduces Karen to the Contessa Magda Terribili-Gonzales, a procurer of handsome young men. The Contessa's prized possession is the petulant Paolo, played by Warren Beatty; portraying the manipulative Magda was another stage and screen legend, Lotte Lenya. The role of Meg, who is jettisoned after Karen takes up with pretty Paolo, was insignificant; Coral sat back and watched Leigh and Lenya fight it out for

TOP LEFT Bossy from the start: two year old Coral in her grandparents' garden, Sunshine.
TOP RIGHT Coral's maternal grandfather, William Bennett — the H V McKay man
BOTTOM A class apart: Coral (*front row, centre*) and the ladies of Claremont College

TOP AND MIDDLE Worlds apart: Hocking Street (now demolished) and 'Fernhurst', 2007.
BOTTOM This desirable residence: Victoria and Leslie Brown (and Mr Chang Pooh),
outside 'Fernhurst', Kew

Coral +++

Miss Coral Brown, daughter of Mr. and Mrs. L. C. Brown, of "Lesvic," Hocking street, Footscray, who at the age of 14 gained a diploma of A.L.C.M. for elocution in the recent examinations.
Ruskin photo.

Yearston TABLETS Regularly!

PUNCH

April 30, 1931 —— No. 3286. No. 1457 (New Series)

WERNER'S

A NEW THEATRICAL "FIND"

TOP Acting like a lady: Coral and friend, early 1920s
BOTTOM LEFT A well-spoken girl: a cutting for 'Aunt Teen's' scrapbook
BOTTOM RIGHT Taking centre stage: the 50-year theatre career begins

TOP LEFT A member of 'The Firm', c.1931   TOP RIGHT Gregan McMahon, c.1905: 'A face like Humpty Dumpty'   BOTTOM 'He taught me more than I ever learned in my whole life': Coral and Gregan McMahon at 'Fernhurst', 1934

The Arts Centre, Performing Arts Collection, Melbourne

Kevin Scullin collection

Garry Gillard

TOP 'Mother and child'
BOTTOM LEFT The embryo Sphinx   BOTTOM RIGHT Cover girl, 1935

Beatrix Lehmann

Miss Nora Swinburne

One of our loveliest stage and
stars who is now playing a lea
part in " The Old Folks at Ho
at the Queen's Theatre, re
a secret of success.

" There is nothing more irritat
to a theatregoer than that slip
the programme which says :
" Owing to indisposition Mi
Dash's part is being played a
this performance by Miss Blank.'
But to avoid disappointing her
public a star has to make care-of-
health a whole-time job. And no
slacking ! At this time of the year
oranges are the one thing I really
rely on to keep away influenza.
I eat plenty of oranges — and drink
them, too. And I consider that
fresh fruit of any kind is the basis
of real beauty
culture."

Nora Swinburne

Eat More Fruit

TOP Mystery girls? LEFT Mary Morris RIGHT Beatrix Lehmann
BOTTOM LEFT Good advice from Nora Swinburne – just before understudy Coral Brown replaced her
BOTTOM RIGHT Paul Robeson, 1930s

Blossoming into Coral Browne

TOP Coral charms *The Amateur Gentleman*
BOTTOM LEFT All mouth and trousers: with Felix Aylmer in *Heroes Don't Care*
BOTTOM RIGHT Gunning for trouble in *The Gusher*

'The Sphinx', 1940

TOP LEFT 'May I kiss you?': Maurice Chevalier, 1937
TOP RIGHT Coral makes her contribution to the war effort
BOTTOM 'Firth is my Shephard'

The main course: *The Man Who Came to Dinner* serves up a star

'The most beautifully dressed woman on the London stage'

'A camp near Dover': Philip Pearman, 1940s

TOP Like sister and brother: with Michael Wilding in *Piccadilly Incident* (1946)
BOTTOM 'Now you can go on for me': wedding day (1950), with Suzzie and Jack Buchanan (*right*)

"I make sure of good sleep by drinking
Ovaltine"
says
CORAL BROWNE

CORAL BROWNE writes—

"Acting which appears natural on the stage has been termed 'the ... which conceals art'. It is true that each 'natural' gesture or inflex... has had to be carefully studied. Long and exacting rehearsals ... necessary, and at each performance, too, concentration must never be lo...

"It is not to be wondered at, then, that all this can cause tiredn... and strain.

"Sleep, I find, is the only really effective remedy. I make su... of good sleep every night by drinking Ovaltine; thus I have restored to ... the energy I have lost and have a sense of well-being to face each new day...

TOP LEFT Viva España: Mr and Mrs Pearman on one of their last holidays   TOP RIGHT Coral reveals her steamy bedtime secrets   BOTTOM LEFT With Paul Rogers, as Lady Macbeth, 1956   BOTTOM RIGHT Helen of Troy, getting ready to play Vera Charles

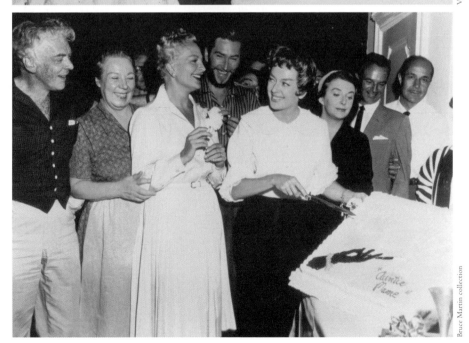

TOP 'Another photo of me going down to some old queen…' at the Old Vic, March 1958
BOTTOM 'Life is a banquet': Coral, Rosalind Russell and cast celebrate the completion of *Auntie Mame*

screen supremacy – a battle won by Lenya, who walked off with the pick of the reviews and was Oscar-nominated as Best Supporting Actress (she lost out to Rita Moreno for *West Side Story*).

Plans to make the film in Rome were abandoned when the Italian Minister for Tourism and Spectacle denied permission on the grounds that the film portrayed Rome as a corrupt city. An entire Roman street was hastily constructed in Elstree Studios. Similarly, Vivien Leigh had not been first choice to play Karen Stone, but Tennessee Williams had prevailed on this matter. She soon had cause to wish he had not intervened on her behalf.

Preparing to play her first film role in seven years, Leigh was in a fragile emotional state: work began shortly after the dissolution of her 28-year marriage to Laurence Olivier, and his subsequent wedding to Joan Plowright. She had recently undergone electric shock treatment for her manic depression: as Geoffrey McNab observed, 'She is not just playing a lonely actress terrified that she has lost her bloom: that was her plight too.'[17] Leigh endured a strained relationship with her onscreen 'gigolo' and his then girlfriend Joan Collins, hired as an extra, and survived a potentially fatal riding accident when her white stallion bolted with the terrified actress into a wood of thick pine trees. At the 'wrap' party, held on the film's nightclub set in full black tie and evening dress, Leigh distributed the end-of-shoot presents she had spent £1000 on, with each gift decorated with the recipient's initials. Sadly, when the film was released on 29 December 1961, the critics weren't as kind to Coral's friend as she had been to her colleagues: most concurred with the view that, 'Vivien Leigh seems…completely miscast and misdirected.'[18]

After the failure of *Toys in the Attic*, Coral starred in the more successful comedy *Bonne Soupe*, with Nigel Davenport and Peter Bowles (and originally Peter Sallis). Félicien Marceau's comedy, which had been a huge success in Paris, told the story of Marie-Paule, 'a demi-mondaine with a heart of brass',[19] 'who tells a Monte Carlo croupier the story of her social ascent.'[20] Coral played the older version of Marie-Paule, and Erica Rogers her younger incarnation. The play spanned 20 years, and featured 22 different settings, from Monte Carlo to Paris. The show toured in Oxford and Brighton but, before the show opened in the West End, producer Donald Albery made some personnel changes: Peter Sallis was replaced by Peter Bowles. 'I think he was cheaper than I was,' Sallis later mischievously suggested. 'And I *didn't* sleep with Coral Browne – I wasn't in the show long enough…'[21]

Milo Sperber had been the original director but, for the London run, Albery hired Eleanor Fazan: 'I'd worked a lot for Donald Albery, and he didn't like the director, so he said, "You've never let us down, you've got to do this."'[22] Fazan's appointment was potentially problematic, for Coral had rather old-fashioned views about a 'woman's place' in the theatre: 'I don't like women directors. It's not a woman's job in the theatre to boss men around.'[23] But then Fazan was at least as accomplished and respected in her field as Coral was in hers: as she said with justifiable pride, 'I twice had three shows on simultaneously in the West End.'[24] Moreover, she was fresh from directing the show which, according to most pundits, launched satirical comedy on the British stage – *Beyond the Fringe*. Fazan understood Coral's view: 'It was very much part of the time: we were Fifties housewives…women would probably have preferred to have a male director. And I think it was a credit to us both that we got on very well and professionally. When I used to go round and give notes to them, I had to creep past Coral's dressing room, because I rarely had notes for her. But if she heard I was there, she would call me in and want to know everything I thought: she was so dedicated to her work, completely and utterly. She felt that I knew what I was doing, and I knew that she knew what she was doing.'[25]

This *entente cordiale* had not extended to all members of the company, as Peter Stenson explained: 'I had a friend called Bill Corlett who was in *Bonne Soupe*; he told me a story about the girl who was the ASM [Carolyn Parish], who was petrified of Coral. And one day, Coral sent for her to come and see her in her dressing room – she was shaking with terror…but Coral said, "Now, I'm a fucking stupid old woman and I don't mean half of what I say, so take no notice of me." And they were friends from then on.'[26] *Tout bien* – that just left the play to tackle. '*Bonne Soupe* was a curious piece and that was very much to do with the times,' explained Eleanor Fazan. 'In those days, we went to France for our holidays, we watched foreign movies, we did our hair like Anna Magnani…we were far more involved with France and Italy. And this was a *very* French play. But I think because Coral wasn't English – and I was born in Africa – it does help: you never feel totally English.'[27] John Heilpern had observed this trend in post-war Britain: 'There was an extraordinary post-war influx of French drama that neatly avoided having to deal with the reality of England at all…in a single London season in 1954 an astonishing seven Jean Anouilh dramas were playing in translation, while Jean Girandoux had an estimated eight productions… Francophilia reached such fashionable heights that high-minded literary reviewers routinely wrote in chunks of French.'[28]

Most of the reviews of *Bonne Soupe* steered clear of French epithets: 'This glossily old-fashioned entertainment has only one discernible merit. Miss Coral Browne gives a capital performance as a hard-bitten woman of the world,' said *The Times*.[29] However, the *Observer* revelled in watching what it called a '…twenty-year trot with a vulgar mind: the mind of its heroine. There is a lot of bad blood in her but none of it sluggish. Neither is the play. Its dirty water flows vigorously between its filthy banks. I enjoyed every minute of it because it is entertaining, laughable and frank…'[30] Not all critics were *d'accord*: in their annual review, *Plays and Players* decided *Bonne Soupe* was one of the 'plays we should like to have missed'.[31]

Still, Coral was enjoying herself: Peter Stenson said, 'There was a young actor in it – Michael Johnson; it was his first big West End juvenile role and he used to arrive at the stage door with a sheepskin coat flung over his shoulder and dark glasses. One day, Coral was waiting for him and said, "Come with me." And she walked him out of the theatre, and down the road to Trafalgar Square which, in those days, was *very* cruisy and full of young men – all with sheepskin coats over their shoulders and dark glasses…and Coral said, "Now look at all them, Michael – what do you think you look like?!" And he never looked like it again…'[32]

By the end of June 1962, enthusiasm for *Bonne Soupe* cooled to vichyssoise temperature, and Coral left for Paris to make a brief appearance in a film set in warmer climes. *Tamahine* was an inconsequential tale of a young woman (Nancy Kwan) from Tahiti who, after her father's death, moves to England to live with her cousin and learn how to be a 'proper young lady.' Coral played Madame Becque, an old friend of Tamahine's father, who takes the girl to Paris, where she introduces her to couturier clothes – and young men. These scenes, complete with a Rolls Royce and a borzoi dog, were shot on the Champs Élysées and at Les Deux Magots restaurant. *Tamahine* was, as Howard Thompson said, 'an amiable, unimportant movie that skips nearly all the way'.[33]

Coral's next film was anything but amiable. In *Dr Crippen*, she played Cora, aka Belle Elmore, the wife and victim of Hawley Harvey Crippen (Donald Pleasance), hung for her murder in 1910. The Crippens had moved from America to England in 1900, where Hawley (called 'Peter' by his wife) worked for a pharmaceutical company. As Belle Elmore, Cora Crippen failed in her ambitions to be, first, an opera singer and then a music hall performer – one of her few bookings was on the same bill as George Formby Sr in Dudley. In February 1910, Belle disappeared. Crippen told everyone, including the police, that she had left him and gone back to America. With unseemly haste, his secretary and mistress, Ethel Le Neve, moved in. In fact, as history tells, Cora was dead: Crippen had burned her limbs and bones in their kitchen stove, dissolved her organs in a bath of acid and put her head in a handbag and thrown it overboard while en route to Dieppe for a day out. What was left of Cora was buried – and later retrieved by police – under the cellar floor in their home at 39 Hilldrop Crescent, north London.

The film mixed scenes of a dreary and unhappy domestic life and Crippen's burgeoning relationship with Ethel, with scenes from the resultant court case. Belle, frustrated by her husband's sexual rejection, yet still hankering for Hawley, turns to their young male lodgers for comfort. It's one of these chaps who tells the Crippens over dinner, 'That fellow Marconi's gone and done it. Sent a wireless message across the Atlantic' – it was this device, of course, which led to Crippen's arrest when he and Ethel attempted to escape to America on the *SS Montrose*.

As the slatternly but seductive Belle, Coral dwarfed Pleasance, as he played Crippen as a man diminished by his drabness. Yet she still managed to make Belle a more sympathetic character than the 'other woman', Ethel Le Neve (Samantha Eggar). In this version, Ethel is no gullible innocent: she tells Crippen that if he ever makes love to his wife again, she'll kill herself, while positively oozing animosity towards her rival: 'I hate her…I could strangle her.' Only one thing could really provoke such a reaction: Coral's attempts to sing. But since Belle Elmore wasn't meant to be very good, it didn't matter that she wasn't.

Dr Crippen stuck to the story he gave in mitigation at his trial – namely, that he administered a small quantity of the narcotic hyoscine to Belle, to sedate her and thus avoid having sex with her, but accidentally spilt an overdose's worth in the sugar bowl without realising what had happened. Erik Larson, in his book *Thunderstruck*, dismissed this implausible explanation, and, like trial prosecutor Richard Muir, expressed grave doubts about Ethel Le Neve's innocence. It all made for dismal viewing – except for one element: 'Thank heaven for Coral Browne,' cheered the *People*.[34] Cecil Wilson admitted, 'I find it hard to hate any character played by Coral Browne. And no easier to believe so comely a woman could fill her husband "with such revulsion that I could hardly bear to look at her".'[35]

Coral was able to cast off Belle's shabby threads and get back into some serious couture for her next film role. She appeared in the British comic crime caper *Go to Blazes*, as the proprietor of cash-strapped Colette's Dress Salon in Berkeley Square. The shop is burned down as part of a not-too-cunning plan by hapless crooks, posing as firemen, to raid the bank next door. Coral was briefly reunited with her former leading man, Robert Morley, who gave a suitably hammy performance as twisted firestarter, 'Arson' Eddie Mountbatten ('no relation'). She also made a new chum: Maggie Smith, playing one of Colette's faux French shop girls. *Go to Blazes* got some favourable reviews, but didn't set the world on fire.

It didn't concern Coral: she was soon on her way to New York again to appear in what, on paper, looked failsafe. Early in 1963, she agreed to star in a Broadway production of *The Lady of the Camellias*, written by Terrence McNally and Giles Cooper from the novel by Alexandre Dumas *fils*, and directed by Franco Zeffirelli, who had won plaudits for his *Romeo and Juliet* at the Old Vic. But, within days of arriving in New York, Coral was hot-tailing it back to London, in tears, and at her own expense – including $300 for excess baggage. According to John Gielgud, '...she found a different script to the one she read in London. I hear "whore" is said every few minutes and "piss" several times.'[36] Well, even an effing lady had to draw the line *somewhere*. Offstage, of course, it was a different matter – for it seems likely that Coral and Giles Cooper may have sought some comfort with each other over the debacle. According to his son, Ric Cooper, 'My mother [Gwyneth Lewis] was VERY SNIFFY about Coral and what she and my father "had got up to", which was unusual for Gwyneth, usually such a generous actress.'[37] As things turned out, despite her bitter disappointment, Coral had had a narrow escape: *The Lady of the Camellias* was lambasted by the critics, including one who decried the writing as 'needlessly explicit and coarse'.[38]

She was back on Broadway before the year's end, with a play by a French writer she had long-admired – she even named one of her chihuahuas 'Antigone' (Tiggy for short) in homage. Jean Anouilh was, she observed, 'probably the first of the modern "black comedy" playwrights'.[39] So she was delighted when asked to star in one of his blackest: *The Rehearsal* with Alan Badel, Adrienne

Corri and Keith Michell. The play is set just after the end of World War Two, when the Count and Countess are preparing to give a performance of an old comedy, Marivaux's *The Double Inconstancy*, during a ball at their chateau. The cast of this play within the play includes Villebosse, the Countess's bore of a lover; the Count's current mistress, Hortensia, and Lucile, an innocent young woman of poor birth with whom the old goat has now, apparently, fallen genuinely in love. This does not sit well with his wife (despite a mutually-agreed 'open marriage' arrangement), his mistress or his inebriate friend, Hero, who drinks because he cannot forgive or forget the betrayal committed against him by the Count many years earlier. During the 'rehearsal', Hero finally finds a way to gain revenge by striking at the Achilles' heel of the Count's newly-discovered true love. Anouilh's use of the play-within-a-play device enabled him, as one critic noted, 'to develop his theme…in *The Double Inconstancy* there is a conspiracy against pure love; in Anouilh's darker modern approach the theme turns into a sophisticated and elegant crime against pure love.'[40].

The role of the manipulative and sharp-tongued Countess was perfect for Coral: high comedy, with an elegant exterior that concealed a callous heart and an unattractive underbelly. The show had been a great success in England a year earlier, with a 12-month West End run followed by a regional tour. But Alan Badel, who played Hero, was the only one of the five principal players from that production to repeat their role on Broadway. Like Coral, Badel came from an industrial region of a major city – Rusholme in Manchester – and, like her, found his way into the theatre via elocution lessons, encouraged by Robert Donat's father, a family friend. A scholarship at RADA was followed by active war service in the paratroop regiment. It was said that Badel was 'known as an able but occasionally difficult actor, a reputation he has by no means completely lived down'.[41] His daughter, Sarah Badel, said, 'Coral didn't know quite what to make of my father – "Moonface," she called him. I think she found him rather eccentric and different. But I think she loved him.'[42] Badel clearly relished the opportunity to revisit the play, now under Peter Coe's direction: 'I had to relearn my lines, which probably was all to the good. I think I found some things I missed earlier. In any case, I think I'm better in the part now.'[43]

The show ran for two weeks at the Theatre Royal Brighton before heading for New York's Royale Theater – where the nearly all-British cast found themselves at the epicentre of a row fuelled by the American Actors Equity

Assocation. There had been growing disquiet among its members about what they believed was a disproportionate number of British actors appearing on Broadway in roles which could easily be played by homegrown performers. When the cast of *The Rehearsal* was announced, Equity responded by asking the US Immigration Department to deny visas to the British actors, on the grounds that 'they are not essential to the production'.[44] They cited the 1952 Act which stated that 'alien actors may gain admission to the United States if they are considered of distinguished ability and if they are hired for roles which unemployed American actors could not fill as capably'.[45] Equity's spokesman William Gibberson said, 'The producer [David Merrick] had not made any attempt to cast the show here. There is nothing about the play that demands British actors.'[46] The American actor Alan Hewitt complained that 'nine of the 25 theaters now open on Broadway are showing imports from England, either with complete British casts or with imported actors in the principal roles. Two years ago alien actors were estimated to have earned $2 million here in theater salaries.'[47] It was, of course, a classic application of double-standards: for decades, innumerable American stage stars, from Tallulah Bankhead to the Lunts, had appeared regularly in the West End, without encountering such hostility. Equity's plea went unheeded by the US Government and Coral and her colleagues descended on Broadway, where they mostly won over the critics – if not their fellow actors.

When the show opened, the New York drama critic of *The Times* reported 'only one player reaches a truly lofty peak – Coral Browne as the countess; in contrast with this queenly figure, all the rest seem like shifty plebeian shop-keepers'.[48] But others strongly disagreed, giving the entire cast the thumbs-up: Alan Badel played Hero 'faultlessly'; Jennifer Hilary brought 'an extraordinary luminosity' to Lucile; Keith Michell was 'mercurial', while Coral and Adrienne Corri 'have an admirable scene where, as jeweled predators, they thrust at each other with velvet claws'.[49] According to Adrienne Corri, Coral didn't keep her claws in when it came to the Broadway audience: 'The well-minked matrons in the stalls were savaged every matinee.'[50] And some of her fellow actors were not beyond a good scratching either: one member of the cast remembered a scene which put Keith Michell under Coral's scathing scrutiny. Listening to it on the speaker system in her dressing room, Coral noticed that Michell's delivery was unusually slow and decided to tackle his fellow player: 'What's that fat cunt up to? What's with all those long pauses?' She was informed that the 'long pauses' were occurring because Michell's character was attempting seduction. Coral was unimpressed: 'Don't like it. I'm going to buy a fucking alarm clock and shove it up his arse.'[51] *The Rehearsal* ran for a relatively modest 110 performances – though critically acclaimed, it may indeed have suffered from the 'anti-Brit' backlash. As Sarah Badel observed, 'It wasn't a very happy production – but it *was* a success.'[52]

While Coral was in New York, a milestone was being made at the Old Vic. On 22 October 1963, the National Theatre Company made its debut. It boasted a permanent company of 100 actors, including Maggie Smith, Joan Plowright, Michael Redgrave and Diana Wynyard, hired for a basic weekly wage of £14, plus £1 per performance. But one notable name was missing from the impressive roster – when, years later, Coral was asked by a reporter why she had never been asked to join the National Company, she said, 'They don't say things like that to me.'[53] This wasn't strictly true: in 1965, Laurence Olivier wrote to her, apologising for being unable to offer her anything at the National, and expressing how much he wanted to have her with the company. But, as Sarah Badel observed, 'She wasn't a company person – not in the mould of Stratford or anything, really.'[54] In truth, although Coral claimed to enjoy being part of a touring company, she was not a natural, permanent 'company' animal – in any case, not for the sort of money the National was offering.

She was determined to continue living in the style to which she and Philip were now accustomed. She bought a new home in Belgravia which, improbably, was even more elegant and desirable than their previous homes: Flat C on the second floor of 16 Eaton Place – a street later immortalised by the 1970s drama *Upstairs, Downstairs*. It was reported that Coral had decided to sell Chester Row 'because she has a house in Brighton, spends much time abroad and doesn't really need two houses. So she is looking for a *pied-à-terre* in London – "just a couple of rooms".'[55] This decision to 'downsize' ended the 'temporary' tenancy of Arthur Marshall, but he quickly made a similar arrangement, this time becoming 'housekeeper' to Emma, elder daughter of his old friend Victor Rothschild, in the Chelsea house her parents had bought for her.

Coral and Philip's beautiful home in one of the most exclusive parts of central London was much-envied: Jill Melford said it was 'wonderful...very theatrical and very elegant – full of antiques and wonderful things', while Vincent Price later quipped he would have married her just for the flat. But,

Melford explained, Coral decided to make one slight 'improvement': 'There was a wonderful terrace and she decided to get Loudon Sainthill to turn it into a conservatory. But he didn't do it quite right, nor did he get permission from the Grosvenor Estate, and it was full of plants. It was freezing in the winter and boiling in the summer.'[56]

Elsewhere in her life, Coral continued to ring the changes. A couple of years earlier, the readers of *She* magazine were asked to put forward nominations for a list of the 'world's most beautiful women'. The top three were Princess Grace, Nina (of the Danish singing duo, Nina and Frederick), and 'Actress – Coral Browne'.[57] Ever mindful of her public image, she started to veer away from being clothed mostly by Molyneux, and towards Jean Muir. Coral first got to know Muir via her husband, Harry Leuckert, a former actor. From 1962, Coral subsequently became a loyal and much-loved client and friend of the designer, and a prominent proponent of Muir's trademark 'little black dress'. Coral was equally appreciative of the self-taught dressmaker's disciplined approach to her craft and her flexibility: 'She'll make things especially for me,' she explained. 'See, I have a 14 top and a size 12 bottom.'[58] Of course, had things turned out differently, Coral might well have enjoyed a similar career: 'I would love to make my own clothes,' she admitted. 'I had taken art courses in school and one part was devoted to design, cutting and dressmaking.'[59]

In reality, there was no time to pursue such ambitions. Shortly before moving to Eaton Place, Coral began rehearsing a new play. *The Right Honourable Gentleman*, written by Michael Bradley-Dyne, was a rather old-fashioned drawing room drama – 'a moth-eaten piece of ersatz Victoriana',[60] according to Alan Strachan.

As the subject matter for his first stage play, Dyne, who had written more than 150 dramas for American television in the previous decade, chose a real-life royal scandal concerning the private life of eminent Liberal statesman Sir Charles Dilke. Anthony Quayle starred as the beleagured politician, once tipped as a future prime minister, whose career was curtailed by a sex scandal in 1886, after he faced allegations of adultery with a Mrs Virginia Crawford. When the Crawfords' divorce case came to court, Dilke's lawyers stopped him giving evidence, as they feared that his colourful private life would become subject to too much scrutiny. As a result, Mr Crawford got his divorce, although, illogically, Dilke was ruled not to have committed adultery with Mrs Crawford. And that would have been that – except that the moralising journalist W T Stead decided to wage a campaign against Dilke, publicly deriding his failure to give evidence in the case. This goaded Dilke into having the case reopened by the Queen's Proctor – this time, he had to give evidence, as did Mrs Crawford. While she was an exemplary witness, Dilke was a disaster and the jury decided to let the divorce stand. Dilke subsequently lost his seat in the 1886 general election but continued to try to clear his name (the subject of the second act of Dyne's play). In the fullness of time, the general consensus was that, although Dilke was hardly a faithful husband, Virginia Crawford was not one of his conquests and that she had been coerced into lying – but by whom, and for what purpose, became the subject of speculation. It was rumoured that Mrs Crawford confessed all to Cardinal Manning, prior to her conversion to Catholicism in 1889.

Coral had been reluctant to appear in the play: while she was still on Broadway in November 1963, the producer Emile Littler sent her the script. Unimpressed by what she read, she turned it down, as she did a month later when it was sent to her again. Then, in February 1964, she learned that Glen Byam Shaw was to direct the play; this, and some judicious rewrites, persuaded her to change her mind. However, as she explained, since 'the part was a smaller one than I usually take, I insisted on a short get-out clause and…negotiated a six months clause, terminable thereafter by four weeks notice on either side'.[61]

Coral was cast as Mrs Rossiter, Dilke's former mistress; it is her daughter, Nia Crawford (played by Anna Massey), whose claims include not only her alleged affair with Dilke, but also that he forced her to have sex with a female servant in what the tabloids would later dub 'three-in-a-bed romps': 'Yes, we slept together. In the same bed! All three of us!' was the rather quaint way this was revealed in the play.[62] Dyne's dramatic disclosures also included Nia's revelation that her 'cuckolded' husband Donald (Richard Leech) is impotent. In hindsight, it was all rather tame stuff. But in May 1964, this sort of subject matter was enough to ensure that the play, for all its conventional construction, got unconventionally good audiences. Rival producer Peter Daubeny sniped at what he said were Emile Littler's 'sensational' publicity tactics for the successful production: 'There are 10 signs outside the theatre saying "not suitable for children". It is doing great business because it is all about a sexual scandal,' he seethed.[63]

The strong cast featured two young actors in minor roles who, like so many others before and after, were familiar with Coral's formidable reputation. One was Jill Melford who was playing Helen Garland: 'I met her the week before we started rehearsing – I thought, "Oh my God…do I need this…" But she was divine, and we became instant best friends. She became my surrogate mother.'[64] The other, Terence Bayler, playing Captain Forster, remembered that, 'She was shrewd and trenchant, but she was always very kind to me, and very encouraging. For instance, I had one brief, rather difficult melodramatic scene with Anna. As her soldier lover, I told her I was ending the relationship; she slapped me, then clung to me, whereupon I flung her to the floor and exited. When I did this at an early rehearsal, Coral passed me in the wings. She said, "You'll never rehearse that scene again." She saw my startled look – was the scene cut, was I to be replaced? – so she quickly added, "You've got it right. Very good!"'[65] Even better were Coral's first-night courtesies: 'She carefully chose appropriate first-night cards for everyone,' said Bayler. 'She gave me a card with a cut-out print of army officers, inscribed "You're the pride of the regiment!!! Good luck for tonight and ALWAYS." To Richard Leech – who was playing Crawford the impotent husband – she gave a card on which was printed "Sorry You Couldn't Come". I asked her how long she had searched for a message so appropriate to that character and she said, "I bought it years ago, but I was never able to cast it…"'[66]

The show would provide many such memorable moments for its cast: Anna Massey recalled how, during rehearsals, the cast had lunch at a fish restaurant in Shaftesbury Avenue, where they were duly served minnow-sized portions. As Coral was leaving the restaurant, the gushing head waiter asked if she had enjoyed her meal, whereupon she informed him that she would be returning the next day – to feed the fish. However, Massey soon found herself suffering a similar fate to the hapless water. Jill Melford explained, 'Coral knew what was "period", and what wasn't. And she was very angry because Anna refused to wear corsets – and of course, you sit and walk totally differently in corsets. So there Anna was striding about…and she was very good in it – but it just didn't look right.'[67] So, of course, Coral responded to this in familiar fashion: a story that got back to Massey (and which she would subsequently tell at her own expense) was that Coral had seen her photo in a newspaper, with the caption: 'What's Anna Massey Looking For?'; 'Her chin,' was Coral's answer.[68]

After the opening night, Massey – like her fellow cast members – could hold her chin high, as they dodged the barbs hurled at the play and picked up a few compliments for themselves. One critic dismissed *The Right Honourable Gentleman* as 'an out-dated piece of upper-crust rubbish...one was grateful for the presence of Coral Browne, who seized upon the few witty lines with the skill of a Gabor opening a jewel case.'[69] *The Times* concurred: the play was '...another sturdily mediocre drama from British legal history...[Bradley-Dyne's] best writing comes out when he is dealing with women...he has enabled Coral Browne and Anna Massey to show a snake pit flourishing in the undergrowth of the drama.'[70] There was much appreciation of its leading lady: 'With Coral Browne playing this fascinating and beautiful woman, the relationship becomes charged with electric undertones of sexual attraction.'[71] 'Her playing was delightful perfection...the play itself bore the appearance of a sort of bastion erected in defence of the English stage tradition against the onslaughts of such as Pinter and Wexler. The mannered elegance of writing and acting was savoured by some theatregoers and dismissed by others'.[72]

Despite its subject matter, the show attracted its fair share of royalty (as well as the theatre queens in the cheap seats): Maria, the Queen of Spain watched one performance, attending a drinks reception afterwards, hosted by the cast. This caused another outbreak of Browne bitching: Coral told Ned Sherrin that, while she had provided the drinks for the event, her co-stars' contributions left much to be desired. Anna Massey's, she insisted, amounted to a solitary lemon, while Anthony Quayle had stumped up half a bottle of tonic water – 'and the next night, he came in to ask if there was any left', she concluded.[73] For many years after, Sherrin would send her a souvenir present on her first nights – comprising a single lemon and half a bottle of tonic water.

The lemon would turn bitter when other queens made their way backstage to see Coral. Many theatrical pundits have wondered why, with her glamour and flair for comedy, Coral was never a Coward leading lady. In fact, her career had rather mirrored that of the Master's beloved Gertrude Lawrence, whose charisma and talents never quite translated to the screen. In 1963, James Roose-Evans produced a popular revival of *Private Lives* at the tiny Hampstead Theatre with a young, unknown cast including Rosemary Martin and Edward de Souza. Coward was keen for it to transfer to the West End, as was the impresario Peter Bridge, who offered Roose-Evans the choice cast of

Ian Carmichael and Coral to play Amanda and Elyot. Instead, Roose-Evans chose to stay loyal to his young cast and was vindicated when the production ran for nearly a year. However, Coward commented that the production was 'very well done on the whole but not quite *elegant* enough' – a quality Coral could have provided in abundance.[74] Then, shortly after *The Right Honourable Gentleman* opened at Her Majesty's, Coward came to the first mid-week matinee. As Coral explained, the reason for his visit was soon apparent: 'He came round afterwards and said, "Oh it's rubbish, it's the worst play I've ever seen" – he had Joyce Carey with him and Graham Payn. And he asked me if I would do *Hay Fever* at the National Theatre – he wanted me to play the lead. And I said, "I don't think I can, Noël. I'd be delighted but I think this play will run…" – they were starting rehearsals of *Hay Fever* in six weeks time. "Oh, this will be off!," he said. And it ran for 18 months… So I never did play it – Edith Evans played it. And I never did a play of Noël's.'[75]

As it transpired, there would be little comedy in Coral's life in the next twelve month, as two major real-life dramas unfolded. During the rehearsals of *The Right Honourable Gentleman*, Philip Pearman felt increasingly unwell. He underwent an array of tests, all of which proved inconclusive. But his health continued to deteriorate – Olive Harding and Ronnie Waters had to take over his roster of clients – until eventually and, much too late in the day, he was told he had lymphatic cancer; this rapidly spread to his stomach and liver. Alan Bates said that Coral nursed her husband 'with great devotion when he was fatally ill'.[76] But it was all over too quickly: Philip died on Tuesday 13 October 1964, at St George's Hospital, Hyde Park Corner, aged just 53. That afternoon, as usual, his weekly order of roses for Coral turned up at Eaton Place. A brief report, headlined 'Miss Coral Browne's Husband Dies', explained her absence from a performance the day after Philip's death.[77] Paradoxically, Jill Melford remembered the night of Coral's absence as 'one of the funniest nights of my life – Albie [Albert Finney] did a cabaret. I came back from the theatre – obviously, I was working that night – and Albie collected Coral and we all went for dinner, and laughed hysterically, as one does when something awful has happened. Albie was brilliant. He adored Philip.'[78] As did Peter Willes, his old friend and comrade in arms, who understood too well what Philip's loss meant to Coral: 'I thought of the luncheon just before I left when he looked so well and, alas, to a discerning eye was very ill. "When you came to see me," he said in passing and he talked of a time I went looking for him in an armoured car in Libya 25 years ago. I, who had so little, and he who had you and so much. It seemed very unfair. Then I thought of you and the loneliness and of your Sundays and getting back from the theatre…You have lost a great big enormous part of yourself…but you haven't really, because his love for you is still all around you and nothing can take that away.'[79]

Jill Melford, Albert Finney and Vicky accompanied Coral to Philip's funeral at Golders Green crematorium, which provided its own moments of black humour. 'Coral had this hat which had on a sort of wiggling stand, like a daisy,' said Melford. 'She said, "Do you think I've gone too far?" and I said, "No, it could save all our lives, actually" – it was hysterical… Her mother said, "You can't wear that, you'll look ridiculous." But, of course, it kept me and Albie going through the funeral – every time Coral sobbed or something, this terrible thing would wiggle…'[80] One repercussion from the tragedy would be no laughing matter: the failure by doctors to diagnose Philip's cancer at an earlier stage engendered Coral's subsequent obsessive paranoia about developing the disease herself. A few months after his death, she admitted: 'I have seen three specialists over the last three or four months… At one time I feared that I was suffering from the same illness which caused my husband's death.'[81]

Laurence Evans sent Coral a cheque for £3600 – one year's, tax-exempt salary – from London Artists, 'as a token of our great appreciation of everything Philip did for us over the years'.[82] This, together with the £11,000 left to her by Philip, was small consolation for Coral's great loss – it was certainly one of the few times in her life when money matters would be immaterial. After 14 years of unconventional but immensely happy marriage, losing Philip left Coral devastated and depressed and in an emotional void which not even her closest friendships could fill. She believed, then, that she would never marry again, or find another man with whom she could enjoy the same sort of relationship. According to Victoria Price, even 20 years after his death, Philip was one of the few people about whom Coral would display great sentimentality: 'How much she loved him was fairly evident.'[83]

There was to be no respite: within months of losing Philip, *The Right Honourable Gentleman* would produce an offstage court case to rival the one at the core of its story. The show had been running for more than a year and bookings were being taken up until October 1965. Then came a bombshell: on 23 June 1965, London Artists Ltd, who represented not only Coral, but also co-stars Anthony Quayle, Anna Massey and Corin Redgrave, gave four weeks' notice to its producer Emile Littler that their four clients would be leaving the play – all on the same day.

An aggrieved Littler had his suspicions about what lay behind this development.

When *The Right Honourable Gentleman* opened, Her Majesty's was owned by Stoll Theatres, the company headed by Emile's brother, Prince Littler. Then, early in 1965, the theatre was taken over by ATV, part of the mighty Grade Organisation – which, by coincidence, also owned London Artists. Unfortunately for Emile Littler, he didn't keep his suspicions to himself: he revealed at a press conference that he had written to the four actors, expressing his dismay at their actions – and claimed that Quayle, Massey and Redgrave had agreed to consider staggering their periods of notice. It was reported that 'Coral Browne said her doctor would not allow her to stay on'.[84] The great impresario then decided to read out parts of the letter: 'Her Majesty's Theatre new directorate wish to get our play out of theatre,' he declared. 'I am being put into a position by my landlords Associated Television Ltd, whereby withdrawing all Grade star labour the play must close down on the date which these notices expire.'[85] In short, he was alleging that the actors had been part of a conspiracy by ATV to deliberately bring the play's run to an early end. The *Daily Telegraph* duly printed substantial parts of the letter – whereupon London Artists and Associated Television Ltd sued both Littler and the *Telegraph* for libel. They hired specialist lawyer Peter Carter-Ruck (later both the butt of jokes and *bête noire* of *Private Eye*) to represent them.

Jill Melford, however, claimed that, 'It all happened because I discovered I was pregnant. [She was then married to actor John Standing.] I thought I'd better tell Emile as, eventually, I'd have to go. Two weeks later, I was fired. Coral was incensed; we both had the same agent at the time – Ronnie Waters – and Ronnie had to ring me and tell me I'd been fired. Everybody was in a fury – Emile was not popular, it was not a good way to behave. Then Coral and Corin and Tony Quayle realised that they were in dead trouble if they wanted to leave.'[86]

Coral worked with Carter-Ruck and his legal team to draft a statement of the evidence she would give in court. She revealed that, following Philip's death, 'I was obviously subject to severe emotional strain but I continued to act in the play because I wished to have something to do and some work to occupy my mind and time. I continued in the play despite medical advice and warnings from friends that I was subjecting myself to too much strain, until my health has now deteriorated to such an extent that I have to leave the play.'[87] Then she said, 'Jill Melford had informed Mr Littler that she was pregnant but could go on working until November…but a few weeks later [she] was given, on a Thursday, notice to leave the next Saturday. Had she not informed Emile Littler that she was pregnant she could have given him four weeks notice but as it was she was deprived of the minimum of a fortnight's salary on which she was wholly dependent.' She continued, 'As a personal friend Mr Littler is charming but I would not want to cross him in the business field as he seems to have the attitude that he must have complete control of everything irrespective of the opinions of others. At no time did my agent attempt to persuade me or even indeed advise me as to whether I should leave and if so at what time. I did not know that ATV were the landlords of Her Majesty's Theatre as I thought this was owned by Prince Littler. I have received no formal bribe or other inducement from London Artists, ATV or anyone else.'[88]

The four actors who had given notice were called to give evidence when the case was heard in the High Court. According to Peter Carter-Ruck, 'they were, without exception, impeccable witnesses'.[89] Jill Melford remembered things rather differently: 'Coral was completely useless in the witness box, Corin refused to swear on the Bible – it was a farce.' But a farce with a happy ending: 'I got a call one night from the lawyers, saying, "Don't worry, you'll never be in the witness box." And we won the case.'[90] Emile Littler and the *Daily Telegraph* had to pay undisclosed damages and costs. Coral subsequently left *The Right Honourable Gentleman* on 24 July 1965, and immediately went to the Algarve for a long-overdue holiday. She was replaced by Margaretta Scott, who continued in the show until its closure on 9 October.

Incredibly, after all the assorted dramas and bad memories associated with the play, Coral agreed to star in a revival of *The Right Honourable Gentleman* opening in New York the same month as the London production closed. With the so-called 'British invasion' continuing unabated, it would be one of six British plays opening on Broadway before the end of the year, including *Entertaining*

Mr Sloane by Joe Orton and John Osborne's *Inadmissable Evidence*. However, this production would have happier consequences for Coral, including a close friendship with its director, Frith Banbury. He and Coral's former leading man, Robert Morley had appeared together in the 1938 comedy *Goodness, How Sad!*, which played at the Vaudeville Theatre for eight months. Together with Peter Bull, they had previously founded a repertory company in Perranporth, Cornwall. Banbury had met Coral briefly when he used to pop round to see his chum Morley during the run of *The Man Who Came to Dinner*. Through his company Frith Banbury Ltd, founded in 1948, the highly respected actor, director and producer worked with and promoted playwrights such as Rodney Ackland, Emlyn Williams and Terence Rattigan. As a director, he had coped with the vagaries of Edith Evans, Sybil Thorndike, Peggy Ashcroft, Ralph Richardson – and all the Redgraves. No one could have been better equipped to cope with any problems *The Right Honourable Gentleman* might pose in New York. 'Glen Byam Shaw, for one reason or another, wasn't going to go do it,' explained Banbury, 'and Coral asked for me to do it. So then I got to know her very well indeed.' It was a friendship that worked well professionally: 'She was really comfortable with Frith – or "Frithy", as she called him,' said Sarah Badel. 'She felt he was the right director for her. She felt secure with him.'[91]

In a move which would please American Actors Equity, only three members of the cast would be coming from England – the rest would be recruited from American actors and the show would rehearse in New York. Before she left London, Coral treated herself by ordering some new outfits from Molyneux; when they weren't finished in time, couturier John Tullis acted as her own personal courier when he left for New York on business a few weeks later.

Frith Banbury vividly recalled the effect Coral's elegance had on her fellow actors: 'At the first reading, Coral appeared looking like a million dollars. I could see the American actors think: "Oh Lord, this is going to be a star lady who chucks her weight about, who won't learn her lines, and is much too grand," and so on. I could see the effect this had. Next day, Coral turned up to rehearsal in old slacks, and was "hail fellow, well met" with everybody – unless they did something she didn't approve of, and then she wasn't! In her work, she was quite marvellous with younger people – she and Sarah Badel had a very good relationship in *The Right Honourable Gentleman*.'[92]

Badel was playing Nia Crawford: 'I was in *Robert & Elizabeth* with John Clements [at the Lyric Theatre] and it was John who engineered it for me to go to New York to do *The Right Honourable Gentleman*. I only had a very small part in *Robert & Elizabeth* – Bella Hedley – but Coral came to see it; she was sort of vetting who might do it.'[93] Both Coral and Frith Banbury had the added pleasure of having another old friend and colleague on board, Charles Gray – who, in New York, had to be billed as 'Charles D Gray', because an American actor had the same name. Gray and Coral had chummed up when he played Achilles in the 1956/7 New York production of *Troilus and Cressida*, and he had appeared as the messenger Mercadé in Banbury's 1954 production of *Love's Labour's Lost*. Within two years, Gray had gone from messenger to leading man. For most of his career, especially in films and television, Gray played toffs, smooth-talking cads and well-heeled villains, including Blofeld in *Diamonds Are Forever*. The reality was rather different: he was a Bournemouth boy, who in his youth looked all set for a career as an estate agent. He would say, 'I'm not in the least aristocratic in real life, I much prefer a pint at the local.'[94] For many years, his 'local' was the Ennismore Arms, where he would often be seen in the company of his next-door neighbour in Ennismore Gardens, Ava Gardner – no stranger to a 'pint' herself.[95] Gardner bought a jukebox for the Ennismore – and stocked it with nothing but records by her ex-husband, Frank Sinatra. Alistair Cooke remembered Gray and Gardner as 'a sort of raucous Nick and Nora from the Thin Man movies'.[96]

In the latter years of their friendship, Coral would often admonish Gray for appearing in what she called 'rubbish' films and television, instead of working more in the theatre. It was all very well saying this – but, ever the disciplinarian, she must have known that her friend's prodigious consumption of alcohol was hardly conducive to maintaining a regimen of eight performances a week. Frith Banbury was acquainted with the after-effects of Gray's over-indulgence – after one unspecified incident, he received a letter: 'Dear Mr Banbury, I hear you were unwise enough to dine with a certain "gentleman" the other evening (who has subsequently been taken into the yard and shot) and I have been asked where you would like your clothes sent for cleaning. Mr Gray's last wish – we are told – indeed cry was "SEE TO FRITH'S CLOTHES". There was a gentleman with him at the time who declined to comment and has left the country. Xxx Sorry.'[97] Frith Banbury said, 'Charles Gray, who was a smashing actor – to my mind, much more interesting than Anthony Quayle had been in the part in London. We also had another facet of that production which, to my mind, was an improvement – two things, in fact. I persuaded the author to do a lot more work on the script; and I saw the original at Her Majesty's and thought it was pretty drab the way it was put on. So Loudon Sainthill was engaged – and he was the most wonderful designer and did the clothes and the sets.'[98]

The show previewed at the Billy Rose Theater from 7 October; when it opened on 19 October, the critics were almost unanimous in their praise, with Sarah Badel and Charles Gray sharing the accolades with Coral. The production was subsequently nominated for two Tony awards. Leonard Lyons declared, '*The Right Honourable Gentleman* is unquestionably the town's newest hit. It's the first historical whodunit in years.'[99] The *Evening Standard* reported that 'Broadway finally has a successful hit of the new season and the stars Charles Gray, Sarah Badel and Coral Browne are the toast of the theatre district.'[100] The *New York Times* critic was at Coral's feet: 'What is lacking in pulsing flesh and blood becomes brilliantly manifest in the role of Mrs Crawford's mother and the performance of Coral Browne. Miss Browne makes every line count and in the glint of her eye and the toss of her head she conveys meanings and emotions between the lines.'[101] None of the critics would have been aware of the heartache the leading lady was going through: on 13 October, Frith Banbury found Coral in her dressing room, sobbing her heart out. She explained that it was the first anniversary of Philip Pearman's death.

Sarah Badel had one theory about why this production of *The Right Honourable Gentleman* was so lauded by the New York critics: 'It was so very redolent of the Christine Keeler affair, so the Americans loved it because that had all just happened – it was still very fresh.'[102] This Keeler analogy was spot-on: Rex Reed said that Virginia Crawford was a girl 'who, in two acts and seven scenes, destroys the lives of almost all the other characters onstage, rocks England with one of its spiciest political-sex scandals and possibly changes the course of British history.'[103] But some of the audience were concerned for the show's young star: 'Youthful and pretty Badel…on opening night, a woman reportedly said, "How could her father allow a young girl to go onstage and say such filthy things?"'[104]

The 'young girl' Badel was more worried by being alone in New York: 'I was so unhappy. A strange role I had never played, a cast I had never met, I didn't know a soul, my hair was standing on end, my dress was wrinkled and I had food poisoning. I went straight to the Piccadilly Hotel, locked the door and cried myself to sleep with dark glasses on.'[105] At which point, Coral went into her best 'Ma Browne' mode with Badel: 'It was just us three Brits – Coral, Charles and I – and the rest of the cast were American. They were both so kind to me – because they were completely out of my age group or experience – and she sort of looked out for me. She had almost a motherly instinct to encourage some younger people. She would foster people. Not many older actresses would do that. She was alarming – but so kind and very protective. She had been in New York with my father [in *The Rehearsal*] and she wrote to him, with little progress reports about "Baby", as she called me, which was very sweet and generous of her. "The Baby's coming on – she's going to be alright" – and, "Don't worry, we'll look after her." I was very touched that she'd done that.'[106]

This side of 'Ma Browne' came as no surprise to others who knew Coral: 'She would adopt theatre companies,' said Sheridan Morley. 'It was part of the old-fashioned star quality – if you were the star, you took on the show and the company and became their kind of den mother. Coral was an amazing combination of den mother and grand dame – she was cosy and cuddly, AND at the same time formidable.'[107] 'Ma Browne' fussed over her 'children', and kept a watchful eye on them, particularly pertaining to their appearance: 'Of course, she always looked sensational,' said Sarah Badel. 'She used to tick me off – "Don't be a scruff, make an effort, do your hair, put something decent on." And she'd say, "Watch it, the pounds are creeping on" – because I'd arrived looking like a stick insect. And then as the run progressed, I'd be at Sardi's and various other places and delicatessens… Coral was very fond of Michael Bradley-Dyne – she called him "Old Mother Dyne". He cooked a beautiful Christmas lunch for Coral and myself.'[108] 'Baby' wasn't the only nickname conferred on Badel: after one reviewer likened her to a 'bantam Bette Davis', she was always referred to as 'Bantam Bette' by Coral.

'Bantam Bette' always remembered fondly the kindness and encouragement she received from such a theatrical heavyweight, but felt that Coral kept the best of her personality out of her performances: 'She was an extraordinary woman, because she was such a blazing personality – an acerbic wit – more daring offstage than on. I always felt there was a constraint about her on stage. She always said to me, "I don't know why I do it, really. It's somewhere to go in the evening." You were longing for her to burst out in a performance and set the house ablaze.'[109] Patrick White also sensed this tendency in Coral to be a tad 'buttoned-up': in 1962, he wanted her to appear as the earthy but poignant Nola Boyle in a London production of his play *A Season at Sarsaparilla*, set in a fictitious Sydney suburb. He told Ronnie Waters, 'I know what is *inside* Coral, and how it would pop out if she got into that part.'[110] However, this didn't stop her inflammatory backstage antics: 'I never saw her take wing and be her as we knew her in the party afterwards or in the dressing room. She would be stark-naked in the dressing room, because she liked to disconcert people. So when the chaps came in, there she would be, with just her wig and her hat on…it amused her, to see their faces and to see what their reaction would be. Wicked old thing… Nothing was sacred – she could demolish anything or anyone.' But Badel could see where these sharp-tongued torrents sprang from: 'I think she had a very low boredom threshold – if someone wasn't entertaining or amusing. I don't think it was frivolity, it's just that she was so quick herself, she could not bear to be bored. She needed a sparring partner – I think she had it in Charles. And that's what the theatre provides – that kind of coterie.'[111] The camp camaraderie of the 'Coral and Charles Show' kept Badel – and everyone else within earshot – highly entertained: 'She loved gossip: "Nothing happening in the cot," she would observe – which meant no one was sleeping with anyone, which she always thought was a pity…the Algonquin was "the All Gone Queer". And she and Charles posed for a photograph once – they were supposed to be engaged – and she said to him, "Oh, Charles, your mother *will* be pleased!"'[112]

The critics were ecstatic, the cast were happy – what could possibly mar the collective joy? Any number of things, of course, but in this case, it was first a blackout – and second a walk-out.

First, there was 'The night the Manhattan skyline disappeared'[113] – on 9 November, a major power failure hit the Eastern seaboard. 'We were there at the time of the big blackout,' said Sarah Badel. 'I was in Macy's – I was a terrible shopper – and suddenly the lights went out. I made my way along Broadway to the theatre – everyone had managed to get there. We made up by candlelight, but obviously nothing was going to happen.'[114] And things got blacker: on New Year's Day 1966, workers on the New York bus and subway went on strike. The situation quickly deteriorated: union leaders were arrested and the New York Board of Trade asked Governor Rockefeller to consider calling out the National Guard to drive the buses. Some taxi drivers responded to the crisis by doubling their fares into Manhattan. Most off-Broadway shows closed until the dispute was over; Manhattan cinema attendance dropped to almost nothing, and the subsequent retail losses alone were estimated to be $40 million a day. In all, the 13-day strike cost businesses, the city and the state and federal authorities $1000 million – the producers of one of the shows affected, *Funny Girl*, tried to sue for damages for loss of revenue. Coral, who, walked to and from the theatre during the dispute, claimed her own 'damages': 'I tell you what the strike did. I walked so much [my feet] went from 8 and a half-AA to 10-BBB.'[115] But, all levity aside, the cast quickly realised the dispute meant doom for *The Right Honourable Gentleman*: the management of the Billy Rose Theater announced that, as a result of the strike, cancellations had caused attendance to 'fall apart'.[116] In a noble attempt to ride out the storm, the cast agreed to take a cut in salary, and the play continued until 29 January, when the producers finally brought the curtain down.

Sarah Badel decided to do something to cheer everyone up: 'I wanted to do a party for them, and I thought, what would be fun? So I went to a little museum where they had a film of excerpts of Eleonora Duse and Sarah Bernhardt. I got them to set it up, and gave a little party and invited the company to see this film – Duse in *Cenere* [1916] – and I have to say we all just laughed our heads off. It was very irreverent...'[117] The actors would have trouble keeping straight faces at another event which demanded decorum. On 10 February, Billy Rose, the great theatrical showman after whom their theatre was named, died. The cast of *The Right Honourable Gentleman* were invited to attend what they thought would be a memorial service being held three days later in the auditorium, and so Coral, Sarah Badel and Charles Gray went to pay their respects. However, after the 700 mourners had assembled, the curtain rose – and there, centre-stage, was Billy Rose in his coffin, with his family and close friends in the orchestra pit. After a 40-minute service, the coffin 'exited' and was taken to Westchester Hills Cemetery for burial. Badel and Coral left for London on 24 February, aboard the liner QE2; Coral departed New York with an impressively excessive 23 pieces of luggage. 'Of course, Coral was in first class and I was down in the "steerage", said Sarah Badel. 'But I used to dress up in the evenings and slither on my stomach under a little gate she'd told me about, and be given a *very* nice dinner by Coral.'[118]

Before they left New York, Coral and Frith Banbury had already decided to work together again. He recalled, 'We had a plan to try and get a Tennessee Williams play, *The Milk Train Doesn't Stop Here Anymore*, which had never – and to this day, never has – been done in the West End. But Tennessee, whom I knew, had written three or four different versions of this play, one of which was done, as it were, Japanese Kabuki style in San Francisco – and Tennessee was, not to put to fine a point on it, on the drugs at that time, and it was impossible to get hold of him. We made appointments; he failed to keep them. And I wanted to know which of the versions he wanted done. It had been done twice in New York; once with Hermione Baddeley and then with Tallulah Bankhead. So in the end I said to Coral, "We're in trouble with trying to cope with this." And Tennessee Williams wasn't – isn't, even to this day – *per se* an enormous draw – it's the stars who appeared in his plays, like Vivien Leigh, that made the plays go in England.'[119]

After a few months at home, Coral left for Paris, where she was to play a supporting role opposite Charles Gray in the film *The Night of the Generals* – an unpleasant, crass and rather pointless effort, with a plot which managed to combine a Jack the Ripper-type murder case, the 1944 plot to assassinate Hitler *and* the siege of Warsaw. Coral was playing Eleanore von Seidlitz-Gabler, wife of one of the three generals suspected of being the murderer of several prostitutes, and mother of a daughter, Ulrika, who (for unspecified reasons) hates her mother – 'quel Vic', as Coral was always fond of saying. During one scene – a soiree hosted by Eleanore – Coral had to utter in passing, 'I remember the Führer saying to me…' The film starred Peter O'Toole and Omar Sharif, but its stellar cast were badly adrift in a story correctly summed up as a '…silly and lengthy epic…long, disorganised, disjointed and basically dotty.'[120]

Much more to Coral's liking was the chance to play Mrs Erlynne in *Lady Windermere's Fan* opposite Wilfred Hyde-White, Isabel Jeans and Juliet Mills; it also reunited her with two actors from the London production of *The Right Honourable Gentleman*, Corin Redgrave and Terence Bayler. It was the first time Wilde's play had been staged in the West End for twenty years, and was being directed by Anthony Quayle. Coral explained their approach to the play's central premise – the mother who sacrifices her own reputation for her daughter's happiness: 'We take it quite fast and we guard against a sentimental, hearts-and-flowers approach. Another problem is there's so much repetition in the writing. Mrs Erlynne…keeps using the same phrases: "Go back to the husband who loves you".'[121]

Cecil Beaton (who, unbeknownst to Coral, had hoped that Vivien Leigh would be playing Mrs Erlynne) was brought on board by producer Binkie Beaumont to design the show: he had performed the same duties for the 1945 Haymarket production, when he had the benefit of discussing the play with Wilde's surviving son, Vyvyan Holland. With clothing rationing still in force at that time, Beaton only had an allowance of 24 coupons per costume to work with. Now, unfettered by any similar restrictions for this production, Beaton had a rush of blood to the head, and saw red – yards and yards of red. And all of it would be lavished on Coral's 'scarlet woman', Mrs Erlynne – for whom he rustled up a fairly alarming scarlet outfit in satin, to be worn in the Act Two ballroom scene. When the time came for Coral to try on the vision in red which her ex-lover had run up for her, the air turned blue. According to Terence Bayler, Coral declared: 'Cecil, I'm afraid to open my mouth in case someone posts a fucking letter in it.'[122] After a meeting with Quayle and Coral, Beaton agreed to change the satin to net – but the colour remained. Coral was not impressed:'To think, I gave him my jewel, and what did I get for it? A lot of rotten frocks.'[123] A similar complaint about Beaton's apparent lack of gratitude for sexual favours granted had been made in 1937 by Tallulah Bankhead, with whom he'd had enjoyed a one-night liaison. He was called in to make some last-minute improvements to the costumes for her New York production of *Antony and Cleopatra*. Twenty-four hours before opening night, Bankhead got her first chance to try on Beaton's offerings, which included a capelet made of a fabric woven with plastic. Bankhead's verdict was not dissimilar to Coral's: 'I look like a shower curtain!'[124] Beaton later wrote to Coral, apologising for the 'ugly' dresses and joking that he didn't know he was capable of such vulgarity. In 1985, his biographer Hugo Vickers believed he'd discovered the reason why Beaton insisted on red for her dress: apparently, the designer had been reading Proust and decided that Mrs Erlynne should be like the Duchesse de Guermantes in *The Guermantes Way*, volume three of *Remembrance of Things Past*. But it still rankled – and in 1974, when Beaton suffered a serious stroke, Charles Gray told Coral, 'If Cecil Beaton's stroke proves fatal you could perhaps arrange to have him laid out in that red frock he designed for your *Fan*. It's never too late for revenge.'[125]

Frank Marcus (whose own West End success, *The Killing of Sister George*, would soon be playing its part in Coral's life) agreed with Coral's prescient fears about elements of Beaton's designs. He said 'the interior decorator in him has run amok…the sets are hideous…the acting is equally ill-assorted…Coral Browne has a good old go at playing a *femme fatale*. But surely Mrs Erlynne would never appear at Lady Windermere's ball literally as a scarlet woman?'[126] Others took up the same thread as they heaped on the plaudits: 'Coral Browne presents us with a scarlet woman, in every sense of the word: she brings poise, a voluptuous presence and a touch of genuine feeling to the part'[127]; 'her poise on the razor's edge of sense and sensibility is unwavering and the effect is spellbinding.'[128] Jack Tinker observed, 'So bristling with famous names and extravagant décor is it that the eyes and ears are kept constantly entranced by the myriad details in this brilliant mosaic…it is a commanding performance full of nuances and neat little touches of comedy and pathos.'[129] In 2002, reviewing the Peter Hall production starring Vanessa Redgrave and Joely Richardson, Sheridan Morley said, 'Nothing in this staging overtakes the memory of the great Coral Browne/Wilfred Hyde-White/Isabel Jeans revival of 1966, which remains definitive.'[130]

The 'definitive' production settled in for a long run. And, as with all long runs, to prevent the onset of boredom, some of the cast found it necessary to amuse themselves – and each other – as Terence Bayler recalled: 'Before the ballroom scene, the whole cast congregated in the wings, waiting to make their separate entrances. As a waltz was playing, it was possible to exchange brief greetings and pleasantries. But one night, one actor gave a lengthy account of his involvement in a production of *Toad of Toad Hall* – and Coral nodded politely as she strained to hear her cue… The next night, this actor approached her again and she murmured, "Here he comes – Turd of Turd Hall."…Another evening, during the performance, she told me that a Catholic priest who regularly visited West End theatres – she always called him "Father Arseholes" – had been to her dressing room. She said, "He asked me when I was going to start a family. *Blind* priests they're sending me now…"'[131]

And there were other *divertissements*: on 22 November, Juliet Mills was 'kidnapped' by two students at the end of the performance. The theatre management called the police, who set off in pursuit and found Mills in a Kensington pub – where they discovered she had been 'forced' to sell her autograph for charity as part of a college Rag Week.

In January 1967, Wilfred Hyde-White left the production and Douglas Byng set up camp. *The Times* noted that the play 'has now acquired a rhythm and fluency it lacked on the opening night...apart from the fastidious aplomb of Mr Byng's Lord Augustus, the chief pleasures of the production are still Coral Browne's voluptuous, scarlet-gowned Mrs Erlynne and Isabel Jeans' impeccable comic timing as the Duchess of Berwick.'[132] For contractual reasons, the production finished with a week at Wimbledon Theatre after its West End run finished in April 1967. This was handy for Terence Bayler, who lived in the south London suburb, up the hill from the theatre – which he said, 'at that time was in some disrepair. Knowing I lived in Wimbledon, Coral asked me about it: "Rats as big as the leading lady, I hear," she said.'[133] Bayler invited his 'leading lady' to escape the rats one afternoon: 'I had recently bought a small house and a Victorian schoolroom which adjoined it in Wimbledon village and was working to integrate the two properties. Knowing of Coral's art training, and her interest in design, I ventured to invite her to tea between our midweek matinee and evening performance. She came, and brought a bag of sweets for the children; she approved of them, *and* of the ongoing work on the property – she keenly inspected everything...'[134]

With *Lady Windermere's Fan* – and Mrs Erlynne's controversial dresses – now packed away for good, Coral had a short window in which to see friends before she headed across the Atlantic again. One who gave cause for particular concern was Vivien Leigh: the troubled actress's tuberculosis had flared up again and doctors had ordered three months' complete bed-rest. Visitor numbers were restricted but Coral was allowed entry into Leigh's Eaton Square flat. On 15 June, Leigh sent a card to Coral, saying, 'If I could ever see your beautiful face that is what I should like best.'[135] Leigh's wish was granted: the friends saw each other on Friday 30 June. A week later, on the evening of 7 July, Leigh was found dead in her bedroom, aged just 53. Coral was unavoidably absent from her friend's memorial service, held at St Martin-in-the-Fields on 15 August 1967 because, most unusually, she had received 'the call' from Hollywood, and had flown off to appear in two consecutive celluloid controversies.

Mercy and Madness

1968–1972

Robert Aldrich, it has been said, emerged 'as one of the most distinctive and forceful filmmakers among the new generation who helped transform American cinema in the 1950s with their defiantly individual vision.'[1] As assistant director to the likes of Orson Welles, Jean Renoir and Joseph Losey, Aldrich's technical and political credentials were impeccable. But somewhere along the way, style, substance and social conscience gave way to sensationalism. By 1967, any actress agreeing to star in an Aldrich movie should have known it came with a health warning: 'If you can't stand the heat, get out of the kitsch.'

Twenty years after Aldrich's death, critic John Patterson lamented the dearth of film-makers of the maverick director's ilk – 'tight, punchy, tabloid sensibility, interested in corruption and violence, and capable of rendering slices of the zeitgeist quickly onto film, all while entertaining a mass audience, and making money doing it. If he were alive now, he'd be…integrating his leftwing politics into all manner of raucous genre entertainment.'[2] 'Raucous' was certainly one way of describing Aldrich's most infamous film, the gruesomely gothic *Whatever Happened to Baby Jane?* (1962), starring Bette Davis and Joan Crawford. The cult classic was, essentially, a mud-wrestling match staged between two great ladies of the cinema, who almost managed to rise above the mire. In 1964, Aldrich persuaded Davis to star for him again, this time in the macabre *Hush, Hush Sweet Charlotte*, lining up with fellow screen icons Olivia de Havilland, Mary Astor and Agnes Moorehead. Aldrich always claimed, 'I think I do rather well with women.'[3] But one woman, the much-feared film critic, Pauline Kael, begged to differ: 'his [style] is from nagging to screeching, from hysteria to violence and he has the grace of a diesel. Aldrich directs like a lewd tourist.'[4]

In 1967, Aldrich hit the jackpot when he switched temporarily from divas to bad boys and anti-heroes: *The Dirty Dozen* took $19.5 million at the

American box office, making it (then) the 15th highest grossing film of all time. Flushed with funds from this success, Aldrich bought a studio and, in 1968, his Associates And Aldrich Company announced a five-year plan to produce between eight and 16 films.

Coral didn't find Aldrich's penchant for a mix of kitsch 'n' bitch a deterrent and signed up to make two films with him; the first was *The Legend of Lylah Clare* (1968), starring Peter Finch and Kim Novak. It was Novak's first film for three years, after recovering from the effects of a riding accident, the break-up of her marriage to Richard Johnson and what was politely referred to as 'career indecision'.[5] Her 'comeback' movie would turn out to be a grim farrago, exceptional only for its unbridled awfulness: 'Necrophilia, cancer, cripples, French critics, lesbianism, ignorant producers, nepotism, abortion, "film-artists", Italian studs and TV are the tasty elements Aldrich ghoulishly juggles...'[6] It was filmed between July and November 1967 at MGM Studios Culver City, where an entire section of Hollywood's fabled Brown Derby restaurant was recreated by designer William Glasgow, complete with walls adorned with sketches by studio artists of themselves, their friends and family.

Novak played German actress Elsa Brinkmann, hired by her mentor, director Lewis Zarkan (Finch) to play a dead Hollywood star, Lylah Clare, in a biopic about the late legend. The real Lylah, we learn, was briefly married to Zarkan – *extremely* briefly: Lylah died on their wedding night. Zarkan, of course, falls for his late wife's reincarnation who, like a good Svengali, he has renamed Elsa Campbell. The story had a slight *Rebecca*-ish twist: the housekeeper Rossella (Rossella Falk) falls for the ersatz Lylah just as she had fallen for the real Lylah. Kim Novak's voice was dubbed for most of her lines, as her German accent wasn't considered up to scratch – with the result that what came out of her mouth bore more than a passing resemblance to the possessed Linda Blair in *The Exorcist*.

Coral had originally turned down the role of Molly Luther, the film's 'venom-tongued film-land columnist',[7] but when the production was postponed, and its new starting date fell after *Lady Windermere's Fan* was due to close, she accepted. 'I've played a succession of world-wise women of all types, so many, in fact that these sort of chic but testy cosmopolites have become known in the profession as "Coral Browne roles",' she said. 'I'm very established. Comes the characterisation of a well-dressed drawing room doxie to be cast and my telephone starts ringing. It could be worse. I'd hate to be known in producer's books as "the ugly old dear with the bun".'[8]

In the film, Lewis Zarkan is keen for the Hollywood press to embrace his new protégée – and the approval he most pines for is that of Molly Luther. The much-feared columnist, wielding an ivory-topped walking stick on account of her crippled left leg and surrounded by male acolytes, hisses, 'She may be tame now, Lewis, but will she turn into a slut like the last one?' In their confrontational scene, Molly and Elsa get a chance to give each other some stick. Molly pokes Elsa with hers, and demands to know if she's sleeping with Zarkan. Finally, Elsa loses patience with Molly's malice – she stubs out her cigarette in the ashtray in the columnist's lap and launches her own venomous volley. Snatching her stick – 'your magic wand' – she taps away at the braced leg and demands, 'Is this what you use to dig graves up with? Molly Luther, the Wicked Witch of the West!' Then the cane is flung out – followed by a limping Luther and her squirming sycophants.

After completing her duties on *Lylah*, the 'Witch of the West' headed east, flying to New York before catching a boat back to London. 'I'm returning by boat because one can carry more things that way,' she explained. 'I'm fair game for anything in the convenience food line. And it's been two years since I was last in America so I'm stocked up with a lot of new goodies. I spend a great deal of time in Fortnum & Mason asking, "What's come in from America?"'[9] But Coral wanted more than just convenience food from America: fed up with doing revivals and period plays, she told Margaret Harford of the *LA Times* that she now only wanted to do new plays, either on Broadway or in London: 'Of course I may be forced into doing another revival. But right now, I'm adamant… Most of all, I'd love to get a call from California saying, "Come back."'[10]

In keeping with its subject matter, *The Legend of Lylah Clare* was given a star-studded Hollywood premiere at Grauman's Chinese Theater. But all the glitz and glamour couldn't disguise its shabbiness, especially when the audience started laughing in all the wrong places (not that it had many right places to laugh). Critic Richard Schickel commented, 'The thing that's swell about this picture is the sobriety with which all concerned manage to keep their heads while we keep losing ours…it is not merely awful: it is grandly, toweringly, amazingly so… I laughed myself silly.'[11] His *Time* counterpart, however, was not amused: 'Instead of being outrageously funny, [it is] outrageously silly.'[12]

Coral herself later admitted the film was 'alarmingly bad',[13] while Aldrich conceded that he'd 'botched up' the film: 'I never got the script right, ergo I never got the picture right.'[14]

The Legend of Lylah Clare turned out to be the last film the unfortunate Kim Novak would make in America; it was also the last to be written by Hugo Butler who, as if cursed by the legend, died from a heart attack two months after it wrapped. Of course, like all tawdry trash, the film earned cult status, helped by the fact that, to date, it has never been released on video or DVD. Thanks to the internet and the watchfulness of camp followers of late-night American TV, clips of the main scene with Coral and Kim Novak have appeared on www.youtube.com.

But something else contributed to the film's limited shelf life: namely, lawyers ready and eager to launch legal action. With the portrayal of Molly Luther, Aldrich had made an enemy out of someone who was – unusually in showbiz – everyone's friend. For nearly 50 years, Radie Harris wrote the 'Broadway Ballyhoo' column for the *Hollywood Reporter*, and was a contributor to *Variety* and the *LA Times*. She was a contemporary of Walter Winchell, Louella Parsons and Hedda Hopper but outlived them all: she died in 2001, aged 96. Her innumerable celebrity chums included Vivien Leigh, Gregory Peck, Laurence Olivier and Katharine Hepburn, and she entertained them at the table permanently reserved for her at New York's Russian Tea Room. Another friend, actress Rosemary Harris, said: 'There was Hedda and Louella and Radie. But Radie was always the kind one.'[15] Kind, and unusually conventional: in the opening page of her memoirs, Harris 'confessed': 'I am a totally abnormal columnist. I have never smoked pot, sniffed cocaine, bedded with a lesbian or homosexual, nor had an abortion or gonorrhea.'[16] But tragedy had struck at an early age: when she was 14, Harris had her left leg amputated from the knee down, after a horse riding accident while she was at summer camp in Maine. For the rest of her life, she kept her false leg covered with elegant gowns, but was in permanent discomfort. Her father's friendship with the managing editor of the *New York Morning Telegraph* led to her first job in journalism.

Given that Molly Luther was a Hollywood gossip columnist, with a crippled *left* leg, Harris – not unreasonably – believed this fictitious fiend to be nothing but a monstrous defamation of her well-acknowledged, cuddlier character. She threatened Aldrich with legal action, but the squabble was kept out of the courts. Coral offered her own verdict on the matter: 'She hasn't got a leg to stand on.'[17] The incident gave rise to an amusing, but inaccurate, story that Harris had actually sued Coral for libel – and won. The apocryphal tale arose out of an incident that occurred after Harris made some disparaging remarks about Coral's performance in her next, even more infamous, film. According to Robin Anderson, 'Radie Harris was very, very scathing about Coral when it came out in New York, saying she wasn't acting, it was typecasting, and so on. But Coral never said a word. Some time later, John Schlesinger opened a new musical in London called *I and Albert*, and Coral and I went to the opening night [at the Piccadilly Theatre, 6 November 1972]. Afterwards, there was a party at The White Elephant Club in Curzon Street, so I escorted her. And there's Radie Harris sitting in the foyer, in a crinoline-type dress with three young men sitting on the floor. She looked up rather nervously and saw Coral, who smiled and said, "There you are, Radie – with the world at your foot."'[18] Eventually, Coral and the columnist put their relationship on a much friendlier footing, especially when Coral began to spend more time in America, when she was a regular guest at Harris's star-studded birthday parties in New York.

Controversy notwithstanding, Aldrich told Coral, 'I would just like you to know how very, very much I enjoyed working with you, how wonderful I think you are in LYLAH and that I hope we can work together again soon. Okay?'[19] It was more than 'okay', and Coral's wish for a call back to Hollywood would soon be granted – but not before she took time to catch up with what had been happening in the West End. What she saw made the excessive Hollywood shenanigans of *Lylah Clare* appear prosaic in comparison. In March, accompanied by Charles Gray, she went to the opening night of Peter Brook's production of Seneca's *Oedipus*, translated by Ted Hughes, at the Old Vic. This notorious rendition featured an incongruous piece of casting, where the 63-year-old John Gielgud was playing Oedipus, the son of Jocasta – played by Irene 'Hattie Abrams' Worth, who was actually ten years Gielgud's junior. On stage, the set's pillars and balconies were adorned with real-life caryatids. After Oedipus's blinding, Gielgud was handed a 'symbolic' pair of dark glasses to put on. Worth's Jocasta had to kill herself on a pyramid-shaped spike downstage – which was the cue for the entrance, on a covered carriage, of a 15-foot tall golden phallus, accompanied by a Dixie jazz band tooting out 'Yes, We Have No Bananas'. It was too much even for Coral's camp sensibility: as the music faded, a hushed audience – stunned into silence by what they had witnessed – heard a woman's voice, with just the faintest hint of an Austalian accent, announce to Charles Gray, 'It's no one we know.'[20]

In August 1968 – the same month that *The Legend of Lylah Clare* had its Hollywood premiere – the Associates And Aldrich Company began work on its next production and Coral was again on board. Aldrich was to direct Lukas Heller's adaptation of *The Killing of Sister George*, Frank Marcus's mildly shocking comedy. Aldrich and Heller had worked together on *Whatever Happened to Baby Jane?*, so it was no great surprise that their latest offering featured yet more unhappy harridans going at it hammer-and-tongues – even before filming began trade adverts were trailing 'The Story of Three Consenting Adults in the Privacy of Their Own Home'.

After a controversial debut in Britain, *The Killing of Sister George* had been a hit on Broadway, where Beryl Reid won a Tony for her performance as June 'George' Buckridge, the frumpy, alcoholic actress, who played a bucolic district nurse in a *Crossroads*-standard TV soap. But as with most Hollywood adaptations, Reid wasn't Aldrich's first choice for the film: he approached Angela Lansbury, who refused ('I didn't want to play a lesbian at that time. I wasn't mad about the play either.'[21]), then considered Bette Davis, who seemed keen: 'I have no qualms about playing a lesbian. I have been married four times so I think my track record speaks for itself.'[22] But when his diva dream-casting (of Davis, Olivia de Havilland and Stella Stevens) proved unattainable, Aldrich took a gamble on Reid. She admitted, 'I was surprised when I was offered this great big star part, because I am not what you would call "a film name". I thought they would probably choose someone else but Robert Aldrich had seen me in the play four times.'[23]

The film was a heavily bastardised version of Marcus's more genteel play – for example, the fortune-teller, Madame Xenia, morphed into Betty Thaxter, a high class prostitute. Reid's 'George' would eventually lose her job, her dignity and her girlfriend, Alice 'Childie' McNaught (Susannah York), to the crafty Mercy Croft, a smooth-talking, elegant foil to the hapless George. Coral later claimed that she'd never have taken the role of Croft if Philip Pearman had still been alive, offering the slightly bizarre explanation, 'It was just my mother or the money.'[24]

With her carefully coiffured hair, slim build (like Coral, Mercy was a fanatical weight-watcher) and backless dress, the widowed Mrs Croft was a remarkable antithesis to the stereotyped image of what one of 'those women' was supposed to look like – which was, of course, like the butch, tweedy George. Coral's Mercy remained a figure of fantasy for many women – after the film's release, the actress Amanda Barrie was an occasional visitor to the Gateways Club (where some of its most famous scenes were shot) and later admitted, 'I always rather hoped that Coral Browne would come down those stairs.'[25]

Mercy Croft's second encounter with 'George' and 'Childie' – quite late in the film – came in party scenes shot in the infamous Gateways Club, the tiny Chelsea watering hole which, for over 50 years, was an oasis in the desert of London's male-oriented, closeted gay scene for thousands of lesbians. These scenes, where 'George' and 'Childie' entertain club regulars with a rather lame cabaret turn as Laurel and Hardy, featured 80 real Gateways members. Coral's left eyebrow elevation goes into overdrive here, when Mercy takes her first look at the close-dancing, bum-hugging female couples – and George and Childie in their party drag.

Susannah York said she was unfazed by the smooching women: 'I wasn't shocked at all, but I was surprised and interested… We had a lot of laughs; there was a very good atmosphere.'[26] But, according to one of the Gateways regulars, Coral decided to keep herself to herself: '[she] appeared very superior and wouldn't mix with us at all. Underneath the stairs was a cloakroom. This cloakroom was turned into a dressing-room, and Coral Browne wouldn't move out of that dressing room until she was wanted for filming.'[27] However, one extra put Coral's aloofness down to a combination of a bad toothache and her customary stage fright, while another said, 'Coral just came down on the couple of days when she was going to do her scenes…[she] was very sweet when we got to speak…'[28]

According to York, there was some offscreen tension between her character's two 'rivals': 'They both saw me as someone they could speak to, as they didn't find it easy speaking to each other,' she said. 'Coral would phone most mornings very early before filming and grumble for 20 minutes. It took me a while to realise that I could leave the phone on the table and get on with my breakfast, just saying "yes" every now and again, because she only did monologues. She could be very caustic and Beryl was waspish sometimes, but they both had their hearts in absolutely the right place.'[29] Yet it was York who would soon be the target of Coral's caustic comments.

Before filming began, when asked whether she had any qualms about playing a lesbian role, Beryl Reid said, 'If you agree to play a part, you play a part. It's no good having qualms about it…'[30] However, she refused to do a sex scene involving George and Childie: 'Robert Aldrich, for reasons of his own – which proved to be right – thought there should be very sexy moments between George and Childie. I completely disagreed… I just couldn't do it. The thought made me sick. It may be silly, but that sort of physical contact, starkers with another woman frightened me to death.'[31]* So Aldrich turned to York and Coral, who reluctantly complied. Aldrich told Vito Russo that, long before he began filming, he had explained to York that the seduction scene had to be played as written. 'A year later, on the day we were to shoot the scene, she came to me in the morning and said, "I can't do it," and I said, "Susannah, I really want you to like me. But there's no fucking way you're not going to do this scene, or you'll just never work again…" So she did it.'[32] Reid claimed that, when it came the time to shoot the scene, Coral and York wouldn't come out of their trailers for four days; when they did, the scene had to be reshot many times. According to Coral, 'Susannah was very unhappy about it. I'd have been content to have a laugh between takes, and say, "Isn't it a funny way to earn a living?"'[33] York later admitted, 'I found it very difficult to do the semi-nude scene with Coral. But then I would have found it very difficult to do semi-nude scene with a man.'[34] Coral recalled, 'Susannah was feeling sick. She thought the whole thing was disgusting, so she was eating little grapes to stop herself from being sick.'[35] York explained the problems she faced: 'That scene was just two lines of exposition in the script. It said something like, "Alice is on the bed playing with her dolls. She drops them. Mrs Croft sits on the bed and the scene reaches a dramatic climax." That's all it was… You can't do a scene like that without trust. But over a period of two or three days you don't stay at the same level of trust. I worried horribly. It was a difficult period. Difficult for me and for Coral.'[36]

Difficult indeed: Coral, vexed to breaking point, gave vent to her frustrations in one of her most vituperative (recorded) outbursts: 'She's my MOST unfavourite nasty & makes Anna Massey seem breathtaking in altogether loveliness… Get angry Sarah [Badel] isn't working – especially when I have to put up with this dreadful, rude, mannerless, humourless, SELFISH little bitch!'[37] Aldrich had some sympathy for her: 'Susannah was a bitch to her

---

* Aldrich's longtime friend and associate, the composer Frank De Vol, was similarly disgusted with the prospect of the sex scene; he quit the production; and didn't work with Aldrich again until 1972, on *Ulzana's Raid*.

[Browne] because she [York] simply didn't want to do the scene. But in this particular sequence, Coral really, really helped her and therefore helped the movie through a very rough time.'[38] There must have been thousands of men and women who, if asked, would have jumped at the chance of enjoying a steamy clinch with Coral. How unfortunate that such a chance fell to one of the few who found the idea repugnant.

Aldrich tried to pour some oil on the deeply troubled waters. 'It is a true, rare, almost-never happening thing…a collective effort. You are all superb,' he told Coral. 'The picture is extraordinary and I think it is a piece of work we will ALL be proud of for a long long time. Onward and Upward!!!' (This phrase became his epitaph.)[39]

But, despite the best efforts of his actresses, Aldrich was far from satisfied with the rushes: 'When I saw the footage, she [York] agreed that it wasn't good enough. Finally, she asked me if she could do those scenes alone, without Coral on the set. It worked.'[40] Aldrich also brought Coral back to film her side of the scenes, alone and with a body double. In the final edit, the scene comprised footage from all four set-ups: Coral and Susannah York; Coral on her own; Susannah on her own; and Coral with the double.

Right from the film's inception, Aldrich had anticipated that this scene would cause trouble – although he didn't think it would be on the set: on the first day of shooting, he predicted, 'It is going to give a lot of self-styled critics a field day.'[41] The trailer for the film 'coming to a cinema near you this Christmas' featured almost the whole of the cut sex scene as a backdrop to clips which focused on anything remotely to do with 'down there' – even a scene where Childie pours water inside George's trousers. Interestingly, 'lesbian' was only said once throughout the entire film, as was 'dyke'.

Even before the film was fed to the critics, there were other obstacles to overcome. The sex scene – all 119 seconds of it – was expunged from the final version in several American states and the film was given an 'X' rating (revised to an R in 1972), despite Aldrich's offer to the censors to make more cuts. The British Board of Film Censors ordered a total of three minutes' worth of cuts, but many London cinemas decided to ignore this missive – as did the cinemas in, of all places, Berkshire. In America, Aldrich had trouble getting TV stations and newspapers to run advertisements for the film. He took legal action against the *LA Times* and Golden West Broadcasters but the lawsuit failed.

And so to the opening. Coral had attended a private screening, and said, 'I found it a particularly stark movie. I knew the play well but was completely unprepared for what I saw. The lesbian bit came out much stronger than I'd anticipated. After this one, I really don't know what they will be able to do on the screen.'[42] William Hall, reporting for *Photoplay Film Monthly*, said, 'We had no suspicion, the 600 of us invited for the world premiere of *The Killing of Sister George*…that when we left it would be in a stunned silence, that our palms would be sweating and that we would feel as if we had taken part in a kind of mass voyeurism.'[43] Mike Tomkies reported that York and her husband, Michael Wells, waited in the cinema until the audience had left. The stunned actress told him, 'I remember hoping that there would be nobody outside. I couldn't face anybody; couldn't talk to anybody… I was really shaking as I hung on his arm on the way out.'[44] Beryl Reid needed no support: in a full-length pink satin gown and ermine fur, she took the audience's applause and declared, 'It's an honest film.'[45]

It was greeted with brutally honest opinions. Late in the film, June Buckridge catches Mercy and Childie in flagrante, and unwittingly (and accurately) predicts, 'What a perfect little gem for the Sunday papers!' And not just the Sundays. Alexander Walker chided, '[Aldrich] would do better to involve himself, if he can, with the problems of more normal women, for on the evidence of recent pictures he is well on the way to acquiring an unenviable reputation as the screen's number-one hag-monger… Misses Reid, York and Browne…have been directed with an over-emphasis that would be better suited to cabaret revue… Aldrich…doesn't give any evidence of caring for his characters as suffering human beings – but only as elderly freaks.'[46] And, as for 'that' scene: the *New York Times* declared that it '…sets a special kind of low in the treatment of sex – any sex – in the movies now. Miss Browne approaches the breast with a kind of scholarly interest… like an icythologist finding something ambivalent that has drifted up on the beach… It is the longest most unerotic, cash-conscious scene between a person and a breast there has ever been on screen and outside a surgeon's office.'[47] *Variety* said that the sex scene 'is unnecessary, gratuitous, offensive and crude'.[48] In the *New Yorker*, Pauline Kael's review was headlined, 'Frightening The Horses.'[49]

Photoplay Film Monthly splashed its cover, 'The Killing of Sister George – Can Movies Go Much Further Than This?'[50] Felix Barker salivated, 'You may be disgusted. You may be licking your lips. You may pretend to be bored.

But ignore it you can't... [it] pushes the frontier of the permitted further than ever before!'[51]

John Russell Taylor believed it would have been better if Aldrich 'had gone the whole hog, Americanized the story and cast a high-powered trio like, say, Bette Davis, Joan Crawford and Stella Stevens...only Coral Browne sails satisfactorily through it all...'[52] Another view was that 'It is dislikable [*sic*] because it is pitiless, and in a grating, grinding way...the whole experience is inhuman...'[53]

An unrepentant Aldrich later said, '*Sister George* was maybe the best directing job I ever did.'[54] Derek Malcolm sounded a lone voice of critical approval: 'It is a remarkably funny film and ultimately a moving one too.'[55]

Any sympathy or goodwill was reserved for the film's three leading ladies: 'The considerable talents of all three have been crudely served by Robert Aldrich's gaudy and lumpish direction.'[56] There was nothing lumpish about Coral's acting: as Mercy Croft, she glided about the sets, stately as a galleon, while everyone else galumped around – and the critics were not oblivious: Judith Crist wrote, 'Coral Browne, as always a complete performer, transmits the ruthlessness of a woman confident of her control and calculated in her releases by the flicker of her eyelid, the merest movement of her mouth...'[57] Others concurred: 'To watch Coral Browne being carried along by her impeccable technique is also a pleasure';[58] Pauline Kael said, 'Coral Browne plays the seduced like Basil Rathbone at his most villainous – hooded cobra eyes, cruel mouth and all.';[59] 'Coral Browne, of course, is a joy as the cool BBC menace,'[60] came another, while William Hall said, 'For myself, I remember Coral Browne's magnetic, lust-filled eyes...'[61]

Aldrich rose above his own disappointment and hurt, and wrote to Coral, commiserating on her lack of an Oscar nomination: 'You should have been a shoo-in.'[62]

The shocking impact made by *The Killing of Sister George* cannot be over-estimated: June Buckridge brought lesbianism stomping and swearing into the general public consciousness, as did the Gateways scenes – where audiences began to see that Mercy Croft's interest in Childie might indeed be, as George puts it, 'anything but poetic'. Poetic was hardly the tone of some of Coral's correspondence once the film was released: 'I have been badgered by kinky women,' she complained. 'Too many ladies have been very persistent, very demanding, writing these sordid letters, and I don't like it. It really has been the most terrible experience. One lady came all the way from Canada, if you don't mind, and another from America and they arrived on the doorstep and started insulting the maid, shouting, "I'm going up!" – though I don't know what they thought they'd see when they got up.'[63]

The film brought woe unto others: in March 1969, Joseph Sasso, the manager of the Cheri Cinema, Boston, was sentenced to six months in prison and fined $1000 for screening the movie. At Sasso's trial, Judge Elijah Adlow declared, 'This is not good and does not appeal to decent people, but it is of great interest and causes laughs for morons that attend…one lesbian scene is unsightly and lewd.'[64] The film's notoriety continued to claim some unlikely victims: on 29 September 1975, eleven pupils, aged around 12 and 13, at the Grove girls' boarding school in Hindhead, Surrey, ran away: 'The walkout, it is believed, was a protest at not being allowed to watch the film *The Killing of Sister George* on television on Sunday night. Police said last night that they believed the girls were still together and not in any great danger.'[65] The runaways were found the next day, alive and well but rather damp after spending the night in a ditch, five miles from the school. They were sent to bed, apparently 'none the worse for their experience'.[66]

The Killing of Sister George and its subsequent controversies didn't harm Coral's film career as, in truth, there really wasn't much of one to harm. Besides, she was hardly a stranger to notoriety. Unfortunately, the leading man in her next stage venture was.

∗

For Coral, 1969 was indeed, as she said, 'The year for the kinky stuff!'[67] – hard on the heels of *The Killing of Sister George*, she agreed to star in the posthumous production of Joe Orton's last play, *What the Butler Saw*, with Sir Ralph Richardson, Stanley Baxter and Julia Foster, directed by Robert Chetwyn and produced by Oscar Lewenstein and Binkie Beaumont. Orton had been dead for a year when Coral was approached to play the part of Mrs Prentice – by which time, as she told Frith Banbury, she had considerable misgivings: 'Sir Turnip [Richardson] will be v slow and fuck it up so it won't run long and I HATED Mr [Robert] Chetwyn's "Importance" so don't fancy him either AND I've cooled on the play. It's hung fire too long.'[68]

The play is set in a private psychiatric hospital, presided over by the twisted Dr Prentice (Baxter), who triggers an insane chain of events when he tries to hide his attempted seduction of young secretary, Geraldine Barclay, from Mrs Prentice. She has upset his plans by returning early from a night out at a club 'primarily for lesbians' – she is exempt on the basis of her unsatisfactory relationship with her husband. Prentice's mantel as the biggest lunatic in the asylum is taken by the visiting psychiatrist, Dr Rance (Richardson). Even Winston Churchill did not escape Orton's mischief: we learn that Geraldine's step-mother has been killed by a very particular piece from a statue of the former Prime Minister, destroyed by a gas mains explosion. In Orton's script, it was his moulded manhood – but, for Ralph Richardson, the statuesque Churchill's missing member became a boner of contention, and so he decided it should be a cigar.*

Despite her reservations about the play, Orton's work had the same sort of appeal for Coral as her beloved Anouilh – the dark humour, the cynicism and frankness about the concept of romance and sexual relationships. When Hero tells the Countess in *The Rehearsal*, 'My talent lies at the bottom of a glass. Sadly, I can never remember which one,'[69] he doesn't sound too different from Mrs Prentice declaring, 'A woman doesn't like facing the fact that the man she loves is insane. It makes her look such a fool.'[70] Ruth Leon observed, 'In a way, Orton was the latter-day Wilde – high comedy. It was, at the time, very shocking. But it wasn't, for Coral, that much of a departure.'[71] Coral did admit, though, that, 'It's very difficult to learn his [Orton's] phraseology – he uses words in unusual places, for counterpoint.'[72]

By the time the final curtain descends on *What the Butler Saw*, all the characters, having survived the mayhem wrought by misdiagnosis and mistaken identity, are in a state of partial undress – and, in some cases, cross-dress. Typically, Coral decided that, even if the role demanded that she be *en déshabillée*, that was no excuse for inelegance: she insisted that the producers paid for Balmain to design her an £800 mackintosh and matching lingerie: 'I was in terribly good taste,' she said. 'I'd been on a diet for three years; oh yes,

---

* It wasn't the first time that Churchill had been at the centre of a theatrical controversy since his death: in 1967, the National Theatre wanted to stage Rolf Hochhuth's play *Soldiers*, which inferred that Churchill, to appease the Russians, had approved of the 1943 murder of the head of the exiled Polish government. The theatre's governing board agreed that the play was insulting to Churchill and deemed it unsuitable to be an NT production.

it was very nice underwear. Going on stage with nothing but your undies at my time of life, you've got to be wearing something very pretty and delicate, otherwise you look like old Frilly Lizzy, or a can-can girl.'[73] Coral's old friend, Angus McBean, took the stills of her clad in her expensive lingerie (one of the last plays he was to photograph) and, in 1981, used this image for one of his famous McBean Christmas cards.

It was Orton's lover, Kenneth Halliwell, who had originally suggested Coral for Mrs Prentice, a choice endorsed by Orton. Oscar Lewenstein favoured Ralph Richardson to play Dr Rance, but Orton had his misgivings – he believed the venerated actor was 'a good ten years too old'[74] and not possessed of the comic skills the part required; he believed Arthur Lowe would be better. He also favoured getting Binkie Beaumont on board as producer because, according to Lewenstein, 'Through Binkie, we thought we'd have a good chance of getting the sort of cast we required.'[75] However, Beaumont's first act as producer was to veto Lowe as Rance, and cast Stanley Baxter in the role. Lewenstein considered Baxter 'a good comedian but wrong in the same way that Kenneth Williams had been wrong for Truscott in *Loot*'.[76]

As it turned out, Orton would be proved right – but he didn't live long enough to enjoy his vindication: he was brutally murdered by Halliwell in August 1967. Orton had given Lewenstein the *What the Butler Saw* script just a week before his death, though it's doubtful this version would have been the final draft. Coral said: 'The greatest loss to the English theatre was the death of Joe Orton. He was a genius, in tune with today and only just getting started.'[77] The music played at Orton's funeral was The Beatles' 'A Day in the Life'. One of its verses had been inspired by the death, in a car accident in 1966, of John Lennon's friend Tara Browne – stepson of Coral's *My Sister Eileen* co-star, Sally Gray.

Ralph Richardson was enthusiastic about *What the Butler Saw* – he considered it to be 'Literature, beautifully written…flicks like Restoration comedy'.[78] As was his habit, Richardson had memorised the script by writing it out on large pieces of music paper, assembled on a music stand. Coral told Orton's biographer, John Lahr, 'He learned it in rhythm and turned over each page as if it were a musical score. Sometimes it was difficult for him to learn because he had no idea of what the words meant. He couldn't get nymphomaniac right because I don't think he'd heard of one of those. He would refer to it as "nymphromaniac".'[79] Richardson also found the set's bars and cages somewhat clumsy, so eschewed the door through which he was supposed to make his entrance, and instead came hurtling through a revolving door at the back of the set – which, according to Coral, 'confused the audience and made it seem like he'd come from outer space'.[80]

Richardson was, indeed, in alien territory. When the company embarked on a short provincial tour to Cambridge and Brighton, all hell broke loose. In Cambridge, Irving Wardle reported that 'a rich crop of disgusted letters from broad-minded mothers of two and farm stock dealers appeared in the *Cambridge News* which went off to tick off its own critic for failing to war the public against "trash".'[81] Then came a week in Brighton: Coral told John Lahr, 'I've never seen anything like it. He was attacked. People were writing him letters. Ralph got terribly depressed, terribly down, thinking he'd made a mistake. Taking a part in a "dirty" play. He replied to every one of those letters.'[82] Stanley Baxter remembered that 'there were old ladies in the audience not merely tearing up their programmes, but jumping up and down on them out of sheer hatred'.[83] (Brighton audiences had reacted with a similar outburst of outrage when 'local boy' Paul Scofield appeared as the gay character Charlie in Charles Dyer's *Staircase* at the Theatre Royal in 1966).

Orton's agent, Peggy Ramsay, saw the production in Brighton and said, 'nobody in the cast is enjoying the play, which never flows, and which doesn't seem to have any fun about it. Sir Ralph just seemed quite frozen in Act One.'[84] Peter Stenson also caught the show in Brighton: 'It was cast very high, with a lot of grand actors, and they played it like Oscar Wilde. And I don't think Joe Orton works if you play it like that…you have to play it very naturalistic for it to work.'[85] However, critic Jack Tinker saw the play during its Brighton run and hailed it as 'both cruel and devastatingly funny… Actresses with Coral Browne's impeccable sense of style and nuance are rare.'[86]

When *What the Butler Saw* opened at the Queen's Theatre on 5 March, things got worse for Richardson, as the barracking continued, with cries of 'Filth' and 'Give back your knighthood!' echoing around the gallery.[87] Coral said, 'It's quite monstrous. An actor can't answer back. It's like throwing a stone at a little dog.'[88] Lewenstein had no regrets about the casting; he said that Richardson 'brought a quality to the mad Inspector Rance the like of which we will not see again. I do not think casting him was a mistake.'[89] Ruth Leon observed, '[Richardson] could do very off the wall stuff, but the level of zaniness involved in Orton was very hard for him – because he was so mad that the combination of Orton madness and Richardson madness was too much.'[90]*

Orton, of course, would simply have loved it all.

The play's reviews were decidedly mixed, on a 'love it or loathe it' basis – most veering towards the latter. Philip Hope-Wallace witnessed the audience reaction on the opening night: 'This was something like the pattern of the old style first night: a piece received at first with loud guffaws by the sophisticated stalls…and which finally incurred the unfriendly groans of those arbiters of theatrical taste, the Gallery First Nighters. They found it all trivial and indecent, a charge which might well be substantiated, though there were many pleasant and compensating sallies of Wildean wit…but this is dubious farce overstretched.'[91] John Russell Taylor deemed it to be 'a very bad play…no one else but Joe Orton would have written a play that was bad in quite this way',[92] while *The Times* sniffed, 'The general effect is vulgar in the wrong way…the play gets the Whitehall farce treatment.'

One critic who spoke out in favour of the play was Frank Marcus – as author of *The Killing of Sister George*, no stranger to controversy himself. Under the headline, 'A Classic Is Born', he wrote, 'Some 18 months after his tragic death, Orton managed to antagonise a section of the audience so much that the final moments of the play were acted – valiantly, it should be said – to an accompanying rumble of opposition. Coral Browne balanced quite brilliantly anxiety with poise… Unfortunately, the marvellous last moments of the play were brutally spoiled by the audience.'[93] And when it closed, Marcus again leapt to the play's defence: 'Last night the curtain fell on the final performance…the failure of this play raises some important questions. Never in recent years has a play been more brutally damaged by a first-night audience. Not content with bleating at the end, they interrupted constantly during the crucial last 10–15 minutes, thus rendering the denouement incomprehensible. The notices were predominantly hostile…'[94] In another truly Ortonesque twist, *The Killing of Sister George* opened in London cinemas during the run of *What the Butler Saw* – prompting one wag to report that, 'Miss Coral Browne will be unable

---

* The play did seem to bring with it a curse of mental illness: in 1995, while appearing in the National Theatre's production, Nicola Pagett started behaving erratically; her condition was ultimately diagnosed as acute manic depression. During this time, she developed an obsession with – of all people – Alastair Campbell, Tony Blair's bellicose press secretary.

to attend the premiere tonight of the film in which she plays a lesbian as she will be busy at the theatre playing a nymphomaniac.'[95]

Despite the tribulations of *What the Butler*, Coral was still keen to continue appearing in new plays. She returned to the stage with a slightly safer subject – royal scandal – in *My Darling Daisy*, directed by her friend Frith Banbury and written by Christopher Taylor (Banbury's longtime companion). Based on a book by Theo Lang, the play concerned the Countess of Warwick's attempt to raise £100,000 by threatening to publish 200 love letters written to her by Edward VII when he was Prince of Wales.

Coral made many suggestions to Taylor for rewrites and adjustments in several key speeches, especially when it came to what she called 'Daisy Warwick's "moment" – the moment of TRUTH...she loved, she gave and wasn't a paid tart. Come what may Daisy is your heroine and this speech is of vast importance. It must be about HER...'[96] Taylor endeavoured to take Coral's suggestions on board. But then there was disagreement about some of the casting: Coral wanted their mutual chum Charles Gray to play the male lead, Arthur Du Cros MP, but Banbury did not agree. Coral wrote to him about her concerns: 'The suggestions for Du Cros like Sean Connery, John Mills etc wouldn't do it and the people who might are unknown and it leaves me up on that stage trying to carry the play like Atlas with a part not capable of doing so. I love you so deeply and value your friendship and loyalty more than you will ever know – but now I can see clearly there is no point in doing what I thought I was capable of doing and that was to "agree to disagree"... The rehearsals would be misery, our friendship would suffer under the strain and if you lost money I would feel utterly guilty...what I feel is deep in my bones and I can't talk myself out of the deep rooted conviction that Daisy is not right for me to do it as it is... I'm upset – very – at having to write this.'[97]

The cast featured fellow Australian émigré Lloyd Lamble, who reminded Coral that he, too, had started his stage career in a Gregan McMahon production (*Fresh Fields*), and that they had met in McMahon's office. Coral replied that this was hardly surprising since, as she delicately put it, the director was 'fucking the arse off her' at the time. *My Darling Daisy* also featured a young actor who was involved with Coral: Christopher Cazenove. A mutual friend of both of them confirmed, 'She fell deeply in love with Christopher. She was completely besotted about him. She suddenly turned into a sort of gypsy teenager... She was dotty about him.'[98] Other friends correctly predicted it would end in tears:

Patrick White told Ronnie Waters, 'Poor Widow Pearman with a young lover: She'll have it coming to her.'[99] And, although the relationship was indeed short-lived, Coral was 'dotty' enough about Cazenove to name him as one of the main co-beneficiaries of a will (subsequently revised) she made in 1969.

My Darling Daisy wouldn't bring her any lasting happiness either: its problems continued on the provincial tour. 'We had to get a new leading man – we had an Irish actor who failed to do what the play needed,' explained Frith Banbury. 'Then we had dear Robert Flemying, who I loved dearly, but it was not his best performance – he only had a very short time to rehearse it. He took the part after two weeks on the road and came into London with it.'[100]

When the production opened at the Lyric Theatre, one notice, setting the general tone for others, got straight to the point: '*My Darling Daisy* creaks.'[101] Herbert Kretzmer complained: '[the] direction is slow and stodgy…none of it is much fun…it provides an undistinguished and dullish evening.'[102] Others agreed: 'The author's mistake has been to suppose that because there was drama in the real life incidents there must necessarily be drama in a stage version of them.'[103] Robert Ottaway waspishly observed, 'The whole thing is so full of deals and contracts that the actors could be fired and their roles taken over by their agents.'[104] And there was no let-up from Coral's old *bête noire*, Milton Shulman, who believed that 'Coral Browne seems far too hard and calculating to make her credible as the woman who captivated the simple heart of Edward VII.'[105] In response to Shulman's review, a *Standard* reader, Michael Johnson, wrote to the paper, defending her: 'Nowhere in the notices for the play can I find any kind of assessment of Miss Coral Browne's performance. I have long felt that few critics can differentiate between a good part and a good performance, but one would have had to be blind or demented not to be dazzled by the brilliance, the warmth, the energy, the discipline and the beauty of Miss Browne's performance. It was a lesson to every actor, and every drama student in London should have been directed to the Lyric Theatre.'[106] Coral kept several copies of this in her cuttings scrapbook.

In fact, some reviewers had admired her performance: 'Coral Browne is deliciously beguiling and naughty as the Countess. She sweeps through the part with great aplomb, enjoying some of the best lines in the play'[107] But the play was doomed: after a run of two weeks, it closed on 4 July. Coral told a reporter, 'God knows what makes a success in the West End these days.'[108] Whatever it was, *My Darling Daisy* didn't have it. 'It couldn't have been more of a flop, really. It was a disaster,' Frith Banbury admitted later. 'However, it didn't seem to ruin our relationship.'[109]

And their friendship also withstood another professional disappointment. Later that year, Coral finally got her long overdue invitation to star in a National Theatre production: a revival of George Bernard Shaw's *Mrs Warren's Profession*, directed by Ronald Eyre. It was a play that she and Banbury had planned to stage several years before, on Broadway and in the West End. Coral was adamant about who she wanted to play Mrs Warren's daughter, Vivie: Julie Christie. She told Banbury, 'I don't want to do Mrs Warren with anyone else – as when one gets the idea of someone like Julie – who would be so utterly right in EVERY way – it's difficult to scratch around and become interested in any other young women.'[110] Lew Grade was also interested in making it for television. But Christie, in the wake of her huge screen successes *Darling* and *Dr Zhivago*, was a 'hot property' in the movies and had film commitments until December 1968. And, as Christie's agent, Olive Harding, told Banbury, 'What Julie will want to be doing by 1969 is anyone's guess. There are times when she says to me that she wants to live an ordinary family life by then – whatever that means!'[111] After many months of fruitless negotiation, the idea was dropped. And at the time the National production was mooted, Frith Banbury also had other commitments.

In Shaw's play, written in 1893, Kitty Warren's profession is revealed as being the madam of a number of high-class European brothels; she uses the income from this to raise and educate her fatherless daughter Vivie, a 'modern young lady' in England. The play was banned by the Lord Chamberlain because of its subject matter, and was not performed until 1902 at the members-only New Lyric Club; its first public performance in London was not until 1926. It was one of three plays which Shaw labelled *Plays Unpleasant*, because they forced audiences to face up to unpleasant issues, such as prostitution and slum housing.

Shaw had assembled a deceptively genteel arena wherein Kitty and her daughter, Cambridge-educated, cigar-smoking Vivie could slug it out over their respective moralities: Vivie says, 'I like working and getting paid for it'; Mrs Warren declares, 'I must have work and excitement' – a motto also appropriate for Coral.

Ronald Eyre said, 'The sort of plays I like directing are those in which the stage is like a gladiatorial arena where the actors carve up their ground and stand on it and compete… Most of the best English plays need casts of individualists.'[112] And Coral was nothing if not an individualist.

Eyre decided to follow Shaw's stage directions to the letter, including the arrangement of the prop furniture. Now there was just the matter of getting the right cast. According to the actor and critic Jonathan Cecil, 'Coral wanted someone who could stand up to her as Vivie – she said of one of the suggested female juvenile actresses, "I'll have her for breakfast".'[113] Less easily consumed was 'Bantam Bette' Badel, who was duly cast as Vivie: 'I was doing a two-hander with George Baker at Guildford – we'd been on tour. Ronnie Eyre came to see me in it; I think Coral recommended me.'[114]

For once, Coral abandoned her diet discipline: 'I'd like her to be massive,' she revealed. 'For once in my life during rehearsals, I've abandoned any sort of controlled diet and I've already put on about 12 pounds. Everyone would be very happy if I put on three stone, but they know what they can do. I suppose I could really do with a couple of extra chins but then I might lose a few friends, and besides, I've got to live with myself.'[115]

It was a heavyweight role for her in every respect: 'Ronnie's tried wonderfully to get me away from myself and it's been bloody hard work all round because Mrs Warren is just about my first shot at a character part. She's like a great big pigeon, all puffed out, wobbling along. It's interesting because she's got to be vulgar but at the same time have a certain amount of Continental good taste – you know, sort of *chic* gone terribly wrong.'[116] Coral's Kitty Warren was certainly no English rose: she was a glorious, swaggering, gravel-voiced galleon, with dropped aitches and all.

The production opened at the Old Vic on 30 December 1970 and Coral's first – and only – stint as a 'National Theatre player' was an unqualified triumph. In this production, Roddy McDowall said she gave 'one of the ten greatest female performances I ever saw. She had all of her experience, all of her elegance, all of her tawdriness, all of her bawdiness, all of her fear and anguish to put into that role, and she made it just spin.'[117] He wrote to her, 'To this observer, your Mrs Warren is full of strength, wry humor, invention, elegance, sensual distinction, world weariness, humanity and pain; tinged with the common but never vulgar – deliciously available toward sentimentality but never wallowing within. It is riddled with "moment to moment" involvement (a most difficult accomplishment with Shaw because most performers sink with the volume of his ideas and words) – laced with surprise and floats upon lively regret. It is a vibrant study in opposites and at its conclusion one longs to see her in the environs of Ostend, Brussels, Vienna and Budapest. One cares for the survival. It is a definitive interpretation, dear Coral.'[118] Jonathan Cecil said, 'She was absolutely perfect for the part; you could imagine her as a society lady – *and* as a brothel madam.'[119] Simon Callow declared the production to be one of 'a series of brilliant achievements by great soloists who had come to work with the company'.[120]

The critics agreed: *The Times* said, 'There could be no greater opening contrast than between Miss Badel's coldly virginal graduate and Miss Browne's grimly overdressed madame with her raspingly vulgar address.'[121] The *Daily Mail* declared the production to be 'a glowing ornament to our National Theatre',[122] while the *Guardian* said, 'Miss Browne is regal, harsh, blighting and as handsome as hell in velour and broderie anglaise.'[123] The combination of Browne and 'Bantam Bette' was perfect: 'the central duet between Mrs Warren and her daughter, Vivie, is splendidly played by Coral Browne (the foremost wicked lady of the British stage) and Sarah Badel.'[124] The *Daily Telegraph* praised both leading ladies: 'Coral Browne as a steely-eyed virago with the appearance of a duchess and the rapacious sentimentality of a sob-sister… As Vivie, Sarah Badel rises to her finest performance.'[125]

Mrs Warren's Profession stayed in the National Theatre company repertory until 1 July 1971, although it was limited to just two performances on Thursdays. And, despite the universal acclaim, there wasn't even a sniff of an award for Coral's performance.

With only two shows a week, Coral was able to break her own rule about not mixing filming with theatre. She made a short documentary, *On Reflection: Coral Browne on Mrs Patrick Campbell*, broadcast on LWT on 14 February, a discussion with Caryl Brahms about the life and influence of another great stage diva. On 9 April, she began recording the television version of *Mrs Warren's Profession* for BBC2. And there was even a rare film role – in *The Ruling Class*, Peter Barnes's own adaptation of his successful black comedy, with Peter O'Toole and Alastair Sim, directed by Peter Medak. O'Toole himself optioned Barnes's play for the screen, and took the lead as the severely deranged Jack, who becomes the 14th Earl of Gurney when the 13th Earl's evening hanging ritual goes fatally wrong. Coral played the sexually frustrated Lady Claire Gurney, aunt-by-marriage to Jack. Lady Gurney takes Jack's eccentricities in her stride and later finds the young loony strangely attractive. But, by the time she is about to consummate her passion for Jack, he's decided he's actually Jack the Ripper, and she becomes his first victim. Being murdered in movies was now becoming almost routine for Coral – and she also complained that, in agreeing to make the film while still doing *Mrs Warren*, 'I nearly killed myself.'[126] When it was released in 1972, *The Ruling Class* died a bit of a death, despite being Britain's main entry at the Cannes Film Festival and winning accolades for its supporting players: 'Rarely have I seen so many star performances in one supporting cast.'[127] One critic said that O'Toole 'is coming to look more and more like a bloodhound with a spectacularly bizarre past.'[128] Paul D Zimmerman went a bit further: '*The Ruling Class* might just be the most odious, trying film ever aimed at the British aristocracy...without any redeeming wit from the screenplay by Peter Barnes, who tries without success to write black comedy like the late Joe Orton. The cast plays with the pluck of the doomed Light Brigade...only Coral Browne's elegantly erogenous matron and Arthur Lowe's W C Fieldsian butler survive Medak's dermatological close-ups and overheated style.'[129] Overlong and overstated, the film has not withstood the test of time.

More successful for Coral were her performances in the television adaptations of *Mrs Warren's Profession*, with Robert Powell and Penelope Wilton, and *Lady Windermere's Fan*, featuring Sîan Phillips. Her performance in the latter was, she felt, one of her best, and was much-praised: 'Poised to the last syllable, superb in irony and disdain...it was a performance which Wilde himself would surely have applauded.'[130] Sadly, anyone who didn't see the broadcast will never know how good it was: in their infinite wisdom, someone at the BBC decided to wipe the master tape. Coral was distraught when she was told: 'They went down into the cellars or wherever they go to rub off a few tapes and they rubbed that one off by mistake. And no copy. I was upset because it's not often I do something that I feel is all right.'[131] In 1986, she got some vestige of revenge: when she was asked to participate in a gala evening, to celebrate the BBC's 50th anniversary at New York's Museum of Broadcasting on 17 November, she revealed the fate of the recording, saying, 'So now I truly can say it was the greatest performance of my career and no one has any proof to the contrary.'[132]

During the taping of *Lady Windermere's Fan*, Coral, as was her wont, befriended one of the younger actresses: Liza Goddard, then best-known for playing second fiddle to a kangaroo in the Australian children's series, *Skippy*. Goddard was understandably nervous: 'I worked with quite a few ladies like that – Sonia Dresdel was the same and her reputation was horrific – I did *Arms and the Man* and *The Importance of Being Earnest* with her. They were all very formidable, those women. But Coral was lovely to me; I never had any trouble at all.

'She was always so glamorous; she'd arrive at ten o'clock in the morning, at the Acton Hilton, which is not the most salubrious of places…always immaculate, with the shoes to match the bag, the gloves and the hat. She and Sîan Phillips wore something different every day – Sîan mostly wore Yves St Laurent and Coral wore Jean Muir and Chanel. When we were in the studio, Sîan and Coral never sat down in their frocks; they didn't want to crease their dresses. They called me "Chunky"…Coral and Sîan were the first really glamorous women I worked with – it's not just the clothes, it's something inside, and the way they are. And it's hard work being glamorous – it takes a lot of effort to look that good all the time.'[133] One of Coral's older chums, Charles Gray, was also in the production – and unwittingly caused a spat between her and another cast member and old ally, James Villiers, a veteran of the 1956/7 New York *Troilus and Cressida*, who had also just played Coral's son in *The Ruling Class*. According to Liza Goddard, 'Jimmy had taken Charles out drinking one night in some dive, and he'd [Charles] picked up some leather boy. He was found in the street by the milkman the next morning, with a gash in his head. It needed 16 stitches. So there was a terrible frost in the rehearsal room that day. Coral blamed Jimmy, you see, and she wouldn't let him speak to Charles again.'[134]

Unlike *Lady Windermere's Fan*, the recording of *Mrs Warren's Profession* survived, and in 2006, was released on DVD. After its original broadcast on BBC2 on 3 October 1972, Leonard Buckley of *The Times* enthused: 'Cedric Messina's production was a model of how a classic should be transferred… Coral Browne as Mrs Erlynne…elegant, composed, yet somehow pathetic, she was everything that Shaw could have wished for the part… I confess that I wept for the tender beauty, the humour and the sadness…'[135] *Variety* praised '…a sterling cast of which the standout was the veteran Coral Browne. In appearance, movement, inflection, she offered a stellar rendition of the woman with a past for whom the gents all panted – and the ladies all knocked.'[136]

Another critic knocked some other ladies: 'Other actresses, among whom Maggie Smith shall remain nameless, should take a long look and painlessly absorb a few hints on how not to go over the top on the tube.'[137]

'This is Mrs Vincent Price'

1972–1979

The Seventies had started well for Coral, with some of her greatest professional triumphs – but, in many aspects of her life and career, she had reached an impasse. Since Philip's death, she had known passion and attraction, but not wholeheartedly reciprocated love and devotion from one man. And there was still the constant presence of 'Mother' – ever crabby and ever critical. 'Do you know my mother still doesn't understand me?,' she told a reporter. 'She doesn't understand any part of my life. She wouldn't miss seeing me act for anything in the world, but she thinks it's just a lovely life where you wear a lot of lovely clothes and make it up.'[1] Concerned about her future, Coral consulted a man she had become acquainted with in 1962 when participating in a 'novelty' feature for *Tit-Bits* magazine. A group of actors, including Donald Sinden and Coral, had agreed to have prints of their right palms read by 'hand analyst' Mir Bashir, who then rang to convey his findings.

Certain revelations had some resonance for Coral: Bashir told her, 'When you were about 26 to 28 there was a lot of muddled emotion, and a heartache.' She refuted the claim that there had been any heartache – but it was certainly during this period of her life that she was ending her relationship with her female lover and becoming involved with Firth Shephard. Next, Bashir said: 'At the age of 18–19, there was quite a strain mentally and emotionally. Some conflict with relatives.' She agreed with this assessment – at that age, she was abandoning her art studies and taking up acting as a profession. He then told her that, 'At 19 you would behave like a woman of 28. From 27 to 28 there was a very definite step forward.' Again, Coral concurred with this: in 1941, at the age of 28, *The Man Who Came to Dinner* had made her a West End star.[2]

She was sufficiently impressed by what Bashir had told her then that in late 1971 she asked him for another palm print 'reading'. In hindsight, many of his predictions were spookily prescient: 'From early '72, especially 3 May a new phase promises a lot of travel… Old person, a new emotional link-up…important change may go live in another place – still active in different way. VERY active four year period. Happy period is next 18 months. Between 62 and 65 do job in far off place – much money – Always work, never retire – work will come but quality DIFFERENT between 60 and 63. Near 61 money and old person will have died. Likely live up to 84. 1972 Love & affection – 10–12 years good.'[3]

This was all very well – however, it was not immediately obvious where all this work, love and happiness would come from. Coral had some idea of the sort of new play she wanted to do – one that was about 'The rich jet-set life. Nobody's writing about it. And funny. I like a laugh a minute, one on every page. But it's easier said than done.'[4] She claimed, 'I have three stage plays which I'm considering at the moment. I get offers all the time… It's a matter of considering what's best for me and what's best financially. The play's the thing. It's no good having a whacking great role if the play's no good. I don't ever plan to retire. But then acting is the sort of profession where one can be retired and not know it…'[5]

The prospects for staving off such involuntary and unwitting retirement did not look promising: she was not being offered any new television dramas or comedies, and the British film industry didn't have much to offer the 'divine monsters' of her theatrical era. Indeed, that breed of 'divine monster' was becoming an endangered species. On stage and screen, Coral was being usurped by a new generation of actresses who, at that time, were not of the 'grand dame' persona: Glenda Jackson, Eileen Atkins, Maggie Smith, Claire Bloom, Sîan Phillips, Judi Dench, Vanessa Redgrave, Helen Mirren and Diana Rigg. In the early Seventies, some of these names would appear most frequently on any producer's casting wish-list – and certainly a good deal higher up the list than the name of 'Coral Browne'.

It was symptomatic of a bigger problem: between 1968 and 1971, British-made films had dropped by a quarter and British studios were struggling to attract American investors. By the early Seventies, the British film industry consisted primarily of Ken Russell's pomps, big-screen versions of popular TV comedy series (*Dad's Army*, *Up Pompeii!*, *Please, Sir!*, *Mutiny on the Buses*), the *Carry On* series, which did what it said on the label, and James Bond capers. Elsewhere, explicit sex and violence was now *de rigueur*, from *Performance* to *A Clockwork Orange*. It was the era in which Joseph Losey and Lindsay

Anderson made their last British feature films; John Schlesinger shone a rare ray of light, with *Sunday, Bloody Sunday*, as did Nicolas Roeg's disturbing *Don't Look Now*. But, by the end of the decade, Schlesinger and Losey were among the film-makers who put their names to a 'Save Our Industry' open letter, as British-made movies playing in the cinema slumped to an all-time low. Coral believed she knew the root cause of the industry's problems: 'The worst things that happened to the acting profession were the Actors' Studio and the candid camera,' she said. 'Now they expect actors to have pockmarks and scratch a lot. Elegance is gone… I don't believe audiences want kitchen sink stuff. I should like to do a play about the jet set – rich, well dressed and elegant. I wouldn't even mind if we had to send it up.'[6]

But, ever-astute, Coral was aware of other obstacles. 'Actresses change physically every five years,' she explained. 'First you are the "anyone for tennis" ingénue, then at 25 you're too old for tennis; at 30 you're a young mother with a child, and at 35 you've a teenage daughter. And so on. Actresses are put into categories in the way that actors aren't.'[7] And she knew which category she fell into: 'I think I suggest, in character, a certain sexuality. I'm not what you might call an English rose nor are the roles I play. I'm more full-blown in many ways, and I represent a certain kind of woman. I mean, it's rather difficult for producers to find ladies of a certain age whom the audience can believe in as capable of performing sex in a way which isn't revolting. Audiences tend to think that anybody over 50 can't be having any of the other and should therefore be put in cold storage.'[8]

Despite everything, Coral was good pals with some of the 'competition', including Maggie Smith and Eileen Atkins. 'She liked Jean [Marsh] more than she liked me,' said Atkins. 'She thought Jean was glamorous and I wasn't; she liked people who were glamorous. And I think she was irritated by my refusal to do the whole "actress" bit. But then she was of that Binkie Beaumont era – and she was a very "Binkie Beaumont" type of person, if you know what I mean. They were all very bitchy. She was a wonderful mixture, there could be this amazing bitchy streak, and then she could be very maternal. I never thought she was beautiful – she *made* herself into this beauty.'[9] And, according to Charles Gray, another of the 'competition' passed muster: 'Helen Mirren thinks she knows you already and is keen to meet you. She's <u>OK</u>. <u>Very</u>. I like her a lot and she can go in the good book with Badel & P [Penelope] Wilton and is quite as different from them as they are from one another. She has a disturbing dress sense (gypsy musical comedy with platform shoes) but a nice style everywhere else…'[10]

When she got the chance, Coral still took her holidays in Spain, as she and Philip had always done, but her destination of choice was now Ibiza, an island which increasingly attracted stage and screen stars. According to Peter Burton, secretary (and sometime ghost writer) to Santa Eulalia resident Robin Maugham, 'Everyone met up at Sandy's Bar, run by a gregarious Irishman called Sandy Pratt. On any given day, Sandy's Bar was more like a theatrical green room than a Spanish bar, as the likes of Diana Rigg, Terry-Thomas, Lionel Bart, Denholm Elliott and Leslie Phillips met and swapped the latest gossip.'[11] Coral, of course, was a most welcome addition to this colony comprised of her peers – but it was the resort's resident peer of the realm who could be more of a drama queen than the lot of them put together. When Coral was invited to Maugham's villa for dinner with Denholm and Susie Elliott, Maugham initially left his secretary to entertain the guests, claiming that he had had 'a small heart attack'. However, when the gathering was in full swing, a flush-faced Maugham appeared, announced he was feeling much better, and perfunctorily dismissed Burton to his room. 'He was not best pleased that his party could continue to go with a swing even though he was not present. The sound of our laughter had been the last straw.'[12]

At home, however, there was considerably less swinging. 'I don't entertain,' said Coral. 'I don't like being left with a lot of washing up to do at two o'clock in the morning. Anyway, I hate social obligations. I'm known as being rather anti-social. When my husband was alive, we used to have at least one dinner party a week – he cooked… I have five or six real friends, but sometimes six months go by without seeing any of them – still they're there and there's never any question of the friendship.'[13] Among the 'real' friends was John Schlesinger: he recognised that Coral was, as he aptly described, 'something of an acquired taste'[14] – but she was very much to his taste, with her wit, her style and (as he later discovered first-hand) her professionalism when it came to the job in hand. In London and LA, they enjoyed lunches, dinners, parties and first-night openings, and maintained a regular correspondence, full of gossip and goodwill, that continued from the late Sixties (when Schlesinger was spending more time in Hollywood) until Coral's death.

Her friendship with Schlesinger brought added benefits, in the form of new pals such as his long-term partner, Michael Childers, and Noel Davis, the actor-turned-casting director. Caroline Cornish-Trestrail, who worked for Schlesinger for more than a decade, said Coral and Davis 'just sparked off each other; Noel had such wit, he just knocked you sideways – he'd say things like, "My dear, if she had any more brains, she'd be half-witted."'[15] It was common knowledge in the business that Davis marked up his own copy of *Spotlight*, the actor's directory, with comments next to each actor's photo; they could range from the mild, 'Should be useful ten years from now,' to the malevolent: 'She's death, death, death!'[16] 'A lot of people thought he was "Mrs John Schlesinger", but he wasn't,' explained Caroline Cornish-Trestrail. 'Once, Noely was taken ill with kidney stones and John rushed him off to St Mary's, groaning. Afterwards, he came back [to Schlesinger's home] and never really left. And he would act as a sort of host for John's dinner parties – he was such a court jester. John would be in the most terrible pit of depression: and one word from Noel, and he'd be tipping over.'[17] Eileen Atkins observed that, 'His sarcasm, delivered with the most precise timing, appealed to John's ribald sense of humour.'[18] However, Schlesinger's biographer, William J Mann, maintained that Davis was often insulting to women and resented Schlesinger's boyfriends, especially the long term companions, such as Michael Childers.

Swapping *bons mots* with friends was all very well – but it did nothing to assuage Coral's dissatisfaction with certain aspects of her life. In 1972, she decided to ring the domestic changes and give her home a radical makeover – she decided it had become 'a period piece'.[19] Jill Melford disagreed: 'She had a wonderful flat in Eaton Place, which was very theatrical and very elegant – full of antiques and wonderful things. But then some disaster happened; she decided she'd reinvent herself and had the whole thing done up as modern. She wanted a change – she was obviously unhappy – and the whole environs changed.'[20] Coral was inspired by her friend Jean Muir's sparsely-furnished flat behind the Royal Albert Hall – and the dressmaker's philosophy applied to life and work: 'Just as I begin a dress from the proper proportions of the body and resist additions, I have learnt to simplify my life in all directions,' she said.[21] Muir's home was decorated with 'the many shades of white…her shiny white vinyl floor and walls hung with interestingly textured papers and fabrics, but then painted over in ivories and palest creams'.[22] Jane Mulvagh said that the effect of this was to turn the flat into an 'antiseptic abode',[23] where visitors had to remove their shoes so as not to mark the white rubber floor. Apparently, this was all very much to Coral's liking; she decided she wanted something similar and called on bespoke interior designer Robin Anderson: 'She came to me through a mutual friend of ours, Johnny Gallagher –he'd seen some of my work – and out of the blue I got this phone call. She said, "I hear you're very good – and very expensive." I replied, "Oh, Miss Browne the actress! Congratulations on your film" – I'd seen *The Killing of Sister George* – and she said, "Don't sweet talk me, come and see me." So I arrived, and she had this horrendous Victorian-style place. She told me, "They're all doing it, dear. They're all going off in fucking space ships, so I want a space ship."'[24]

Like all visitors to Eaton Place, Anderson couldn't help but notice Coral's impressive collection of nearly forty sphinxes and Egyptian obelisks. 'She said, "I like me sphinxes – I must have been Cleopatra, spending a lot of time on the Nile on a barge…" I said, "Cleopatra, dear? Instead of barging up the Nile, she would have preferred to have been feluccad." So Coral replied, "Very feluccan funny, dear."' And it went on like that all the time – it was an absolute joy to work for her.'[25] As part of Coral's new modern minimalist motif, Anderson housed many of the Egyptian collection in two obelisk-shaped acrylic towers, either side of a glass coffee table, supported by four Sphinx figurine 'legs'. When Coral decided they were too brown, Robin Anderson improvised by applying some black boot polish. '"What are you doing?," she said. "Turning them into a minstrel show!?"'[26] According to Anderson, this new coffee table would become a yardstick by which Coral would, literally, measure the efficiency of her maid, Mrs Edwards: 'After she'd been in, Coral would check the coffee table position. She'd say to me, "I've got me measure, dear – she's just dusted – and if it's an inch out…after all, an inch is important to a girl."'[27]

Coral was keen to show off her new 'space ship', which cost £17,000 to 'launch'. A visiting journalist enthusiastically reported that, 'The apartment is stunning, with mirrored walls and a parrot green colour scheme. There is a tall plant against the wall. She says there are two worms in the soil. "Adrienne Corri gave them to me. From her garden."'[28] However, Jill Melford, an accomplished interior designer herself, was less impressed: 'I walked in: it was stark and white – and I said, "I get the feeling you're going to perform an appendectomy here." Because all the goodies had gone, and all sorts of pretty things and memorabilia, which were all very Coral. And all of a sudden, we were in this operating theatre!'[29] But Coral was happy, and she became good chums with the creator of her 'surgery' – though, sometimes, their friendship was tested.

'I'd just done Coral's flat and Roy Miles, the gallery owner, was giving a party,' recalled Robin Anderson. 'He wanted her to come for a drink, but Coral and I were having dinner with John Schlesinger. "Oh, it would be *marvellous* if you could bring her," Roy said. So I asked Coral – I told her it would only be half an hour – and she said, "Oh yes...Gloria Gallery wants us to go for a drink, does he?" So we went, and Roy was quite effusive over Coral when we first arrived – but then he was swanning around, and there was Miss Browne sitting on the sofa, with a face like thunder, sitting between two very young men looking at her with total adoration. Eventually, I did say to Roy, "Look, you asked Coral to come here, I think you should make some sort of fuss over her." So he went over to her and said, "Oh Coral, *there* you are – a rose between two thorns!" To which she replied, "Yes dear, and I'm waiting to see which one has the bigger prick..." And with that, she got up and walked out.'[30]

Such social slights would soon be forgotten, as some of Mir Bashir's predictions started to transpire. In 1972, Coral agreed to appear in, of all things, a horror film being made in London: *Theater of Blood*. She only accepted the part at the urging of old pals Robert Morley and Jack Hawkins, who had already signed up. The cast also featured Coral's ex-lover, Michael Hordern; it was during the funeral scene for his character, the first 'murder victim', that she got her first glimpse of the film's star – an actor who had come to epitomise the horror genre, and would now be cast as the new leading man in her life.

Like Coral, most of the world knew only one facet of Vincent Price: 'Mr Hammer Horror', the star with the creepiest voice in films. But the Vincent Price behind the Halloween mask was a man of wit, style and erudition, a gourmet cook, a wine connoisseur and an expert and enthusiastic art collector and curator. His daughter, Victoria Price, said 'People underestimated his intelligence until the day he died: this was a man who could remember a Schubert lieder he learned when he was 14 and knew as much about art as anyone I've ever met.'[31] Born in St Louis, Missouri, on 27 May 1911, he was the youngest of four children; his grandfather invented the first commercially manufactured baking power, while his father was a sweet manufacturer and President of the National Candy Company. The prodigious Price was barely in long trousers when he started his art collection with a first-state Rembrandt etching, aged 12; he went on to study art at Yale University and then at the Courtauld Institute. During his time in London, he started his stage career, playing a Chicago policeman at the Gate Theatre. He was then cast as Prince

Albert in Laurence Houseman's *Victoria Regina*; the young actor played opposite Helen Hayes when the show was taken to New York and ran for nearly two years on Broadway. In 1938, Price made two 'firsts': his first film, *Service de Luxe*, and his first marriage, to the actress Edith Barrett who, as Victoria Price observed, 'was a huge star in the Twenties – she came from theatre royalty.'[32] In August 1940, the couple had a son, Vincent Barrett Price Jr, known as Barrett. Vincent Price's career in horror films began in 1953, with *The House of Wax*, followed by *The Fly*. In fact, only 20 of his 70 films were of that genre – before 1953, he had acquitted himself well in classic dramas such as *Laura, The Private Lives of Elizabeth and Essex* and *The Song of Bernadette*.

His marriage to Edith ended in divorce and he married his second wife, the designer Mary Grant, in 1949; their daughter, Mary Victoria – always called Victoria – was born in 1962. During the Sixties and early Seventies, he continued to plow the horror furrow, mostly in low-budget Edgar Allan Poe adaptations for American International Pictures (AIP) directed by Roger Corman. He also augmented his income with memorable guest appearances in such cult television series as *Batman*, where he played the follicularly-challenged villain Egghead, who eggselled in cracking *œuf*-related yolks. But then Vincent Price relished any opportunity to lay on the ham. He was also a familiar face and voice in an eclectic – or, as Egghead would say, 'egglectic' – range of commercials, promoting everything from Monster Vitamins to Best Western Motels. Sometimes, they landed him in trouble: in April 1957, six Baptist students – four of them ministers – picketed Louisiana College where Price was giving a lecture. The 'dry' protesters objected to a magazine advertisement he'd appeard in for Smirnoff vodka. For most of his professional career, Vincent was a regular on the American television chat and game show circuit. His chat show party piece was demonstrating a recipe for cooking trout in a dishwasher: this required shallots, parsley, lemon, white wine, olive oil, seasoning and thick foil, and cooked on a full cycle, no soap. Don't try it at home, viewers. Each TV appearance usually resulted in a deluge of mail from fans, containing cuttings on art, cookery and wine. No matter what he was performing in, or lecturing about, Vincent received fan mail and invitations to everything: award ceremonies, horror film conventions, charitable benefits, fundraising dinners, wine symposia, culinary festivals and requests to sit on visual art committees and foundations. When he appeared on the *Tonight Show* in 1968 and made some disparaging remarks about America's rail services, he was invited to become a member of the National Association of Railroad Passengers.

When it came to work, the word 'no' didn't seem to be in his vocabulary. 'I love being busy and I believe in being active,' he said. 'I know some people think I've lowered myself as an actor, but my idea of "professional decline" is not working.'[33] His daughter Victoria said, 'Boredom for him was the eighth deadly sin.'[34] But these jobs also provided a means to an end – namely, providing funds with which he could add to his art collection. 'You do some awful things so you can have the privilege of doing other things,' he said.[35] His passion for fine art was one shared by fellow actor Edward G Robinson, another cultured actor who spent most of his career typecast – in his case, as a gangster. In October 1956, the two stars were celebrity contestants on CBS's quiz show *The $64,000 Challenge*, and ended up splitting the prize after a complicated four-part question on the subject of paintings created by two or more artists. Five years earlier, Vincent and Mary had founded the Vincent and Mary Price Gallery and Art Foundation at East Los Angeles College, donating funds and hundreds of works of art. He served on America's Department of the Interior's Indian Arts and Crafts Board for more than ten years. In 1962, he was contracted by mega-merchandisers Sears to supervise the purchase of 55,000 pieces of art, priced from $10 to $3000. In attempting to upgrade its image, the chain store borrowed an idea from its past: in 1895, Sears offered oil paintings for sale to customers at prices starting at 90 cents. Now, Vincent was given carte blanche to acquire any works he considered suitable for the scheme. The artworks in the Vincent Price Collection were offered to Sears' customers on an instalment purchase plan, similar to the one which had helped the 12-year-old Price acquire his Rembrandt etching. By 1971, more than 50,000 pieces in the Collection had been sold. Occasionally, Vincent's well-known passion for art brought some freakish fallout: one John Light, Head Counselor at the Indianapolis Skills Center, wrote to him with the news that he'd had a dream: 'I am personally convinced that you were Leonardo da Vinci in a past life, and that you can paint in the same manner again if you are regressed to the full memories of that life.' Light's offer to achieve this, by regressing Vincent via the medium of prayer, was not taken up.[36]

In any case, there was no time to be Da Vinci – in between art and acting, there was his fascination with food: 'I believe there is art in everything. Cooking is definitely an art,' said Vincent.[37] To prove the point, he and Mary wrote the best-selling cookbook, *A Treasury of Great Recipes* – 'Famous Specialties of the World's Foremost Restaurants, Adapted for the American Kitchen'. This was rather bold: Vincent's public 'coming out' as a dab hand in the kitchen was decades before heterosexual men felt they could safely enter a kitchen and marinate to their heart's content, without it besmirching their manhood. This, then, was the man who, when Coral first saw him at Michael Hordern's 'funeral', looked nothing more than a scruffy, dirty old gravedigger.

In *Theater of Blood*, Vincent Price played Edward Lionheart, a hammy actor-manager who wreaks Shakespearean revenge on the cruel critics who, he believes, have ruined his career by failing to bestow their Best Actor Award on him two years previously. He delivers his own deadly verdicts, murdering each critic in turn by a method drawn from Shakespeare; for instance, one is forced to eat a pie containing his 'children' – his pet poodles – cooked to a recipe copied from *Titus Andronicus*. The film's tongue-in-cheek promotional materials featured a 'souvenir programme, London Critics' Circle, Presentation of Awards 1970' with 'nominations' including 'Best Actress, Anne Seymour in *They Won't Shoot Horses Will They?*'[38] The 'programme' listed the president and members of the 'Circle' – Peregrine Devlin (Ian Hendry), Hector Snipe (Dennis Price), Horace Sprout (Arthur Lowe), Trevor Dickman (Harry Andrews), Oliver Larding (Robert Coote), Meredith Merridew (Robert Morley), Solomon Psaltery (Jack Hawkins) and Miss Chloe Moon – Coral, the Circle's sole female scribe.

Filming began in London on July 10, and finished on August 17 – but those few weeks would provide more drama and twists than the film itself. First, producer Sam Jaffe had to iron out a minor dispute about who would receive top billing – Vincent or Diana Rigg, who was playing Lionheart's daughter, Edwina. In the end, their names appeared on the same line in the credits. Then, the Edwardian Putney Hippodrome – derelict since 1958 – had to be turned into Lionheart's 'Burbage Theatre', and dusty Shakespearean costumes stored under the stage at the Old Vic were hauled out to add a touch of authenticity. Industrial cleaners spent a weekend driving out the Hippodrome's resident pigeons and cleaning up the detritus before 500 old cinema seats, bought for 50p each from the Croydon Odeon, were fitted.

The film's designer, Michael Baldwin, had some challenging tasks, including 'providing duplicate sets of shirts and sports jackets to be soaked in blood for Dennis Price's death scene, to supplying full evening dress for the meths drinkers who finally impersonate the almost defunct Critics' Circle.'[39] But, as Baldwin revealed, supplying Kensington gore and alcoholics' attire was nothing compared to dealing with a certain diva's dress demands: 'I rang her up and said, "Good afternoon, Miss Browne, my name is Michael Baldwin and I'm designing the costumes for *Theater of Blood*." And she said, "Well, good luck!" – which rather took my breath away; I couldn't think what to say. So I asked if she minded if we met and talked about it – she said, "My dear, I only dress in Jean Muir and you can tell your producer John Kohn that's what I want." When I told her I didn't think we had the budget for Jean Muirs, she said, "I don't give a fuck, darling. You go and talk to Johnny." So I told him, and he went off on one: "The woman's mad, that's impossible!" Two days later, he rang me and said, "Michael, can you meet Coral at Jean Muir's?"'[40] John Kohn wasn't the only one to bend to Coral's will, as Baldwin recalled: 'You could tell the other actors were very much in awe of her. One day, we were doing a scene on top of a skyscraper by the river, near Vauxhall Bridge. Ian Hendry was late, and she was striding up and down a bit. And when he turned up, he was *absolutely* pissed… She said, "How DARE you come here late, with all these people waiting!" – she was really fierce!'[41]

Coral's fate as Chloe Moon was to be electrocuted under a salon hair dryer, in an approximate simulation of Joan of Arc's burning-at-the-stake in *Henry VI Part I*. It may well have brought back memories of Coral's own experience while filming *Auntie Mame*. This time, the criminal crimpers would of course be Vincent Price and his assistant, Diana Rigg, disguised with sunglasses and two alarmingly awful afro wigs. The scene where Chloe Moon goes for her fatal hair appointment provided one of cinema's campest moments: Vincent introduces himself with a cheery, 'Hi! I'm Butch!,' and Coral responds with an expression, punctuated by her trademark left eyebrow, which sums up what everyone else is thinking: 'Like hell, you are…' To add to the fun, Vincent, for medium and close-up shots, would slip on a comfortable old pair of carpet slippers. Soon, Coral would be telling Frith Banbury, 'I'd let *him* leave his slippers under my bed…'[42]

Vincent was looking forward to sampling some of Coral's acid wit, which had been given a big build-up by Diana Rigg: 'The third day of shooting, Diana put her back out and had to be hospitalized. I went to visit her with a bottle of champagne. Diana said, "Oh, you're going to work with Coral tomorrow.

Be sure to take down every word she says." The following day, I told this to Miss Browne whereupon she promptly clammed up.'[43] Coral's appointment with 'Butch' was filmed in the basement of a Knightsbridge salon – which, as luck would have it, had been designed by Robin Anderson. 'I designed this hairdressers in Knightsbridge called Derek Rowe. It had circles in the wall and all sorts – it's *so* dated now. One Sunday morning, the phone goes and it's Coral. She said, "Thank you for singing happy birthday to me…" I told her I didn't realise it was her birthday. I asked, "Where are you?," so she said, "I'm sitting on a film set in a most fuck-awful hairdressing salon in Knightsbridge…" I said, "Coral, I designed it…" but she continued: "I've just been burned up under the hairdryer by Vinnie Price. You'd better come and see me, bring me a bottle of champagne and a straw." She had all this gauze and stuff over her face, you see. When I got there, she was being *so* rude about Vincent: "Look at him, look at what he's done to me, and there he is, having a good time with the rest of the cast…" A couple of weeks later, she came to lunch at Morton's and said, "Darling, I'm in love." I nearly choked.'[44]

Coral explained: 'Our first date was a disaster. It was my birthday [July 23]. It was also the day I was supposed to be fried to death by Vinnie in the movie. The makeup men had just spent hours putting black makeup on all parts of my face so I would look like I had burns…he asked me out to lunch. I thought he was madly attractive but I couldn't go on our first date that way.'[45] Vincent had said to Diana Rigg, 'I understand it's Miss Browne's birthday. What could I get her?' To which Rigg replied, 'Well, I know what she wants. You!'[46] Vincent had become stuck on Coral, 'the Great Barrier Reef – beautiful, exotic and dangerous', as he described her.[47] He later said, 'When I was courting Coral, the first gift she gave me was a photo of herself simply signed: "Remember Coral" – not really a challenge, as the problem was: how could you forget her?'[48] The pair had fallen passionately in love – and proceeded to put the 'sex' back into 'sexagenarian'.

It was a fairytale romance – or would have been, except for one thing: Vincent, of course, was still married to Mary. She and daughter Victoria, then only 11 years old, came to visit him in London that summer, staying at the flat he had rented at 1 Eaton Square – awkwardly, just round the corner from Coral. Vincent behaved as though everything was perfectly normal and his family returned to America, none the wiser. But he couldn't keep up the façade: after filming on *Theater of Blood* finished, he returned to the States and embarked on a month-long art lecture tour. He returned to London briefly, to do over-dubs on *Theater of Blood*, during which he spent every night with Coral at Eaton Place. This time, when he returned to LA, Mary realised all was not well with the marriage, and offered him a divorce: he agreed with almost unseemly haste. Excruciatingly, that autumn, on 9 November 1972, they had to play 'happy families' when Vincent was the subject of *This Is Your Life*, which of course featured Mary, Victoria, Barrett and his wife Rini. In a fine performance, Vincent betrayed no hint of the emotional turmoil about to engulf them all.

Later that month, he and Coral met up in Washington DC; in the meantime, on Thanksgiving Day, Mary told Victoria about the impending divorce. Vincent later said, 'I suspect the failures of my first two marriages were the biggest failures of my life. I've been very lucky that I've loved three ladies, but I'm not proud of having stopped loving two of them.'[49] Victoria Price made an interesting observation about Vincent's 'three ladies': 'All three of my father's wives were very fearful people, yet they all masked it in different ways. His first wife, with an obsessiveness and an addictive personality; my mother, with rigidity and control; and Coral, with this larger than life personality.'[50] Some of Coral's friends also recognised this trait: 'Coral had a mask,' said Sheridan Morley, 'and she wore it to cover up the insecurities, and the fear, and the dreads.'[51] But, according to Victoria Price, there were other similarities between the women her father married: 'Style was a *huge* part of Coral's appeal. It was definitely something my father was drawn to in women. Coral and my mother both had that thing that can't be taught: that gut instinct and sense of what is cutting edge and what is stylish; it was just something they carried with them. He was also drawn to these women who were both extremely intelligent – not in the conventional sense, and not in the same way he was. The women that he was with were, in a way, daunted by his intelligence, because it was a more upper-class intelligence. And in Coral's world, that made her gravitate towards those who weren't going to look down on her – the gay men, the theatre people – for whom her wit would be recognised as a form of intelligence.'[52] Of course, with the intelligence and style went Coral's not inconsiderable beauty, which Vincent appreciated on all levels. He once wrote, 'Every once in a while in profile I see in my wife Coral's face the cool assurance of her beauty, the same look the Venus de Milo throws down the corridor in the Louvre... Coral admires herself as others admire her – it is a classic beauty, strictly adhering to the primal precepts of this kind of woman – caring simplicity in everything she does.'[53] Coral was a work of art, whose construction and pleasure could be appreciated sexually and aesthetically. His fascination with her face was manifest in the sketches of her face with which he adorned letters, cards or any scrap of paper to hand.

In the summer of 1973, the Price home at 580 North Beverly Glen was sold: Mary and Victoria moved to an apartment in the San Fernando Valley and Vincent moved to their beach house on Nicholas Beach Road. However, when Mary offered her husband a divorce, she had no idea that he was involved with Coral, and he managed to keep the affair secret from her and his children for almost a year. In the early days of their relationship, only one or two of Vincent and Coral's friends were let in on the secret. Coral told John Schlesinger, 'V went back to Malibu a few days ago…we're v happy and hate being parted for a second…but he phones almost every day and is very dear to me.'[54] Robert Hanley, who'd been the designer on *Auntie Mame*, was a friend of both Coral and Vincent and, according to Victoria Price, 'became their go-between. When Coral came to LA while my parents were still married, she stayed at Bob Hanley's. He remained a close friend of both my father and Coral, particularly during the early years of their marriage.'[55] Another mutual friend let in on the secret was Eileen Atkins, who had got to know Vincent in 1969 when they starred in a BBC *Play of the Month* production of *The Heiress*. 'I was in LA once and Vincent came to collect me,' she explained. 'As he got out of the car, he said, "I've got a surprise for you…" And there was Coral, lying down in the back seat, with a carpet on top of her! We made lots of jokes about her being like Cleopatra…Vincent said, "She can get out now", and then we drove somewhere miles away for dinner – because at that time, their relationship was completely clandestine.'[56]

Almost forgotten amid the subterfuge and sex was *Theater of Blood*, released in April 1973. The American press wallowed in the gore: 'A superior film in every way.'[57] The *LA Times* called it 'A triumph of stylish, witty Grand Guignol… It allows Vincent Price to range richly between humor and pathos… and his performance revitalizes that tired-out adjective, magnificent.'[58] Judith Crist thanked 'all involved, for restoring that fine sense of fun to a genre more honoured of late in its exploitation than by a creative exploration of its intelligent entertainment values'.[59] However, the film had a few detractors: Anitra Earle wondered 'why anyone as rich, celebrated and allegedly

Coral embraces the 'little black dress' style, early 1960s

A long way from Footscray… the drama queen at her most majestic

'Oh Charles, your mother *will* be pleased!' – Coral and 'fiancé' Charles Gray in New York, 1965

There she blowsy: as Cora (Belle Elmore) Crippen in *Dr Crippen* (1962)

TOP LEFT 'Bantam Bette' Badel and her 'parents' in *The Right Honourable Gentleman*, 1965
TOP RIGHT A (lifted) face fit for Hollywood: Molly Luther in *The Legend of Lylah Clare* (1968)
BOTTOM On a friendly footing: Coral and Radie Harris (*right*) with Christopher Cazenove

No Mercy: as Mrs Croft in *The Killing of Sister George* (1969)

TOP 1972: 'She was obviously unhappy…she wanted a change'
BOTTOM The 'space ship' with its resident sphinxes: 16 Eaton Place, early 1970s

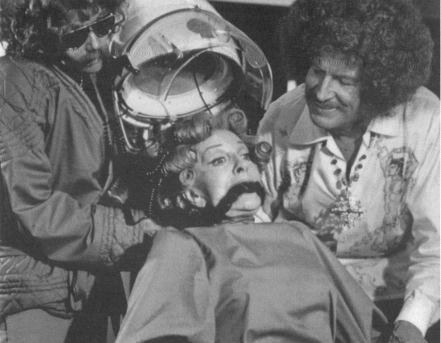

TOP Mad about the mad boy: as Claire Gurney in *The Ruling Class* (1972), with Peter O'Toole
BOTTOM Coral's first 'date' with Vincent Price (with Diana Rigg), *Theater of Blood* (1973)

Vincent Price, the cultured connoisseur

TOP Vincent tells chat show host Gary Collins, 'And when I saw her,
I was like a bird dog pointing, saying, "That's for me!"'
BOTTOM 'Our dining room area is sufficient for exactly six people': Swallow Drive, 1980s

Victoria Price collection

Author collection

Victoria Price collection

Kevin Scullin collection

TOP LEFT Coral lives dangerously in Hawaii   TOP RIGHT John Schlesinger, Coral's favourite Englishman, at home and abroad   BOTTOM LEFT The good life: Roddy McDowall snaps a happy Schlesinger and Coral in LA   BOTTOM RIGHT 'The mask made v. heavy carrying': Best Actress, BAFTA, 1984

TOP With 'Alan Bites' in *An Englishman Abroad* (1983)
BOTTOM 'It comes to us all…', playing Tom Conti's mother in *American Dreamer* (1983)

Death-defying glamour, 1983

Author collection

Author collection

Author collection

TOP A struggle to age: as Alice Hargreaves in *Dreamchild* (1985)
On the town: BOTTOM LEFT With publicist Rupert Allan at the premiere of *Zoot Suit* (1981)
BOTTOM RIGHT Coral and Vincent at an LA opening of a retrospective of work by their friend, David Hockney

TOP Celebrity chef Wolfgang Puck with fellow gourmands
BOTTOM LEFT 'From the Pole to the Panama Canal': the cruising couple, 1983
BOTTOM RIGHT Second time around: Coral and Vincent celebrate their church wedding, 1984

TOP Fading, but still 'caviar for the general', 1990
BOTTOM Vincent Price and his 'elegant lady wife'

distinguished as Vincent Price continues to fiddle around playing ghoulish lunatics in potboilers'.[60] The British press concurred: 'Coral Browne...and the rest of the cast should devise some diabolical death for the scriptwriter.'[61]

Having foreseen a new love in Coral's life, another Mir Bashir 'prediction' came true. She was, at last, offered a new stage play by one of the current crop of British writers who had helped dispatch the drawing room dramas and costume comedies she had made her name in. And, as the icing on the cake, she would be making her debut at the Royal Court, which had nurtured those same 'angry young men' of the theatre. However, there were some drawbacks: one day, when Coral was walking down the theatre's front steps with a friend, she was accosted by a young director from a struggling provincial theatre, who asked if she would star in his next production. She turned to her companion and said, 'You see, you work here and people think you'll work anywhere.'[62]

In Edward Bond's *The Sea*, Coral starred as Mrs Rafi, 'the local queen bee, brought up to bully all who cross her path'.[63] The play was set in a tiny seaside community in 1900s East Anglia, where one of the local young men has drowned after his boat overturned. Ian Holm played Hatch, the village draper, 'a sad, mad little man full of fears that visitors from outer space are stealing people's brains and replacing them with bits of machinery...'[64] Coral relished the challenges set by Bond's idiosyncratic use of language: 'It is such a good play. Probably the hardest I've ever had to learn. Really, nearly impossible. The words he uses are so right – but not at all what one would ordinarily say.'[65] Or sing: the role of Mrs Rafi required her to perform 'as an improbable Orpheus...a rendition of "There's No Place Like Home" just before she is rowed across the Styx to the tune of the Eton boating song "Jolly Boating Weather".'[66] This request hit the wrong chord with Coral, and cued another cavil, this time to Robin Anderson: 'She rang, and said "I've got to sing descant, dear. I don't want to sing *descant*..." *Everything* was a drama...'[67]

Bond's play was hailed by *The Sunday Times* as 'the most exciting event in an exhilarating week...from Ian Holm and Coral Browne [come] superbly controlled modulation.'[68] Another critic said, 'Mrs Rafi is given to Coral Browne to exercise her incomparable gift for economical hilarity in.'[69] However, Sheridan Morley said the play was 'mainly notable for giving Coral Browne the chance to go into training for Lady Bracknell', resembling 'an eery crossing of Daphne Du Maurier Cornish Gothic with Terence Rattigan High Comedy'.[70] As it turned out, Morley wouldn't have to wait long to see Coral as Lady Bracknell – as she told John Schlesinger, 'Am going to give my Lady Bracknell on the box. Gielgud thinks I'll be disaster.'[71]

Coral's time at the Royal Court provided her with a chance to be one of the first people ever to experience the 'Time Warp': another show – an obscure, low-budget musical – opened in the Court's upstairs theatre on June 16, a week before *The Sea* closed. And, because of the 'downstairs' play, this noisy upstairs show couldn't start until 10.30pm. On its opening night, Coral and Vincent decided to sneak upstairs to find out why the theatre seemed to be staffed entirely by ghoulish cinema usherettes. What they saw was a theatrical phenomenon in its infancy: Richard O'Brien's *The Rocky Horror Show* was enjoying its first run, and Coral and Vincent enjoyed its timeless combination of camp humour and horror movie references. The show's designer, Brian Thomson, doubled-up as their usher: 'I took them through the other ghouls. I remember a load of the seats fell over where we hadn't screwed them to the floor. Anyway, they loved the show, really loved it, and so I asked them to tell the cast that. I took them back to this tiny room where everyone was crammed in, all in their knickers and underwear. In they went and Vincent said his bit, in that great voice. The cast loved it.'[72] When the show was later produced in Australia, its programme notes proudly reported that Coral and Vincent, 'London's newest and handsomest lovebirds guffawed as loudly as two Tallulahs.'[73]

The lovebirds were able to spend a good deal of time together that spring and into early summer: Vincent was in London on several work fronts. He was making Jim Clark's *Madhouse*, yet another horror film, in which he played a horror film actor – the appropriately named Paul Toombes. For him, its only positive outcome was a friendship with Coral's chum, and fellow art-lover, Adrienne Corri. Then there was *The Amazing Nasrudin*. For many years, the animator Richard Williams had been trying to make a film about the legend of Nasrudin; at various times during the project's development he had hired big-name actors to provide 'scratch tracks' – temporary dialogue recordings to help animators work out the timing of sequences. Vincent had been one star to provide the voices for these tracks. However, after Paramount withdrew their backing from the film, Williams had to start all over again – including new 'scratch tracks' in London in 1973. It gave Vincent a legitimate opportunity to be in town and enjoy some 'illegitimate' activities with Coral. Victoria Price said, 'I recall that he was going back and forth quite a bit to do dialogue work for it. I remember because it was a cartoon, which was a lot more interesting to me than the horror films. I'm sure his enthusiasm for going to England was increased by the prospect of Coral at the other end! Also, it was right about that time that Sears was coming to an end. It was a difficult time for a man who was perpetually fearful of being penniless. Losing the Sears income right as he was getting a divorce and getting together with a woman of high style must have been terrifying.'[74]

One thing he didn't pay for was a new king-sized bed for Eaton Place, which he and Coral went shopping for together, thus creating another oft-quoted anecdote. Like the ten-shilling story at the Old Vic, versions vary: but, whether it was Heal's or Harrods, the hapless assistant had to inform Coral that the bed wouldn't be ready for at least four weeks. Coral pointed at herself and a tired-looking Vincent (possibly as a result of their bedroom activities) and cried, 'Look at us – do you think we've got that long!?'[75]

Time was, indeed, running out – Vincent and Coral's relationship was becoming public in more places than the bed departments of London stores: in August that year, the *Sunday Express* ran a story, headlined 'Are Theatre of Blood Stars Vincent and Coral to Marry?'[76] Finally, the jig was up when the October 14 issue of *National Enquirer* contained a rather unflattering photograph of Vincent and Coral, captioned 'Vincent Price Admits He's Fallen In Love', together with an 'exclusive interview' with Price.[77] Victoria Price said her mother Mary saw the magazine at a supermarket checkout – and this was how she discovered the identity of her soon-to-be ex-husband's new lover. It was the type of cruel twist that would not have been out of place in an Anouilh play – so it was not entirely incongruous that, soon after this incident, Coral accepted the opportunity to star in one of her favourite playwright's works.

In late 1973, it had been rumoured that Coral would star in a revival of the melodrama *Gaslight*, but this never materialised. Instead, she was cast opposite Trevor Howard in a West End production of Anouilh's *The Waltz of the Toreadors*, a typically bittersweet tale of 'an aging general who has kept the love of his life waiting for 17 years to endure daily abuse from a bed-ridden wife'.[78] General St Pé (Howard) believes he has a chance to marry his love Ghislaine (Zena Walker) when he discovers his wife has a passion for the family doctor. However, his dreams are shattered when he learns that Ghislaine has – not surprisingly – tired of waiting and fallen in love with his male secretary. It was a play which, according to Sheridan Morley, was 'situated midway between Pinero and "Virginia Woolf".'[79] Rehearsals began in January 1974, but Coral was far from happy: uncertain and insecure about the future, with Vincent now back in America, sorting out his divorce arrangements, she was missing him terribly. Nearly every day, she wrote him letters, embellished with a signature lipstick 'kiss': 'Are you still smoking – what do you look like? What do you do in the aeroplanes on those endless journeys. How much do you REALLY love me – <u>enough</u>???????????? Do I get Tig [her dog] injected for US regulations? I don't know – I don't know anything much… Lewis Fiander* forgot to send me a card!!! Also MOTHER! I only have one up & that's yours. Wish I had something else of yours up – think mine has grown together. Its UTTERLY twitchless…I want to be JOLLY & potter about & eat a lot of prawns & chicken & COCK – so there…I want you so – am <u>V</u> uptight & could do with a lot of your attention…there is absolutely NO substitute for your clever sucking drill – NONE AT ALL – & I sure can't make it for myself, out of ANYTHING. I hold you passionately tenderly & cry out loud for your nearness Oh soon, soon – SOON??'[80]

Meanwhile, her co-star Howard, facing his first stage play for ten years, had his own concerns: 'I'm only off the stage for one and a half pages of dialogue! Then I have a scene where I have to carry Coral Browne off the stage and literally ten seconds later, I am supposed to be sitting down, perfectly relaxed… I tell you, it's a terror.'[81] Both Coral and Howard, believing they needed more rehearsal time, asked for its opening date to be postponed, but this was refused. She told Vincent, 'It really is an awful mess…its all so TASTELESS & POLISHLESS… [Trevor & I are] both too old hat at the game to kid ourselves that we have any kind of respectable offering. Its depressing, to say the least.'[82] Even the size and state of her dressing room was cause for complaint: 'It hasn't been cleaned for months. You never know what you are going to find when you open a drawer. And there is a dead mouse under the table.'[83]

However, when the play opened at the Haymarket, as scheduled on February 14, her negativity was not shared by the critics. Harold Hobson commented, 'Coral Browne, rising in vengeance from her bed…lifts this most piercing of Anouilh's plays to a height from which it never afterwards falls.'[84] Jack Tinker agreed: 'Coral Browne mines all the rich black comedy buried

* Melbourne-born actor who appeared in *Waltz* in Australia in 1959.

in the role of the recriminating wife.'[85] Garry O'Connor said that, 'Trevor Howard and Coral Browne's one long scene of marital in-fighting is worth the rest of the evening's three brief acts put together: it's stunning.'[86] Even mardy old Milton Shulman managed to pry out something veering on the positive: 'Coral Browne, with her face powdered to look like Marcel Marceau's mother, had one good outburst.'[87] Looking back over the year's plays, Eric Johns said the production was '...gripping, fascinating, almost frighteningly alive...Coral Browne had one of her finest parts and gave one of her finest performances... and made the woman stir the mind keenly, as well as touch the heart.'[88]

Coral welcomed the reviews but, as she told Vincent, 'Not that I want the bloody thing to run ONE night but having suffered so much I would have liked it to have passed fairly flawless under my jewellers glass.'[89]

That February was a good month for Coral: *The Importance of Being Earnest* was broadcast on BBC1 on 17 February, as a *Play of the Month* presentation, and the critics didn't agree with John Gielgud's 'disaster' predictions. The women shone brightest in this production, with Gemma Jones and Celia Bannerman superb as Gwendolyn (played correctly as a younger version of her mother Lady Bracknell) and Cecily – and, of course, Coral simply glorious, especially in the last act: 'Her Lady Bracknell was a dragon, but an elegant, middle-aged one.'[90] Leonard Buckley of *The Times* said her entrance in the first act 'was the moment for which we had been waiting...hers was an unfussy, finely chiselled performance designed to show us how well Wilde wrote and how elegantly Miss Browne could speak his words. It lacked perhaps the sheer majesty of Dame Edith [Evans] but somehow its restrained dimensions enlarged the other characters so that we saw afresh what treasuries of wit and wisdom Wilde had offloaded on them as well.'[91]

Vincent and Mary's divorce became final in April 1974: according to Adrienne Corri, 'Coral mourned that the divorce settlement had left him with little of his legendary art collection – "nothing but the Canalettos and the Rembrandts".'[92] By now, Vincent had bought a house just off Sunset Boulevard, at 1359 Miller Drive, for $95,000 – a '2 story English Country mini estate'. A real Hollywood home, it was built as a honeymoon cottage by Angela Lansbury's first husband, Richard Cromwell, and subsequent owners included Greta Garbo and Cole Porter. It had nine rooms, a half-acre garden with views over Hollywood – and parking room for ten vehicles. Anticipating an imminent move to America, Coral made plans. She revised her will again and mulled over who should inherit the lease of Eaton Place: 'It was left, as you know, divided between Corri and Jill but I think it had better be left to you now,' she told Vincent.[93] 'I've still got Building Society money quite a bit which is O.K. thank God... V. lucky you didn't take up my offer to live on what I HAD such a short time ago – we'd have got around to the garage & the fumes from the car sooner than I'd anticipated...the share market has gone & everything I have almost valueless...'[94] But they were still arguing about where they should be based; the *Evening News* reported that Vincent had decided to live in London with Coral: 'Friends say she has told Price she won't live in California.'[95] Vincent admitted that he had become somewhat disillusioned with California life: 'The smog, the city that became physically enormous but never grew with it. You don't feel safe there anymore... The ideal thing would be to live half the time in London.'[96] In private, Coral told Vincent, 'OF COURSE we could survive a long spell together in 1359 or 16 – Isn't that what we both want...The sooner the better...as you say "I want to enjoy my life with you – whats left of it" – I say just that to you & I've told you SO often its ALL I want.'[97] However, she made one thing crystal clear: 'I'm too old to turn into that cleaning type of wife-mother-slave-dogsbody – & <u>especially</u> as C2 [Mary] had fucking well everything from houseman to laundry woman...'[98] As she did with most things, Coral eventually got her own way on this matter; Hungarian-born Marika Kiss became the long-suffering housekeeper in the Price household.

Apart from their domestic arrangements, there was also the welfare of a 12-year-old daughter to consider – who, at that time, was still being kept in the dark about Coral. When Victoria Price first visited her father at his new home, she was told that the lady sunbathing topless by the pool was 'a house guest'. 'My dad was extremely worried about losing me – and he wrote to Coral about that a lot – so she knew up front how much I meant to him. One thing that probably irritated the hell out of Coral was that, at Miller Drive, they had a pool house which was quite a way from the regular house. Coral would sleep in the guest room and I would share my dad's bed, which was a big king size. So I would come into the house and literally displace her from her bed – which in retrospect was probably not his best decision... Also, because Coral's persona was so carefully constructed – so that people saw what she allowed them to see. And there was I, this little girl, who would spend two weeks with them sometimes, and was getting to see the things that other people didn't. For example, I saw her without make-up – how many people saw Coral without make-up? She spent an hour putting on her "face", as she called it – it was a whole ritual. On the one hand, it inevitably brought us closer, probably because it brought to mind being backstage with a younger actress – and I was interested in the theatre – but on the other, it was allowing someone who she didn't choose to see her behind the scenes and to see her vulnerable. And very few people got to see that. I mean, I saw that she was not young – because she looked unbelievable when she had make-up on. She looked unbelievable without it, too – but she looked like a regular person, not this "construct".'[99]

As soon as *The Waltz of the Toreadors* closed on April 13, Coral flew off to LA to see Vincent and finalise their plans. But in her hurry to get away, she didn't notice that her passport had run out, and consequently wasn't allowed to board her flight. Otis 'Dick' Blodget, Vincent's London agent at ICM, reported on the ensuing drama: 'It was indeed a bit traumatic getting Madam out of the country. The scene at the airport must have been divine and what the poor officials at Petty France thought of the language by the time she reached there to get her passport renewed, god alone knows.'[100]

However, once the oaths and curses had finished, Coral and Vincent made their decision: by the end of the summer, she would move into Miller Drive. The finality of the decision couldn't be questioned when Coral took Tiggy to LA with her: 'I brought my dog from England, and he knew that was it,' she said.[101] She was the first in a long line of toy dogs to occupy the Price household: after Tiggy died in 1980 (on Vincent's 69th birthday), their pets included Fendi, who enjoyed rutting a toy rat; Maile, named after a Hawaiian town; Licky and two Schipperekes, Kiki and Willie. Coral would make sure the dogs sent 'Daddy' birthday and Father's Day cards. Now, she was eager that the 'children' should live in a 'legitimate' household. In public, she said that, 'It's wishful thinking to say we are going to get married. I had one happy marriage that was divine and you can't win the pools twice.'[102] In private, she was putting Vincent under increasing pressure to marry her, whatever the cost. She wanted a Catholic church wedding; but, knowing that Vincent's recent divorce would be an impediment, she made a suggestion which was at best thoughtless, and at worst despicable: she wanted Vincent to persuade Mary to agree to an annulment of their marriage. Coral even sent their priest to Mary's house to exert his 'holy' pressure – twice. Understandably, the request was turned down. For now, they'd have to content themselves with 'living in sin' – and, doubtless, a few extra visits to the confessional.

In July 1974, Coral and Vincent flew to Italy, where he was filming *Journey into Fear*. In Genoa, they were on their way back to their hotel when an Italian youth snatched Vincent's shoulder bag, which contained $15,000 in cash plus assorted credit cards. Vincent gave chase – 'I intended to catch the little punk and throttle him'[103] – but the pursuit ended in a dead-end alley. Now, the elderly actor – more used to terrifying young people – found himself in the dangerous situation of facing not one, but four, youthful robbers. Fortunately, the culprits ran off with their loot, leaving 'Mr Horror' more than a little shaken.

Journey into Fear would be the last film Vincent made for nearly five years. Coral had persuaded him to stop making sub-standard movies and consider a return to the stage. She wasn't always as good at taking her own advice, as evident when she agreed to take a small part in *The Drowning Pool* (1975). It was a mediocre private-eye thriller starring Paul Newman and Joanne Woodward, a sequel to the earlier hit *Harper* (1966), largely dismissed as '…a lacklustre workout'.[104] She told John Schlesinger, 'Did three days on a Paul Newman movie – played Richard Derrs 84 year old SOUTHERN mother and HATED IT!'[105] Coral was playing Olivia Devereux, a Louisiana matriarch who refused to sell her land to a greedy oil baron. Almost unrecognisable in a cheap grey wig and spectacles that wouldn't have been out of place in a joke shop, and demonstrating a pretty poor Southern accent, Coral went through the motions. 'I was in a birdcage all day, where birds did things in my hair and on my face. It was just horrendous,' she said.[106] But at least the horror was short-lived: Olivia Devereux was killed off less than twenty minutes into the film.

This stinker also spoiled Vincent's surprise plans for their special day: after confirming the dates she would be needed for her scenes in Louisiana, he told Coral that he had secretly arranged their wedding to take place one of those days. However, it only meant a temporary postponement: 'When I got back he said, "Let's get married tomorrow" – we'd had the blood tests, which you have to have in California – and we got into the car and drove to Santa Barbara.'[107] At the courthouse, though they had a marriage licence, they had no witnesses, no ring – and no judge. But these were mere details: and, on 24 October, at Santa Barbara County Courthouse, Coral became the third 'Mrs Vincent Price'. 'When we got back,' said Coral, 'we had Maggie Smith, John

Standing and Julia Foster coming to dinner so I put the marriage licence up on the fireplace so they'd know it was all all right and they weren't coming to a house of ill fame.'[108] 'But the crowning glory came the next day when the announcement appeared in the Los Angeles Times. It said that Vincent Price had married "Cora Perlman, artist".'[109] Just in case there was any confusion, she cabled a simple message to her London agent Ronnie Waters: 'We are married. All love, Coral and Vincent.'[110] Some of the juicier details were saved for John Schlesinger: 'We're "legal" and now I'm stateless or statusless as Somerset House won't send Philip's death certificate and the US won't make me a permanent resident until they know I'm "clean". Even had to get a blood tests to show I couldn't pass German Measles onto <u>our</u> offspring before they'd marry us (the VD one didn't seem so important).'[111]

Several weeks later, Coral and Vincent went on a honeymoon cruise, accompanied by Peter Marshall, host of the US quiz show, *The Hollywood Squares* (another of Vincent's regular gigs) and his second wife, actress and former *Playboy* centrefold, Sally Carter-Ihnat (aka Marya Carter). On the first morning, Sally met Coral and Vincent and mischievously asked how their 'honeymoon' night had been. She got more than she bargained for in reply: 'As a matter of fact, darling, we were talking about you,' said Coral. Vincent smiled, gently patted Mrs Marshall on the chin and told her, 'We were just saying what a nice little tidbit you'd make for Coral and me.'[112] The 'tidbit' got her own back on Coral a few years later when they were all were having dinner at the home of Jerry Shaw, *Hollywood Squares* director. Coral had neglected to bring her spectacles and, while she was chatting to Sally, picked up what she thought was a dainty piece of black bread. It fell to Sally to tell her gently that this 'tidbit' was actually a burnt cork coaster – at which point, Coral calmly announced her intention to tell their host not to use 'stale fucking hors d'oeuvres when entertaining friends'.[113] When they got back from their cruise, Liza Goddard called Coral to ask her how the wedding had gone – and instead got a typically blunt verdict on the wedding night: 'Well, darling, it was like getting a marshmallow into an old leather box, but we managed…'[114]

Throughout their marriage, tongues wagged in LA and London about the 'true' nature of the third Mr and Mrs Price's relationship. Rumours about Vincent's sexuality, fuelled by his sometimes effete manner and speech, had been doing the rounds for decades. However, as Victoria Price said, 'My father's bisexuality was like a rainbow with no pot of gold at the end of it. The best I can come up with is that my father loved men. Whether there was a sexual component, or how important the sexual component was, I don't know... But then he loved women. And he loved the company of women. How you label that I have no idea.'[115] Many gossips speculated that his marriage to Coral was one of sexless 'convenience' – a claim easily disproved by Coral's passionate letters to Vincent. Obviously, as the passage of time and increasing ill-health took their toll on both of them, their physical relationship waned, but their affection for each other didn't – even when, as in Coral's case, it morphed into a destructive and divisive jealousy and thirst for control. Vincent explained, 'I think you can love more intensely and abstractly when you're older, whereas when you're young, your love for somebody might be very personal and have to be satisfied emotionally and sexually. But when you're older, you can have a friend with whom you really feel terribly close and love extremely much without having the relationship require any satisfaction other than being able to love and be loved in return.'[116] And, when they were both in their seventies, he revealed, 'There's still a wonderful thing of being terribly fond of each other that is very sexual, very sexual, really more so than sex. To be really fond of someone, to touch them, to feel them, is wonderful. Something that does last forever.'[117] According to Liza Goddard, the couple would amuse each other by flicking through the pages of *Spotlight*, the actors' directory, and commenting, 'Had her', 'Had him', 'Had her', 'Had him...'[118] The majority of their friends believed they were a perfect match – sophisticated, witty, glamorous, and personally and professionally unconventional. Robin Anderson said, 'When she was effing and blinding, Vincent would always refer to her as his "elegant lady wife". But then as I said once, "She even swears in style..."'[119]

There was one crucial area, as Victoria Price pointed out, in which the couple were not evenly matched: 'He was more famous than her – and I think that came as a horrible shock to her. I don't think she understood my father's fame. She thought he was some sort of lovely, charming, erudite, handsome, gentle, gay-seeming man, and she didn't really understand the degree to which he was beloved. She liked that about him – but she *hated* what it took away from her.'[120] And, similarly, Vincent had fallen for the public, fabricated creature who had become 'Coral Browne'. 'She was completely her own creation, even down to the fact that she reconstructed her face,' observed Victoria Price. 'I once read a book by a sociologist who defined "alienation" as the state that occurs when somebody can no longer distinguish between their private self and their public persona. Those words just jumped off the page at me: at first I thought of my father, who was this persona "Vincent Price". But I think that's what he and Coral had most in common, and I think it was a much larger stretch for Coral. My father came from a wealthy family and had a lot of status, so for him to create this persona wasn't so much of a stretch. I think my father was enamoured with Coral's persona, and with who Coral was in the British theatre. I think there was a part of him, right from when he was a young man in London in *Victoria Regina*, that was so enamoured with that world that he fell in love as much with that, and the entrée she provided him into that world, as with Coral, and that persona she created.'[121]

However, when it came to money, it was a non-contest: for little did Vincent know that he was now married to a *very* wealthy woman. On top of her salaries from plays, films and television, her fortune had first begun with the money bequeathed to her by Firth Shephard in 1949. There was also money from Philip's will in 1964; then 20 years later, Philip's sister, Joan Pearman, left Coral £10,000. In 1967, she was informed by the Office of the Public Trustee in Australia that she was entitled to a share of the estate of her uncle, George Reginald Brown, who had died intestate. Coral made judicious investments with her money: just before she married Vincent, her portfolio of stocks and shares were valued at around £63,000 – a sum worth, in 2007, around £625,000. Money was transferred regularly to an offshore, tax-free account with Rea Brothers on Guernsey, and to several high-interest savings accounts in banks on the mainland. In 1974, her collection of paintings – which included works by Matisse, Graham Sutherland, Jacob Epstein and Lowry – were valued at just over £15,000; in 2007, this would be worth, at a conservative estimate, around £100,000. Even Coral's beloved Sphinx and obelisk collection was valued at £2500 – a sum worth over £18,000 in 2007.

Very occasionally, she would reveal some details of her finances to Vincent: 'I'm trying to get out of death duties on the flat – All very complicated but I'll tell you all about it at length. I've transferred 50 thousand pounds to my Wetherly Bank so I'm working HARD – I seem to be richer than I imagined by quite a bit you'll be pleased to hear so I can afford to take you to Venice AND Paris...'[122] But money was to become one of the prevailing twin themes in their marriage. Of course, the workaholic Vincent's earnings were not small, but his financial commitments included child support and two lots of alimony to pay to the women Coral ungenerously called 'those man eating wives'.[123] And now, of course, he was expected to meet his new wife's luxurious demands. For example, his income for the year 1980 was $845,901 – but out of that, he paid $124,965.25 in alimony and $16,744.93 on 'jewelry, furs and fine arts'.[124] Victoria Price said, 'The number of times she complained to anyone who would listen that my father was not working hard enough to supply her with the $700 shoes that she liked to wear, or the Chanel and Armani suits, was beyond number.'[125] Coral kept meticulous records of even her most miniscule outgoings – everything from magazine subscriptions to her grocery shopping at Safeway.

For the time being, she decided against selling Eaton Place, and rented it out to a succession of tenants. She told Frith Banbury, 'I'll be leaving the place as it is at present except I may take away the sphinxes in sitting room & the books.'[126] When she needed somewhere to stay during her London visits, she was a welcome guest at John Schlesinger's Kensington home, 10 Victoria Road. 'Its nice being here as I have a lovely room & bath,' she told Vincent. 'Its well-heated & there is a man driver, 2 daily maids & an excellent cook so everything is nice & clean & tidy the way I like it to be & John is a lovely host & I'm not pressed – there is always lunch & dinner & bfast & it can be served me any time.'[127] Her frequent visits to the house led to a close friendship with Caroline Cornish-Trestrail: 'We just hit it off. She would come down into the office in just her dressing gown, with no make-up on – she did have the most extraordinary skin – and she'd come and sit, and have coffee and a gossip. She was very interested in people, especially their relationships – who was doing what with whom. She loved any form of wickedness or scandal… John had lots of houseguests – and some of them were so taxing – but they really looked forward to her coming to stay. It wasn't a chore at all.'[128]

Meanwhile, with Coral's relocation, 'Mother' had been moved to a residential care home, Delves House Nursing Home at 31 Queens Gate Terrace in Kensington – which, naturally, she complained about non-stop. After nearly 20 years in London, having moved there of her own volition, she still hated all things English: 'English folk are cold I think, quite unlike Australians and Americans – I never did like England much in any way.'[129] She sent Coral and Vincent regular 'we're all doomed' missives in California: on the 1976

Central American earthquake, she declared, 'All of these events are mentioned in the Bible and coming true. Keep well and happy...'[130] She found a more sympathetic listener in Vincent than her 'beloved Coral', especially regarding her various physical ailments: 'Delves House goes from bad to worse...if ever I can move again [after a bad fall] I shall certainly leave this dreadful hole... Unless you lived here one could never believe it. The days are long and nights worse. Thank God Les is not alive!!!'[131]

As Coral and Vincent settled into married life, they made a few concessions: she applied to be a US citizen, and he converted to Catholicism. Years later, while on yet another tour, he told Coral, 'I must say I do enjoy the service it seems to put everything right or at least into perspective – I should have become one years ago.'[132] If their Catholicism seemed at odds with their lifestyle and personalities, their parish church matched them for incongruity. They worshipped at St Victor's (named after the first African pope) on 8634 Holloway Drive, just off Sunset Strip in West Hollywood, an area known for its large gay population. In 1994, St Victor's became the only church in the Archdiocese with an AIDS Memorial Chapel. From 1929 until 1976, the pastor of St Victor's was Monsignor John J Devlin – former head of the Legion of Decency. 'Ours is a <u>V</u> funny church,' Coral told Alec Guinness, 'It's absolutely <u>full</u> of Kweans – the hissing sounds remind me of being a child – about 5 – & throwing myself down in the "shivery grass" to listen to the gentle breeze blooming the blades.'[133] Other worshippers at St Victor's included Vincent's fellow *Batman* scene-stealer – and confirmed 'kwean' – Cesar Romero.

Coral made another concession to LA life: she learned to drive. 'She couldn't drive at that point,' recalled Jill Melford, 'and she bought herself a car to learn to drive in, which was a Daf. I know it was, because I bought it from her – she'd very nearly demolished it by then... Then Vinnie bought her some large automatic drive car. She never quite worked out clutches and brakes, so she had entered quite a few brick walls... She hated the whole thing of HAVING to drive to get anywhere.'[134] And feared it: 'Coral never let anyone drive with her,' said Victoria Price. 'She was terrified to drive anyone. She drove my dad when it was necessary but I was never in a car where she drove me. And my mother was afraid of certain things too: she wouldn't go uphill, she wouldn't make left turns. There were these odd little things that they had in common.'[135] Occasionally, Coral's exploits behind the wheel brought her to the attention of the LAPD: in 1977, she told Frith Banbury, 'Am in court tomorrow for SPEEDING!!! Guilty!!!'[136]

Coral's closest male friend in LA was Roddy McDowall, who dubbed her the 'OK Coral'. In fact, McDowall appeared to be everyone's best friend and most trusted confidant, not least because of his loyalty and discretion. No one could keep a secret like Roddy. This capacity for confidentiality extended beyond the grave: at his death in 1998, all his personal papers were left to Boston University – with the proviso that they would not be publicly accessible for 100 years. The collection was sealed until the year 2098 – all will presumably be revealed to anyone left alive then who's thirsting to discover the intimate secrets of his friendships with Elizabeth Taylor, Lauren Bacall, Bette Davis, Montgomery Clift *et al.* Rupert Everett became friends with McDowall in 1984 during the filming of *Another Country* after McDowall, an accomplished photographer, asked to take some pictures of the young star on set. 'Knowing him was definitely a key into the forbidden city,' said Everett. 'He had an extraordinary talent for friendship and he was genuinely funny. He pioneered the role of the gay best friend.'[137] Certainly, only someone with a true genius for friendship could have managed to keep onside with both Sybil Burton Christopher *and* Elizabeth Taylor – respectively, the first and second (and third; they remarried) wives of Richard Burton.

Dominick Dunne praised McDowall's 'innate gift for intimacy, there was nothing you couldn't tell him… He kept a lot of secrets for a lot of people.'[138] McDowall's bungalow at 3110 Brookdale Road in Studio City, on what Rupert Everett called 'the unfashionable side of Laurel Canyon' was the centre of an LA social circle that embraced old and new Hollywood.[139] The exotic and eclectic company more than compensated for the uncomplicated food McDowall served at his gatherings: hotdogs and hamburgers frequently graced the tables. But, as Dunne explained, 'The food wasn't the point. The conversation was.'[140] However, Coral sometimes found McDowall's soirées as uninspiring as his nibbles: 'Went to a surprise party for Roddy's awful Wanker Paul – all asked at 6 to some remote canyon – the Wanker arrived at 8…at 11 the hostess announced the food for the party had FALLEN OFF THE TRUCK.'[141]*

---

* Like Coral, McDowall was a collector – not of sphinxes but, with a nod to his British roots, Toby jugs. But his most notable items of bric-a-brac were in his sloping, rose-filled garden.

The new Mr and Mrs Price became a much-loved double-act throughout much of Hollywood's social circle; Coral's wicked wit went down particularly well with LA's circle of prominent gay ex-pats, including Christopher Isherwood and David Hockney. A month after her wedding, Coral gave Frith Banbury a thumbnail sketch of the Prices's social life: 'Going to Chris Isherwood's Sunday for a chop with Gore Vidal so you see I'm moving up socially & tonight I'm cooking for the Axelrods [George and Joan].'[142]

They were especially chummy with another Hollywood double-act: Joan Rivers and her husband, TV producer, Edgar Rosenberg. The Rosenbergs had got to know Vincent first, through *Hollywood Squares*, as Rivers also made regular appearances on the show. She said of Coral and Vincent, 'There are so few people that you dare, in our business, to tell the truth. And you could tell them the truth and you knew you'd get great advice. You knew they were on your side. There was no question about that.'[143] However, Rivers was not oblivious to some of her friends' weaknesses, particularly at restaurants: 'One dinner in fourteen there would be a half-hearted attempt to pick up the check. They were not generous that way.'[144] This came as a shock to Victoria Price: 'That really surprised me when Joan said how cheap they were. When he was married to my mother, he would *always* pick up the tab.'[145] Vincent said that, when the sharp-witted Rivers and Coral were pitted together, 'They cancel each other out. It's like being in a pot of syrup. They're all sweetness and light.'[146] But, apart from their barbed tongues, the two women had much in common, including a fondness for all things nip-and-tuck. 'I think everybody should keep tweaking,' said Rivers. 'Look at any actress over 60 who doesn't have jowls. They say they've done nothing, but they're lying. I go to my surgeon once every two years, like you service your car, or you repaint your house. We're in a business where it counts, and don't tell me that it doesn't.'[147] And she was as diet-conscious as Coral: 'I started my first diet the day Hannibal crossed his first Alp.'[148] The two women had something else in common: stage fright. Rivers later said, 'I hate anyone coming in to see me in the dressing room

---

At the top, visitors could sit and gaze down at the house, perched on a bench from the set of *Lassie*, while outside the back door stood a 20-foot statue of the primate 'Caesar', purloined from the set of *Planet of the Apes* – a sight guaranteed to put Coral's left eyebrow, and tongue, into overdrive. Caesar now stands guard in the Roddy McDowall Rose Garden at the Motion Picture and Television Fund Wasserman Campus retirement home and hospital in Woodland Hills, California.

before a show. I've been on Broadway now four times and I still think I'm going to forget my lines.'[149] They could also have fun swapping stories about Coral's former paramour, Cecil Beaton: Rivers had once been a 'Girl Friday' to the designer when he was working in New York. He seemed to have grown out of his 'red' period by this time, and advised the fledgling actress that, 'Onstage, you must always have pink lights above, blue lights below, and grey velour behind you.'[150]

Vincent was readily accepted into Coral's circle of friends in England, where his charm and wit were much appreciated. However, as Alec Guinness said, 'Although I was charmed by him and liked him enormously, I never felt I knew him intimately.'[151] And Ned Sherrin said that, 'Vincent seemed to shrink when in the company of actors.'[152] Victoria Price noticed one way in which these new friends and acquaintances changed her father: 'He became a name-dropper. He was always fascinated by famous people – and Coral came with all these famous people attached to her. So every note to me was, "Had dinner with Larry Olivier," that sort of thing. So he totally bought into Coral's world.'[153] The couple were visited by a steady stream of old friends and colleagues from England, including Robin Anderson, Frith Banbury and Jean Marsh. Sheridan Morley said, 'They were a perfect couple in an alien community which they both made the best of. They ran a sort of court in California, for English exiles. It was the first place you went in LA.'[154] Eileen Atkins also visited – once she'd manage to track them down: 'One time, when I was there, I was breaking up with someone, and I wanted to get out of LA, but I had no money. I was desperate. I had Vincent's old address so I took a cab there. And, of course, his ex-wife was there – and I asked to see him and she was absolutely vile to me because, of course, he had left her. Anyway, I traced him and turned up at the house. Vincent wasn't there, but Coral was: I said, "I really need some help. Could you give me a cup of tea?" And she said, "Cup of tea? You look as though you need a double vodka!" She was so wonderful to me – I told her about the whole thing. And she said they'd lend me the money to get home, no problem, and so on… I was going to go, but she said, "You're not leaving here like that; we're going out tonight and you're going to come with us." And they took me to Roddy McDowall's.'[155] As Robin Anderson observed, 'Coral, for all the nonsense, was a sweet person, and terribly compassionate and *worried* about people.'[156]

Sadly, all this care and compassion was not bestowed on Vincent's nearest and dearest. Vincent's son Barrett and his family bore the brunt of Coral's hostility and resentment, but many family members and friends who had featured large in Vincent's 'pre-Coral' life came a cropper, and many of these emotional rifts hadn't healed by the time he died two decades later. In her 1999 biography of her father, Victoria Price revealed in great detail the depth of the problems she and her family experienced with Coral. She wrote, 'My stepmother and I had always had a rocky relationship. Although she loved me, she was extremely jealous of my close bond with my father and often made all of our lives quite miserable as a result.'[157] In the early days of their relationship, Coral had tried to help Vincent as he fretted about maintaining a good relationship with his daughter: 'Just be happy with her in a natural manner and she will be doubly so with you…I know how much you miss her.'[158] But this insight wasn't applied to her own behaviour: 'What became painful was the fights we had and how difficult she made it,' recalled Victoria Price. 'I would think, "I haven't done anything wrong, why is she picking on me?"'[159]

It was Barrett Price and his family who came off worst, as Victoria explained: 'Barrett doesn't suffer fools gladly. He has always had a very low tolerance level for people who are full of shit; and there was a big part of Coral that was *full* of shit – completely insincere and only interested in social-climbing. And, to my brother's credit, he wasn't going to kiss her ass: he would have done whatever it took to keep the peace, and he loved my father tremendously and wanted him to be happy. But once he saw how badly he was being treated, *and* his wife and kids, there was no way he was going to suck up to her… I was 14, and that's what you do when you're 14, you try to make people like you! So I was in a completely different place; had I been older, and Coral treated me like she treated them, I would have been in the same boat. I mean, she treated them *horribly*.'[160] Vincent, the husband, father and friend at the epicentre of the perpetual battle, usually acquiesced to Coral. 'Why *did* my dad put up with some of the truly horrible things that Coral did – for example, the fact that she cut my brother out of my Dad's life and, worse, his grandchildren? People have said to me, "Of course, your father didn't like to fight." And that's a family trait – I'll go 40 miles to avoid a fight. And I think that there was a real dynamic in their relationship…there's this thing that people do: that you convince yourself that all those things aren't problematic.

And yet it changed him – it changed him *completely* – and I think he chose to focus on the parts of Coral that were extraordinary – and, of course, there were many.'[161]

Yet, paradoxically, Coral could still be generous to those she regarded as her primary 'competitors' for Vincent's attentions: in 1986, when Victoria was putting herself through graduate school, it was Coral who agreed to stand guarantor for her $3000 loan from the New Mexico Educational Assistance Foundation. And, when Victoria came out as a lesbian, she found a supportive ally in Coral: 'When she tumbled to the fact that I was gay, suddenly she felt much better. In her mind, I was no longer a threat. I came out to my father in my early twenties. We were driving down the hill from his house and I blurted it out in the car. "Oh, I know," he said, calmly negotiating a hairpin turn. "Coral already told me." Shortly after my father told Coral the news, she presented me with a coming-out gift – a box of 40 silk bow ties! Coral's lesbian fashion sense remained stuck somewhere around D-Day. Coral lent a sympathetic ear to my romantic troubles. Both were eager to meet anyone I brought home, though my stepmother rarely missed an opportunity to flirt outrageously with my girlfriends or to comment on their looks or style. One woman, she told with a very knowing smile, "does it very well".'[162]

Such sweetness and light were rationed. 'Coral was vile to his daughter,' said Eileen Atkins. 'She called her "a fucking truck driver". After Coral died, I was doing *A Room of One's Own* in LA. Vincent was terribly ill by then, but he came to see the show – booked his own tickets and everything. And with him was this gorgeous young woman – and he said, "This is my daughter"; I couldn't believe this was the same woman Coral had been so rude about.'[163] 'I think she had a terrible time because Coral didn't like her – and that's not an easy thing to cope with,' said Jill Melford. 'And Coral, not being a maternal sort of person, didn't realise that you have to get on with your husband's children...'[164] Victoria Price had no illusions about Coral's duplicity where she was concerned: 'As time wore on, I would come in and out of favour with Coral – and I know for a fact that she referred to me as "Vincent's dyke daughter" to all of her English friends. What kind of a description came after that I can only image. When I met her English friends after her death, they would all look at me and say more or less the same thing, "You can't be Victoria. You're beautiful." I came to find the whole thing rather amusing – one can't help but look fabulous to someone who is expecting Quasimodo to show up at the door...'[165]

A certain amount of resentment and bitterness was also caused by Coral having to live in a city she despised. 'I can't imagine her in LA at all because she was so direct,' observed Jonathan Altaras. 'And the only way you can exist as an English person in the LA film community is to know that every single word they say is a lie – it's not just one in ten words, it's *every, single, word*. If you understand that, then you can survive. And I can't imagine that suited her at all.'[166] Jill Melford agreed: 'She always called it "that bloody horrible place" – she really hated it there, I think, because no one knew who she was. That didn't go down well: she was used to being the centre of a salon and it didn't suit too much just being "Mrs Vincent Price".'[167] Coral preferred San Francisco to Los Angeles; she told Tom Silliman, director of the Vincent Price Gallery, 'It can't possibly be part of California, it's too sophisticated!'[168]

John Schlesinger observed that, 'Irony is a word that doesn't exist in America.'[169] This didn't stop Coral using it to pillory some of the more preposterous aspects of life in LA. In January 1975, Charlton Heston and Vanessa Redgrave opened at the Ahmanson Theater in Peter Wood's production of *Macbeth*. 'The stage is actors' country,' said Heston. 'I've always felt the need to go back, to have my passport stamped.'[170] However, after seeing the show, there were many who felt his 'passport' should be permanently revoked. The production made abundant use of 'Kensington gore' and, according to Heston, 'H R Poindexter [the designer] gave us a great swooping stone structure down which I could stumble, half-naked, drenched in blood and horror-struck after killing the king.'[171] It was said that the audience howled with laughter at this point, as they did when Macbeth's prop head was brought out on a pike. The presence of Heston ensured the show's two-month run was a sell-out – as Coral discovered when, sensing it might be a rip-snorting stinker, she rang the box office:

'This is Coral Browne. Can I have seats for the first night of Charlton Heston's *Macbeth*?'

She was told there were no seats left for that night and hung up. Seconds later, she rang back.

'This is Mrs Vincent Price. Can I have two seats for the first night of Mr Heston's *Macbeth*?'

This time, 'Mrs Price' was again politely informed, no seats were left.

'All right, I'll have two for the second half.'[172]

Robin Anderson recalled another Charlton Heston vehicle which Coral treated with similar disdain. Ava Gardner had asked her to go to the premiere of *Earthquake*, the disaster movie she had made with Heston, complete with full ear-thumping Sensurround. Ava played Remy, the alcoholic wife of Heston's construction engineer. 'Coral said, "We've been invited to the premiere by Ava. She wants us to go, dear, so we must go and support her. Do you know about Ava? She's had quite a long romance, dear – with the vodka bottle…" And I thought, oh dear, here we go…' At the movie's climax, with the city of LA flooded and its survivors struggling for survival in its drain system as the water swirls in, Heston's character is faced with the choice of saving himself, or holding on to Remy and perishing with her. Nobly, he opts to die with her. Gardner had done all her own stunts for the movie's dramatic action sequences – and, according to Robin Anderson, some of her friends found it more than a little convincing: 'After the film was over, Ava asked Coral what she thought of it. So she said, "Ava darling, you were *so* genuine going down the drain…"'[173]

The new Mr and Mrs Price were champing at the bit to get back on the stage, and launch themselves as a successful theatrical husband-and-wife team, akin to the Oliviers and the Lunts. Unfortunately, the only similarities with the Lunts concerned their offstage activities: like Vincent, Alfred Lunt was a gourmet cook, and he and wife Lynn Fontanne had long been the subject of rumours and speculation about their private lives. However, Coral and Vincent's respective agents were on the case: Milton Goldman told Ronnie Waters, 'I spoke with Coral Browne yesterday…and she asked me to find out from you about a play that has been commissioned by Eddie Kulukundis and is being written by Alan Seymour under the supervision and direction of Eric Thompson. It is being especially written for Vincent and Coral… Coral and Vincent are desperately looking for a play to do together. I have suggested a revival of *The Play's the Thing*.'[174] Eventually, Coral thought she had found a suitable vehicle for herself and her new husband; once again, she looked to Anouilh and decided that *Ardèle* would be just right. As it turned out, it couldn't have been more wrong.

She asked Frith Banbury to direct the show – but, although he agreed, it was with some reservations: 'Vincent and Coral wanted to work together but they really were on different planes,' he explained. 'One was a serious actress, the other had a commodity to sell, which was all those horror films, and that was simply not suited to acting in straight plays. *Ardèle* is a tricky play to do. It had been done in London with a certain success with Isabel Jeans and Ronald Squire, but had been a three-night flop on Broadway. But Coral said, "Why don't we do it there?" I approached Robert Whitehead, and he said, that's a good idea. So we all four gathered in New York, and the idea was it should be done in the States to start with, with quite a long tour on the road and then hoping to bring it to Broadway. But when Robert went to the theatres, they didn't display what *he* would have thought to be much enthusiasm about the idea, and therefore he didn't manage to raise any money from them.'[175]

One of the reasons for investors' reluctance was that Charles Gray, whom Coral wanted in the show, was not considered to be a big enough name by American producers. Instead, Ralph Richardson, Christopher Plummer, Paul Scofield, Anthony Quayle and Alec Guinness were some of the bigger names approached to take the role of The General. Many of these were unavailable; others weren't right as far as Coral was concerned: 'Chris Plummer NOT weighty enough – too "light" for V – Sinden a possible – Ralph might die on us but would be lovely on the bill,' she told Frith Banbury.[176] Robert Morley was also considered but Coral put the kibosh on this idea: 'No, no, I really could not cope with Robert M AND the tour. His bad acting would ruin the delicate play, and drive me crazy!'[177] Coral was adamant: 'Let's face it, old Charlie would be better than anyone as he's in LOVE with the play and THAT makes a change and he'd pull his finger out (and I'd see he KEPT it out!)'[178] However, it emerged that it wasn't only Gray who producers were unimpressed with – they didn't think American or British theatre audiences would flock to see Vincent Price, and Banbury and Whitehead were concerned about how to break this news to Coral and Vincent.

'After a long delay, I told them I'll see if there's any chance of getting it on in London – and there I had more success, so I then had to get together with them again. I said to Vinnie, "If you do this play, to make it viable you will have to accept much, much less than you are used to earning, so I must lay it on the line before we go any further." He said he was prepared for that.'[179] In September 1974, Banbury had to tell Coral that he didn't think that the

West End atmosphere boded well for their plans, given that it was chock-full of shows called *Let's Get Laid, The Bedwinner, Pyjama Tops, No Sex Please We're British* and *Why Not Stay for Breakfast?*. It was certainly going to be hard to get West End audiences interested in the story of the scandal caused when a hunchback (who's never seen on stage), the 'old maid' of a wealthy family, falls in love with her tutor – also a hunchback. The outrage of her relatives is shown up as rank hypocrisy, since they are all having affairs.

During one of her visits to London, Coral tried to reassure Vincent: 'Ardele London prospects wonderful. Blodgett thinks career wise brilliant idea. I think morale wise super.'[180] Then her own morale took a dive: during her stay, she was told that Vicky had been diagnosed with cancer. To cheer her up, Robin Anderson and his friend, the actor Barry Justice, took her out to Morton's for dinner – and disaster struck again: 'Coral was having Dover sole, and a little fishbone got stuck in her throat,' said Robin Anderson. 'So we got her in a taxi and took her to St George's; we got her into A&E and she was doing this whole number, "I'm choking, I'm going to sue!" She was so busy talking about what she was going to do, she forgot about the fishbone... Then, of course, they needed to fill out a form for her. And they said, "Miss Browne, your age?" – and she suddenly became very discreet... But she was actually quite ill – we had to take her to see a throat specialist.'[181]

There was better news regarding *Ardèle*: it was given the go-ahead and, after a regional tour, would open at the Queen's Theatre that June. Coral told a reporter, 'I play the Countess and Vincent is the Count. Careful how you spell that, darling...'[182] 'They came over, and we got a very good cast. Charles Gray was marvellous in it,' said Frith Banbury, 'But there was an in-built problem with the play: the amusing characters played by Coral, Vincent and Charles departed just before the end and there was a long scene between two young people while the audience were thinking, "When are the others coming back?" And that didn't ever happen. Another difficulty is that Ardèle is the hunchback and she never appears – she has to be addressed offstage, which is very difficult.'[183]

Performing in England posed other problems for Coral, still in the process of obtaining 'American resident' status. She told Frith Banbury, 'My accountant...tells me I must NOT be in England more than 90 DAYS per year for the next 3 years from last April to avoid paying British Income Tax.'[184] And, despite her assurances to Vincent, she had any number of reasons for resisting a West End run: 'It is not worth it financially and the flat's a bit SMALL for us and we DON'T want to be away from home – dogs in kennels, etc – AND the part's not good enough for me…so as you can see I'm not all that keen to say nothing of bombs, misery and being in England with Mother there!!!'[185]

But it was all set: auditions to find the rest of the cast were held at the Phoenix Theatre on 11 March and four weeks' rehearsal began on April 28. 'Our rehearsals were at Westminster Abbey – in the Community Centre,' said Coral. 'All those people playing badminton…'[186] To counter this, on the first day of rehearsals, Coral and Vincent took over a restaurant and made lunch for everyone: while Coral chopped and dressed the salad, Vincent prepared the chicken and nut stuffing for stuffed crêpes and sour cream dips, periodically asking, 'Have you found my thumb yet?'[187]

Soon, the joking would stop, as it became apparent to Banbury that there was a serious problem: 'In the first week, Vincent, instead of rehearsing his own part, kept on saying how wonderful all the other actors were. And I realised that he hadn't actually got a method for serious work any more – you could almost say he didn't know how to work on a part any more. Coral was absolutely on to it like a knife. And about the third day, after rehearsals, she came privately to me and said, "He can't do it, can he? You and I will have to support him in every way we can." So I had to step in and treat him, in some ways, as if he were a student. He had an idea of what to do but he didn't seem to know how to do it. In the first act, he was OK, because the part of the Count has many amusing and sarcastic one-liners on the action all the time. But when it came to the second act, when he had what I would describe as an "aria", technically and vocally, he simply couldn't do it. I called two long rehearsals for him alone – I was almost reduced to saying things like, "Put your left foot forward first, not your right." It was very sad, and when it came to it, he didn't pull it off. It didn't get very good notices – and Vincent said, "It's all my fault. I've let you and Coral down." I didn't know what to say.'[188]

The play opened at the New Theatre, Oxford on 26 May, then ran for a week at the Theatre Royal Brighton. Coral said, 'I'll be glad when the bloody thing opens. We've done a tour and previews and you begin to feel like a pregnant woman wondering if the baby will ever be born.'[189]

The first 'baby' from the Price marriage was, sadly, stillborn: Herbert Kretzmer said, 'The presence in the cast of the Hollywood actor, Vincent

Price, not to mention his wife, the grand and imperious Coral Browne, may encourage curiosity-seekers to attend this... But its long-term chances must be considered doubtful.'[190] Milton Shulman was harsher: 'This revival's impact struck me as merely petulant and fleeting';[191] while the Daily Mirror said, '*Ardèle* is not so much a play as a debate on the theme What Is Love? ...seems better suited to the radio than to the stage.'[192] In *The Times*, Charles Lewsen declared the production to be 'as edifying as a dish of scarecrow in aspic'[193] and that Price was 'as legato as a London taxi driver reaching to stop his meter'.[194] Vincent bore the brunt of the criticism: 'Mr Price has a witty, deprecating presence and a good pettish way with one-liners, but handed anything more complex he mumbles. This is the West End recumbent.'[195]

During the play's run at the Queen's Theatre, Frith Banbury, sensitive to Vincent's guilt and the onslaught from the press, wrote to his leading man, expressing his admiration for the way he had pressed on regardless, despite the difficulties encountered, and saying he would never regret doing the production.[196] Sheridan Morley was kinder to the show which provided 'an evening of stylish bitchery built around a plot which looks like Rattigan crossed with Charles Addams. What follows, predictably, is Miss Browne's evening: pausing only to take occasional umbrage the way lesser women take aspirin, she sails through the drama in full rig... Mr Price, in by far the most thankless of the leading roles, exhibits commendable skill and charm...'[197] Years later, Morley said, 'I think it was a very unhappy choice – it's a very obscure piece. It was a bridge too far. Had they chosen an easier, drawing room comedy, they might have coasted home. It wasn't what the public wanted – an obscure Anouilh is not what you want to see Vincent Price and Coral Browne do.'[198]

The production seemed doomed, especially when real disaster struck one of the cast. 'There was a new character, a mad wife who appeared only in the last 20 minutes, played by Valerie White, who was marvellous, and that brought the play right up again,' said Frith Banbury. Indeed, White had been critically acclaimed for her performance as the character 'who bursts on the company with an extraordinary *Cold Comfort Farm* speech of gloating sexual disgust'.[199] Tragically, White suffered a heart attack during the Thursday matinee in Brighton, and was replaced by her understudy for the London run. White died in December 1975.

Coral and Vincent enjoyed a smaller, but more successful joint venture during the problematic run of *Ardèle*: they recorded the melodrama *Night of the Wolf* for BBC Radio 4, which began – predictably – with standard BBC sound effect, 'howling wolves'. Vincent played an American judge, Deakin, in Cambridge to search for his student son, believed to have killed himself, but with no body to prove it. Coral played Mrs Northcote, who lived in the house where his son was allegedly last seen, grandmother to Dorothy, Robert's 'constant companion'. His grandmother refutes the charge that Robert was a friend of Dorothy. They were both praised for their 'committed performances.'[200] There was talk of making a film version of the play, but this never materialised.*

After the failure of *Ardèle*, Vincent mused, 'Coral and I have survived a play. I guess this marriage will last forever.'[201] Sadly, 'forever' was not the word on Coral's mind, as her worst fears about Vincent's health started to be realised. During *Ardèle*, doctors discovered a malignant tumour in his digestive tract, for which he had surgery. To recover from the traumas of *Ardèle* and Vincent's surgery, that September he and Coral went on a fortnight's Swans Hellenic cruise to the Greek islands, Turkey and Egypt; their fellow passengers included Coral's old 'Bottom', Frankie Howerd and his partner Dennis Heymer. A year later, Coral appeared on Howerd's *This Is Your Life*: 'We all enjoyed seeing you on the telly,' Charles Gray told her. 'You simply looked ravishing, and what bona drag.'[202]

Meanwhile, their run of bad luck continued: while they were away, burglars broke into 16 Eaton Place. As Coral and Vincent made their way back to London, Robin Anderson and Jill Melford surveyed the damage and tried to clear up: 'It was such a mess of overturned furniture and forced locks that we simply couldn't let Coral return to see it,' said Anderson.[203] Using the photographs Anderson had taken when he refurbished the flat, they were able to ascertain exactly what had been taken. It included fur coats, jewellery

---

* Coral found some other small diversions: one day, a young man working at the Queen's mentioned that he and his boyfriend were going to a bring-and-buy sale to benefit a lesbian and gay organisation. Coral insisted on accompanying them. This same man later took home the umbrella Vincent used in the show and gave it to a friend who, many years later, reported: 'At work one day I happened to mention my umbrella's previous illustrious owner – whereupon, the entire office rose from their desks and went to the cloakroom where they stood silently staring at my umbrella. I'm not sure what they expected it to do; possibly to turn into a vampire bat and bite the General Manager on the neck. But at that moment I understood the extraordinary power of celebrity.'[204]

and silverware, though the fussy felons had eschewed the bulkier paintings and sculptures. And Vincent was delighted when he believed he'd found other valuables that had been overlooked: 'When we got back, I opened the drawer and it was filled with silver. "Look!," I said. "They didn't get the silver after all." Then I looked closer and it said "Savoy", "Dorchester", "Claridge's". It was a sit-down service for 90. She'd taken it from all over.'[205] Coral always believed that the burglars had 'cased the joint' by studying photographs of the flat published in a magazine. Her paranoia about this travelled with her to LA: Tom Silliman and some East LA College students were once visiting the house and started taking photographs for a newspaper article about the Gallery. Silliman told Kevin Scullin that, 'Coral flew into a rage. "Stop it, stop taking pictures...do you want the world to know what we have? They can find everything!"'[206]

After returning to LA, the couple were still determined to stage a professional partnership. They were offered the lead roles in a play called *Curtains!*, but opted not to take it up. Eventually, they signed up for a touring production of *Charley's Aunt* with their friend, Roddy McDowall; Coral took the part of Donna Lucia d'Alvadorez, reprising the role she played in a 1969 BBC TV production with Danny La Rue, and Vincent was Stephen Spettigue. The small-scale tour opened in Ann Arbor on 10 May and ended in Milwaukee on 26 June, and the regional critics were impressed with Coral: 'Miss Browne brings a stately and unexpectedly warm presence to the role of the real aunt';[207] 'She performs with such restrained wit and genuine warmth we can only wish she had more to do.'[208] Behind their backs, Coral was being less than complimentary about some of her colleagues: 'Vinnie and Roddy are first-class – the others ought to be made to walk home!'[209]

She was similarly unimpressed with the behaviour of some other American actors when she starred in a short-run of *The Importance of Being Earnest* and Tom Stoppard's *Travesties* at LA's Mark Taper Forum. She told Gregg Hunter, 'Here, it seems everybody is very much out for himself. You wouldn't catch me moving a hair during someone else's line, but I observe American actors indulging in all kinds of extraneous "business" when another character is speaking... I'm accustomed to being called for rehearsal when I'm needed. When we were preparing the two plays at the Taper there were many days when I drove the 45 minutes to the Music Center and then sat for four, five, six hours before actually rehearsing a scene. It made for exhausting long and boring days.'[210] But there was more to it than that: Coral wasn't in the best of moods because she had been recently been rejected by the management at the Ahmanson, responsible for the infamous Charlton Heston *Macbeth*: 'They want no part of me...because I'm not a "name" here,' she said. 'I was eager to play the aunt in Anouilh's *Ring Round the Moon*. She's supposed to be an imperious old crone ruling her household from a wheelchair. I didn't get the part, of course.' (In fact, it went to Glynis Johns.)[211]

The shows were being produced together as 'companion' pieces, with a company that included David Dukes and Coral's friend, Jean Marsh. Stoppard's fiercely intelligent and funny comedy has at its root an obscure historical fact – specifically, that an amateur actor called Henry Carr performed in a 1918 production of *Earnest*, staged by James Joyce, who had been stranded in Zurich after war broke out. Stoppard being Stoppard, he arranged for these characters to cross paths with Lenin and his wife, Nadya, living there in exile. Coral was lukewarm about her role: 'Actually, playing Mrs Lenin is rather a bore. I just have a few lines in Russian at the beginning of the play and then I sit in my dressing room for ages while everyone else is out there being terrifically energetic. Then I have to go out there and match that energy through a very long complicated speech, full of dates and places – everything that Nadya says is totally factual.'[212] Amusingly, as Nadya, Coral had to speak more Russian than she had during the entire 1958/9 Shakespeare Memorial tour.

As well as Lenin's wife, Coral was cast as Wilde's most famous *grande dame*, a prospect about which some had their reservations. Even her friend Frith Banbury thought 'she wasn't right as Lady Bracknell'.[213] And, as Coral revealed, 'Sir John Gielgud told me I should never play Lady Bracknell because I was too good-looking. Dear John, I love him. Practically every time he opens his mouth all his feet go in it. But I've never listened to that sort of advice. I was told not to try Lady Macbeth and when I did it was one of my triumphs... I was told I was too tall for Helena and that performance was one of the most satisfying to me personally.'[214] Later on, however, Coral did go right off the role: in 1987, she was asked to appear in another television production of *Earnest*, but turned down the offer to play 'Lady Rotten Bracknell – who is a man anyway'.[215]

The LA critics found nothing rotten in either of her performances. In *Travesties*, she '...proves she is a first-rate actress of enormous range by making the small role of Lenin's wife touching and believable'.[216] Edward Parone of

Variety enthused. 'The performances are, without exception, expert-plus',[217] while Dan Sullivan said, '*Earnest* is OK. *Travesties* is a joy.'[218] Coral was more than 'OK' as Lady Bracknell: 'It is precisely Coral Browne's potent charm that puts her Lady Bracknell in a ruling class by herself,' said one critic.[219] The *LA Times* said that her portrayal '...gives us the weight and the cutting edge that Wilde wants...not only does the audience perk up when she's on, so does the cast. At last, someone to act against.'[220] Ron Pennington enthused, 'Browne easily achieves exactly the right qualities – she is haughty, stern and shrewd... it's a beautifully modulated performance.'[221]

Unfortunately, according to Coral, there was nothing beautiful about the performance which her friend Roddy McDowall came to see: 'Roddy and Paul saw a very good Act I and a disaster Act II,' she told Vincent, who was away lecturing. 'That fat bummed Dukes sat on "my" chair and broke the leg off just two seconds before my entrance so I had to STAND all the act and got in everyone's way and I missed quite a few things. I was LIVID. It would happen when Roddy was there.'[222] Happily, this performance was missed by the *LA Herald-Examiner*, who declared, 'She is a delight in every scene. Her performance should and will be remembered next year when awards time comes around for the Los Angeles Drama Critics Circle.'[223] Remembered it was: Coral won the 1977 Los Angeles Drama Critics' 'Featured Performance' Award for Lady Bracknell. It was the ultimate irony: the only stage award she won in her 50-year career was for a role that she didn't particularly care for, which some of her friends didn't feel she was right for, in a country were there is no such thing as a 'handbag'.

Her next role was one that Coral wasn't always comfortable with, but which she would now perform most often – 'Mrs Vincent Price'. She took a back seat as Vincent embarked on a challenge which, on the evidence of *Ardèle*, appeared to be beyond him. In fact, it would prove to be his biggest critical success, and more than compensate for the bitter disappointment of his last stage outing. *Diversions and Delights* was a one-man show about Oscar Wilde, written by John Gay. Set in a Parisian theatre in 1899, a year before Wilde's death, the ruined writer speaks to the paying 'audience' about his triumphs and tragedies, while sipping 'absinthe' – in fact, a glass of water coloured with a foul-tasting vegetable dye. Its first performance was on 11 July 1977, at the Marines' Memorial Theater, San Francisco, after which Vincent toured the play through America until December the following year. After this, he took the show on an intermittent global tour, giving 800 performances in 300 cities (he was still receiving requests to perform it in 1985). One memorable stop in this international itinerary was in 1979, when Price performed it at the Tabor Opera House, Leadville, Colorado on the same stage where Wilde had lectured the miners about art in 1883.

Late in Vincent's career, *Diversions and Delights* was a triumph, providing him with the sort of critical acclaim that had escaped him when he attempted to forge a stage partnership with Coral. In 1992, he reflected that 'my role as Oscar Wilde was my greatest achievement as an actor'.[224] He was not alone in this assessment: 'Price could win an Oscar for his Wilde show,' declared the *Chicago Daily News*, while the *Hollywood Reporter* said, 'If the first act shows Price as a great performer of the comic, the last act shows him as one of the nation's great dramatic actors'.[225] However, almost inevitably, the show was not a success when it reached New York. Richard Eder of the *New York Times* said, 'Mr Price gives a most delicate and touching performance…' but said the second half of the show 'drags, and loses color and contrast'.[226] The show closed just two weeks after opening on Broadway. Vincent told Bernard Drew, film critic for Westchester Rockland Newspapers, 'I'm not bitter or depressed. I thought New York had had it with one-man shows. And now I know it. My only anger is for the producers who didn't advertise it properly.'[227] One notable omission from his itinerary was London. Mindful of her husband's mauling at the hands of the critics during *Ardèle*, Coral persuaded him not to risk performing the show there. She said, 'I see no reason for him to do it. I think the critics could be tough on an American doing Wilde – Vinnie might be shot down – & for what – not for MONEY that's for sure…'[228]

Coral, for her part, was seemingly content to play the dressing-room wife, supporting Vincent and welcoming the many backstage visitors who beat a path to his door. She told Don Lane, 'He's a workaholic, it's essential for him to work; it's not essential for me to work. It's more essential that we should be together. We're very fond of each other; we get great pleasure from each other and being together; we have the same interests and that's splendid. We see art galleries and play around and have a very happy time. I think he would be miserable alone and also it's very difficult to do a one-man show.'[229] But the play was starting to take its toll: 'I feel very much the country bumkin being away from "home" (if that's LA) and long to get on some kind of even keel,' she told John Schlesinger. 'Have been away from any permanent spot since last June and it does seem a long time living in a couple of suitcases and not speaking much to characters. V is terribly tired and I feel is not at all well. I've got a long line of doctors and dentists "at the ready" – it's repair time.'[230] And there were other curious ill-effects: 'A strange thing has happened to my voice,' Vincent revealed, 'I got a recording of him reading "The Ballad of Reading Gaol" and Wilde had a very high voice, so I pitched my voice higher. It's very difficult now for me to bring my voice down lower to its natural pitch. I'm stuck with the voice of Oscar Wilde.'[231] Or, in all likelihood, that of an impostor: in 2000, the British Library announced it had proved the recording was a fake.

In 1977, Coral was asked to do *The Importance of Being Earnest* in New York but, as she told Frith Banbury, 'I'm not going to do that – it is May, June, July, Aug, Sep and Vinnie does his one-man play on Wilde opening San Fran July 8 and will want someone to talk to every night. A one man-er is depressing – no chums to call on or talk to.'[232] But there was another reason, as she revealed to John Schlesinger: 'You've probably heard – I've been cut up something shockin' – but cured. Had a melanoma on my ankle. But the professor of cancer surgery got at me and took no chances. My doctors' words are "You've been BUTCHERED" – I now go around looking like George Sand or Puss in Boots, take your pick. Am going to London Sep 16 – Oct 8 to get a lot of long drag from Jean Muir and see Mother!!! Jean flew all the way from NY to be with me when I was so ill – I was v touched. Poor Vinnie was filming in Fiji at the time.'[233]

Some of Coral's friends believed then, as now, that there had been no need for her to be 'cut up' at all. According to Victoria Price, 'Adrienne Corri really felt that what Coral called the cancer on her leg wasn't that at all; but *she* was convinced it was and so she had this whole chunk taken out. But then to say she was fixated on illness would not be too strong…and that was fear. And Adrienne could see it – and because she could see it, she would call it with Coral. She would say to her, "OK, you're coming over to dinner tonight and you are not going to mention the word 'cancer'." And Coral would be *mute.*'[234]

The silence wouldn't last. Now, as Coral had suffered what she perceived as a major health scare, 'poor Vinnie' got an earful, as his wife articulated her concerns about his hectic work schedule and the pressures this was bringing to bear on *her* happiness, *his* health and *their* marriage: 'WHAT is the point of all this if the end is Forest Lawn – I simply couldn't cope with my life without you & we should have a few years left, with any luck so PLEASE see to it that we do...I love you my darling SO much – HATE being away from you...'[235] One of her biggest concerns was the state of Vincent's health; she was constantly trying to get him to stop smoking: 'Knock off the fags – in all senses,' she chided.[236]

That September, she went to London to sort out her finances, see friends and attend to 'Mother'. As usual, she stayed *chez* Schlesinger; while she was there, he hosted a party in her honour: '40 guests – "The Grange" doing the food – 10 waiters & the household staff on top of that which brings the total to 15 slaves in all.'[237] Unfortunately, several of her best friends were out of town and those who were around did nothing to dispel her gloom: 'Still jolly depressed,' she told Vincent. 'I HATE being here in London. Its too depressing as Vick is so much older & awful & its all sad & sordid... The daily visits to Delves & lunch with Mother are killers for me – to say nothing of the look of everybody in the street – dirty, downcast & zombie like...'[238] Schlesinger himself had to leave mid-visit and fly to LA, to attempt to raise the finance for his next film, *Yanks* – which, according to Coral, was 'a very little film about little soldiers & little waitresses in the last war (in England). I think we've had that subject over too many years – & not a part good enough for a "name".'[239]

Coral had her own financial matters to sort out, having meetings with her accountants, the Inland Revenue and her banks. She also went to see a doctor about the prognosis for a recurrence of a melanoma and was told 'like 99 p.c come back the stomach or liver etc: could have done without that good news', she told Vincent.[240] And the cavils continued: she dined with Charles Gray and Ava Gardner at the Carafe and, she told Vincent, 'He's flat broke & I saw Ava give him some money before we left her place... I think Charles will step out of the world fairly soon as he's in a bad way indeed...there doesn't seem anything for him to live for. He thinks acting is a load of "rotten rubbish" & all his friends have deserted him (I suppose because of his drunken insulting behaviour) & says only Ava speaks to him now...'[241]

Coral took some of her misery out on her absent husband: 'Maybe if my name was Ethel Pisshouse, of Trash Alley you'd get up at 7AM & write to me...feel very neglected by no telegram or a word from you. I know how the work is – but one fucking overnight telegram isn't going to be the straw that broke the camel's back. You're awfully thoughtless in that way. Rotten about the little things like flowers & thinking ahead to send a card.'[242] However, she cheered up a bit when she went to to see Ralph Richardson and Celia Johnson in *The Kingfisher* at the Lyric; she thought he was 'absolutely super & for my money better than Gielgud, Larry, Alec & the lot rolled into one. He was so happy to see me afterwards & I thought I'd be raped over the wash-basin.'[243] In fact, Richardson asked Coral if she was interested in doing the play with him in New York. But, as she told Vincent, 'It's a 2 character play so don't think I'd ever be able to learn THAT!! Its about 2 people of 65 & 73 getting married & FUCKING!!!'[244]

In February 1978, they managed to find time in Vincent's busy schedule to move to their new home in the Hollywood hills: 9255 Swallow Drive. Naturally, the address got the left eyebrow and the tongue going. Robin Anderson recalled, 'She said, "I'm married to Vinnie Price, one of the biggest closet queens in Hollywood and we're moving to *Swallow* Drive. And furthermore, dear, he's sold the Roller. And guess what he's got instead? A camper van! So there I am, with Vinnie Price in *Swallow* Drive, in a *camper!*'[245] She told Alec Guinness they sold the Miller Drive house 'to the man next door who wants to put his Mother in the pool house – with the heat there in the summer & the cold & damp in winter he's hell bent on pushing her thru the pearly gates at the earliest possible.'[246]

In true LA fashion, arranging the move was a nip-and-tuck affair: 'Vinnie only has from Feb 19–29 off until about October so I pray the move will happen when he's back to help.'[247] She told John Schlesinger they had moved to 'A rather ordinary, no atmosphere, Californian semi-middle class house which I find much to <u>my</u> liking – air conditioning, lots of cupboard space, decent size kitchen on one level and no pool (the latter only being a plus because of me 'ole not fit to be seen). It's what's known as "Birdland" by the squares and the Swish Alps by the belles below Sunset in the faggots' flats. It's the last street on top of Doheny. NOT yet unpacked because Vinnie's been flashing his Oscar in NY And SF and is now doing Damn Yankees for 3 weeks then from Sep 10 to Dec 11 he does 58 cities with Oscar.'[248]

Lindsay Anderson thought the couple's new home was 'cool and elegant and spacious – but not pretentious…it is a picture of harmonious tranquillity, of European civilisation, infinitely relaxing'.[249] Coral told a reporter, 'Our dining room area is sufficient for exactly six people…we have a king size bed with barely enough space to get in and out of the bedroom. Closet space is limited to put it politely...'[250] There was art everywhere, of course – even the garden contained Romanesque statues. 'The house was wonderful and very pretty,' said Jill Melford, 'It was a tiny doll's house, a little gem... And of course she complained about it non-stop... "fucking Vinnie's paintings everywhere"...and they were, they were stacked up. But then she complained about everything! She was always having a moan – but it was a funny moan...'[251]

This was more than could be said for the moans of 'Mother', which grew more desperate and emotional. 'I expect you do not have any idea when you will come home – That is my longed for wish,' Vicky wrote to Coral.[252] 'I am so very depressed, loneliness is an awful state... I only wish you loved me more, then you would understand... Somehow I must put my letters badly to you because I never seem to do anything right – I do try because I love you so much...'[253] For Coral's birthday that year, she sent her daughter a diamond ring: 'Dad gave it to me when we had been married 25 years... <u>You</u> are all I ever wanted but life has not been that kind to me – it is the way God works things out I expect.'[254] That October, Coral went to London where, she told John Schlesinger, she had to 'deal with Mama who's gone "funny" and thinks she's got no lolly and is trying to trip up Arabs with her walker to flog her diamond rings – must get power of attorney and all that'.[255]

One of Vicky's friends, Lily Henry, interceded in the battle of wills: she told Coral, 'She is extremely complex, no one sweeter when she's in a good mood but when she gets aggressive she can be quite impossible...she's always accusing people when she's in a bad mood... I think she resents her life as it is now after the luxury of former years... I really would not worry much. Delves seem to be doing what they can but Vick is not exactly easy.'[256]

And, sometimes, nor was being Coral: the offers of work were now few and far between. 'I work a bit on the Coast but since I married Vincent, I sit in California and read scripts till I'm blue in the face, waiting for this gorgeous play that absolutely requires me but they simply aren't writing plays for actresses like me any more. They are in London. I am offered all sorts of things there alone but Vincent is based in California and I didn't marry him to work in London.'[257] She was asked to consider playing the part of Miss Balfour the housekeeper in Billy Wilder's *Fedora*, but admitted to a certain relief when Frances Sternhagen was cast: 'I didn't fancy an <u>Old</u> Mrs Danvers pushing a wheelchair all over Europe in every shot!', she told Frith Banbury.[258] It appeared that, in Hollywood at least, her only starring role would be playing 'Mrs Vincent Price'. But what neither she – nor, indeed, Mir Bashir – could have predicted was the imminent creation of *the* most perfect part for her: yet another version of 'Coral Browne'.

'Unless a Job Comes for Coral'

1979–1983

As the decade drew to a close, and Coral approached her own seventies, her work prospects appeared inauspicious. To make matters worse, ill health – and the *fear* of it – were beginning to cramp her and Vincent's style. As Coral said to Robin Anderson, and many others, 'Old age isn't for sissies!'[1] 'After 50, life seems to be one long trip to the dentist or the optician,' she complained. 'I've done it so often I don't know which bits of me are real any more. You get prone to peculiar diseases and it's another ache and another pain.'[2] Coral continued to wage her endless war against the ravages of time with regular cosmetic corrections – eyes, cheeks, even, at one point, major reconstruction of her teeth (in 1985, Vincent had $25,000 worth of dental treatment). Little was left untouched by the surgeon's scalpel; she even persuaded Vincent to succumb to a nip-and-tuck on his neck. She told Alec Guinness: 'Vinnie went into hospital to have the "waggle" removed from under his chin – or is it wattle, no that's Australian for mimosa – anyroad, it's now been planted behind his ears and he's home looking like he's off to the Pole – some kind of Nanook of the North head dress – most unbecoming…'[3]

In 2001, Dame Diana Rigg said, 'I had a nip about 10 years ago, but I can't be bothered now. I let Coral be a warning. She had her face done to the extent that when she smiled it was a terrible effort to get the lips back over her teeth again.'[4] And, of course, there were the endless dietary attempts to keep in shape. In 1980, Coral discovered the Scarsdale Diet; she told Alec Guinness: 'I lost 10lb in two weeks – I look rather good & you can see the cheek bones & I've a remarkably small waist now – Also look younger I'm told…DIDN'T find it difficult to do for the two weeks.'[5] She became a sworn advocate of the regime, recommending it to everyone from John Gielgud to the Olivier family: she told Alec Guinness (who she was also trying to 'convert', 'The Scarsdale Diet has been a huge success with Lady Blowright (lost 8lbs in a week) Richard Olivier (lost 14lb in a week).'[6]

Five years in Los Angeles had brought about other alterations – not the surgical or physical kind, but just as effective: the metamorphosis of her identity from Coral Browne to Mrs Vincent Price was now virtually complete. The once-glittering British stage career – occasionally interrupted by a quirky but memorable film role – meant nothing in Hollywood, and occasional offers from Britain to revive her old Shakespearean parts for television didn't appeal. 'They [the BBC] phoned me recently and said would I be interested in playing the queen in Hamlet, in this big new television series.'[7] The cast included two actors, Derek Jacobi and Patrick Stewart, who had given superb performances in another BBC drama, I, Claudius. But Coral wasn't interested: 'I don't think they're very good on television, I really don't. Doesn't show the work...'[8] Claire Bloom accepted the part of Gertrude. Coral also revealed that, in 1979, she turned down a chance to work with her friend Alec Guinness: 'I was asked to do The Old Country in London; Alan Bennett wrote it with me and Alec in mind. But it would have meant four weeks rehearsal, then four weeks out [of London] then six months in London. I know he [Vincent] wouldn't mind, but he's a workaholic and it's much more important that he should be kept happy than I should be, really...'[9]

In 1979, Coral and Vincent were offered another chance to work together, this time fronting a sci-fi TV series for Warner Brothers, created by Ivan Goff and Ben Roberts, the men behind Charlie's Angels and Logan's Run. Time Express (speeded up from its original title, Time Train) had a one-track premise: 'Ever dream of changing your past? Aboard the Time Express... It's possible.'[10] The 'Express' was a train, presided over by husband-and-wife Jason and Margaret Winters, which departed Los Angeles Union Station and took its passengers on a journey 'back in time' to relive a momentous episode in their lives. Jason Winters was described as 'Dapper and elegant, he's loftier in manner and more cynical in his thinking than Margaret, but she has a way of warming him up and bringing him down to earth. As a couple, they're made for each other.'[11] Margaret Winters 'is beautiful, elegant and lovingly devoted to Jason, though she's not above gently chiding him for his occasional lapses into cynicism. She's warm, intuitive and emotionally supportive of the passengers.'[12]

Filmed at Burbank Studios and at various locations in LA, guest stars booked for the series included future Dallas players Steve Kanaly and John Beck. The first episode, aired by CBS on 26 April, featured another husband-

and-wife team, Jerry Stiller and Anna Meara, and James MacArthur ('Book 'Em' Danno from *Hawaii Five-O*). Stiller played a tycoon who takes the Express back to the moment when he found two million dollars in cash – and kept it – while MacArthur was a man who tries to find the one person capable of curing his terminally-ill wife. Unfortunately, *Time Express* couldn't get the critics to come on board: 'Let's say five nice words about *Time Express*: Vincent Price and Coral Browne. The real-life married couple promises wit, sophistication and a certain droll, darling-we're-only-in-it-for-the-fun... And we get them – for maybe five minutes. Then there's the other 55 minutes, which only seem longer. This isn't just a disappointment, it's a waste.'[13]

Coral and Vincent's five minutes of wit and sophistication were appreciated by viewers – one wrote, 'We loved it and with Coral Browne and Vincent Price this show should be a tremendous success. The appeal of a married couple working together still holds, as did the *Thin Man* series, the magic of the Lunts also.'[14] 'Both of you are like a breath of fresh air, especially the way Mrs Price dresses, so womanly,' gushed another fan.[15] But these viewers were in the minority, and the *Express* came off the rails after just four episodes.

A few months later, they turned down an offer to play David and Judith Bliss in a production of *Hay Fever* for the McCarter Theatre Company in Princeton the following spring. Despite the McCarter's good reputation, appearing together on stage no longer had the same appeal – even if it was physically possible. It was easier to accept less demanding roles: in March 1980, they were joint MCs at the LA Drama Critics Circle annual awards dinner, where the guest of honour was Julie Harris. *Evita* cleaned up most of the awards, but the dinner's most memorable moment came when they presented a special gong to Quentin Crisp for his one-man show, 'for exemplifying personal courage and self-reliance, as well as enabling theatre audiences to gain a richer awareness of themselves through his wit and wisdom'.[16]

Perversely, Coral began accepting parts in movies predestined for the video bargain bin even before a single frame had been shot – the very thing she had always been trying to dissuade Vincent from doing. In 1980, she provided the heavenly voice of Hera in *Xanadu*, a costly musical remake of *Down to Earth*, starring Olivia Newton-John and Gene Kelly, in what would be his last film role. Intended as a vehicle to cash in on Newton-John's huge success in *Grease* two years earlier, the movie's producers splashed out: the set of the Xanadu club – the place 'where dreams come true' – cost a million dollars alone. But the Xanadu 'dream' turned into a nightmare: the film was a gargantuan critical and commercial failure. One reviewer summed it up in a single line: 'In a word, Xana-don't.'*

To escape the frustrations and dearth of inspiration in LA, Coral frequently visited New York, usually staying at Wyndhams Hotel on 42 West 58th Street, becoming friends with its owners, Suzanne and John Mados. There, she would catch the latest shows – she and Jean Marsh saw the Broadway productions of *Amadeus* and *Piaf* together – and meet up for a dine-and-gossip with friends, including visitors from England and New York residents such as Marti Stevens and Lillian Hellman. She told Alec Guinness, 'Went to a bun-fight at Marti's last Sunday for Lillian Hellman… [she] was in fine fettle but its sad to see her blind. She can't find the food with the fork & if she strikes it lucky & manages to stab & get it to the mouth the teeth seem to buck at that & the chewing becomes a major problem.'[17] In April 1980, she and Vincent both went to the city for a party being given by Joan Plowright, who had been appearing in the comedy *Filumena* on Broadway, directed by Laurence Olivier. Plowright's first appearance on the New York stage had not been a raging success: the show closed after 33 performances. But at least the party was memorable: 'It was SO jolly – never seen so much food in my life,' Coral told Alec Guinness. 'There were a lot of young folk who ran in & out in a state of undress – that brightened up Vinnie's old eyes. A great deal of night tennis was played on the roof of their hotel and I suspect hanky-panky in the sauna and feelies in the pool…the OLD folk consisted of Jimmy Coco – us – Joan – Jeremy Brett (!!) & his live in what-you-call-him & Max Schell – I HATE him a treat so that called for several vodkas & a bad day to follow. Went to Marti's [Stevens] for that where George Cukor sat for three hours with his flies undone & was generally forgetful – Christopher Isherwood his usual 14 year old <u>superb</u> self – such a dear, funny BRIGHT boy – Gavin Lambert hot from Tangier & complaining about the inflation here – I presume the meat rack on Selma has gone up.'[18] In LA, she continued to rub shoulders with the glitterati: 'Had dinner last week at Rupert Allan's for Princess Grace,' she told Alec Guinness. 'V small, only

---

* Movie producer and campaign copywriter John Wilson saw *Xanadu* when it played as one half of a double-feature with *Can't Stop the Music* (another musical movie mishap), and was inspired to create the Razzie Awards, 'honouring' the very worst achievements in film. Appropriately, the very first 'Worst Director' Razzie Award was given to *Xanadu*'s director, Robert Greenwald.

ten of us. She is VERY beautiful & the press don't do her justice. She was also very nice & your ears should have been burning a treat.'[19]

Occasionally, the hint of a job offer would come: she told Alec Guinness, 'VERY nearly got into Charlie Chan & The Dragon Lady [*Charlie Chan and the Curse of the Dragon Queen*] – a certain Welsh actress [Rachel Roberts] has had a LOT of difficulty – I suspect the bottle, the "change", the inadequate lover & a few more disastrous happenings, got the producers to call me. She'd been rehearsing for three weeks + the last gasp was loss of voice – "They" had hoped on the first day of filming she'd <u>finally</u> fall over so I was engaged IF that happened, to be paid fifty thousand dollars – I need hardly say the day came + she DID get through it + I got a nice <u>bunch of roses</u> + thanks for learning the part + being a trooper!! It's too much. I've got to the stage of wondering if I'll EVER be able to do "it" again – or if I'll ever get an "offer" here.'[20]

There was one offer that Coral would gladly have declined but simply couldn't: Vincent had said 'yes' to a tour of *Diversions and Delights* – in Australia. Despite refusing to accompany Vincent to Sydney four years earlier, when he was making for a series of TV commercials there for Hitachi, this time she felt the tour was too arduous for him alone, so she reluctantly agreed to go. Frith Banbury said, 'I remember Coral saying "He's going to do it in *Australia*" – and she loathed Australia, *loathed* it! I said it wasn't so bad when I went. But when they went, I got a card saying, "You are wrong. Australia is every bit as horrible as I knew it would be!"'[21]

Vincent's two-month, 46 show tour of Australia began on 30 June, and took him (and Coral) to Sydney, Adelaide, Canberra, Melbourne, Brisbane and Perth. In Sydney, they appeared on the *Don Lane Show*, where Vincent repeated his 'how to cook a fish in a dishwasher' party piece, and visited Coral's old friends, Thelma Scott and Gwen Plumb, at their Whale Beach house. Melbourne was memorable for many reasons: it was the hundredth city Vincent had performed the play in – and it ran at the Comedy Theatre, Coral's old stomping ground. During their two weeks in the city, they took time out to inspect the construction of Melbourne's new Arts Centre (Coral refused to wear the requisite hard hat when having her photograph taken). They paid a brief visit to Footscray – in Sydney, Vincent had told Don Lane, 'I'm terribly excited I'm going to see the slum where she was born.' There wasn't much to get excited about: 'We went to see the house where I lived,' said Coral, 'but that had been knocked down and the remaining aunt we were going to visit dropped dead a week before we got there.'[22] In her suite at the grand Hotel Windsor, Coral gave an interview to Frank Van Straten, head of the Arts Centre's performing arts collection for their oral history files. Van Straten also asked Coral whether she would be willing to donate – either then or at some point in the future – her collection of papers and photographs. Surprisingly, she agreed.

There had been changes to her homeland in the last 20 years: as Clive James observed, 'With the advent of Gough Whitlam's government, in the 1970s, Australia had begun to esteem itself... The cringe became a snarl. Tub-thumping was heard in areas where a reasoned tone might have been more suitable.'[23] Whitlam had put a great deal of dollars and determination into helping his country develop an independent identity and lose its Britishness. Even Patrick White was temporarily converted from cynicism: 'I had become enthusiastic about Australia for the first time in my life during the Whitlam regime.'[24] Australian art, literature, film, food and wine were all starting to lose their reputation for being 'naff'. Australian culture, from the backyard 'barbie' to full-bloodied reds, from the Kylies to the Thomas Keneallys, was being wholeheartedly consumed by younger generations of post-colonial Poms. Still, old prejudices die hard, especially late in life: for Coral to embrace her home country would be to take a step backwards – and that was neither her style nor her nature. Indeed, Coral's opinions about Australia weren't greatly altered by the visit: 'Friends said you'll see how much it has changed but, apart from the Sydney Opera House, which I love, it hasn't changed at all in 50 years.'[25] But she was, at least, cognisant of its burgeoning new wave of cinema, and what this meant for Australian actors. She admitted, 'I'd love to do a film here... there are more theatres here now than when I was here... I think you'll find a lot of good Australian actors will stay here...they'll go and make a movie, but they'll come back. Unlike the old days when you had to go – and stay.'[26] At the end of August, she left her home country – for the last time.

Back in America, when Vincent wasn't busy with *Diversions and Delights* duties, he was busy with his lucrative art lecture tours; at one point, he was the highest paid lecturer in the United States. Coral's most frequent diary entries became 'V away' or 'V leaves' – and she was feeling increasingly anxious and neglected. She wrote to her husband, 'You must know, if you stop to think about it, that I have been a woman, not spoiled, but always in demand professionally & personally & to find myself deprived of both a place which is not a capital city but a village & to have nothing but you & two dogs isn't much – especially when I don't have you around much these days & when you do come home I have a tired out ill man who is shut in an office answering letters & checking contracts, who doesn't want to celebrate in any way, hates taking me out to a movie or any jolly evening & frankly is a bore, unless other people are around…somewhere it isn't right & now its ridiculous & utterly selfish… It worries me to death the way you are working – that more than anything contributes to my unhappiness… God knows I'm not perfect & must be hell to live with…'[27]

And there was enough 'hell' to go round: in the autumn of 1980, she went to London, to get fitted with new bifocal contact lenses and to check on Vicky. Now, when she was in town, she always told 'Mother' she would be arriving a few days after she actually did, so she could have a few peaceful dinners with friends. But it brought little respite – she told Vincent, 'Mother not being at all nice & picking on me all the time because I wear pants & now insists I get up at dawn to put my hair in curlers as she's taken against berets or the nice little soft hats I got in Melbourne. She is VERY strong & VERY well – more so than in the last ten years & therefore has much more strength to be vile.'[28]

Vincent helped her recuperate from the horrors of 'Mother' by taking her on a Christmas and New Year cruise, taking in Barbados, Devil's Island, Rio, St John's Antigua and Fort Lauderdale. Although, as she told Frith Banbury, 'I like travel – it gets me out of housework',[29] her professional frustration started to manifest itself physically. Early in 1981, she began to suffer severe abdominal discomfort. She spent a week in hospital undergoing tests and X-rays, including 'the final insult of eight tablespoons castor oil followed by five enemas' which, she told Alec Guinness, 'nearly succeeded in having me join the feathered choir.'[30] It wasn't, as she'd feared, cancer but a peptic ulcer. She told Caroline Cornish-Trestrail, 'We've had a christening and I've called it Ulcer-on-top-of-the-hill!!!'[31] 'I presume the boredom of living on the top of the hill, alone, watching local TV & being in the bullseye of an intellectual desert eventually got to my gut,' she mused. 'Vinnie is still laughing at the bad joke of me getting an ulcer, me wot loves eating – Imagine how you'd feel!!! We're very alike when it comes to grub & a little drinkie.'[32]

The timing was unfortunate: she was offered, albeit at extremely short notice, a chance to return to Stratford, Ontario to take two roles, including Volumnia in *Coriolanus*: 'Start rehearsing next week & stay there through

September!'[33] However, she decided it would have caused too much domestic upheaval, as she explained to Alec Guinness: 'Have the dogs, the builders re-building & adding a study & whirlpool tub for Vinnie – Vinnie's 70th birthday in May – when he <u>finally</u> finishes this lecture tour – It isn't like getting an offer from the National when you live in Eatonstrasser – and BRIAN BEDFORD directing.'[34]

With Coral's ulcer under control, she and Vincent temporarily left the 'desert' and took to the high seas again, this time for a Royal Cruise Line trip to the Far East on the *Golden Odyssey*, where they were booked as guest hosts/lecturers. Passengers were invited to 'Join Vincent Price on an Odyssey into the Mystery of China and the Orient'. After their oriental odyssey, Coral prepared herself for a dressing-down: she had a supporting part in an American TV drama, *Eleanor, First Lady of the World*. The story concerned itself with the latter years of former First Lady Eleanor Roosevelt (played by Jean Stapleton, best known as Edith Bunker in the TV series *All in the Family*), when she played a crucial role in getting the United Nations to pass the first Universal Declaration of Human Rights in Paris in 1948. Coral was playing Roosevelt's great friend, Lady Stella Reading who, among other things, founded the British Women's Royal Voluntary Service. It is Stella who explains to Mrs Roosevelt the problems faced by the millions of Europeans displaced by the war that prompts the former First Lady's humanitarian efforts. Coral had never heard of Lady Reading: 'There's apparently only one photograph of her extant,' she told Alan Bennett, 'and they've given it to make-up, so I fear the worst. They've kitted me out in some Oxfam clothes, furs with alopecia, plus I have to wear these invalid shoes.'[35] Despite her worst fears, Coral's scenes managed to inject the soapy drama with a much-needed frisson of glamour and sharpness – even in the final scene, where Lady Reading witnesses the 'First Lady of the World' fulfilling an earlier pledge made to her grandson, by taking a running slide along a particularly slippery corridor floor. Coral moaned to Alec Guinness about the rigours she'd endured: 'When I've worked the hours have been 'orrible – from 7AM until 10–11PM – they get away with murder here…' but then admitted, 'I've enjoyed doing the TV & hope I'm good. It's five years since I worked & I've missed it terribly.'[36]

Five years – yet it seemed five days didn't pass without Vincent receiving more offers and invitations. Coral was still enraged at his propensity for saying 'yes' to everything offered and filling up his diary with work that would have financial, but little artistic, merit. And, apparently still oblivious to Coral's hidden wealth, he went for the money. Some of the requests were more unusual than others: Milton Goldman, Coral's American agent at ICM (who had now taken over London Artists), asked Vincent, care of Coral, to contribute 'a drawing or doodle or sketch of any kind on plain paper', for the New Dramatists' annual charitable auction. Coral duly passed the request on to her husband, and asked, 'Please do this – any old doodle of your cock would help.'[37] Vincent ignored her suggestion and submitted a more tasteful doodle consisting of stars and the figure '20'. In March 1982, he attended the ultimate envelope-opening ceremony – the 54th Academy Awards – where he presented the Oscar for Best Make-Up to Rick Baker – appropriately, for the modern horror flick, *An American Werewolf in London*.

The years of putting her marriage and Vincent's welfare first, together with the calibre and scarcity of work she was offered, rankled. Half-hearted ideas for the couple to work together again came to naught; one suggestion, mooted by Christopher Taylor and relayed to them by Frith Banbury, was a play about the friendship between Edith Wharton and Henry James. However, Coral told Banbury, 'Can't get Vinnie interested enough in the James thing – he has too much to do. If he was at home moaning about having nothing coming up I might get him to it.'[38]* Producer Sam L Irvin Jr was keen to discuss a script by Brian Clemens (writer of many episodes for *The Professionals* and *The New Avengers*) for Vincent and Coral. The project didn't materialise, but then the title alone might have condemned it to failure: *Stiff*. Another offer came for them to do a show at Granny's, a 700-seat dinner theatre in Dallas. Rather misjudging the type of venue, Vincent and Coral suggested *The Waltz of the Toreadors*; this was rejected and the Harry Kurnitz comedy *Once More, with Feeling* was suggested instead. Yet again, nothing came of the idea.

In the meantime, financial affairs continued to weigh heavily on Vincent's mind. 'He's having a v difficult time making his WILL,' Coral told Alec Guinness. 'He finds it tedious I think. By Californian law half of everything he has is mine & its driving him mad thinking what Adrienne Corri will do with it when I join the feathered choir!!!'[39] Then, in 1982, Vincent got an offer which, in just two takes, could have set him up for life financially. He was asked to

---

* In the mid 1990s, Irene Worth – Coral's detested 'Hattie Abrams' – devised and performed a two-hour monologue, *Portrait of Edith Wharton*, based on the writer's life and works. The show was notable for having no props, costumes or sets – characters were created entirely by voice.

perform, in his best tones of terror, a couple of verses of rap on the title track of Michael Jackson's new album, *Thriller*. For his efforts, he was offered a flat fee of $20,000, or a percentage of the royalties. Swayed by what must have seemed, at that time, a tempting lump sum, he went for the flat fee – and in doing so, kissed goodbye to what could have been his 'pension'. *Thriller* went on to sell a Guinness-estimated 104 million copies and, when the title track was released as a single in 1984, it too was a million-seller. According to Victoria Price, her father contacted Michael Jackson, seeking retrospective remuneration from the track's phenomenal success. Jackson responded by sending Price a gold album – but no cheques. There's no record of Coral's response; but in 1993, when the singer settled out of court over allegations of child molestation, a still-miffed Price joked to his friends, 'Michael Jackson fucked me too, and I never got a dime over it.'[40]

Coral's frustration with her supporting role was evident. Scheduled to accompany Vincent on a *Diversions and Delights* tour to Denmark, Finland, Russia, China and Japan, she told Alec Guinness, 'One always says, "Unless a job comes for Coral," but as I've only had one TV film in five years it's fairly safe to say I'll send a card of a tree all covered with white blossoms…'[41]

There wasn't much joy for her in London. First, there was the declining health of 'Mother': 'My mother is v ill indeed and I don't think anything can be done for her,' she told Caroline Cornish-Trestrail. '[The] doctors say it could be any minute or three months.'[42] And there was another nasty shock in store when she decided to pay a visit to her London agents. Jonathan Altaras explained, 'They were very grand at ICM in those days. One day she arrived in London, and she went to their office. And the girl on reception said, "Who are you?" – and so Coral walked straight out again. She came to Dennis van Thal, who was the head of London Management, who I worked for. I was a "baby" agent – I'd worked as assistant to an agent and he left nine months after I started there, so I ended up with Irene Handl, Eric Porter, Paul Rogers… I had quite a grand list of clients. Dennis was sort of slowing down then, and I don't think the idea of representing Coral appealed to him, but he'd known her from the old days. So he said to me, 'I've got just the sort of person for you…' It was a sort of mismatch, but it *did* work, and we got on really well. But I'd never heard of her – I knew nothing about her at all.'[43]

Altaras quickly discovered he wasn't the only one: 'Nobody knew her – although there were a *select* number of people who knew her, she was way out of fashion. They knew her at the National and the Royal Court, but pretty well nowhere else. She'd done the Anouilh play but it hadn't been a huge success. So I threw a cocktail party for her at the Savoy, because I didn't know how else to promote her – she obviously couldn't be sent around to meet people. And that's how I got to know Vincent; he came, and he said, "I've never known an agent do anything as sweet as this. Can I come to you too?" So I represented him in London too. But you know that old adage about not representing husband and wife... I mean, even with them, I'd get Coral on the phone and say, "Actually, I've rung to speak to Vincent," and she'd get very snappy about it...'[44]

There appeared to be no end to the indignities Coral had to endure. But the multiple humiliations of being offered nothing except playing faceless deities or charitable titled ladies in forgettable films were about to end: Alan Bennett had been busy creating something truly memorable.

◆

In the summer of 1981, Coral had spent a weekend with Alec and Merula Guinness at their home near Petersfield, Hampshire. Guinness was then starring in the West End, in a new play by Alan Bennett, *The Old Country*, about an English defector's life in Russia. During Coral's weekend, Bennett visited the Guinnesses, and the discussion turned to the subject of British spies. 'Alec and his wife were preparing tea and we were out on the grass,' Coral later recalled. 'I happened to say to him, "Oh I met Guy Burgess in Russia." We discussed it for about five minutes, no more than that. [Bennett said the story was told to him at an after-theatre dinner at the Mirabelle in 1977.] I never thought another thing about it. Several months later, he sent me the script and said he'd written up the things that I'd told him and would I mind if he went on with it.'[45] She didn't – and the conversation prompted her to rummage in her 'big black case' to retrieve something she thought Bennett might be interested in seeing: Burgess's letters, her original notes of his measurements and his uncashed cheque for £6. She sent photocopies of the documents to Bennett, who duly incorporated pertinent facts and telling phrases into his script: for instance, Burgess's request and specifications for pyjamas, as 'Russian ones cannot be slept in – are not in fact made for that purpose', are almost verbatim from a letter he sent to Coral on Easter Sunday, his birthday.

When she received Bennett's script – now entitled *An Englishman Abroad* – Coral mentioned it to her old chum, John Schlesinger (for whom Bennett had written his first film script, an adaptation of Evelyn Waugh's *A Handful of Dust*) and casually enquired whether he could envisage it as a film. Schlesinger said he couldn't – but he *could* see it as a single drama for television. Bennett's first draft was duly dispatched to the director – but not before it was offered it to BBC producer Innes Lloyd, to slot into a series of new plays. When Schlesinger explained that he wouldn't be able to fit in with the series production timetable, Lloyd agreed to give *Englishman* a slot as an entirely separate entity.

As usual for a Schlesinger project, the task of assembling the actors for *An Englishman Abroad* was left to his friend and casting director, Noel Davis. Performers suggested for some of the supporting roles included Rupert Everett ('for Foreign Office man'); Christopher Biggins ('for fat Foreign Office man – is a fat man, lots of sparkle'); Timothy Spall and Kenneth Branagh. For 'Claudius', Anthony Quayle, Eric Porter, Donald Sinden, Joss Ackland, Tony Britton and Robert Hardy were all considered.[46] The role of Guy Burgess was first offered to Robert Stephens, who wasn't available, so Noel Davis started making a 'shopping list'. To play Burgess, his poison pen inked in Jeremy Kemp, Ronald Lacey, Alec McCowen, Denis Quilley, Anthony Hopkins, Keith Michell and John Standing. His final shortlist was an entertainment in itself:

> *Alan Bates; I believe he would be great, appearance?*
>
> *Michael Caine:* CAN *do the accent*
>
> *Tom Baker: is very debauched*
>
> *Edward Fox: can he be made to look less handsome?*
>
> *Dirk Bogarde: prissy – self pity.* NOT JUICY.[47]

Schlesinger himself wrote to his, and Coral's, old pal, Charles Gray, and offered him the role of the actor playing Claudius: 'It is not an enormous part in the film but he does have a few civilian scenes away from the theatre with her. In any case, it would be a great pleasure to work with you, even though we shall all be freezing our tits off in Dundee and Glasgow which are our grey and forbidding locations.'[48] Dundee was to be the substitute location for wintry

Moscow – which it did remarkably well with, said Schlesinger, 'a lot of salt and luck with the weather.'[49] Dozens of locals – some of them members of Glasgow's Polish Club – were recruited as extras, donning greatcoats and fur hats to play ordinary Muscovites suffering from the effects of the cold weather, and the Cold War.

There was really only one part that had proved easy to cast: 'Had a strange card from Alan [Bennett],' Coral told Alec Guinness. 'He seems to think I know something about doing his TV play – well, I don't, but I DO know I'd like to do it.'[50] It was, in fact, Bennett who had suggested Coral play herself, as early as November 1981 – her only concern was that she was too old, but she then decided 'age didn't come into it'. John Schlesinger said, 'I couldn't see anyone other than Coral playing the part. It would have been pointless.'[51] And so it was decided that the 69-year-old Coral Browne would play the 45-year-old Coral Browne. The curious experience of playing herself would present Coral with one of her most intriguing acting challenges: 'I found that intensely difficult. I kept on saying to myself all the time, "Who am I? This sounds like me." When I learned the lines and acted them with Alan Bates I became an actress, but in the beginning it was a very strange experience.'[52]

Despite her positive outlook and best efforts, age *was* coming into it: she was then suffering from a bad back, and was waiting for a new bridge to be fitted to replace broken false teeth. She complained to Vincent: 'I looked liked an old merchant from Ceylon flashing the gold stumps on my "bridge".'[53] 'The teeth just won't stay on – three times in the last week. I am in despair about it...'[54] But the despair would be short-lived: by August 1982, Bennett told Coral she would soon be receiving the latest draft of the screenplay. 'I've asked for a couple of "one liners",' she told Vincent, then filming in London, 'as I felt the last text wasn't overburdened with any "funnies" for me.'[55]

At home there were still amusements to be had at other people's expense. On 23 August, 66-year-old retail millionaire Alfred Bloomingdale died of cancer at his Santa Monica home. His body was barely cold when reports surfaced in the tabloid press about his sado-masochistic bedroom rituals with Vicki Morgan, his mistress for 12 years who had been kept in a style to which she'd become *very* accustomed, complete with luxury apartment and all the trimmings (Morgan subsequently lost a $10 million lawsuit against the Bloomingdale estate in September 1982 and, less than a year later, was murdered by her gay roommate, Marvin Pancoast). Mrs Bloomingdale also worshipped at St Vincent's, and Coral was able to tell Vincent, 'Betsy Bloomingdale looked VERY happy in church on Sunday…made up as the Flag in red-red, white & blue outfit with a face made up to match. The funeral had only been a week previous but "He" left her ALL his lolly & the papers say it was well in excess of 50 million.'[56] However, her letter omitted to mention another observation she made as The Widder Bloomingdale entered the church: Coral hissed, 'Here comes Betsy Bloomingdale – thin as a *whip*.'[57]

On January 5, Coral arrived in London, and happily settled into a suite at her old home, the Savoy. 'I have a superb room,' she told Vincent. 'I could have a couple of hundred people in for drinks and no crush…'[58] Old friends had laid on a floral welcome in her favourite white blooms: the room was adorned with 'so many flowers I may just be dead – a million white roses from Adrienne Corri – a huge display of white narcissus and white tulips from Alec [Guinness], a white azalea tree from my lovely girl dress designer [Amy Roberts]…'[59]

However, the film's £300,000 budget would leave room for no luxuries: still recovering from a bad back before she set off for England, Coral told John Schlesinger that, though her back was better, it was 'not strong enough to stand the disgusting suggestion of the BBC to go the cheapest and pinched-up way. I'm so pissed off I feel like telling them to shove it as they want to give me £35 a day for the HOTEL AND ALL MY FOOD AND EXPENSES. To say nothing of the fee which is disgraceful and NOT what they pay other people I know of. I'm real CROSS.'[60]

She wasn't the only one cursing the BBC; she told Vincent that she had had 'a nasty time with John Schlesinger on the phone. He screamed and shouted and carried on a treat, so I said I'd pick up a red velvet frock at Bermans and he could get into that and take himself to Covent Garden and be a prima donna there and throw powder puffs… I called in on Caroline [Cornish-Trestrail] today on my way to Vick and she said he's dreadfully bad tempered at present, as he hasn't been allowed to pick his assistant or anyone else to work with and has been denied EVERYTHING he's asked for…and now is LIVID he ever got involved in the project and is taking it out on everyone in sight. He went to Dundee and Glasgow yesterday with Casanova Bennett so I phoned Alan and told him to take a large bottle of oil to pour on all waters to quiet John down as NOBODY wants noisy rehearsals and scenes all the time. <u>V.</u> boring indeed.'[61]

But bigger problems were about to emerge: on January 16, the day before rehearsals started at Acton studios, Coral rang John Schlesinger and told him she been to see her doctor. She had a found a lump in her right armpit.

⁂

Alec Guinness recalled that, when Coral had been staying, she had experienced a strange sensation, which felt like water flowing down her arms. He believed that may have been the first symptom of what, it now transpired, was a serious problem.

A few days before Coral called John Schlesinger, she wrote to Vincent and – after first filling him in on all the gossip – revealed, almost as an afterthought, 'I spent all yesterday haunting the Nuffield in Bryanston Square, as on Sun, I discovered a lump in my armpit – that gave me the shits – so I saw [Dr] Janvrin at 9 on Mon; and he sent me straight away for blood tests and X rays at the hospital. Today the results: – OK lungs – bad arthritis in the neck and top of spine – lovely. I have to phone on Sat re the lump (which is a lymph gland). He hopes (and Christ knows so do I) that it will go away by then as he thinks it may be caused by my back exercises pinching the nerves in the arthritic neck which causes that awful "running water" & "burning" sensation I've been complaining of & that in turn, with any luck, could have caused the glands to swell. Certainly don't want anybody cutting into me pits at this time…'[62] A few days later, she had to tell him that, 'My arm is v bad today and the lump is v. tiresome indeed. It's a terrible worry – I'm to see the cancer surgeon at 5 on Thursday. The blood tests were OK but I've gone thru all this with Philip [Pearman]. His tests were OK when he got the lumps in the armpits so it's difficult for me as I'm living the nightmare of his illness over and over.'

To help her through the nightmare, she told him, she had gone to confession where 'all I got was two hundred Hail Marys and Our Fathers and NO mass.'[63] Her faith was being sorely tested: after spending years waiting to be offered the perfect film role, she had been offered one that was – playing herself. Now the project was in serious jeopardy, threatened by the very thing she had always feared would strike, just as it had struck her beloved Philip.

A week before shooting on *Englishman* was scheduled to begin, it was obvious that, quite soon, someone would indeed have to start 'cutting into her pits' – but not before she finished the job in hand. A round of discussions began between director, producer, doctor, agent and leading lady about what should happen next. 'She phoned me to say, "Should I do it or shouldn't I?",' said Jonathan Altaras. 'And of course, being a rather ambitious agent, I said, "Yes, you should do it – it's the story of your life and you'll never be happy with someone else doing it." *Now* I would say, "Don't even think about it – go to hospital!"'[64] But the final decision was Coral's – and she decided that even cancer wasn't going to interfere with her work. 'She was bloody angry about being ill,' said Jill Melford, 'It interfered with her life. But I think that anger kept her going.'[65]

Dr Alan McKinna, consultant cancer surgeon at the Royal Marsden Hospital, told Vincent what he had told Coral on January 22: 'The X-rays of the breast show a small tumour in the right breast and she is taking one of the best new medicines for such tumours – this is called Tamoxifen and there is a very good chance that it will bring about some regression before surgery...she has gone off to film in Scotland with less pain in the arm and with good spirits and great courage. We have provisionally made arrangements for her to have an operation in the Fitzroy Nuffield Hospital on Thursday 24 February.'[66]

Typically, Coral appeared to be more concerned about costs and comfort than cancer: 'I think it's better to do the tests from the Savoy instead of hospital – the Savoy is £50 a night and the Nuffield £250,' she told Vincent.[67] Although her husband had rescheduled his latest American art lecture tour so he could be in London for the operation, Coral was concerned and angered by his belief that she would be well enough to travel back with him in time for his tour to recommence on March 7: 'That's NOT time enough for healing, stitches and leg strength to return – one also loses a lot of blood on breast ops I understand... I think Janvrin and the surgeon will want to see a proper healing.'[68] And a phone call to her doctor in LA brought more bad tidings: 'After the surgery here and my return [to LA] I will have to start a programme which will last several months of that awful chemotherapy – the one that makes your hair fall out and makes one feel so ill,' she told Vincent. 'Thought you should know this now and check with him <u>as I don't think it's the sort of thing I could cope with alone</u> and you may have to get out of some of those Carlton Sedgley (and cruise?) things if you have any...chemotherapy is something I've always dreaded. It kills the cells but it nearly kills you in the process – oh God, what a bore.'[69]

However, as scheduled, the three weeks of filming *An Englishman Abroad* began on 31 January. In Coral's absence, Vincent was able to spend some quality time with Victoria. Coral sent regular bulletins from the 'Russian' front: 'It's perishing cold,' she complained, 'terribly icy strong winds and NOT conducive to acting – fur hat leaping about like a mad bird and silver fox in my eyes, mouth, etc.'[70] Other locations served as 'stand-ins' for Moscow venues: the interiors of Polesden Lacey in Great Bookham served as the inside of the British Embassy. Coral's 'Russian' hotel room was a bit nearer to home – the Great Western Royal Hotel in Paddington. Scenes set in the hotel's 'lobby' were actually shot in Senate House, while L'Ecu de France restaurant in Jermyn Street stood in for the Caprice.

The story depicted in *An Englishman Abroad* was largely as Coral had related to Alan Bennett. For dramatic purposes, he decided to have Guy Burgess make his uncouth entrance in Coral's dressing room rather than Michael Redgrave's (an early draft of the script had Burgess saying to Coral, 'I'm a friend of Michael's') and Redgrave didn't appear as a character. Bennett also said that he had 'taken a few liberties with the facts. The scene in the British Embassy, for instance, did not occur – but since the Shakespeare Company were warned by the British Ambassador to "shy away from that traitor Burgess, who's always trying to get back to England", it seemed no great liberty.'[71]

Several scenes in the original script which didn't make it onto film included one where Coral, in her Moscow hotel, declares, 'I feel as if I'm in *King's Rhapsody*. It's all too Ivor Novello for words,' before breaking into a verse of 'I can give you the starlight, I can give you the moon'; and another in a London hatter's where Coral, being shown round a room lined with shelves of labelled hat blocks, enquires whether they keep every client's block. The hatter reveals that they are only retained until the client's death – and that they hadn't expected to need Burgess's again. There was another, last-minute change to the script: the revelation that Coral had almost married Jack Buchanan was only made casually to Bennett just before filming began. In the film the same revelation is made in the scene where Coral is stuck in Burgess's flat for several hours, during which he has repeatedly played to her his record of Buchanan singing 'Who?', and this provided *Englishman* with perhaps its greatest moment of poignancy. Bennett observed, 'It's the kind of coincidence which, had it been invented, would have seemed sentimental.'[72]

Bennett, with the cast and crew on location in Dundee, kept Alec Guinness abreast of their adventures. He told how, one day during a blizzard that made it feel even more like Moscow, he and Coral took shelter 'in a Glasgow Seamens Rest', where 'Miss Browne got on like a house on fire with the old tars. This can perhaps be put down to her colourful vocabulary. The first mate of a freighter out of Mombasa with a cargo of jute remarked that it was a pleasant surprise to him personally that a member of the acting profession could be so refreshingly foulmouthed.'[73] And there were more dangers to be faced by the cast: 'Sandbags are presently being installed round the windows and barbed wire over the bar against the imminent arrival of Mr Gray (well known to be "a bit of a card").'[74]

Coral insisted on no concessions being made to her illness. Every day, she was up at 5AM and didn't finish work until 7 or 8pm. She was in every scene of the film, except for the final shot where Burgess parades his new outfits walking across a bridge in 'Moscow'. Her American doctor had told her to 'have a couple of hours REST each day at lunchtime, etc. Well, I can see poor John having to do THAT with me running up and down "Moscow" and the BBC breathing down his neck.'[75] John Schlesinger told Roddy McDowall, 'In reality, she was frightened and exhausted from her treatment before surgery, but I have never witnessed such courage and professionalism in the shadow of impending disaster.'[76]

Friends and colleagues in London, shocked by the severity of her illness and moved by her fortitude and professionalism, were responding to the situation: 'Everyone is being SO kind to me. I'm thoroughly spoiled,' she told Vincent.[77] She was particularly touched by the care and consideration shown her by her leading man, Alan Bates. She told Vincent, 'I do want to give Bates a wallet like I gave Schlesinger as nobody in my whole life (except my husbands) has done more for me than Bates. He spends every waking hour and I suspect a few sleeping twitches thinking of what he can do for me in an unobtrusive way. He always takes me to eat, buys me some wine and makes me laugh a great deal. A VERY tender and SOFT and GENTLE man – the girl costume designer has also been wonderful… [she] took me to all the specialists and tit hospitals, etc and has even asked me to stay at her place if I have to stay in London for treatments after the op – of course, everyone else has been incredible – to TRY and make it easier for me.'[78]

At the end of the shoot, Alan Bennett wrote to Coral, thanking her, 'For letting me write the story for a start and never pulling rank by saying, "It wasn't like that," or, "I didn't feel like that at the time." For playing yourself so wonderfully and so well… And especially for being so brave but without being "brave" about it. You made us all forget you were facing an ordeal in the most selfless way, and let us laugh: I don't think I remember laughing so much on a production before.'[79]

As planned, with filming finished, and with Vincent now in London, Coral entered the Fitzroy Nuffield Hospital on 23 February and, the following day, underwent surgery to remove the tumour. Once again, friends rallied: John Schlesinger sent flowers, as did Alec Guinness and John Gielgud. Michael 'Old Mother' Dyne wrote to Vincent, whom he had never met, from his home in Pennsylvania, offering assistance: 'I am wondering, without wishing to be intrusive, if I could be of any help in hopping over to be on hand to peel grapes and wave bedpans etc…it would be no trouble for me at all. I have hardly seen Coral in the last few years but I am devoted to her and it distresses me greatly that she should have to undergo such an ordeal.'[80]

To keep her amused, Alan Bennett wrote to her with an 'account' of his meeting with a Finnish TV producer at a BBC Sales conference in Edinburgh: 'Charming English playsmith Ellen Barnett…tell me he has written play about Gay Poges. I tell you, we in Helsinki are all on tiptoes for seeing *This Englishman Aboard*. When is screening this film by John Frankenheimer about Gay Poges and Carl Braun? I had only just escaped from Mr Turdasson (I do not lie) when I fell into the clutches of a gentleman from Bavarian television… I have a sneaking suspicion he thought you were related to the other Miss Braun with whom Herr Hitler was walking out… I hope you're not feeling too bad and are beginning to sit up and *assert yourself*.'[81]

Laid up in London, Coral was missing all the fun at home in California, where the Queen's visit to the state was making news. A group calling itself the American-Irish Unity Committee had paid for a series of commercials, accusing police and British soldiers of terrorising civilians in Northern Ireland, which were shown on CNN during the visit. A gay bar in San Francisco marked the occasion in more fitting fashion with a 'Royal Family look-alike' competition. The monarch was entertained in true Hollywood style by the showbiz presidential couple, Ronald and Nancy Reagan. At the 20th Century Fox studio, a gala dinner was held in her honour and the cream of the British

LA community were lined up as guests, and the 'entertainment' featured an impressive roll-call of Hollywood's more follicularly-challenged stars. As Clive James observed, 'Perry [Como] ruffled his hair to prove that it really grew on top of his head, even if it had started its life somewhere else.'[82] Alan Bennett kept Coral well-informed about the royal variety show: 'Very depressed by HMQ in Hollywood – all those terrible English. And so many toupes – Fred Astaire, George Burns, Frank Sinatra – poor dear, she must have thought they were showing her round a mink farm.'[83]

When Coral was well enough to leave hospital, she went, at John Schlesinger's invitation, to recuperate at Victoria Street, where she was cared for by Caroline Cornish-Trestrail. 'John said to me, "Could you come and live here to look after Coral?" On that Friday night, I had a lot of people coming round for dinner and I said, "John, I can't cancel all these people." So he said, "Well, you can have the dinner party at number 10. I said, "Well, what about my boyfriend?" – because he was an ex-lover of John's. So he said, "That's alright, you can bring him too..." So off I went to fetch Coral in the BMW. And down she came – remarkably perky, considering she'd just had an operation on her breast. And it had just become compulsory to wear seat belts in front seats – so I said, "You'll have to belt up, Coral." She said, "What?! Well, if a policeman stops us, I'll tell him I've just had my fucking tit off." So as a concession, she held the belt so it looked like she had it on. We got back and she went to bed. So I had this dinner party, for eight people, and she wasn't well enough to come down, but she was hungry. So I said I'd send the courses up, and so the men were dispensed with the food up to what we called "The Green Room". And they'd go up – and they just didn't come down! I'd have to call them for the next course... They would just walk in and there's this living legend, propped up in bed, looking gorgeous, despite the fact she'd just had major surgery, and she'd say, "Come and sit down and tell me all about yourself." And these were men in their thirties...'[84]

On Sunday 20 March, Coral and Vincent returned home to California, where she was due to start a course of chemotherapy. Among the post waiting for her was some literature about the Hospital Santa Monica, on the Californian/Mexican border – 'A Haven For Those Who Have Been Told "You Have An Incurable Disease"' – which had been sent to her by the writer and director Curtis Harrington. Among other things, the hospital offered Live Cell rejuvenation treatment. Sticking to more conventional treatments, she made a good recovery. In July, she signed a directive to doctors, forbidding any attempts in the future to be made to artificially prolong her life if she was suffering from an 'incurable disease'. This done, she looked forward to the 70th birthday party Vincent had arranged for her; it was held at Roddy McDowall's home, as, she explained to John Schlesinger, 'this place is too fragile with those bloody pots and figurines all over the place'.[85] It seemed only LA's intolerable heat was getting her down: 'It's as hot as a fox and I find that trying,' she told Caroline Cornish-Trestrail. 'I get up at 6.30 and water the garden, get the paper, make the coffee and run like a bat out of hell to the laundry or post office or the market in an endeavour to get back before noon and remain in the air conditioning until night. V. bored by letters from London asking me if I'm really on my way to the pearlie gates. I'm too fat and look too well!'[86]

Meanwhile, it had been announced that *An Englishman Abroad* was to be premiered at the London Film Festival on November 21, prior to its BBC broadcast eight days later. John Schlesinger asked Coral to attend the screening but, as she explained to Caroline Cornish-Trestrail, she was worried about how expensive the Savoy – her hotel of choice – would be: 'What do you think the De Vere or any of those dumps charge? I think £250 a week is about my price. I have hungry Ma to feed all too frequently to say nothing of Corrie [*sic*] and Amy and Jill Melford, Charles Gray and all the OTHER out of work actors I know.'[87] Regardless of her worries about expenditure, Coral came to London where she fulfilled a range of PR duties to publicise the film, including a major profile in *Radio Times* and, on 12 October, an appearance with Vincent on Russell Harty's eponymous ITV chat show. Their fellow guest on the sofa was Boy George; the three of them may also have enjoyed the programme's other feature – the final of the "Woman's Realm Wonder Wife" competition. During his interview, George coquettishly made his infamous (and, as it turned out, staggeringly dishonest) remark that he preferred 'a cup of tea' to having sex. 'How long do you think he'll last?,' Coral later asked a reporter from the *Glasgow Herald*, 'It's so difficult to tell with that sort.'[88]

With her *Englishman* PR duties completed, Coral and Vincent left for Paris where she had yet another health scare, this time suffering an allergic reaction to some antibiotics. Once she'd recovered from this setback, they proceeded to Venice where, to celebrate their wedding anniversary, they were attending a week-long gourmet seafood cookery course with Marcella Hazan at the Hotel Cipriani restaurant. Vincent was in seventh heaven, as they learned how to make new fish sauces, risottos and entrees; visited the Lamberti winery and olive oil pressing plant and were introduced to fine Italian wines selected by Marcella's husband, Victor. Coral told Caroline Cornish-Trestrail that, 'Vinnie has put on 10lb and I dare not look at the scales (which I have brought WITH me).'[89]

After their gourmet week, Vincent returned to the States to begin yet another lecture tour. Coral had to travel to Paris for three weeks' playing Tom Conti's mother – 'It comes to all of us,' she wryly observed.[90] The maternal performance in question was for the '...fanciful but unspectacular romantic comedy'[91], *American Dreamer*, starring JoBeth Williams as a housewife who, after an accident, believes she is the heroine of a thriller novel, called (of all things) *The Priest Confesses*. Coral was playing Margaret McMann, author of the popular 'Rebecca Ryan' thrillers, but who is the 'front' for her son Alan, the books' real writer. 'It's about chasing spies,' said Coral, who remembered the experience chiefly for a scene that involved her 'leaping on and off a train with about 5000 commuters watching'.[92] When it was released, the film was a critical failure; as the *New York Times* said, *American Dreamer* wasn't 'funny or romantic or suspenseful. It's not even trashy. It has no identity whatsoever...'[93]

On 29 November 1983, *An Englishman Abroad* was broadcast on BBC1; it was pitted against a new film by David Hare on ITV, *Saigon: Year of the Cat*, starring Coral's former colleague and lodger, Judi Dench. For many viewers, it was their first glimpse of Coral onscreen for more than a decade, since *The Killing of Sister George*. But there was also a new audience, a generation too young to know about her theatrical glory days, who might well have greeted her appearance with the same question as a crooning Jack Buchanan: 'Who?'

All the questions would be answered: and all the worries about casting, the bitching about budgets and the horrors of health problems were swept away, as plaudits rained down on *An Englishman Abroad* – and on Coral. *The Times* said it was 'a beautifully controlled exploration of a secret life in a secret world...a brilliant, bitter-sweet comedy... Alan Bates...is as memorable a performance as one could wish...a truly outstanding film which justifies all the ravings of the critics.'[94] The *Telegraph* observed that Coral was 'wonderful in what must have been a very puzzling role to play,'[95] while Julian Barnes in the *Observer* quipped, 'Coral Browne was certainly everyone's idea of Coral Browne.'[96] Nancy Banks-Smith declared: 'If all concerned are not immediately showered with encomium I shall buy six Old Roedeanian ties and exit stage left.'[97] Ronald Bergan also paid tribute to most of those concerned: 'The humour comes from a combination of the 4 Bs, Burgess, Browne, Bates and Bennett.'[98] Even Coral's most reluctant, hard-bitten admirers caved in: American agent Charles Baker told Lindsay Anderson, 'I never thought Coral was a great actress, she's a lovely person of course and I adore her, but thought she was quite wonderful in that…so clever…the most original thing I've ever seen on television.'[99]

Jonathan Altaras observed, 'I don't think people were at all prepared for *An Englishman Abroad*, because those who remembered her remembered her being camp and loud. I don't think they remembered the subtlety of her acting – being camp and loud wasn't ultimately what she was about. And underneath that exterior she was a very decent, caring person – remarkably sensitive actually, which wasn't something I was expecting.'[100]

There were very few voices of dissent on the subject of *An Englishman Abroad* – though they hardly counted as 'dissent'. David Robinson, film critic of *The Times*, had met Burgess in Moscow and voiced his surprise at how the messy his flat was onscreen: 'I only remember it being kept spotless by an adoring *babushka*, and Burgess saying, "Never breathe it in London, dear boy, but there's no servant problem in Moscow." It was better furnished, too, than in the film since Burgess had his own English furniture with him. "Foreign office shipped it out. They've been awfully decent about some things."'[101]

Liza Goddard – who would play Coral when *Englishman* played in the West End as one half of Alan Bennett's double-bill, *Single Spies* – noted accurately that 'It didn't make her nearly rude enough. I mean, she had a mouth like a *docker*!'[102] And Eileen Atkins said, 'There was only one thing wrong with *An Englishman Abroad* – everywhere she went, people stared at her, because she looked so grand.'[103]

Any genuinely disparaging words were dealt with by Coral in her usual manner. At a party in Los Angeles, she was talking to a second-rate American screenwriter. The conversation turned to *An Englishman Abroad*, and the hapless hack said, 'I thought you were wonderful, darling, but I wasn't too sure about the script.' Coral's response was entirely apt: 'You weren't too *sure* about the script? *You* weren't too *sure* about the script?! You couldn't write "fuck" on a dusty Venetian blind!'[104]

Curtain Calls

1984–1991

Nineteen-eighty-four got off to an inauspicious start for Coral, with yet more surgery, this time to remove a melanoma from her leg: just weeks after seeing in the New Year on a 'Pole to Panama Canal' cruise, on 1 February, she 'Had a great chunk of my thigh removed.'[1] She recovered from the surgery in time to fly to London for the BAFTA ceremony, where *An Englishman Abroad* was nominated in virtually every category. The BBC had responded by repeating the film on 21 January. Before the BAFTA event, the Broadcasting Press Guild announced on March 22 that *An Englishman Abroad* had won three of their awards: Best Single Drama, Best Actor and Best Actress. The gongs were handed out later at a luncheon ceremony at Whitbread Brewery's Smeaton Vaults, Chiswell St on 13 April.

But first, there were the BAFTAs on March 25, held at the swanky Grosvenor House Hotel. Among the glittering throng, clad head to toe in black, was Cher, whose performance in *Silkwood* had strengthened her claim as a serious actress. Coral decided that she looked like 'a burnt out twig from the stake of Joan of Arc'.[2] *An Englishman Abroad* romped home: it won eight awards out of the BBC's total haul of 19 BAFTAs, including Best Single Drama for John Schlesinger, Best Actor for Alan Bates, Best Costume Design for Amy Roberts, Best Design, Best Film Sound, Best Film Cameraman, Best Original Film Music and the Writing Award for Alan Bennett. And, of course, Best Actress for Coral Browne, up against two of her stage 'successors', Judi Dench (for *Saigon: Year of the Cat*) and Maggie Smith (for *Mrs Silly*). 'I don't think any of them had any idea of the sort of success it would have,' said Jonathan Altaras. 'At its screening, the audience got up and applauded – I've never seen that before. And I was quite surprised, because, although I knew it was wonderful, while I was watching it, I wondered, "Can anyone else see the point of this?" And then the awards started to flood in…'[3] Like all floods, it caused some damage: 'I've had a lovely evening,' Coral told Alec Guinness, 'and the mask [the BAFTA award] made v. heavy carrying... A Bennett had mislaid his dinner jacket trousers a couple of years ago – here he thinks. But someone came to the rescue with a respectable pair – sadly tho' an unfortunate waistcoat. I'd given Alan a bit of a grub the evening before in the Savoy Grill – v. unfortunate as it must have been too rich and he fell over the door knob the moment he reached home, and was wearing a most macabre heavy white sticking plaster across his face when he was presented with the award, so one couldn't see if he was pleased or nay.'[4]

However, within weeks of collecting the BAFTA 'mask', she confessed to Alec Guinness, 'I'd rather be struck with the ITCH than see "Englishman" again. Twice was MORE than enough & I thought I was absolutely lousy in it – dull & altogether lifeless and piss-poor.'[5] And she wasn't saving all the brickbats for herself – she had plenty to spare to aim at the actor she always referred to as 'Lord Puddleduck': 'Saw "Voyage Round Dad" last week [*A Voyage Round My Father*] – THAT should have been stopped...Larry was VERY lively, very unboring, undull and altogether HATEFUL. I thought little Elizabeth Sellars should have put that v. fat ass of hers over his face & smothered him to death. Even Vinnie, who thinks good of all God's creatures, goes purple on the face and shakes if you mention Larry's performance & the only other person who has such a disastrous effect on him is President Regan [*sic*].'[6]

She soon had another target to aim at: that September, she was informed that she had to demolish her conservatory which, it now transpired, had been constructed without proper permission, planning consent or adherence to building regulations. Coral made a retrospective planning application, but to no avail. She suggested replacing it with a new roof terrace; the issue dragged on for months. 'The fucking roof is causing me a LOT of trouble, everybody out to "do" me,' she complained to Caroline Cornish-Trestrail. 'I was hoping it would be underway about a week after I got there but there's a bit of hanky panky going on and I may have to call in Lily Law – my solicitors.'[7]

Meanwhile, Coral had to hold her tongue and ready herself for another round of promotional duties for *Englishman* prior to its US television broadcast that autumn. The well-meaning Radie Harris had given it an early plug in her column, but erroneously reported that the film was based on Coral's meeting with Guy Burgess 'during her filming of *Nicholas and Alexandra* in Moscow'.[8] Predictably, Coral was full of complaints: she moaned to John Schlesinger, 'Worked my ASS off for a week in NY for Exxon [sponsors of the cable

TV broadcast]. Ten hours a day with three big TV interviews (Exxon paid four night at the Wyndham and my fare – no hamburger money OR danger money!).'[9] During her stay in New York, she and Vincent attended Radie Harris's birthday party held in the Wyndham Hotel penthouse of John and Suzanne Mados, where fellow guests included Alec Guinness, Sir Richard Attenborough and John Huston.

But all the work was worth it. In a rare joint venture between cable and public channels, *An Englishman Abroad* was premiered simultaneously on WNET's 'Great Performances' and on the Arts & Entertainment cable channel, on 2 November, to ensure the biggest possible audience. And once again, the critics were elbowing each other aside to confer the biggest compliments. Howard Rosenberg of the *LA Times* declared *An Englishman Abroad* to be 'perhaps the best single hour of TV this year'. Rosenberg's colleague, Rick Du Brow, concurred: 'I never saw a better TV drama. Never.' The *New York Times* said it was 'a superb little tragicomedy…this hour long production works brilliantly.'[10] Coral couldn't wait to tell Schlesinger: 'Englishman SENSATIONAL! The phone has never stopped ringing and TONY RICHARDSON even called it your greatest work and perhaps Bates greatest work. I love you and am so HAPPY to tell you how much this country has given you for all your hard work on the Englishman – you're real hot cock stuff.'[11]

Unfortunately, the same didn't seem to apply to Coral: as Jonathan Altaras explained, producers weren't exactly beating a path to her door: 'They were interested, but it didn't particularly convert into a job. I suppose it then put her on the Peggy Ashcroft level, who was always going to get jobs before Coral – so maybe it even limited her. But it gave her a profile that she hadn't had in England for many years – which she was incredibly happy about.'[12] In fact, Ashcroft nearly pipped Coral to another choice role – one which proved that her performance in *An Englishman Abroad* was no fluke – and one which, in many ways, even surpassed it.

Dennis Potter had written *Dreamchild*, a screenplay which, he explained, stepped away from the cosiness long associated with Lewis Carroll's *Alice in Wonderland* stories: 'Charles Dodgson has been locked up in the nursery far too long,' said Potter. 'I'm sick of films made for teeny tots or adults who never seem to grow up.'[13] Potter's script took, as its starting point, an event which occurred to the real 'Alice' – Alice Hargreaves, née Liddell – near the end of her life. In 1932, Hargreaves was invited to New York by Columbia

University to attend their centenary celebrations marking the centenary of the birth of the 'real' Carroll, Charles Dodgson, and to receive an Honorary Degree. The University was exhibiting the original *Alice's Adventures Under Ground* manuscript, which Dodgson had given to his Alice.* Hargreaves was accompanied by her surviving son Caryl (her two other sons were killed in World War I) and her sister, Rhoda Liddell, on her trip to New York, where she was greeted by a wildly enthusiastic American press and given a police escort to her suite at the Waldorf-Astoria. She was made an honorary Doctor of Letters in a private ceremony and on May 4 (her 80th birthday), donned in mortar board and gown, addressed an audience of 2000 at Columbia in a speech broadcast nationwide by NBC. She said: 'If the children expect to see a young girl such as I was, like the one in the books, I am afraid they will be disappointed.'[14]

Potter being Potter, he used this charming but innocuous event to explore the true nature of the relationship between Dodgson and the young Alice – what it meant to both of them, then and in later life, and its emotional and psychological impact. For dramatic purposes, Potter removed Hargreaves's son and sister from the story, and replaced them with a young, naïve paid 'companion', Lucy (Nicola Cowper), who falls for ambitious reporter, Jack (Peter Gallagher). Jack sees the old lady from Britain as his meal-ticket to fame and fortune, and uses Lucy to gain access to her – but, despite his greed, Jack's affections for the put-upon young woman turn out to be genuine.

Potter and his director, Gavin Millar, had one name at the top of their wish list for the part: Peggy Ashcroft, who had starred in their 1980 television play, *Cream in my Coffee*: 'I'd worked with her before and we'd kept in touch, so it seemed the obvious way to go. There were slight cavils about it because she wasn't a "known" movie star – despite the fact she was one of the great actresses in the world. But you know what it's like, that old snobbery between movies and the theatre…'[15] Ashcroft was recovering from the rigours of a late-life purple patch, winning accolades and awards for her roles in *A Passage to India* and *The Jewel in the Crown*, and was having mobility problems because of a troublesome hip. And it wasn't long before Coral was in contention. She told the screenwriter Ed Naha, 'I read the script three or four years ago and loved

---

* Many years later, the widowed Alice Hargreaves was strapped for cash and the manuscript was auctioned by Sotheby's; it was bought by one Eldridge R Johnson for nearly four times the reserve price.

it. I never thought I'd get the part. I thought I was too young for the role, and they'd probably cast a "name". I supposed most of the actresses who were really 80 wouldn't have had the stamina to do the story.'[16]

Coral was an unknown quantity to Millar: 'I didn't really know her personally – and to be absolutely frank, I hadn't seen an awful lot of her on screen, and not too much in the theatre, either, so she was a slightly unknown quantity to me. But, obviously, she was so highly spoken of in lots of other circles there was no problem with being very happy to get her interested. And as soon as her name was mentioned, everybody's face lit up and they thought, "What a good idea." So getting Coral was a delight.' Millar said that, from beginning to end, working with Coral was 'a joy': 'People said she could be rather sharp and brusque, but anybody who said that in a dismissive way seems to me not to have understood her. Of *course* she could be sharp and brusque, and she didn't suffer fools gladly – but it was *because* she was a very sharp, funny, witty woman, who wanted to fill every hour with good fun and laughs and intelligent moves. So it was a delight to be with her. I never had a moment's difficulty with her, socially or professionally.'[17]

Coral had no difficulty with understanding what was required of her in *Dreamchild*: 'It was patent from the script what was going on and the sort of person Alice was,' said Gavin Millar. 'We had short discussions about the attitudes which she expressed as an old lady – she'd read bits of the biography about Alice – but really the delicate part of the acting was manoeuvring her through the stages of Alice's reaction to the American experience: the idea that she found it rather bizarre and extraordinary, and couldn't understand what all the fuss was about. And then she was affronted, and then *intrigued*, by the idea of making money out of it. Plus the intimations of mortality...' Indeed, there was a slight but amusing crossover between the Alice character and Coral herself: when an acquisitive reporter tells Alice she could make a lot of money out of her fame, she thinks for a moment, and then asks, 'Pounds or dollars?'

But, according to Gavin Millar, Coral's understanding came from more than mere monetary considerations: 'Dennis's idea, which Coral quite quickly caught hold of, was that Alice would be able to confront a lifetime of experiences through the device of a little girl remembering what she was, and what Dodgson had really meant to her, which she'd never really thought about – and that revelation comes to her right at the end. So it was nursing her through those changes of mood and pace – but I had to do very little.'[18] Coral's own experience gave her particular insight into one of the film's underlying themes – the reaction of Alice Liddell's mother to her daughter's close friendship with Dodgson. 'The letters he wrote to Alice were torn up by her mother,' she said. 'We don't know what was in them. Why should she do so unless there was something terribly wrong?'[19] Of course, Coral had the answer to this one: jealousy, pure and simple. She knew only too well how a loving, but bitter and envious, mother could and would strike at the very roots of what she perceives separates her from her child – viz. Vicky's caustic, constant criticism of Coral's lifestyle, performances and appearance, and even her adopted country.

In fact, it was Coral's appearance that would give Gavin Millar his only real problem with her. Alice Hargreaves was described as being 'of medium height and build, grain-haired...she spoke in low tones and had a quaint sense of humour...she used two canes in walking...'[20] The use of canes was eschewed, but Coral still had to look convincingly like an 80-year-old woman. According to Millar, 'She was actually 70 at the time and looked 60 – if that – and we had to make her look 80 plus. So we were putting twenty years on her – which is always hard for a woman who's still bonny and very well-preserved. But there was absolutely no temperament about that.' Not until the physical realities kicked in, at least. The lack of natural lines on Coral's face was remedied by applying layers of latex. She said, 'At the end of 10 days I looked like a street accident. I was bleeding under the eyes.'[21] 'Her skin went very raw within a couple of days. So she was very uptight and nervy about that – but all it was, was that she wanted to get it right and not damage her skin. So we had to go another route,' explained Millar, 'so Jenny Shircore [the make-up supervisor] had to devise a natural make-up job, which was extremely time-consuming and took longer than the prosthetics would have taken. So Coral was a bit edgy for the first week or so with all that – but in the long run, Jenny just fell for her, because she was so affectionate, and gave her a wonderful present at the end of the shoot.'[22]

It wasn't the first time a role's 'ageing' factor had caused Coral to think twice: just before *Dreamchild*, she told Alec Guinness, 'I've been offered a pilot for British TV called "The Battle of the Grandmothers". Nobody but a fool would offer me a piece with a title like that!!!'[23] Three years earlier, *Love Story* director Arthur Hiller offered her a part in his *Romantic Comedy*. 'He said I'd have to age,' she told Alec Guinness. 'It was a <u>strong</u> lady of 80. Said "No" as I felt one cancelled the other out. Suppose it will be said that I didn't want to look 80 – wouldn't mind that at all, but don't expect to be believed.'[24]

Filming on *Dreamchild* commenced at Elstree Studios in June 1984, and continued until the end of August. For once, Vincent played 'consort' to his wife for most of this period, during which they were based at the Savoy. Coral announced, 'I'm pleased to be back here but I can't call up friends and say, "Let's get the vodka out," until September 1.'[25] Before filming began, however, she and Vincent managed to see John Schlesinger and Alan Bennett, and squeeze in Sunday lunch with Maggie Smith as guests of Alec and Merula Guinness: 'We managed to keep lunch going until 5.30PM and then it was time for church.'[26]

And then it was time for work: Coral's days began with a two and a half hour make-up session at dawn with Jenny Shircore. At Elstree, she spent two weeks shooting her scenes with the grotesque creatures that Jim Henson had created to bring some of the 'Wonderland' characters to life, as Alice Hargreaves starts to relive her childhood memories. 'My first day on the film, I had to act with a giant caterpillar,' said Coral. 'It was huge, and it was moved by remote control. There was no one inside.'[27] Gavin Millar said, 'She rather liked that – she loved the idea of the Tenniel characters coming to life and being part of her memories and part of her nightmares.'[28] Other scenes shot at Elstree included one of the film's best, where Alice Hargreaves, having agreed to make a lucrative radio commercial, struggles with the ludicrous things she's being paid to say.

Then it was up to Liverpool, which was standing in for New York: St George's Hall, opposite Lime Street station, was playing Columbia University, where the Carroll centenary was celebrated. 'The audience was mostly composed of unemployed Liverpudlians,' recalled Gavin Millar. They got very stroppy towards the end of the day – because they didn't realise that a film day is *very* long – and they started throwing coins at the platform. When it came to do Coral's close-ups, we'd got rid of most of them by then.'[29]

The climax of the film came with a moving speech by Alice Hargreaves, in which she acknowledges, and embraces, the affection lavished on her as a child by 'Mr Dodgson'. But both director and leading lady were quite clear that this scene did not require an excessive show of emotion from the character: that was inherent in the text. 'The speech was quite critical, obviously, and we discussed how to do it,' said Millar. 'When we'd done one take, the producer came up to me and said, "That was a bit dry – a bit low key." So I said Coral, "You know what she wants, don't you?" And she said, "She wants the fucking hankies out, does she?"

'It was too much – she knew it, I knew it – that wasn't the way we wanted to play it and it didn't need it. This was a tough old bird, who was expressing something honestly and was moved by it, but was damned sure she wasn't going to show she was overcome by it.'[30] In the end, Millar did another take, as requested, with Coral giving the speech – with the 'hanky' treatment – but ended up using the first.

With hankies safely tucked away, *Dreamchild* was completed; now, its cast and crew could enjoy themselves – all except one: 'There was this rather comic scene at the end of the shoot,' explained Gavin Millar. 'We had a wrap party at the hotel in Liverpool and after about an hour, Coral came up to me and said, "I don't know what the fuck is going on, but no fucker will talk to me." I said, "What do you mean, Coral?" She said: "Well, they just ignore me. They look at me like I'm a complete stranger." Then I realised what had happened: nobody had recognised her – because she would be there at 5.30AM every morning and, by the time she went on set, she was this old lady. So for all the weeks we were there with the crew, no one knew who she was – so I had to take her round and introduce her!'[31]

It was happy endings all round: even Dennis Potter, renowned for being a perfectionist who demanded more from his actors and directors than some could give, was delighted with the realisation of *Dreamchild*. According to Gavin Millar, 'It was a tricky film to assemble, because the way Dennis had written it, it didn't hang together – we had to change the order. But he was absolutely fine about it: he loved Coral, loved what she was doing. She was very funny with him; she knew that he was a bad-tempered old sod but she also knew that he was very unwell – more unwell than she'd ever been – so she was indulgent in that sense, as we all had to be.'[32] Potter wrote to Coral, complimenting her performance: 'Your playing of it is everything I hoped for, plus a good many other things I didn't even suspect were in the part!'[33]

While the lengthy process of editing *Dreamchild* continued into 1985, Coral had the usual ways to keep herself and Vincent amused. That September, she accompanied him when he was star guest on a 'Mystery Cruise' from New York to the Bahamas on the SS Bermuda Star; the trip featured a screening of *The Abominable Dr Phibes*. The cruise company were given very explicate instructions for their special guests' comfort: 'Please make certain that his stateroom has a bath rather than a shower. Second, he and Coral do not like to sit alone at dinner…'[34]

They returned to New York on October 5, and made their way back to LA, where they had to prepare for a very special event. Ten years after their low-key civil ceremony, Coral finally got her longed-for church wedding. It nearly happened in 1978, while Vincent was in New York with *Diversions and Delights*: 'Might get married,' she told Alec Guinness. 'Never did like that rotten bit of paper we signed in Santa Barbara so think St Pats could easily see us limping up the aisle.'[35] In the end, Coral had to wait another six years to 'limp up the aisle' at St Vincent's; the ceremony took place on their 10th anniversary. It was not, however, an occasion for happy families: none of Vincent's relatives, not even Victoria or Barrett Price, were invited to attend.

Apparently there was room for just one 'child' in Coral's life at that time: *Dreamchild* had opened in the US on October 12, to reviews that could only have been better had she penned them herself. The *New York Times* declared, 'Coral Browne gives a performance of indomitable dignity, in which reserves of warmth and vulnerability are constantly crackling through the chilled exterior of Victorian propriety.'[36] When it opened in Boston, local critic Jay Carr said, 'It's only January, but I doubt if the rest of 1986 will give us a film so satisfyingly drawn from a celebrated literary source.'[37] Stephanie von Buchau of the *Pacific Sun*, declared that the 'Best Acting I've Ever Seen in Any Movie, Ever, Period' was 'Coral Browne in *Dreamchild*, awakening to the realization of what Lewis Carroll's love really meant.'[38] Even the ultra-cynical Pauline Kael was bowled over: 'Nothing I've seen Coral Browne do onscreen had prepared me for this performance. In the past, this Australian-born actress seemed too bullying a presence; she was too stiffly theatrical for the camera, and her voice was a blaster. Here, she has the capacity for wonder of the Alice of the stories…'[39] Peter Rainer summed it up: 'Coral Browne's performance is a marvel. Forget Meryl Streep – *this* is the female performance of the year.'[40] Four years later, Rainer included it in his pick of the best film performances of the 1980s.

It all seemed to be too good to be true – and, tragically, it was. Gavin Millar reflected, 'Sometimes I look back at the reviews and think, "Gosh, this was a huge success." But of course it wasn't – financially, it was a disaster. Thorn

EMI collapsed at the very moment it was released, so they didn't have any money to put behind it. Universal [its distributors] weren't interested in paying for anything, so it just sort of limped across the Atlantic and opened in New York in one cinema, and in LA and Boston and one or two other places – but with absolutely no fanfare and no publicity behind it. It became a sort of cult – it was taken off when people were still queuing round the block in New York. People were ringing me up and asking me why it still wasn't on. And it was so sad for her, because she'd just had the best reviews – and she never got proper industry recognition for *Dreamchild*. They [Universal] wouldn't put fourpence behind it…'[41]

'We'd been playing to wonderful audiences and then they whipped it off so they could show this *Brazil* that they'd been getting into trouble over,' said Coral. (*Brazil*'s release had been held back because of a disagreement between director Terry Gilliam and the producers about the ending.)[42] Michael Musto, reporting on *Dreamchild*'s failure at the box office, observed that 'Universal gave the film such an underwhelming push that Browne had to take it upon herself to call Gene Shalit [of *The Today Show*] and Joel Siegel [of *Good Morning America*] to ask why they hadn't reviewed it… Browne even facetiously suggested to Universal that she dress as a Salvation Army girl "and disrobe in front of the theatre – anything that will attract attention".'[43] Coral ruefully told columnist Roderick Mann (once the fiancé of her *Lylah* co-star, Kim Novak), 'I think *Dreamchild* is one of the three best things I've ever done – the other two are *Macbeth* which I did in New York and *Waltz of the Toreadors* – so I'm upset they're not advertising it more. I volunteered to commit a nuisance and get myself arrested outside the theatre but nobody seems keen on the idea…'[44]

Reg Williams, EMI's overseas PR director, did his utmost to put a positive slant on matters in his weekly updates: 'Engagements continue strongly in San Francisco, Seattle, Denver, Toronto, Berkeley, Palo Alto and San Jose. Chicago run stars today with Boston next Friday, Washington coming up soon after and a reopening in LA in the works. The Film Advisory Board (LA) is giving the production its Award of Excellence with a special award to CB for her performance at its annual luncheon at the Beverly Wilshire on February 2.'[45] In LA's *Reader*, critic Andy Klein pinpointed the problems the film faced: 'This little gem was more or less orphaned by Universal. Everything that made it good also made it a pain to the market. It had no big stars, it appeared to be a children's film but wasn't, and…it couldn't easily be sold in a few words.'[46]

That January, *Dreamchild* was finally given its theatrical release in the UK, where it and Coral were accorded the same critical acclaim. *Photoplay* praised the film for containing '…plenty of sinister undercurrents and perceptive asides which make this apparently quite simple story restlessly disturbing but always fascinating.'[47] And as for 'Alice': 'Coral Browne gives a simply towering performance,'[48] '…a formidable tragic-comic performance'.[49] 'But for *Dreamchild* being an ensemble triumph, it would be Ms Browne's film. She's superb – regal, malicious, pathetic, funny, haunted – frequently in the same breath,' gasped the *Daily Mail*.[50]

Meanwhile, in Hollywood, Coral was being linked with yet another man: Oscar. Bridget Byrne, a producer on *Entertainment Tonight*, observed that in the cocktail party discussion of nominations there was a certain boredom about the same names coming up every year – these included Sissy Spacek, Meryl Streep and Jessica Lange. 'I hear people saying that someone should get behind non-traditional choices – Coral Browne in *Dreamchild*, Vanessa Redgrave in *Wetherby*, Miranda Richardson in *Dance with a Stranger*.'[51]

People Weekly reported that Coral was in a list of 23 actresses who were 'legitimate contenders' for an Oscar that year, including Lange, Redgrave, Cher, Maggie Smith, Jane Fonda and Anne Bancroft. However, there was a problem: 'So far it's a case of what if we made a movie and no one came.'[52] And there was more vocal support for Coral from the Hollywood press: Gregg Kilday of the *LA Herald-Examiner* announced to any Academy members who were reading, 'We'd like to nominate Coral Browne for your consideration as best actress…if the proper attention is paid, she could more than hold her own among the more usual Oscar contenders.'[53]

Universal made a token gesture by holding two screenings of the film for Academy members on December 11 and January 9 – but little else. The company sent 'a terribly young man' to meet Coral: 'We had a sort of lunch together and he told me how they wanted the Oscar for Meryl Streep [for *Out of Africa*, co-produced by Universal]. Never mentioned anything else. And that was the last I saw of him.'[54] An advert appeared in *Variety*: 'For Your Consideration. Best Actress, Coral Browne.' It was paid for – by Coral Browne. As Gavin Millar observed, 'We all know what the Oscars are about – if you don't get a studio behind you…'[55]

Aljean Harmetz of the *New York Times* correctly predicted that Coral's 'widely praised' performance in *Dreamchild*, and another, Norma Aleandro's in *The Official Story* (a performance which won the New York Film Critics Circle award for Best Actress) would be gypped out of their just rewards for one reason only: money. Harmetz said, '*Dreamchild* has a major studio behind it, although it was released by Universal. While [it] has ended up on the 10-best lists of many critics in the 10 or 12 cities where it has played, it is an art film with a limited audience. It cost $3.8 million and has sold $490,690 worth of tickets. Universal, understandably, has more interest in its own $28 million… in fact, in order to get Universal to release *Dreamchild* in the first place, EMI had to pay for the prints and all the advertising costs.'[56]

The parsimony continued: when the film opened in London, Coral had to pay her own air fare to attend the screening. Alec Guinness accompanied her to the Curzon Mayfair (yards from her old home at number 36) on 24 January 1986, and to the party held afterwards at the White Elephant Club. 'Saw "it" last night,' she wrote to Vincent. 'It is an enchanting movie & looks beautiful – sure will get <u>good</u> reviews – critics will love it – God knows where the audiences will come from – <u>Cried a lot</u> – it really is v. moving. I am really V E R Y good & didnt put one foot wrong – it <u>should</u> be a lady of Peg's age but the make-up is excellent – difficult to judge myself but I really know when Im pleased & we all know that's not often!'[57]

As history tells, Coral did not receive a Best Actress Oscar nomination for *Dreamchild*; Meryl Streep did – for Universal's *Out of Africa* – and duly won.

There was some small compensation for Coral: on 25 January 1986, at a ceremony held at the Savoy, she was presented with the Evening Standard British Film Award for Best Actress. Dennis Potter's screenplay was nominated but lost out to Robert Bolt for *The Mission*. Appropriately, Coral received her award from 'Alan Bites' who introduced her as 'An actress of great originality – we have no one like her.' In her acceptance speech, Coral thanked 'the people so responsible for my performance' – which included Jonathan Altaras, Kenith Trodd, Rick McCallum and Dennis Potter. But then she stumbled: Verity Lambert's first name came out as 'Valerie'; Coral tried to cover up her faux pas with a joke: 'I don't like to be on familiar terms with you at the moment.' Alan Bates thought he was to blame for the error: 'I made a rather extravagant announcement, as one does on these occasions, and she came to the stage, suddenly a Coral I had not reckoned with before. The supremely confident Coral Browne was nervous, she forgot the name of someone she thought highly of and very much wanted to thank, and was, in short, suddenly vulnerable.'[58] Coral conquered her nerves long enough to thank the make-up artists 'who gave me my face – and Jane Robinson who gave me the clothes to match', and Gavin Millar who was 'a joy to work for'.

An Englishman Abroad and now *Dreamchild* reminded an older audience of what Coral's years in America had denied them, while introducing her to a new audience, largely oblivious to her long, but ultimately transient, stage career. This mirrored almost exactly what had happened to Peggy Ashcroft – Coral's rival for roles – another stalwart of the London stage, who in 1984 was discovered by a new TV and film audience after her award-winning supporting roles in the series *The Jewel in the Crown* and David Lean's last film, *A Passage to India*. In reference to Ashcroft, Trevor Nunn observed that 'when actors and actresses reach a certain age, it is their life experience that really counts'.[59] The same could now be said of Coral. There was, however, one rather significant difference between Peggy Ashcroft and Coral: one was a Dame, the other wasn't. 'Dame Coral Browne' was a notable omission from the list of veteran stage and screen actresses who had been so honoured, from Sybil Thorndike and Edith Evans, to Ashcroft and even fellow Australian Judith Anderson. There wasn't even a sniff of a CBE or MBE.

According to Victoria Price, Coral told a number of friends that she'd been offered a DBE – but only *if* she went on a goodwill tour of Australia. This, of course, would have been anathema to her and so she declined. Or, at least, this was Coral's version of events. But when Victoria Price was researching her biography of Vincent, she found a rather different version: 'Everyone to whom I mentioned this in England thought it was utter baloney. But Coral certainly said it more than once. She was dramatic and definitely prone to hyperbole, but why on earth would she make up such a thing? I got the sense that this was while she was married to my father – but if it was, he would have *made* her do it. Between his work ethic and his infatuation with all things British, he would never have let her refuse.'[60]

One of Coral's best friends, John Schlesinger, was made a CBE but wasn't knighted, despite persistent lobbying from the likes of Glenda Jackson and Alan Bates. He always maintained it was because he was gay, and that the 'fucking homo kiss' in *Sunday, Bloody Sunday* had been crucial in preventing him becoming 'Sir John'. But Schlesinger's biographer William Mann believed that the reason came from the incorrect perception that 'he had become an American director'.[61] It follows, then, that it is entirely possible a similar misconception applied to Coral after she decamped to LA in 1974 *and* married an American. However, this doesn't explain why an honour of some kind hadn't been bestowed well before then – after all, any established performer with a 50-year stage career behind them could justifiably expect a gong in some shape or form – even if it was only officially given for 'services to charity'. Coral's re-emergence as an internationally-acclaimed performer with the success of *An Englishman Abroad* and *Dreamchild* should have made her a shoo-in, but it wasn't to be. Perhaps, in the end, Palace officials were just too afraid of what 'this fucking lady' might have come out with in front of HMQ.

Putting the vagaries of the British honours system to one side, there was a more serious dilemma facing Coral, as Charles Champlin noted: 'The peril of being a gifted international actress of strong character is that you may well play character roles to great acclaim and enduring respect, but miss the kind of superstardom that moguls understand.'[62] As feared, job offers did not come thick and fast after her twin triumphs. Early in 1985, Jonathan Altaras reported to Coral that he was trying to set up a film for her in England that summer – 'a period film, but not large hats or sipping tea under oak trees'.[623] Coral once told an interviewer that she had 'a recurring urge to play a lady who sits under a great big English tree with a great big English hat on'.[64] Altaras was also attempting to get Vincent a film part, so they could work in England at the same time. In the meantime, Vincent was enjoying himself in a new Disney caper, *The Great Mouse Detective*, giving voice to Professor Ratigan, suspected of kidnapping – *quelle horreur* – a toymaker. This cartoon cad – which Vincent claimed was his favourite role – was the arch-enemy of Basil of Baker Street, a rodent Sherlock Holmes, played by Coral's ex-Old Vic colleague, a distinctly undistracted Barrie Ingham. Ingham and Coral had a brief reunion when he and his wife, Tarne, came to LA for a private screening of the film at Buena Vista Studios. 'We were going to have lunch but Coral couldn't – she had terrible raging toothache,' said Ingham.[65] It was the last time they would see each other.

In the end, the proposed film projects for Coral and Vincent in England failed to materialise, and it was back to the cruise and commercial circuit. For Vincent, this meant plugging the likes of *Time-Life*'s 'Enchanted World' book collection and Michael Forrest Lunaraine's natural dark brown American mink coats (which must have met with Coral's approval). They were also starting to appear in adverts as a 'celebrity couple', including one for Citibank credit card. In the advert, filmed in their garden, Coral thanked Citibank for making their Visa and Mastercard 'better than other banks', and for giving customers bonuses called 'CitiDollars' that could save them up to 40% on items such as a new TV or stereo. She explained that they used their CitiDollars to get something 'strictly for Vincent's amusement': when the camera drew back it revealed…an electric insect killer, which Vincent declared was 'wonderful'. His wife looked considerably less thrilled with the new amusement. Another dual display was featured in a TV commercial for 'Soup Time' instant soup, where Coral gritted her teeth and grumbled, 'My Vincent, he's a stickler for good soup…so I sprung this on him…10 second soup with home style stock. I got an evil look…'[66] Vincent dampened Coral's distaste for the job by telling her she could buy herself, by way of consolation, a new fur coat with her half of the money. Their 1986 cruises included one which took them down the Nile to Cairo, where Coral could see the original of her beloved Sphinx icon, and had something else to complain about when she developed galloping gut rot.

That May, she was back on *Dreamchild* promotional duties, this time in Vancouver, where the film had just opened. For Coral, it was one publicity trip too many: 'I'm entering my fifth week of pneumonia tomorrow,' she told John Schlesinger later. 'Have had an awful time – fucking Cedars and all. Got it in Vancouver when I was with Pat and Michael York. I was flogging Dreamchild and they were flogging Michael.'[67] Before she was struck down by illness, she and Vincent had attended an event in the city, to honour his 75th birthday, featuring his-and-her film screenings.

It was becoming obvious that the decline in their respective states of health was dictating their pace of life. Vincent's health, in particular, was rapidly worsening: he was now taking medication for a thyroid problem, and had developed arthritis. Coral told Lindsay Anderson that they were now embracing the quiet life: 'We generally get to bed at 9.30am. Then we watch a tape, and then the light out by 10.30.'[68] Of course, it was a rather fanciful claim – especially as Vincent had just agreed to appear in what would be Anderson's last feature film. In *The Whales of August*, Vincent would be working with Bette Davis and Lillian Gish who, at 93, was the oldest actress ever to star in a leading role. The melded maturity of the cast did not escape Coral's notice:

Vincent said, 'Coral asked me the name of the production company. I told her it was called Alive. "With you and Bette Davis and Lillian Gish? It should be called Almost Alive!"'[69] After one encounter with Davis, Coral had no great affection for the screen legend. Discovering that they had been invited to the same dinner party, Coral and Vincent arranged to give Davis a lift. According to Lindsay Anderson, 'Coral didn't know her... From the moment she got into the car she was bitchy, insulting, nasty... When they arrived at their hosts, she continued in the same vein. Coral made a beeline for the opposite side of the living room... "To get away from that monster."'[70] Eventually, fellow guest Roddy McDowall marched Davis off to the bathroom and took her to task about her behaviour. The transformation was immense and immediate: Davis was suddenly all sweetness and light, and even insisted that Coral and Vincent stop by for a nightcap on their way home.

Filmed on an island off the coast of Maine in autumn 1986, *The Whales of August* was an adaptation by David Berry of his own play. The story centred on 'two sisters living alone in a comfortable but basic home they have occupied for decades on the striking coast of Maine. Sarah (Gish) is a doting busybody who is obliged to care for her sister Libby (Davis), because the latter is blind. Trouble rears its head in the form of Vincent Price, a White Russian of considerable charm and gentlemanliness who for decades has lived as a "houseguest" of numerous ladies.'[71] When it was released in autumn 1987, *The Whales of August* did for Vincent what *An Englishman Abroad* and *Dreamchild* had done for Coral, namely giving him a belated chance to show there was more to his screen acting than gore and horror. Monica Sullivan enthused, 'Vincent is so irresistible as a charming scrounge who tries to horn in on this pair that when he makes his graceful exit from the plot with resignation, he takes much of the film's lightness of tone with him,'[72] while Roger Ebert enjoyed the character of 'The old aristocrat, down on his luck, played by Price with a self-deprecating humor that creates dignity out of thin air.'[73] The 'O' word was whispered in industry circles but, just like his wife, Vincent had to content himself with the reviews.

After the film's completion, Coral and Vincent had more work – of sorts – on the East coast: on 17 November, they both gave speeches at New York's Museum of Broadcasting as part of a celebration to mark the BBC's 50th birthday. Then they headed to the Strathmore Hall Arts Center, in Rockville,

Maryland, where they were co-hosting 'The Mystery at Strathmore Hall, an evening of intrigue'.

That Christmas, Coral and Vincent spent Christmas with Victoria Price: 'I was living about an hour south of Santa Fe and had driven up to spend Christmas Day with them both. Neither of them was in very good humor. My father couldn't breathe very well at 7500 feet and was really distraught that he would no longer be able to visit one of his favourite places. As for Coral, she was rather peeved that no one in Santa Fe served any alcohol on Christmas Day. At some point, we left my father to lie down in the hotel room and went down to the bar together.'[74] There, Coral launched into her story of the woman she had loved and given up more than 40 years earlier. Victoria explained, 'I had just ended a relationship, and she was in one of her kind, commiserating moods.'[75]

Coral and Vincent were soon back on the cruise circuit: in February 1987, they were special guests on a Princess Line trip to Bora Bora, featuring screenings of *Dreamchild* and *Laura*. On 4 June, they embarked on a trip to China and Japan. 'I hated every minute of it,' Coral told Caroline Cornish-Trestrail. 'Needed A. Bennett, plenty of copy. HATE "Red" countries.'[76] There was another reason why this trip had left Coral slightly less than ebullient: she had recently undergone extensive dental work. However, as Charles Champlin related, 'She had left a new and crucial partial bridge at home. There began a port by port, consulate by consulate, cruise line office by cruise line office struggle to get the missing dentistry airshipped to the next port of call. It did not catch up until the cruise was over. The sequence could have been played in rage – she was forced to eschew some of the ship's most ravishing and chewable cuisine – but her bulletins made it all seem to be a hilarious and suspenseful slapstick misadventure.'[77] Coral was more concerned about the state of her husband's health, as she revealed to Caroline Cornish-Trestrail: 'Vincent isn't really OK – he has "retired" – and I think doesn't know what to do with himself…he has aged a lot recently. Has no ambition and is v.low.'[78]

On 29 April 1987, Coral finally became a naturalised US citizen, and it appeared that becoming officially American helped her reach a decision she had been pondering for some time. 'I'm going to sell the lease of 16 Eaton Place,' she told Caroline Cornish-Trestrail. 'I have till 2014 and am <u>sick</u> of it all – It will go on the market next month. I've left Jill Melford to handle it & she can have the commission. <u>When</u> I know its sold I will have to go over &

see whats to go on the block & whats to come over here.'[79] In due course, Jill Melford sold the flat to a friend of hers – but not before she completed the arduous task of clearing out 20 years of Coral's clutter: 'Cleaning it out was a mammoth job. There were lists that appeared daily of what went to Australia, what went to California, what needed to be sold, and what was to be kept for her. I was given all the drink that was kept in the top cupboards in the bedroom. But what with all the heat, all this Dom Perignon stuff that she'd hoarded had all gone bad… She didn't want any of her old photographs, or anything like that. I started to look at them, and I said, "This is mad – you can't chuck all this out." There were some magical pictures and things, cardboard boxes of stuff…'[80] But off to Australia they went, to the Performing Arts Centre in Melbourne to form part of the 'Coral Browne Collection'. This time, Coral had cleared out rather more than a few letters from her 'big black bag' – she was expunging most of her past.

There was enough to worry about in the LA of the present: along with her worries about Vincent, their friend Joan Rivers was now giving cause for concern. In August 1987, she was having trouble with 'the help', as Coral revealed to John Schlesinger: 'The Guard who carries the gun and guards the house got away with 168 bottles of Lafitte at 150 dolls a throw… He'd been there 7 years but had recently acquired a heroin habit.'[81] Furthermore, Fox had just pulled the plug on her TV chat show, which was produced by her husband, Edgar Rosenberg, and the couple had decided to spend some time apart. Then, on 14 August, came shocking news: Rosenberg had been found dead in a Philadelphia hotel room, from an overdose of prescription anti-depressants. The *LA Times* reported that, only hours earlier, 'He was trying to figure out when he could reschedule dinner with actor Vincent Price.'[82]

It emerged that Rosenberg, temporarily separated from his wife, had previously suffered a serious heart attack, and had undergone quadruple bypass surgery. He was also put on a drug called Halcyon (subsequently taken off the market) which, it was later discovered, caused severe depression – as in Rosenberg's case. 'People had no idea what was going on with this man,' Joan Rivers explained. 'At one point, he was taking 30 different pills a day…I had gone in for a bit of liposuction – they did it in hospitals then – and some idiot in Philadelphia called my daughter. So Melissa was told this, and then had to come to the hospital to give me the news. She was 16 at the time…'[83] Coral heard the news on the radio and immediately drove to see her friend, clad only in her bathrobe and nightgown. Rivers recalled, 'She was furious with Edgar for doing this to me, but insisted, "All right, darling, you've got to deal with this. You'll get through it."'[84]

The problems were mounting: in March 1988, Vincent had a pacemaker fitted and, within months, was diagnosed with Parkinson's disease; this was treated with a combination of medication and a regime of physical and vocal exercises to stave off its debilitating symptoms. Realising that it was all going to be downhill from then on, Coral told John Schlesinger that they were 'Now trying to get permission to pull down the carport and erect a garage with living quarters above to try and seduce daily help to live in.'[85] Yet still they kept up their busy schedule, filling their diaries with an assortment of events – some for loot, some for love. That February, they had attended a retrospective of their friend David Hockney's work at the LA County Museum of Art, then accepted an invitation to join other celebrity guests at the Bullocks Wilshire, the luxury department store, housed in an impressive art deco building, whose previous customers had included John Wayne, Marlene Dietrich and Clark Gable. However, on this occasion, the 'big name' guest shoppers were the Duke and Duchess of York. Within weeks of this, Coral and Vincent were at sea again, guest lecturers on a Cunard World Cruise on the QE2.

In August, they were back in London, where John Schlesinger hosted a cocktail party for them at Victoria Street; the guest list included Jill Melford, the Guinnesses, Alan 'Bites', Alan Bennett, Frith Banbury, Eileen Atkins and Jonathan Altaras. Maggie Smith was also invited but Coral bitched to her host, 'I expect she won't come as she'll be overacting for money.'[86] She also forewarned Schlesinger about Vincent's increasing physical frailty: 'He can't really deal with more than v few people (like six) as since he's been so ill he finds it terribly difficult to make conversation and he gets into panic. Not easy for me – he may not turn up – or v late because of this so if anyone expects him to be a host we'll have to get a blown-up cut out to stand by the welcome mat.'[87] The party went off smoothly enough, but Coral still wished 'A pox on the nine who didn't turn up.'[88]

Disease and illness had now become the predominant, and permanent, themes – Coral poured her heart out to John Schlesinger: 'V is very NOT well... He has really fallen apart and such a personality change. He is so tired of living and frankly it's so terribly hard for me to cope – his depression is very deep – I haven't had a laugh since we were together in Venice and that's God's truth. I have just returned from a LOUSY cruise – have a cold and was mugged IN THE REVOLVING DOORS at Bergdoff Goodmans in NY – 700 dolls and all the cards and my GOLD rosary gone – Well!'[89] Within weeks of this mishap, Coral and Vincent duly got their 'daily help to live in': their friend, Reg Williams, EMI's former PR man, became Vincent's secretary and moved in to the new quarters above their garage. The only other piece of cheer came in a review of John Schlesinger's new film, *Madame Sousatzka*, which starred Shirley MacLaine as the eccentric piano teacher who, Mame-like, likes to give her pupils lessons in how live. The *Pacific Sun* commented, 'Maclaine is the singular sour note in this otherwise impeccably pitched film. Schlesinger almost makes it to the level of his fabulous *An Englishman Abroad* (what wouldn't Coral Browne have done with the role of Madame Sousatzka!)'[90] What indeed.

Coral did briefly leave an ailing Vincent to go to London to keep an eye on herself. Alan Bennett had adapted *An Englishman Abroad* for the stage; it formed the first half of a double-bill called *Single Spies* opening at the National Theatre in December 1988. The second play, *A Question of Attribution*, was also adapted from Bennett's television play about the exposure of Anthony Blunt, starring James Fox as the Keeper of the Queen's Pictures who was unveiled as the 'fourth man' in the Philby-Burgess-Maclean 'Cambridge spy ring'. What made the play especially notable was that the Queen would feature as a character for the first time ever on a British stage. Simon Callow was playing Burgess, while Alan Bennett made a rare foray onto the stage to portray Blunt, directed by Callow. And to Prunella Scales fell the challenging task of portraying both Coral and the monarch. 'When I was offered the play, I was very uneasy about playing Coral because, apart from anything else, I'm about 5 and a half inches too short – I wore extremely high heels with lifts and so on – and, of course, had seen her play it herself. I wanted to go and see her to talk about the part but she wasn't well enough to see anybody at that time. So one was left with talking to other people and to Alan about her; I watched everything I possibly could, all her screen performances, and I worked very hard on that very specific, particular, accent she had, which was very special.'[91]

As ever, Coral's reputation preceded her: 'She was revered by my generation,' said Scales. 'She had a rather wild reputation as a woman – one had the impression that she had a lot of partners. But she was known as a West End actress – very glamorous, with a great reputation – and also for the things she said about people, very sharp and amusing observations. People on the whole loved working with her – she was fun to work with.' And, though she enjoyed playing Coral, Scales admitted, 'I was very nervous, more nervous about that than I was about playing the Queen. I don't think anybody had played the Queen on stage before…but I was the right height, I had a fabulous wig and costume, and there was masses of footage of her as a private and public person to go on. Whereas with Coral, one had recordings of TV plays and films, but there was nothing of her as herself, doing interviews or anything like that at that time. So there was a certain amount of guesswork involved… Initially, anyway, I found it easier to believe I was the Queen than to believe I was Coral Browne.'[92]

Single Spies opened at the National on Thursday 1 December 1988. Simon Callow revealed, 'A first night is like an operation: you have to have it…but the thought of it gives you nothing but pain. For some reason last Thursday wasn't like that. It would have been had we known the original performers, Coral Browne and Alan Bates were in the audience…and there she was, in the dressing room at the end of the show, looking younger than she did at the time of the events depicted, and possessed of a kind of mythic glamour in the flesh that ordinary actors can only attain on the screen… It was literally breathtaking to see her. She was charming and warm and enthusiastic. But then Prunella Scales didn't ask her, as Laurette Taylor asked Tennessee Williams's mother, upon whom her character in *The Glass Menagerie* was based, "Well, dear – how do you like yourself?"'[93]

Coral liked 'herself' well enough – but even she struggled for words to describe her loathing for what the designers had given 'her' to wear: 'I nearly *fainted.* The prospect of my appearing in a fake fur – and hats that wouldn't have come out of a grab bag after Christmas at the Salvation Army! I was incensed… I consider it defamation!'[94] And the problem never went away: Liza Goddard, who played the Queen and Coral in a 2002 revival of *Single Spies* agreed: 'The clothes were never quite right…'[95] Alan Bennett subsequently revealed that Coral had donated the fur coat she had worn in *An Englishman Abroad* to the National Theatre. But, in 2000, when the West Yorkshire Playhouse asked if they could borrow it for their production of *Single Spies*, it emerged that the coat had been disposed of – not because of space limitations, but because the real fur was considered out of step with the prevailing attitude. Bennett mused, 'I'd like to have heard Coral herself confronting whichever apparatchik it was that made this decision.'[96]

At the National the critics were unconcerned with the production's sartorial shortcomings: Michael Ratcliffe said, 'Scales plays Browne as cleverly as one actress may dare this side of *lèse-majesté*.'[97] Milton Shulman observed, 'Prunella Scales makes no attempt to imitate the delectable Coral Browne but in her own way conveys the pleasure that such a sardonic, high-spirited actress would enjoy at finding herself in such a curious, almost farcical, situation.'[98] However, while Charles Osborne of the *Daily Telegraph* agreed that 'Prunella Scales gives an equally remarkable impersonation of Coral Browne, an actress whom she in no way physically resembles,' he admitted, 'I can't help wishing, however, that we could have had Coral Browne playing herself, as she did in the TV film.'[99]

In February 1989, *Single Spies* transferred to the West End and enjoyed a six-month run at the Queen's Theatre. Coral sent Prunella Scales an unusual first-night present: a papier mâché 'lucky rabbit' that she'd made herself, decorated with postage stamps from England, Gibraltar and other domains – all, of course, bearing the Queen's head. *Single Spies* had been a strange experience for Coral: she had watched another actress play her – a role that she had played, playing herself.

However, when Coral returned to LA, she reverted to playing one of her least popular roles: the 'wicked stepmother'. Victoria Price had decided to ditch academia and try her hand at acting (she had previously spent one term at graduate acting school). Aware of the professional etiquette, which decreed that no actor would ask another to recommend them to their own agent, Victoria was surprised when Vincent said that it would be OK to send her resumé to his agent Pearl Wexler at the Kohner Agency. However, as Victoria recalled, when Coral found out about this innocent development, 'all hell broke loose…they almost got divorced over it. Coral seemed to think my Dad and I had been colluding behind her back. To say she lost it is not an overstatement – she was *furious*. But my Dad, for one of the few times in his life, held his ground. He said, "She's my daughter, and she's interested in doing this – and fuck you: leave me if you want to." And they had a huge, *huge* fight over it. And I never understood it, it was idiotic – I mean, I was just this *kid*. But that was Coral: there was this *incredible* fear and vulnerability. It was inexplicable.'[100]

In time, the dust settled on this ugly episode and, of course, the divorce papers never materialised – when Vincent and Coral made their next public appearance together, they were the picture of harmony. Coral had always said that her husband would attend the opening of an envelope – which is precisely what he did, accompanied by his 'elegant lady wife'. On 29 March 1989, they made their way to LA's Shrine Auditorium for the 61st Oscars ceremony. There, they would have cameo roles in one of the most notorious events in the history of the Academy Awards, a spectacle with so many to choose from. Allan Carr, the man behind hit stage musicals *Grease* and *La Cage aux Folles*, had been selected to produce that year's awards show, and duly devised a special song and dance number. The ten-minute sequence turned out to be possibly the longest and most excruciating ten minutes in the entire history of the Oscars. It began with a shrill-voiced 'Snow White' (Eileen Bowman, fresh from playing the character in a Las Vegas production of the kitsch San Francisco show, *Beach Blanket Babylon*), singing in front of a row of dancing gold stars, while she tried to 'connect' with the assembled firmament in the audience. Worse quickly followed: the stage curtain rose to reveal a tawdry recreation of the famous Coconut Grove Club, where the Oscar ceremonies had been staged during the Thirties and Forties. Merv Griffin – who once recreated the club in his hotel, the Beverly Hilton – proceeded to croon his cheesy way round the tables. These were occupied by an eclectic collection of ageing stars of yesteryear, whom Griffin introduced in turn. Alice Faye, Dorothy Lamour, cow couple Roy Rogers and Dale Evans, Cyd Charisse and Tony Martin all played their non-speaking parts to perfection, and departed the stage as quickly as their faculties allowed. Then the spotlight fell on the next couple who, in tasteful contrast to the lurex and lamé outfits sported by some of their fellow 'guests', looked immaculate in their black suits. On cue, Griffin bellowed, 'Ladies and gentlemen, Vincent Price and Coral Browne!' In these ludicrous circumstances, Coral did the only thing possible in what was to be her final stage appearance: she said goodbye to Hollywood by giving the audience a grand gesture that, on closer examination, was part wave – and part V-sign. It was a fitting farewell.

What the audience would never have guessed from Coral's stylish appearance was that the cancer had returned – with a vengeance. In early February, she had surgery to remove another lump from her breast. On 4 May, she began an intensive course of daily radiotherapy at UCLA's John Wayne Cancer Clinic and, on 6 July, had another tumour removed from her leg. She told Alan Bennett that she felt like '... a fucking sieve. I've got a hole under my arm from the last operation and now another hole in my leg. And that's in addition to the holes that nature gave me.'[101] She was now also making good use of an assortment of wigs and hats to disguise the resultant hair loss.

And then, when it was too late to do her any good, came a death that was only surprising because Coral so nearly didn't live to see it: on 11 November 1989, Victoria Brown died at Delves House, in her hundredth year. Notices were placed in the *Daily Telegraph* and the *Guardian* announcing the death of the 'dearly loved mother of Coral and Vincent'.[102]

Neither of them was well enough to attend the funeral of 'Mother', held on Friday 17 November at Mortlake Crematorium in west London, but a friend of Vicky's arranged for flowers to be sent in their names. At the funeral, Coral did have the final word in the lifelong tussle of wills she fought with her mother: the presiding minister had no idea whose mother Vicky actually was, until one of the six mourners present told him her daughter's first name. Then the penny dropped: 'Brown, Brown, Coral – not *the* Coral Browne!' The ashes of 'Coral Browne's mother' were sent to her daughter. They were not, as Vicky had once arranged, deposited next to Leslie's in Boroondara General Cemetery – her niche remained reserved, but empty.

Coral herself was not quite ready to join 'the feathered choir' and, out of the blue, got a chance to have the final say on her life and career. Late in 1989, the young American film-maker Christopher O'Hare was visiting John Schlesinger in London and spotted a photograph of Coral, resplendent in pearls and furs, taken by Helmut Newton in 1989; it was her favourite photo. Intrigued by the image, O'Hare quickly learned enough about Coral's life and lines to decide a documentary should be made about her. Despite her ongoing illness, Coral, realising it would be a good chance to make her own screen 'obituary', agreed to be interviewed for the programme, *Caviar for the General*.

John Schlesinger himself undertook the role of interviewer, under O'Hare's direction. Coral loaned them material from her many scrapbooks and personal photographs. Copious well-researched and probing questions were compiled in preparation for Coral's interview – from her relationships with Paul Robeson and Douglas Fairbanks Jr to a query about Dame Marie Tempest refusing to tread on Cornish soil during the filming of *Yellow Sands*, and her 'feud' with Radie Harris. But, disappointingly, the answers to many of these tantalising questions were missing from the film. Another problem was that Coral had been asked to retell some of her best-known stories and one-liners which, when uttered on the spur of the moment and in context, had been sharp. When she repeated them on cue, their impact was rather blunted; such anecdotes were more effective when told by contributors including Schlesinger, Ned Sherrin and Anna Massey.

Coral was clearly unhappy with the way things had gone: 'Schlesinger did an interview with me on film – probably look like Grandma Moses & will be sued for every answer to every question…it sure bored me,' she told Alec Guinness.[103] Later, she sent him a card telling how she 'got 6000 dollars for that TV rubbish coming up'.[104] When *Caviar for the General* was screened on Channel Four, on 23 December 1990, Guinness himself had a few cavils to make about the film. He told Coral that Alan Bennett had 'got it all wrong' about *An Englishman Abroad*: 'I told him the story and then brought you both together here and you told him again.' Guinness also felt that the film was lacking some vital qualities: 'What I missed, badly, was someone up there to talk of your KINDNESS and WARMTH. And there should have been at least a passing reference to your Catholicism.'[105] Now, she needed her faith more than ever: in January 1990, she began a course of chemotherapy injections. 'I understand why Doctors say, "It makes the death easier,"' she told Alec Guinness. 'That figures, as you have no desire to live!!! I look very slim & about 50 – never looked so good, never felt so bad.'[106] But the injections had to be stopped: 'My veins have dried up…so next week I go to the John Wayne (!) Cancer Hospital at UCLA & my chum professor Eilber inserts a false vein into the top of my breast and into the heart.'[107] Still, none of this was an excuse for looking like Grandma Moses: 'I've sent him drawings of my breasts & orders as to where I want the "Hinkman line" as I fully intend to continue to wear low cuts if I fancy…'[108] She wrote to John Schlesinger, 'I'm in bed – I used to be at my best there but how things have changed. More hell tomorrow – they implant a very heavy pump into that sad and unforgiving breast which will throw chemo into me unceasing 24 hours day and night for at least two months. I presume I carry it strapped to me and into a KCET hold all.'[109]

Despite her own traumas, Coral was not beyond caring and worrying about her dearest friends: she was distraught to learn about the sudden death of 19-year-old Tristan Bates, the twin son of her beloved Alan 'Bites'. 'I can't think what he'll do,' she told Alec Guinness. 'He brought the twins up from the day they were born – in baskets on the make-up table at Stratford with bottles & nappies as I recall & those boys were his life.'[110] And, of course, her loved ones were now becoming increasingly concerned about her. Friends rallied: Joan Rivers – then rebuilding her life and career in New York – was one of Coral's most frequent, and cheering, visitors: 'It was my job to sit on her bed and make her laugh,' Rivers explained.[111] Ronald Eyre, suffering from cancer himself, wrote to his 'Kitty Warren' with some luvvie gossip to cheer her up: 'You're well away from the theatre scene. *Timon of Athens* (T Nunn with David Suchet) is a lesson in how to soup up a stale dog's dinner.'[112]

Roddy McDowall regularly sent Coral fresh flowers from his garden; Patrick White wrote to tell her, 'Your fantastic films will remain with me till I die. You are indeed one of *the* actresses';[113] and David Hockney sent a touching invitation to tea: an offset litho depicting a sitting room with a blazing fire and a trademark dachshund asleep in front of the hearth. Coral had it framed and hung it in her bedroom. She needed all the comfort she could get: 'Vinnie sleeps a lot and doesn't speak much,' she complained to Alec Guinness. 'In a way I'm lonely… MS tries to get her foot in the door but frankly am not for the social chit chat – especially when the <u>wit</u> is sadly missing.'[114] She was now taking a potpourri of medication that included drugs to prevent the growth of cancer cells, Procan and Lanoxin for an irregular heartbeat and twice-daily pills for the 'ulcer on the hill'. 'I'm on steroids to try & give me strength but <u>I</u> fear it's because my doctor is gay & wants me to look like Christopher Reeve,' she told Alec Guinness.[115]

On 10 September, Coral entered a $600-a-night private room in the Hazel Wilson Pavilion at UCLA Medical Center, where she endured yet more chemotherapy as doctors made increasingly desperate efforts to prolong her life. Now, her diaries, once full of parties, lunches and theatre dates, contained only entries that charted her decline. On November 11, she noted that she was 'weak and shakey and breathless – heart not too good. Lousy.'[116] The same day, she found the strength to write to Vincent: 'My darling love, Take great care of yourself. I love you SO much. Thank you for being so wonderful to me, especially during my illness – You know how I feel – its not for words – I haven't sufficient call on those. But you <u>know</u>. I hold you close forever – Pray for me.'[117]

Before she entered UCLA, Coral had returned to Alec Guinness all the letters he'd written to her throughout their long friendship. Warning him of their imminent arrival, she explained, 'Thought you might like to have them before someone went thru my panties & gave them to Alan Bennett to read on the BBC!!!!'[118] She had, of course, thought of another way they could be used: 'Thank you for all the pleasure your letters have given me – thought you might want them back in case Alan B ever got into my ditty box & made a play out of nothing – he's a v. clever puss.'[119] Guinness duly burned the letters, and promised to do the same to hers. However, a number of Coral's survived the inferno and were later discovered in his father's papers by his son, Matthew. Other friends started to receive 'farewell' packages from Coral: she sent Suzzie Buchanan all her mementoes of Jack, the man they had both loved and, separately, lost.

By the beginning of 1991, Coral was in steep and terminal decline. The cancer had spread to her lungs, and an increasingly unwell Vincent hired nurses to help take care of his wife. In January, their friend, the theatre critic Dan Sullivan, aware of Coral's failing health, wrote to her and suggested that, as they had once discussed over dinner, they start work on her autobiography. Sullivan suggested that Coral could speak into a tape recorder, possibly in the style of the actress Ruth Gordon's memoirs, which were long on anecdotes and short on chronology. Sullivan's suggestion was not taken up: the only things Coral was capable of writing now – in barely legible handwriting – were the heartbreakingly brief entries in her diaries chronicling her demise. Early in 1991, her blood pressure was being monitored on a daily basis, and she noted this down; the last entry was on May 28. In the last few weeks of her life, she stopped speaking. Victoria Price said, 'The last time I spoke to her was on Mother's Day [May 12], when we told each other we loved each other, so that was really fortuitous.'[120]

Vincent decided it was time to put Alec and Merula Guinness in the picture: 'For such a volatile and active lady being confined to bed with never a really well day has been worse than constant pain which, thank God, she's been spared. She has been remarkably tolerant of it but not without a certain despair and resentment…now the invasion of the lungs is the worst of it. I tell you all this as she has sort of hinted she'd like you to know from me…she grows weaker every day – the mind works and can still laugh a little but it just kills me to see her losing out!'[121] Nonetheless, according to the critic Liz Smith, Coral mustered enough strength to deliver one final, damning verdict: 'One of Coral's last acts was to throw across the room the Julia Phillips book

You'll Never Eat Lunch in this Town Again. "Trash! Trash!," said Coral, as she hit the wastebasket on the first toss.'[122]

Vincent's 80th birthday on 27 May was not forgotten in the enveloping gloom. Barrett, Rini and Victoria took him out for dinner, while among his birthday post was a scrapbook compiled by Anthony Timpone, editor of the sci-fi media magazine, *Starlog*. Entitled 'We Honor Vincent Price on his Illustrious Career and Upcoming Birthday', it contained photos and messages from Charlton Heston, Gene Tierney, Robert Mitchum, Peter Cushing, Diana Rigg, Christopher Lee (who shared his birthday with Vincent) and Roddy McDowall. Heston wrote, 'I wish you the warmest of Happy Birthdays, even though you treated my mother so badly in *The Ten Commandments*.' That same day, BBC Radio was repeating *Night of the Wolf*: writing to inform them of the event, Head of Drama John Tydeman assured them, 'The absence of Coral has left a huge hole in British theatrical life.'[123]

Throughout the final days of Coral's illness, Vincent maintained a near-constant vigil at his wife's side. However, on 29 May, two days after his birthday, he had to go to the Vincent Price Gallery to meet Tim Burton, who was starting work on a documentary about his life. While he was gone, Coral slipped away.

⁂

The press paid tribute accordingly, in Britain and America. Charles Champlin's tribute in the *LA Times*, 'Coral Browne: Her Character Survives', said: 'Browne was a delicious raconteuse, one of those women (not all of them necessarily actresses) who see themselves continually at the center of dramas ranged anywhere between farce and tragedy, depending on events, and who report on them with immense verve and humor. She kept a wickedly discerning eye on the follies and idiocies of the world but she was just as amusing as the author of her own mischances.'[124] The British press didn't hold back either: *The Times* declared, 'Coral Browne was one of the wittiest actresses of her generation on-stage and an equally striking personality off it. As a classical actress she had power and authority while her sheer stylishness and her commanding personality lifted many a commercial piece well above its natural level.'[125] The *Daily Telegraph* observed, 'On the stage Miss Browne excelled in playing duchesses or dragons – or, above all, Edwardian women with a past. With her striking dark looks, lustrous brown eyes, blitheness of spirit and an ability to remain poised in a crisis, she had tremendous stage presence, which saw her safely through anything from light comedy to Shakespearean tragedy, from farce to melodrama.'[126] BBC Two's *The Late Show* on May 30 featured a special tribute to her. Alan Bates later commented that the tributes paid to Coral 'were not obituaries, they were the best notices I have ever read for anyone, and rightly so'.[127] Her closest friends paid private tributes: Roddy McDowall told Vincent, 'I don't need to tell you how much I admired and wallowed in her – or how much I shall deeply and daily miss the pulse of her spirit and affection and friendship in my life. You know it all...the experience of the two of you together was a rare one indeed. The value of you alone is an unparalleled treasure.'[128]

Among the many fulsome and fond public obituaries was one in a Footscray newspaper, complete with a headline which would surely have sent Coral's left eyebrow shooting skywards: 'Mrs Vincent Price of Footscray dies at 77.'[129] Months later, another Melbourne paper, *The Age*, ran a belated but touching notice in the 'personal' ads: 'This tribute is from Max Ferguson on behalf of all Coral's relations who were very proud of her achievements.'[130] It appeared that Australia had not forgotten, but forgiven, one of its most reluctant and negligent daughters.

For Vincent Price, there would soon be much to forgive. But first, there was Coral's funeral to endure. 'My Dad, Reg [Williams] and I attended a private viewing shortly after she died,' said Victoria Price. 'Naturally, she had picked out exactly which Armani suit she wanted to be viewed in and Marika made sure it was in perfect condition. My dad had a hard time with it – it was one of the only times I saw him cry.'[131] The funeral mass was held at St Victor's Church, followed by cremation at Hollywood Memorial Park (now Hollywood Forever) on Santa Monica Boulevard – not, as Coral always jokingly predicted, at Forest Lawn. Her ashes were scattered under a white rose bush in the Park's garden. Vincent said, 'I'll always know it. It will be the tree on which all the roses are nodding their heads with laughter.'[132]*

---

* Coral was in good company: Hollywood Memorial's star-studded necrology included Rudolph Valentino, Peter Lorre, John Huston, Tyrone Power, Peter Finch, Cecil B De Mille and even an ex-lover – Douglas Fairbanks Jr. However, a few years after Coral's death, Hollywood cemetery expert Mark J Masek said that the Hollywood Memorial had taken on 'the Norma Desmond role as an aging and forgotten legend, a faded shadow of its former glory.'[133] In 1998, the

But there was to be little to laugh about in the immediate aftermath. In June 1991, the contents of her much-revised will were revealed – and nearly everyone who knew her was staggered to learn that her estate totalled over six million dollars, including a million dollars in US banks and three million pounds in an offshore tax-free account in Guernsey. No one was more staggered than Vincent: he told John Schlesinger, 'The lawyers are confounded by the number of different bank accounts to say nothing of the amounts in them.'[134]

But Vincent wouldn't see much of the money: for Coral had named, as her main beneficiaries, the John Wayne Cancer Clinic at the UCLA Cancer Center and a Californian animal charity. According to Victoria Price, 'What Coral did around money – and I come from a family of people who were paranoid and idiosyncratic at best about money – was the most hurtful thing she could ever have done to my Dad. He was angry, angry, angry – and deeply *hurt*. He felt truly betrayed by her. Oddly enough, though, it seemed that many of her English friends, particularly Jill [Melford] and Adrienne [Corri], knew very well that Coral was loaded, and didn't know how this could have escaped my father's notice.'[135]

'Coral wasn't secretive with anybody,' explained Jill Melford. 'She certainly never *looked* poverty-stricken, and one never assumed she was. And Coral had some very valuable things – paintings, jewellery and fur coats galore.'[136] At the beginning of her relationship with Vincent, Coral told a reporter, 'I expect men to send the Rolls for me and shower me with gifts.'[137] And, as far as Vincent was concerned, it appeared she never wavered from that attitude, despite her claims to the contrary. 'Vincent told me on the phone he was shocked she was so rich,' said Eileen Atkins. 'It hurt him very much. How she worked that one, not telling him, I don't know...and she'd told me once, "I don't want Vincent to dish out money on me."'[138] The real dichotomy – some would say cruel

ruined and debt-ridden cemetery was bought for $375,000 by Tyler and Brent Cassity, the sons of a St Louis mortuary owner. It was renamed Hollywood Forever and the Cassitys immediately set about revamping and restoring their new acquisition. Hollywood Forever was relaunched as a welcoming attraction for celebrity spotters, complete with a gift shop selling celebrity memorabilia, including framed copies of stars' death certificates. Many graveside scenes from the series *Six Feet Under* were filmed there – one of the embalmers even got a job as a consultant on the show. So, in a fittingly bizarre turn of events, Coral's final resting place became a film set.

irony – is that Vincent so often accepted work just for the money, yet Coral constantly berated him for taking on such a heavy workload which put his health at risk and made her unhappy. Perhaps if he'd known about the vast sums she had stashed away in her many accounts, he might have been less inclined to say 'yes' to everything that came his way.

To Vincent, Coral bequeathed her share of their property and the income from her investments, administered under a Trust. Victoria Price said, 'She left my father the interest from her estate, but he only lived long enough to get one payment. He was absolutely determined to get at least *one!*'[139] It was scant consolation. Vincent subsequently amended his own will, and set up the Vincent L Price Jr Family Trust to safeguard his children's inheritance.

Despite the posthumous pain Coral had caused him, Vincent was bereft. He once said, 'I've come to believe remembering someone is not the highest compliment – it is missing them.'[140] And miss her he did. 'It seems so unfair that she should have had to suffer so much and one can only thank God she's out of it,' he told John Schlesinger. 'I feel her all around me and trying to put my life in order without her, she trips me up at every stop. Beautiful lady! Witty lady! I'm lost! I miss her but the last few weeks were so terrible – why her?'[141] But there were still elements of his wife's 'legacy' he could smile about: 'I'm glad I've retired because now I can open the Coral Browne Secondhand Store,' he informed Schlesinger. In her wardrobe, he had found '5000 pairs of shoes, 7000 Chanel everythings from buttons to belts, purses, etc. The make-up went back to Jack Buchanan and further. Bits of money everywhere. The mail is overwhelming from hairdressers to someone who knew her when she was 10 – was she ever 10? 75 single stockings – in case she lost a leg I guess… I'm glad you didn't see her towards the end. So sad, so helpless to get out of it and wanting to so much. The orders of her will are very explicit but not all that easy to carry out. I've given or sold almost all the clothes – you can't believe the amount.'[142] Jill Melford recalled that 'Vinnie rang me up and said, "I'm in the most terrible muddle – do you know what Coral left you?" And I said, "Vinnie, we were all out of the address book so often…" – I mean, if she got cross with you, you were out of the will and of the "back of the address book". She left me the diamond brooch she's wearing in that Newton picture and she left me some other bits of jewellery, including a diamond bracelet. My son went to California and collected them.'[143]

Some of the more straightforward bequests were easier to fulfil: Coral left John Schlesinger her Graham Sutherland oil painting of palm trees. Alec and Merula Guinness were left two Lowry paintings, and Jean Muir received a Graham Sutherland watercolour, 'White Rose'. Vincent donated Manet's 'The Cats' Rendezvous' to the Fine Arts Museums of San Francisco, 'in memory of Coral Browne Price'. Marti Stevens received a sable coat, while, according to Eileen Atkins, 'Coral left Jean [Marsh] a diamond ring – she'd told her once, "I've left you a diamond ring in the will. The minute you hear I'm dead, you come down the hill and bang on the door and say to Vinnie, 'The ring's mine!'"'[144] It had been a close-run thing: Jean had indeed gone in and out of 'the will and the address book'. Coral had once complained to Alec Guinness, 'Still not a word from Jean Marsh & the prospect of leaving my square cut diamond pinkie ring to her gets farther away.'[145] However, it didn't take much for her to relent: 'Had two cards from Jean last week – funny & nice & just in time as I had the ring…insured for its value 30,000 dollars.'[146] Roddy McDowall was given a rug that Coral had made herself. He told Vincent, 'I thought you might like to know where Coral's truly beautiful carpet has been placed. It is under the 'wheel table' in front of the living room fire. I love it and am so proud to have it.'[147] Some pearls, a Cartier watch and three gold bangles, made from a melted down cigarette case that had belonged to Vincent's father and which he had given to Coral, were left to Victoria Price.

Remarkably, after the emotional rollercoaster ride she had alternately endured and enjoyed with her 'wicked stepmother' for nearly two decades, Victoria discovered other 'legacies': 'Not many months after she died, a friend said to me, "You speak of her so well, how can you forgive her for what she did to you?" But it was easy for me to see that what was underneath Coral's meanness was really fear. And when you can see what's at the root of something, it's easy to forgive it. I feel it was extraordinary that I got to know somebody like that; she really was like somebody you read about it in books when you were a kid. She wasn't a normal human being; she was a larger than life character. Joan Rivers said to me, that if I had been someone else's child, Coral would have been my biggest fan. And I think that was the most confusing thing as a child – that Coral could come through for me in a way *no one* else could and she would understand things about me that my parents didn't see at all. And she taught me things – there are big parts of who I am that come more from Coral than any of them. If I'm known for anything in terms of what I do in art and design, it's my sense of style. And I always attributed that to the fact that I had an art collector father and a designer mother. But in fact, it completely came from Coral's panache and sense of style and how she tried to teach me about that. And she would take me under her wing – you wouldn't call it maternal by any stretch of the imagination. But it was loving – and she wanted you to succeed and know the perils that might face you, and she wanted to give you some tips she was fairly sure no one else would – and she did that with me. It was almost uncontrollable with her. But that was the most confusing thing to me when I was a child: which Coral would I get today – the wonderful Coral, or the one that's vitriolic and jealous?'[148]

On 23 July, on what would have been Coral's 78th birthday, a memorial service was held at St Victor's, attended by over 70 people. Letters from friends and admirers were read out, and Roddy McDowall paid tribute to the woman he called 'OK Coral'.

At her memorial service in London, Alan Bates did get to tell one 'Coral Browne' story that, in many ways, told the whole story: 'Before she was confined to bed, I rang up to speak to Coral. Vincent picked up the phone: "She's gone to confession," he said, "and she's going to be an *awfully* long time..."'[149]

Epilogue

Vincent Price survived Coral by two years. He continued to work, when his health permitted. Victoria Price said that, 'His mind remained as vital as ever. So my father's secretary and caretaker, Reggie Williams and I organised a circle of my mostly gay male friends into a group that Roddy McDowall took to calling "the angels". Attractive, interesting and talented all, the angels took turns with Reggie and me in caring for my dad.'[1] The 'angels' included writer Jim Phipps, actor Mitchell Anderson, TV writer Rick Mitz, student nurse Chris Jakowchik and another writer, Paul Brown. In January 1992, Vincent attended a ceremony to receive the LA Film Critics Association Lifetime Achievement Award. He said that Coral would have been amused to see him honoured: 'She would have congratulated me and said, "Congratulations to the LA Film Critics – they got you just in time."'[2] On 25 October 1993, Vincent Price joined Coral in what she always referred to as 'the feathered choir', succumbing to lung cancer, aged 82, at Swallow Drive. His friend Peter Cushing said, 'He was so very lonely since the death of his beloved wife. He is reunited with her now after a splendid innings.'[3]

Many of Coral's nearest and dearest would, like her, succumb to cancer – Roddy McDowall, Charles Gray, Alan 'Bites' Bates, Jean Muir, Michael 'Old Mother' Bradley-Dyne and Alec and Merula Guinness. In his last years, Noel Davis suffered from emphysema. In November 2002, he was admitted to the Chelsea and Westminster Hospital and died there on 24 November. His friend, Gyles Brandreth, had visited him just 24 hours earlier. To Brandreth's surprise and delight, Davis pulled off his oxygen mask and, struggling for breath, told, for one last time – his favourite 'Coral Browne story'.

It seems that, as long as there's an actor with breath in their body, 'Coral Browne stories' will be told, in the green rooms and dressing rooms, the bar-rooms and bedrooms. They are, perhaps, the most fitting tribute to her – only bettered by Barry Humphries' homage to his fellow Australian:

'A Chorale For Coral' by Barry Humphries

She left behind an emptiness
A gap, a void, a trough

The world is quite a good deal less
Since Coral Browne fucked off.

Her beauty and her shining wit
Sparkle beyond the grave
The girl who didn't give a shit
Preposterously brave.

And yet we also mourn for her
Her genius to affront
The phoney and the crashing bore
The coward and the cunt

Loyalty and love she lavished free
On lowly friends and well-born
Like Murdoch, Melba and like me
She was marvellously Melbourne

Uniquely-minded Queen of Style
No counterfeit could coin you,
Long may you make the angels smile
Till we all fuck off to join you. [4]

Notes

Abbreviations

AB   Alan Bennett
AG   Alec Guinness
CB   Coral Browne (Collection)
CCT   Caroline Cornish-Trestrail
JS   John Schlesinger (Collection)
PAC   Performing Arts Collection
VP   Vincent Price (Papers)

Introduction

1   *Evening Standard*, April 20 1984
2   *Evening Standard*, July 20 1979
3   *The Tatler*, December 4 1946
4   *The Age*, April 5 2003
5   *Andy Warhol's Interview*, July 1975
6   author interview
7   *The Sun-Herald*, May 5 1957
8   author interview
9   www.alanbates.com
10   *Caviar for the General*, Channel 4, December 23 1990
11   www.alanbates.com
12   *Independent*, May 31 1991
13   Rupert Everett, *Red Carpets and Other Banana Skins*, Little, Brown, 2006, p159
14   author interview

Prologue

1   www.alanbates.com
2   JS/65/4, JS
3   www.alanbates.com

'Coral Brown Is An Australian…'

1   *The Age*, undated
2   www.clivejames.com, *New Yorker*, March 23 1987

3   author interviews (Gems & Sherrin)
4   Korzelinski, Seweryn, *Memoirs of Gold-Digging in Melbourne*, University of Queensland Press, St Lucia, 1979, p24
5   Macintyre, Stuart, *Concise History of Australia*, Cambridge University Press, 2004, p110
6   *Williamstown Chronicle*, 17 December 1870
7   *Caviar for the General*, Channel 4, December 23 1990
8   Marr, David, ed, *Patrick White Letters*, Jonathan Cape, 2004, p413
9   *Oz and Them*, BBC Bristol January 2007
10   Ibid
11   Humphries, Barry, *My Life as Me*, Michael Joseph 2002, p51
12   Tape C34, oral history collection: interview with Frank Van Straten, PAC
13   *Mail*, May 1 1948
14   Tape C34, oral history collection: interview with Frank Van Straten, PAC
15   Ibid
16   White, Patrick, *Flaws in the Glass*, Vintage, 1998, p155
17   *Mail*, May 1 1948
18   *Mail*, May 1 1948
19   *Mail*, July 1 1980
20   Tape C34, oral history collection: interview with Frank Van Straten, PAC
21   author interview
22   letter, Feb 1948, 1994.95 1 B 17, PAC
23   Tape C34, oral history collection: interview with Frank Van Straten, PAC
24   Ibid
25   Ibid

26   undated cutting, www.garrygillard.net
27   Tape C34, oral history collection: interview with Frank Van Straten, PAC
28   *Mail*, June 30 1928
29   *Mail*, October 26 1929
30   author interview
31   Williams, Lucy Chase, *The Complete Films of Vincent Price*, Citadel Press Book, New Jersey, 1998, p44
32   *Caviar for the General*, Channel 4, December 23 1990
33   Humphries, Barry, *More Please*, Viking, 1992, p254
34   *Table Talk*, September 4 1930
35   C294, oral history collection, PAC
36   *The Melbourne Argus*, September 1 1941
37   www.bbc.co.uk, March 28 2007
38   www.adb.online.anu.edu.au
39   Paul Bentley, *Australian Culture 1789–2000*, www.twf.org.au
40   Porter, Hal, *Stars of Australian Stage & Screen*, Angus & Robertson, 1965, p109
41   Love, Harold, ed, *The Australian Stage*, NSW University Press, 1984, p160
42   Address given by R W Beetham to Old Players & Playgoers' Association, September 10 1941, 1994.95, BOX 1 B 16, PAC
43   Love, Harold, ed, *The Australian Stage*, NSW University Press, 1984, p159
44   Ibid, p160
45   Tape C34, oral history collection: interview with Frank Van Straten, PAC
46   Blundell, Graeme, *Australian Theatre*, Oxford University Press, 1997, p76

47 Caldwell, Zoe, *I Will Be Cleopatra*, WW Norton, 2001, p40

48 *The Australian Handbook*, 1875

49 Tape C34, oral history collection: interview with Frank Van Straten, PAC

50 *Plays and Players*, July 1972

51 Ibid

52 Tape C34, oral history collection: interview with Frank Van Straten, PAC

53 *Sunday Telegraph*, February 10 1974

54 Roddy McDowall, *Double Exposure*, 10 May 1988, JS/65/4

55 author interview

56 *Table Talk*, April 30 1931

57 *The Herald*, May 1 1931

58 *Christian Science Monitor*, February 25 1957

59 *The Bulletin*, undated 1931

60 *Evening Standard*, February 4 1974/*Sunday Telegraph*, January 19 1986

61 *The Argus*, May 25 1931

62 *The Herald*, July 12 1931

63 *The Herald*, July 24, 1931

64 *Smith's Weekly*, February 26, 1932

65 *The Truth*, March 9 1932

66 *Evening Standard*, January 11 1974

67 Tape C34, oral history collection: interview with Frank Van Straten, PAC

68 Ibid

69 Ibid

70 Love, Harold, ed, *The Australian Stage*, NSW University Press, 1984, p161/220

71 Tape C34, oral history collection: interview with Frank Van Straten, PAC

72 *The Truth*, December 15 1932

73 *The Truth*, April 15 1933

74 *Sunday Telegraph*, January 19 1986

75 Price, Victoria, *Vincent Price: A Daughter's Biography*, Sidgwick & Jackson, 2000, p371, and passim

76 Tape C34, oral history collection: interview with Frank Van Straten, PAC

77 undated cutting, *Table Talk*, Scrapbook 1931–54, 1 B 12, PAC

78 *Table Talk*, April 6 1933

79 Tape C34, oral history collection: interview with Frank Van Straten, PAC

80 Ibid

81 *The Graphic of Australia*, October 19, 1933

82 *Smith's Weekly*, November 11, 1933

83 *Table Talk*, December 7 1933

84 undated cutting, 1930s

85 Robert Hughes, *Time*, September 11 2000

86 Tape C34, oral history collection: interview with Frank Van Straten, PAC

87 *Table Talk*, April 6 1933

88 *Women's Weekly*, December 30 1933

89 author interview

90 *Plays and Players*, July 1972

91 www.archivists.org.au/www.portrait.gov.au

92 May 25 1934, 1994.95, 1 B 17 PAC

93 Ada Reeve, *Take it for a Fact*, William Heinemann Ltd, 1954, p200

94 Ibid p200

95 Ibid p200

96 Love, Harold, ed, *The Australian Stage*, NSW University Press, 1984, p160

97 undated letter from Gregan McMahon to CB, 1994.95.362, PAC

98 *Table Talk*, May 2 1935

99 *The Age*, undated

100 letter, April 1 1975, 1994.95 1 B 17, PAC

101 author interview

102 author interview

103 *Plays and Players*, September 1955

104 *Theatre World*, April 1950, p28

105 author interview

106 Shellard, Dominic, *British Theatre Since The War*, Yale University Press, 2000, p7

107 Huggett, Richard, *Binkie Beaumont*, Hodder & Stoughton, 1989, p327

108 www.bl.uk/projects/theatrearchive/cecil.3.html

109 G McM to Dame Sybil, May 25 1934, 1994.95 1 B 17, PAC

110 *The Age*, October 13 1934

111 May 12, 1994.95 1 B 17 PAC

112 Agate, James, *Ego 6*, George G Harrap Ltd, 1944, p52

113 Scrapbook 1931–54, 1 B 12, PAC

114 Box 1 B 12 Scrapbook, PAC

115 *Sunday Telegraph* February 10 1974

116 *Guardian*, May 5 2000

117 *Caviar for the General*, Channel 4, December 23 1990

118 author interview

119 author interview

120 *Guardian*, October 26 1934

121 *The Times*, October 26 1934

122 *Theatre World*, February 1935

123 October 27 1934, Scrapbook 1931–54, PAC

124 Ibid

125 *Independent*, November 3 1934

126 *The Era*, October 31 1934

127 *Everyman*, November 2 1934

128 *Theatre World*, February 1964

129 Undated note, 1994.95 1 B 17 PAC

130 BOX 1 B 12 SCRAPBOOKS Scrapbook 1931–54, PAC

131 Ibid, February 27 1935

132 Ibid, April 3 1935

133 White, Patrick, *Flaws in the Glass*, Vintage, 1998, p55

134 *Woman's Journal*, November 1983

135 *Daily Mail*, February 18 1935

136 *Daily News Chronicle*, February 19 1935

137 *Daily Herald*, February 19 1935

138 William J Quinn, 'Talent, Stamina & Luck: A Great Lady Abroad' [undated article 1994/95/630, Box B 16, PAC

139 *Observer*, April 14 1935

140 *New York Times*, April 8 1935

141 *Daily Telegraph*, April 8 1935

142 William J Quinn, 'Talent, Stamina & Luck: A Great Lady Abroad' [undated article 1994/95/630, Box B 16, PAC

143 BOX 1 B 12 SCRAPBOOKS Scrapbook 1931–54, PAC

144 letter, undated 1935, 1994.95 1 B 17, PAC

145 letter, undated 1935, 1994.95 1 B 17, PAC

146 letter, undated 1935, 1994.95 1 B 17, PAC

147 letter, May 7 from *The Age*, June 12 1935

148 BOX 1 B 12 SCRAPBOOKS Scrapbook 1931–54, May 18 1935, PAC

149 *Daily Mail*, May 28 1935

150 *Northern Dispatch*, May 31 1935

151 Press Book, BFI Archives

152 Ibid

153 correspondence with author

154 author interview

155 Price, Victoria, *Vincent Price: A Daughter's Biography*, Sidgwick & Jackson, 2000, p409

156 Wright, Adrian, *John Lehmann: A Pagan Adventure*, Duckworth, 1998, p168

157 Ibid, p168

158 Parker, Peter, *Isherwood*, Picador, 2004, p251

159 *Diva*, July 1998

160 Noble, Peter, *Profiles and Personalities*, Brownlee, 1946, p70–1

161 *The Times*, January 7 1936

162 *The Star*, May 5 1936

163 undated cutting, *Punch*, Box 1 B12, Scrapbook 1931–54, PAC

164 *Empire News*, June 14 1936

165 *Theatre World*, July 1936

166 *Woman*, July 9 1936

167 *Melbourne Herald*, July 2 1936

168 *Daily Express*, Sep 26 1936

169 Fairbanks Jr, Douglas, *The Salad Days*, Collins 1988, p251

170 *The Times*, January 21 1936

171 undated, unattributed, BFI cuttings

172 *Evening News*, June 19 1937

173 *The Tatler*, June 23 1937

174 *The Age*, October 22 1949

175 William J Quinn, 'Talent, Stamina & Luck: A Great Lady Abroad' [undated article 1994/95/630, Box B 16, PAC

176 *The Times*, August 2 1937

177 undated cutting, Box 1 B12, Scrapbook 1931–54, PAC

178 unknown cutting, Box 1 B12, Scrapbook 1931–54, PAC

179 *Dallas Morning News*, August 19 1976

180 author interview

181 *Guardian*, December 30 1970

182 conversation with author

183 Sherrin, Ned, *A Small Thing Like an Earthquake*, Weidenfeld & Nicolson 1983, p74

184 Speech for BBC's 50th anniversary, File 3 Box 154 VP Collection

185 letter to AG, May 13 1984

186 undated note, 1994.95, 1 B 12 SCRAPBOOKS Scrapbook 1931–54, PAC

187 undated letter, BOX 1 B 12 SCRAPBOOKS Scrapbook 1931–54, PAC

188 undated letter, 1994.95, 1 B 12 SCRAPBOOKS Scrapbook 1931–54, PAC

189 undated cutting, BFI

190 *The Times*, November 7 1938

191 undated cutting, Box 1 B 12 SCRAPBOOK 1935–48, PAC

Firth is my Shephard

1 *Daily Sketch*, August 24 1939

2 Note on cutting, BOX 1 B 12 SCRAPBOOKS Scrapbook 1931–54

3 *Theatre World*, September 1942, p23–4

4 Souhami, Diana, *The Trials of Radclyffe Hall*, Weidenfeld & Nicolson, 1998, p245

5 Sheridan Morley and passim

6 Mitchell, Leslie, *Leslie Mitchell Reporting*, Hutchinson, 1981, p147

7 author interview

8 *Time*, January 24 1944

9 Ziegler, Philip, *London At War*, Sinclair Stevenson, 1995, p41

10 *Evening Standard*, May 11 2005

11 *Theatre World* March 1942

12 *Caviar for the General*, Channel 4, December 23 1990

13 *New York Times*, March 9 1941

14 *The Times*, April 25 1944

15 *Caviar for the General*, Channel 4, December 23 1990/*The Herald*, March 5 1940

16 *SAGA magazine*, September 2003

17 *The Sketch*, November 4 1942

18 *The Times*, November 27 1942

19 *Guardian*, April 16 2007

20 *The Times*, January 21 1940

21 *Sunday Telegraph* February 10 1974

22 *Caviar for the General*, Channel 4, December 23 1990

23 Randall, Alan and Ray Seaton, *George Formby*, W H Allen, 1974, p84–5

24 Ibid, p122

25 Box 1 B 12 SCRAPBOOK 1935–48 PAC, unknown cutting

26 Morley, Sheridan, *Asking for Trouble*, Hodder & Stoughton, 2002, p3

27 *The Times*, December 5 1941

28 *Theatre World* October 1941/ *Theatre World* January 1942

29 *Independent*, May 31 1991

30 author interview

31 *Caviar for the General*, Channel 4, December 23 1990

32 *Theatre World*, July 1934

33 *Theatre World*, September 1942, p23–4

34 *The Age*, undated/Bay Area Reporter, August 4 1977/The Morning News, May 21 1976

35 author interview

36 author interview

37 undated cutting, www.garrygillard.net

38 author interview

39 author interview

40 Porter, Hal, *Stars of Australian Stage & Screen*, Angus & Robertson, 1965, p219

41 Woodhouse, Adrian, *Angus McBean, Face-Maker*, Alma Books Ltd, 2006, p193

42 letter to author, 6 August 2006

43 *Sunday Telegraph*, January 19 1986

44 Vickers, Hugo, *Cecil Beaton*, Little, Brown, 1985, p253

45 Vickers, Hugo, *Loving Garbo*, Pimlico, 1995, p38

46 Vickers, Hugo, *Cecil Beaton*, Little, Brown, 1985, p253

47 *Sunday Telegraph*, January 19 1986

48 Vickers, Hugo, *Cecil Beaton*, Little, Brown, 1985, p506

49 *Radio Times*, November 26 1983/*Sunday Telegraph* January 19 1986

50 Bruce Martin to author

51 *Sunday Telegraph*, January 19 1986

52 author interview

53 *Independent* May 31 1991

54 Rossi, Alfred, *Astonish Us in the Morning: Tyrone Guthrie Remembered*, Hutchinson, 1981, p108

55 *Online Oxford Dictionary of National Biography*

56 January 13 1946, 1994.95 1 B 17, PAC

57 Tape C34, oral history collection: interview with Frank Van Straten, PAC, Melbourne

58 Blundell, Graeme, *Australian Theatre*, Oxford University Press, 1997, p101

59 Ibid, p102

60 John Schlesinger Collection, research notes for *Caviar for the General*, uncredited

61 *Theatre World* October 1943, p4

62 *Tatler & Bystander*, October 13 1943

63 theatre programme, author collection

64 *The Times* October 21 1957

65 Marshall, Arthur, *Life's Rich Pageant*, Hamish Hamilton, 1984, p87

66 Melville, Alan, *Merely Melville*, Hodder & Stoughton, 1970, p132

67 Marshall, Michael, *Top Hat And Tails*, Elm Tree Books, 1978, p111

68 Ibid, p68

69 Ibid, p134

70 author interview

71 Rossi, Alfred, *Astonish Us in the Morning: Tyrone Guthrie Remembered*, Hutchinson, 1981, p104

72 Ibid, p108

73 *Theatre World*, January 1945

74 author interview

75 *The Herald*, January 1 1947

76 Marshall, Michael, *Top Hat And Tails*, Elm Tree Books, 1978, p149

77 *Theatre World*, July 1944

78 *The Times*, June 16 1944

79 *Caviar for the General*, Channel 4, December 23 1990

80 Walker, Alexander, *Fatal Charm: The Life Of Rex Harrison*, Orion, 1992, p347

81 *Theatre World*, September 1945

82 *Theatre World*, January 1947

83 *The Age*, January 24 1947

84 *Theatre World*, January 1947

85 Ibid

86 *The Tatler & Bystander*, July 24 1946

87 BOX 1 B 12 SCRAPBOOKS Scrapbook 1931–54, PAC

88 Ibid, uncredited cutting

89 *Caviar for the General*, Channel 4, December 23 1990

90 Miscellaneous 1994.95, 1 B 10 PAC

91 *The Times*, May 9 1947

92 Marshall, Michael, *Top Hat and Tails*, Elm Tree Books, 1978, p155

93 O'Connor, Garry, *The Secret Woman: A Life of Peggy Ashcroft*, Weidenfeld and Nicolson, 1997, p193

94 *Montreal Gazette*, September 15 1956

95 *Theatre World* January 1948

96 *The Times* November 19 1947

97 *Daily Mirror*, August 7 1948

98 Marshall, Michael, *Top Hat and Tails*, Elm Tree Books, 1978, p155

99   Melville, Alan, *Merely Melville*, Hodder & Stoughton, 1970, p10–11

100 Morley, Sheridan, *Asking for Trouble*, Hodder & Stoughton, 2002, p63

101 Humphries, Barry, *My Life as Me*, Michael Joseph 2002, p68

102 Melville, Alan, *Merely Melville*, Hodder & Stoughton, 1970, p10–11

103 Norman, Barry, *The Movie Greats*, Arrow, 1981, p71

104 Melville, Alan, *Merely Melville*, Hodder & Stoughton, 1970, p10–11

105 *The Times* July 20 1948

106 Melville, Alan, *Merely Melville*, Hodder & Stoughton, 1970, p10–11

107 *Theatre World*, April 1950

108 Mitchell, Leslie, *Leslie Mitchell Reporting*, Hutchinson, 1981, p153

109 Ibid, p147/184

110 Ibid, p147

111 Sherrin Ned, *The Autobiography*, Little, Brown, 2005, p25

112 Read, Piers Paul, *Alec Guinness*, Pocket Books, 2004, p332

113 *Guardian*, November 23 2002

114 O'Connor, Garry, *Alec Guinness the Unknown*, Sidgwick & Jackson, 2002, p297

115 Melville, Alan, *Merely Melville*, Hodder & Stoughton, 1970, p132

116 Marshall, Michael, *Top Hat and Tails*, Elm Tree Books, 1978, p167

117 Melville, Alan, *Merely Melville*, Hodder & Stoughton, 1970, p132

118 *The Times*, December 8 1949

119 Ibid

120 Ibid

121 Ibid

122 Marshall, Michael, *Top Hat and Tails*, Elm Tree Books, 1978, p239

The Englishman, the Irishman and the Gentleman

1   *Varsity Weekly*, Saturday May 14 1932

2   *Varsity*, February 27 1932

3   Price, Victoria, *Vincent Price: A Daughter's Biography*, Sidgwick & Jackson, 2000, p407

5   author interview

6   *The Stage & Television Today*, November 28 1991

7   Marshall, Michael, *Top Hat and Tails*, Elm Tree Books, 1978, p174

8   author interview

9   *The Age*, April 5 2003

10   passim

11   author interview

12   White, Patrick, *Flaws in the Glass*, Vintage, 1998, p53

13   William J Quinn, 'Talent, Stamina & Luck: A Great Lady Abroad'[undated article 1994/95/630, Box 1 B 16, PAC

14   April 1 1975, 1994.95, 1 B 17 PAC

15   York, Michael, *Travelling Player*, Headline 1991, p96

16   author interview

17   Spoto, Donald, *Otherwise Engaged: The Life of Alan Bates*, Hutchinson, 2007, p43/44

18   Ibid, p45

19   *Sunday Telegraph* February 10 1974

20   *Staten Island*, November 9 1956

21   *Birmingham Evening Dispatch*, November 27 1958

22   author interview

23   *New York Times*, March 12 2002

24   *Guardian*, March 12 2002

25   *Theatre World*, December 1951

26   *The Times*, November 1 1951

27   *The Times*, November 1 1951

28   Price, Victoria, *Vincent Price: A Daughter's Biography*, Sidgwick & Jackson, 2000, p388

29   author interview

30   Agate, James, *Ego 9*, George G. Harrap Ltd, 1948, p112

31   Agate, James, *Ego 5*, George G. Harrap Ltd, 1942, p110

32   author interview

33   Williamson, Audrey, *Paul Rogers*, Rockcliff, 1956, p65

34   BOX 1 B 12 SCRAPBOOKS Scrapbook 1931–54, letter to Vicky, undated

35   *Theatre World*, April 1952

36   *The Times*, March 4 1952

37   *The Spectator*, March 7 1952

38   *News Chronicle*, December 3 1959

39   Ibid

40   *The Times*, August 22 1952

41   Ibid

42   *Staten Island*, Nov 9 1956

43   *Evening Standard*, February 4 1974

44   letter to Arnold Weissberger, May 13 1957

45   Bryan, Dora, *According to Dora*, Bodley Head, 1987, p77 /*Daily Mail* August 17 1996

46   Bryan, Dora, *According to Dora*, Bodley Head, 1987, p77

47   BFI pressbook, *Lylah Clare*

48   Garland, Patrick, *The Incomparable Rex*, Macmillan, 1998, p148

49   *The Times*, November 26 1954

50   Shellard, Dominic, *British Theatre Since The War*, Yale University Press, 2000, p36

51   Heilpern, John, *John Osborne: A Patriot for Us*, Chatto & Windus, 2006, p95

52 Tynan, Kenneth, *Curtains*, Longmans, 1961, p92

53 *Time*, December 17 1951

54 Hordern, Michael, *A World Elsewhere*, Michael O'Mara Books Ltd, 1993, p102

55 Harrison, Rex, *Rex: An Autobiography*, William Morrow & Company, NY, 1974, p141

56 *Sunday Times*, October 17 1976

57 Hordern, Michael, *A World Elsewhere*, Michael O'Mara Books Ltd, 1993, p103

58 Ibid, p102

59 author interview

60 undated 1955, *Daily Mail*

61 Hordern, Michael, *A World Elsewhere*, Michael O'Mara Books Ltd, 1993, p103

62 Ibid, p104

63 Harrison, Rex, *Rex: An Autobiography*, William Morrow & Company, NY, 1974, p142

64 undated, BOX 1 B 12 SCRAPBOOKS Scrapbook 1931–54, PAC

65 Forbes, Bryan, *Ned's Girl: The Life of Edith Evans*, Elm Tree Books, 1977, p231

66 *Observer*, July 31 1955

67 *Financial Times*, undated, 1955

68 *Evening Standard*, July 28 1955

69 *Theatre World* September 1955, p8

70 Hordern, Michael, *A World Elsewhere*, Michael O'Mara Books Ltd, 1993, p105

71 Ibid, p105

72 Ibid, p105

73 Rossi, Alfred, *Astonish Us in the Morning: Tyrone Guthrie Remembered*, Hutchinson, 1981, p106

74 *A View of the English Stage, 1944–63*, Davis-Poynter 1975

75 Address by Sir AG at TG memorial, St Paul's Church, June 16 1971

76 *New York Times*, January 15, 1956

77 interview with Frith Banbury, The Theatre Archive Project, British Library, University of Sheffield and AHRB

78 Rossi, Alfred, *Astonish Us in the Morning: Tyrone Guthrie Remembered*, Hutchinson, 1981, p104

79 Ibid, p106

80 Ibid, p106

81 Ibid, p106

82 *Caviar for the General*, Channel 4, December 23 1990

83 Rossi, Alfred, *Astonish Us in the Morning: Tyrone Guthrie Remembered*, Hutchinson, 1981, p106

84 *New York Times*, January 15 1956

85 Joan Sims, *High Spirits*, Partridge 2000, p 69

86 Rossi, Alfred, *Astonish Us in the Morning: Tyrone Guthrie Remembered*, Hutchinson, 1981, p109

87 *The Times*, January 5 1956

88 *New York Times*, January 20 1956

89 Rossi, Alfred, *Astonish Us in the Morning: Tyrone Guthrie Remembered*, Hutchinson, 1981, p110

90 *Staten Island*, November 9 1956

91 *Illustrated London News*, undated

92 *Daily Mail*, May 23 1956

93 *Daily Sketch*, undated 1956

94 Lahr, John, ed, *The Orton Diaries*, Minerva, 1989, p134

95 *New York Times*, October 30 1956

96 *New York Daily News*, October 30 1956

97 Ibid

98 *Caviar for the General*, Channel 4, December 23 1990

99 Lahr, John, ed, *The Orton Diaries*, Minerva, 1989, p133

100 Coveney, Michael, *Maggie Smith: A Bright Particular Star*, Gollancz 1992, p180

101 William J Quinn, 'Talent, Stamina & Luck: A Great Lady Abroad'[undated article 1994/95/630, Box 1 B 16, PAC

102 Rossi, Alfred, *Astonish Us in the Morning: Tyrone Guthrie Remembered*, Hutchinson, 1981, p110

103 *Chicago American/Today*, undated

104 *New York Times* December 17 1956

105 *NY Herald-Tribune*, undated

106 *Evening Star DC*, February 8 1957

107 *New York Times* March 7, 1957

108 Heilpern, John, *John Osborne: A Patriot for Us*, Chatto & Windus, 2006, p93,

109 www.thestage.co.uk/ stage125/profile.php/hall/

110 author interview

111 Tape C34, oral history collection: interview with Frank Van Straten, PAC

112 Tynan, Kenneth, *Curtains*, Longmans, 1961, p185–6,

113 *Shakespeare Quarterly*, Autumn 1958, Volume IX, no.4, The Shakespeare Association of America, p514

114 *Caviar for the General*, Channel 4, December 23 1990

115 *Plays & Players*, November 1957

116 author interviews

117 *Theatre World*, February 1958

118 *Plays and Players*, February 1958

119 McCann, Graham, *Frankie Howerd: Stand Up Comic*, Harper Perennial, 2005, p153

120 *Plays and Players*, February 1958

121 *Theatre World,* February 1958

122 author interview

123 author interview

124 *Theatre World,* April 1958

125 *The Times*, February 20 1958

126 author interview

127 letter to Arnold Weissberger, March 20 1958

128 *Plays and Players*, July 1972

129 undated, VB to CB, PAC

130 *Plays & Players*, February 1955

131 author interview

132 letter to Arnold Weissberger, March 20 1958

133 letter to Mary Gillard, August 11 1967

134 author interview

135 author interview

136 Driberg, Tom, *Guy Burgess: A Portrait With Background*, Weidenfeld and Nicolson, 1956, p1

137 Ibid, p5

138 Ibid, p101

139 Ibid, p105

140 *Birmingham Evening Dispatch*, October 27 1958

141 letter to Arnold Weissberger, May 13 1957

142 letter to Arnold Weissberger, November 12 1958

143 Ibid

144 Kempson, Rachel, *A Family & Its Fortunes*, Duckworth, 1986, p181

145 THM/31/1/1/36, TM

146 *Birmingham Evening Dispatch*, 27 November 1958

147 *Guardian*, October 30, 1958

148 Kempson, Rachel, *A Family & Its Fortunes*, Duckworth, 1986, p181

149 *Daily Telegraph*, 23 December 1958

150 *News Chronicle*, Saturday December 13, 1958

151 Kempson, Rachel, *A Family & Its Fortunes*, Duckworth, 1986, p184

152 author interview

153 Kempson, Rachel, *A Family & Its Fortunes*, Duckworth, 1986, p185

154 Caldwell, Zoe, *I Will Be Cleopatra*, WW Norton, 2001, p102

155 author interview

156 Redgrave, Michael, *In My Mind's Eye*, Weidenfeld & Nicolson, 1983, p192

157 author interview

158 *Observer*, January 11, 1959

159 copy undated letter GB to CB

160 Holm, Ian, *Acting My Life*, Transworld 2004, p65

161 Redgrave, Michael, *In My Mind's Eye*, Weidenfeld & Nicolson, 1983, p193

162 Driberg, Tom, *Guy Burgess: A Portrait With Background*, Weidenfeld and Nicolson, 1956, p103

163 *Daily Mail*, December 3 1983

164 *The Sun*, October 20 1984

165 *Daily Mail*, December 3 1983

166 *Glasgow Herald*, November 28 1983

167 Ibid

168 *The Sun*, October 20 1984

169 Marshall, Michael, *Top Hat and Tails*, Elm Tree Books, 1978, p25

170 copy undated letter GB to CB

171 Costello, John, *Mask of Treachery*, Pan, 1989, p501

172 copy letter 16 April 1959 GB to CB

173 Kempson, Rachel, *A Family & Its Fortunes*, Duckworth, 1986, p185

174 Caldwell, Zoe, *I Will Be Cleopatra*, WW Norton, 2001, p105

175 *The Sun*, October 20 1984

176 *Daily Mail*, December 3 1983

177 copy letter 16 April 1959 GB to CB

178 Ibid

179 Ibid

180 Ibid

181 *Daily Mail,* December 3 1983

182 *The Times*, October 21 1960

183 *The Times* September 2 1963

184 *New York Times* October 24 1984

Drama Queen

1 *The Times*, January 12 1959

2 *Daily Mirror*, January 9 1959

3 *Financial Times*, January 12 1959

4 *Theatre World,* June 1959

5 undated cutting

6 unknown cutting, Scrapbook 1952–59 PAC

7 unknown cutting, Scrapbook 1952–59, PAC

8 *Daily Telegraph*, May 8 1990

9 Marshall, Arthur, *Life's Rich Pageant*, Hamish Hamilton, 1984, p189

10 *New York Times*, February 21 1960

11 *The Times*, November 12 1960

12 author interview

13 *Theatre World*, December 1960

14 *New York Times*, January 29 1961

15 1994.95 1 B 17, October 27 1960

16 William J Quinn, 'Talent, Stamina & Luck: A Great Lady Abroad'[undated article 1994/95/630, Box 1 B 16, PAC

17 *Independent*, July 7 2006

18 *The Spectator*, February 23 1962

19 *Theatre World*, January 1962

20 *The Age*, October 25 1961

21 conversation with author

22 author interview

23 *Woman's Journal*, November 1973

24 author interview

25 author interview

26 author interview

27 author interview

28 Heilpern, John, *John Osborne: A Patriot for Us*, Chatto & Windus, 2006, p95

29 *The Times*, October 24 1961

30 The *Observer*, October 29 1961

31 *Plays & Players*, January 1962

32 author interview

33 *New York Times*, July 16 1964

34 *The People*, August 18 1963

35 *Daily Mail*, August 17 1963

36 Mangan, Richard, ed, *Gielgud's Letters*, Phoenix, 2005, p291

37 correspondence with author

38 *New York Times*, March 22 1963

39 *Sunday Telegraph*, February 10 1974

40 *New York Times*, September 24 1963

41 *New York Times*, November 17 1963

42 author interview

43 *New York Times*, November 17 1963

44 *New York Times*, August 3 1963

45 Ibid

46 Ibid

47 *New York Times*, December 15 1963

48 *The Times*, January 2 1964

49 *New York Times*, September 23 1963

50 *Guardian*, May 31 1991

51 Bruce Martin, www.coralbrowne.com

52 author interview

53 *Evening Standard*, January 11 1974

54 author interview

55 *Evening Standard*, February 20 1964

56 author interview

57 *She Magazine*, March 1961

58 *The Morning News*, May 21 1976

59 Ibid

60 *Independent*, May 7, 2005

61 undated statement, 1965, Miscellaneous 1994.95 1 B 10 PAC

62 *Independent*, May 7, 2005

63 *The Times*, August 29 1964

64 author interview

65 author interview

66 author interview

67 author interview

68 *Caviar for the General*, Channel 4, December 23 1990

69 *Plays and Players*, July 1964

70 *The Times*, May 29 1964

71 *The Stage & Television Today*, June 4 1964

72 *Theatre World*, December 1965

73 Sherrin Ned, *Ned Sherrin's Theatrical Anecdotes*, Virgin Books, 1992, p39

74 Hoare, Philip, *Noël Coward*, Mandarin 1995, p480

75 Tape C34, oral history collection, PAC

76 www.alanbates.com

77 *The Times*, October 15 1964

78 author interview

79 Letters, 1994.95 1 B 17, undated PAC

80 author interview

81 undated statement, 1965, Miscellaneous 1994.95 1 B 10 PAC

82 undated 1964, Letters 1994.95, 1 B 17, PAC

83 author interview

84 *The Times*, June 25 1965

85 *Daily Telegraph*, June 24 1965

86 author interview

87 undated statement, 1965, Miscellaneous 1994.95 1 B 10 PAC

88 Ibid

89 Carter-Ruck, Peter, *Memoirs Of A Libel Lawyer*, Weidenfeld & Nicolson, 1990, p165

90 author interview

91 author interview

92 author interview

93 author interview

94 *Guardian*, March 9 2000

95 Server, Lee, *Ava Gardner*, Bloomsbury 2006, p471

96 Ibid, p471

97 Note to FB from CG, 1973? Box 51.1, FBP

98 author interview

99 *New York Post*, October 21 1965

100 *Evening Standard*, October 20 1965

101 *New York Times*, October 20 1965

102 author interview

103 *New York Times*, November 28 1965

104 Ibid

105 Ibid

106 author interview

107 author interview

108 author interview

109 author interview

110 Marr, David, ed, *Patrick White Letters*, Jonathan Cape, 2004, p356

111 author interview

112 author interview

113 *New York Times*, November 11 1965

114 author interview

115 *New York Post*, January 16 1966

116 *New York Times*, January 4 1966

117 author interview

118 author interview

119 author interview

120 *The Sun*, January 30 1967

121 *The Times*, November 14 1966

122 author interview

123 *Guardian*, May 31 1991

124 Lobenthal, Joel, *Tallulah! The Life and Times of a Leading Lady*, Aurum Press Ltd, 2004, p272

125 August 14, 1974, Letters 1994.95 1 B 17, PAC

126 *Plays and Players*, December 1966

127 *The Times*, October 14 1966

128 *Oxford Times*, undated, 1966

129 *Brighton & Hove Gazette*, August 26 1966

130 *International Herald Tribune*, March 6 2002

131 author interview

132 *The Times*, January 25 1967

133 author interview

134 author interview

135 Letters 1994.95 1 B 17, Card from VL, June 15, PAC

Mercy and Madness

1 Robert Shail, screenonline

2 *Guardian*, June 10, 2006

3 Miller, Eugene L Jnr and Arnold, Edwin T, *Robert Aldrich Interviews*, University Press of Mississippi, 2004, p139

4 Kael, Pauline, *Going Steady*, Temple Smith 1970, p208

5 Silver, Alain and Ursini, James, *Whatever Happened To Robert Aldrich? His Life and Films*, Limelight Editions, New York, 1995, p27

6 *Time Out Film Guide 13*

7 BFI pressbook

8 Ibid

9 *LA Times*, September 27 1967

10 *LA Times*, September 27 1967

11 *Life*, October 28 1968

12 *Time*, August 30 1968

13 *Women's Wear Daily*, February 19 1986

14 Miller, Eugene L Jnr and Arnold, Edwin T, *Robert Aldrich Interviews*, University Press of Mississippi, 2004, p139

15 *Playbill*, February 28 2001

16 Harris, Radie, *Radie's World*, WH Allen, 1975, p1

17 *Guardian*, December 30 1970

18 author interview

19 September 15 1967, 1994.95 1 B 17, PAC

20 passim

21 *Gay News 91*, 1976

22 Considine, Shaun, *Bette & Joan: The Divine Feud*, Sphere Books, 1990, p384

23 BFI, *Sister George* pressbook

24 *The Times*, March 26 1969

25 *Diva*, January 2003

26 Gardiner Jill, *From the Closet to the Screen*, Pandora Press, 2003, p139/144

27 Ibid, p144

28 Ibid, p145

29 *Daily Mail*, November 8 1997

30 BFI *Sister George* pressbook

31 Reid, Beryl and Eric Braun, *So Much Love*, Hutchinson, 1984/Nova, January 1969, p152

32 Russo, Vito, *The Celluloid Closet*, Harper & Row, 1981, p212

33 *The Times*, March 26 1969

34 Gardiner, Jill, *From the Closet to the Screen*, Pandora Press, 2003, p151

35 *Caviar for the General*, Channel 4, December 23 1990

36 *New York Times*, December 29 1968

37 FBP Box 51.2 CB to FB, Aug 23 1968

38 Miller, Eugene L Jnr and Arnold, Edwin T, *The Films and Career of Robert Aldrich Interviews*, University Press of Mississippi, 1986, p 147

39 Letters, October 21 1968, 1 B 17 PAC

40 Russo, Vito, *The Celluloid Closet*, Harper & Row, 1981, p212

41 notes on DVD

42 *The Sun*, March 25 1969

43 *Photoplay Film Monthly*, April 1969

44 *Daily Mail*, March 26 1969

45 *Photoplay Film Monthly* April 1969

46 *Evening Standard*, March 27 1969

47 *New York Times*, 17 December 1968

48 *Variety*, December 18 1968

49 Kael, Pauline, *Going Steady*, Temple Smith 1970, p207

50 *Photoplay Film Monthly*, April 1969

51 *Evening News*, March 27 1969

52 *The Times*, March 27 1969

53 *Sunday Times*, March 30 1969

54 Miller, Eugene L Jnr and Arnold, Edwin T, *Robert Aldrich Interviews*, University Press of Mississippi, 2004, p139

55 *Guardian*, March 26 1969

56 *Observer* March 30 1969

57 *Evening Standard*, December 16 1968

58 *Daily Telegraph* March 28 1969

59 Kael, Pauline, *Going Steady*, Temple Smith 1970, p207

60 *Sunday Telegraph*, March 30 1969

61 *Photoplay Film Monthly* April 1969

62 March 11, 1969, 1 B 17 PAC

63 *Guardian*, December 30 1970

64 *Daily Telegraph*, March 13 1969

65 *The Times*, September 30 1975

66 *The Times*, October 1 1975

67 *The Times*, March 26 1969

68 FBP Box 51.2 CB to FB, August 23 1968

69 *The Rehearsal*, translated by Jeremy Sams, Methuen 1990, p11

70 *What the Butler Saw*, Joe Orton, Methuen 1976, p35

71 author interview

72 *The Times*, March 29 1969

73 *Daily Telegraph*, May 31 1991

74 Lewenstein, Oscar, *Kicking Against the Pricks*, Nick Hern Books, 1994, p126

75 Ibid, p127

76 Ibid, p128

77 *Plays and Players*, July 197

78 *The Times*, December 17 1968

79 Lahr, John, *Prick Up Your Ears*, Allen Lane, 1978, p331

80 Ibid, p331

81 *The Times*, March 8 1969

82 Lahr, John, ed, *The Orton Diaries*, Minerva, 1989, p256–7

83 Lahr, John, *Prick Up Your Ears*, Allen Lane, 1978, p331

84 Ibid, p331

85 author interview

86 *Evening Argus*, February 11 1969

87 Lahr, John, *Prick Up Your Ears*, Allen Lane, 1978, p333

88 *Independent*, May 31 1991

89 Lewenstein, Oscar, *Kicking Against the Pricks*, Nick Hern Books, 1994, p129

90 author interview

91 *Guardian*, March 6 1969

92 *Plays and Players*, April 1969

93 *Sunday Telegraph*, March 9 1969

94 *Sunday Times*, June 1 1969

95 *The Sun*, March 25 1969

96 FBP Box 31 CB to CT, November 15 1969

97 FBP Box 31 CB to FB November 22 1969

98 author interview

99 Marr, David, ed, *Patrick White Letters*, Jonathan Cape, 2004, p366

100 author interview

101 *Illustrated London News*, 4 July, 1970

102 *Daily Express*, June 23 1970

103 *Punch*, July 1 1970

104 *The Daily Sketch*, undated, 1970

105 *Evening Standard*, undated, 1970

106 *Evening Standard*, July 14, 1970

107 *The Stage*, 2 April 1970

108 *Evening Standard*, March 13 1970

109 author interview

110 letter to FB, 13 April 1966, FB Papers Box 29

111 February 10 1967, FB Papers Box 29

112 *The Times*, December 30 1970

113 author interview

114 author interview

115 *Guardian*, December 30 1970

116 *Guardian*, December 30 1970

117 Price, Victoria, *Vincent Price: A Daughter's Biography*, Sidgwick & Jackson, 2000, p373

118 undated, 1994.94.171, 1 B 17 PAC

119 author interview

120 Callow, Simon, *The National*, Nick Hern Books, 1997, p26

121 *The Times*, December 31 1970

122 *Daily Mail*, December 31 1970

123 *Guardian* December 31 1970

124 *New York Times*, January 1 1971

125 *Daily Telegraph*, December 31 1970

126 William J Quinn, 'Talent, Stamina & Luck: A Great Lady Abroad'[undated article 1994/95/630, Box 1 B 16, PAC

127 *Daily Mail* May 24 1972

128 *New York Times*, September 14 1972

129 *Newsweek*, September 25 1972

130 *Daily Telegraph*, March 15 1972

131 *Evening Standard*, January 11 1974

132 Box 154, Folder 3, VP

133 author interview

134 author interview

135 *The Times*, May 15 1972

136 *Variety*, May 31 1972

137 Undated cutting, 1972

'This is Mrs Vincent Price'

1 *The Age*, undated cutting

2 *Tit-Bits*, December 8 1962

3 undated notes written by Coral, Miscellaneous 1994.95, 1 B 10 PAC

4 *Evening Standard*, May 5 1972

5 *The Age*, undated cutting, 1972?

6 *Woman's Journal*, November 1973

7 *Sunday Telegraph*, February 2 1974

8 *Guardian*, December 30 1970

9 author interview

10 letter to CB, undated, 1975, letter 1994.95 1 B 17, PAC

11 Peter Burton, unpublished manuscript, *Another Little Drink*

12 Ibid

13 *Woman's Journal*, November 1973

14 *Caviar for the General*, Channel 4, December 23 1990

15 author interview

16 *Daily Telegraph*, December 9 2002

17 author interview

18 Mann, William J, *Edge Of Midnight: The Life Of John*

Schlesinger, Hutchinson 2004, p125

19 *Evening Standard*, January 11 1974

20 author interview

21 Lees-Milne, Alvida and Moore, Derry, *The Englishwoman's Home*, Collins 1984

22 *Guardian*, September 10 2005

23 *Independent*, May 30 1995

24 author interview

25 author interview

26 author interview

27 author interview

28 *Evening Standard*, January 11 1974

29 author interview

30 author interview

31 author interview

32 author interview

33 *New York Times*, October 26 1993

34 *People*, December 12 1999

35 *Washington Star,* November 6 1977

36 BOX 32 Folder 5: letter to VP, December 12 1973, VP

37 *Television International* magazine, September 12 1984, BOX 45 Folder 3, VP

38 VP OV 3

39 *Theater of Blood*, publicity notes, BFI

40 author interview

41 author interview

42 author interview

43 *Washington Star*, November 6 1977

44 author interview

45 *St Louis Globe-Democrat*, August 12 1978

46 *Bay Area Reporter*, August 4 1977

47 Williams, Lucy Chase, *The Complete Films of Vincent Price*, Citadel Press Book, New Jersey, 1998, p44

48 www.alanbates.com/abarchive/tv/coral.html

49 *USA Weekend*, October 25-7 1985

50 author interview

51 author interview

52 author interview

53 Victoria Price, correspondence with author

54 JS/65/4 July 20 1973, JS

55 correspondence with author

56 author interview

57 *Chicago Sun Times*, April 20, 1973

58 *LA Times*, May 14 1973

59 *New York*, May 14 1973

60 *San Francisco Chronicle*, May 19 1973

61 *Daily Express*, May 23 1973

62 *New York Times*, February 21, 2000

63 *The Times*, May 23 1973

64 John Walker, *International Herald Tribune* May 26–7 1973

65 *Woman's Journal*, November 1973

66 John Walker, *International Herald Tribune* May 26–7 1973

67 author interview

68 *The Sunday Times*, May 27 1973

69 *Financial Times*, May 23 1973

70 Morley, Sheridan, *Review Copies*, Robson Books, 1974, p187

71 JS/65/4 20 July 1973

72 Evans, David & Michaels, Scott, *Rocky Horror: From Concept To Cult*, Sanctuary Publishing, 2002, p73

73 Love, Harold (editor), *The Australian Stage*, NSW University Press, 1984, p260

74 correspondence with author

75 passim

76 *Sunday Express*, August 19 1973

77 www.angelfire.com

78 *The Times*, February 15 1974

79 *The Tatler*, April 1974

80 Box 3 Folder 5, February 7 1974, VP/Box 3 Folder 5, February 11 1974, VP

81 *The Times*, February 9 1974

82 Box 3 Folder 5, February 7 1974, VP/Box 3 Folder 5, February 11 1974, VP

83 *Evening Standard*, March 7 1974

84 Sunday Times, February 17 1974

85 *Daily Mail*, February 15 1974

86 *Plays and Players,* April 1974

87 *Evening Standard*, February 15 1974

88 Johns, Eric, ed, *British Theatre Review 1974*, Vance-Offord Publications Ltd, Eastbourne 1975, p227

89 Box 3 Folder 5, February 1974, VP

90 *Daily Telegraph*, 18 February 1974

91 *The Times*, 18 February 1974

92 *Guardian*, May 31 1991

93 Box 3 Folder 5, February 11 1974, VP

94 Box 3 Folder 5, February 7 1974, VP

95 *Evening News*, September 19 1973

96 Williams, Lucy Chase, *The Complete Films of Vincent Price*, Citadel Press Book, New Jersey, 1998, p43

97 Box 3 Folder 5, February 1974, VP

98 Box 3 Folder 5, February 11 1974, VP

99 author interview

100 Box 149, 25 April 1974, VP

101 C294, *Don Lane Show*, PAC

102 *Evening Standard*, January 11 1974

103 Box 33, Folder 6, undated cutting, VP

104 *New York Times*, June 26 1975

105 JS/65/4, November 24 1974, JS

106 unknown cutting

107 *Evening Standard* June 20 1975
108 Ibid
109 undated cutting, unknown Sydney newspaper
110 undated cutting, CB folder, Theatre Museum
111 JS/65/4 November 24, 1974, JS
112 Marshall, Peter and Adrienne Armstrong, *Backstage With the Original Hollywood Square*, Rutledge Hill Press, Tennessee, 2002, p83
113 B54, Folder 9, letter to VP, October 1 1991, VP
114 author interview
115 http://uk.tv.yahoo.com/001101/128/anxhb.html, accessed 16 April 2004
116 *USA Weekend,* October 25–7 1985
117 *TV Times*, March 11–18 1988
118 author interview
119 author interview
120 author interview
121 author interview
122 undated, 1980 Box 3 Folder 5, VP
123 FBP Box 51.2 CB to FB February 5 1975
124 Folder 2, VP
125 correspondence with author
126 FBP Box 51.2 CB to FB undated 1974
127 Box 3 Folder 5, undated letter 1977, VP
128 author interview
129 letter to VP, January 21 1984, File 3, Box 44, VP
130 Ibid
131 Ibid
132 undated, Letters 1994.95, 1 B 17, PAC
133 letter to AG May 13 1984
134 author interview
135 author interview
136 April 27 1977, FB Box 51

137 Everett, Rupert, *Red Carpets and Other Banana Skins*, Little, Brown, 2006, p155/6
138 *Vanity Fair*, December 1998
139 Everett, Rupert, *Red Carpets and Other Banana Skins*, Little, Brown, 2006, p177
140 *Vanity Fair*, December 1998
141 JS/65/4 August 1978, JS
142 FBP Box 51.2 CB to FB undated 1974
143 Price, Victoria, *Vincent Price: A Daughter's Biography*, Sidgwick & Jackson, 2000, p398
144 Ibid, p466
145 author interview
146 *Women's Wear Daily*, February 19 1986
147 *Independent*, May 11 2005
148 Ibid
149 *Independent on Sunday*, October 10 2004
150 *Observer Weekend*, May 2006
151 Guinness, Alec, *My Name Escapes Me*, Viking, 1996, p112
152 author interview
153 author interview
154 author interview
155 author interview
156 author interview
157 *The Advocate*, November 9 1999
158 Price, Victoria, *Vincent Price: A Daughter's Biography*, Sidgwick & Jackson, 2000, p383
159 http://uk.tv.yahoo.com/001101/128/anxhb.html, accessed 16 April 2004
160 author interview
161 author interview
162 *The Advocate*, November 9 1999
163 author interview
164 author interview
165 author interview
166 author interview
167 author interview

168 author correspondence, Kevin Scullin
169 *The Times*, November 14 1983
170 http://www.moviecrazed.com/outpast/heston.html
171 Heston, Charlton, *In the Arena*, HarperCollins, 1995, p481
172 Morley, Sheridan, *Asking for Trouble*, Hodder & Stoughton, 2002, p184
173 author interview
174 Box 149: November 25, 1974, VP
175 author interview
176 FBP Box 51.2 CB to FB undated 1974
177 FBP, CB letter to Robert Whitehead October 4 1974
178 FBP Box 51.2 CB to FB undated
179 author interview
180 Cable from CB to VP from London: January 6 1975
181 author interview
182 *Evening Standard* June 20 1975
183 author interview
184 FBP Box 51.2 undated letter CB to FB
185 FBP Box 51.2 CB to FB December 10 1974
186 *Evening Standard* June 20 1975
187 *The Times*, April 28 1975
188 author interview
189 *Evening Standard* June 20 1975
190 *Daily Express*, June 19 1975
191 *Evening Standard*, undated, 1975
192 *Daily Mirror*, undated, 1975
193 *The Times*, June 19 1975
194 Ibid
195 *Observer*, June 22 1975
196 Ibid
197 *Punch*, June 15 1975
198 author interview
199 *Evening Argus*, June 3 1975

200 *Daily Telegraph* August 11 1975

201 undated cutting, *Standard*, VP

202 Box 35 Folder 3: Christmas card from Charles Gray, 1976, VP

203 *Evening Standard*, September 30, 1975

204 http://goinguphill.blogspot.com/

205 *Washington Star*, November 6 1977

206 author correspondence, Kevin Scullin

207 *Pittsburgh Press*, June 1 1976

208 undated, *Post-Gazette*

209 JS/65/4 8 June 1976, JS

210 *News-Press*, March 3 1977

211 Ibid

212 Ibid

213 author interview

214 *Los Angeles Herald-Examiner*, February 28 1977

215 letter to CCT, February 1987

216 undated, *New West*

217 *Variety*, February 2 1977

218 *LA Times*, January 31 1977

219 undated, *Free Press*

220 undated, *LA Times*

221 *Hollywood Reporter*, January 28 1977

222 undated letter to VP, Box 3 Folder 5, VP

223 *LA Herald-Examiner*, February 28 1977

224 Williams, Lucy Chase, *The Complete Films of Vincent Price*, Citadel Press Book, New Jersey, 1998, p46

225 undated cuttings, VP

226 *New York Times*, April 13 1978

227 *Westchester Rockland Newspapers*, May 10 1978

228 undated letter, Box 3, Folder 5, VP

229 C294, CB ABC and *Don Lane Show*, PAC

230 JS/65/4 to JS 29 Nov 77, JS

231 *Daily Telegraph*, October 27 1993

232 CB to FB Box 51.2 April 27 1977, FBP

233 JS/65/4 undated to JS, JS

234 author interview

235 Box 3 Folder 5, September 29 1977, VP

236 undated, Box 3 Folder 5, VP

237 Box 3 Folder 5, September 26 1977, VP

238 Box 3 Folder 5, September 28 1977/September 19 1977, VP

239 Box 3 Folder 5, September 26 1977, VP

240 Box 3 Folder 5, September 28 1977/September 19 1977, VP

241 Box 3 Folder 5, undated, 1977, VP

242 Box 3 Folder 5, undated, 1977, VP/September 28 1977, VP

243 Box 3 Folder 5, undated, 1977, VP

244 Ibid

245 author interview

246 letter to AG, January 17 1978

247 Ibid

248 JS/65/4 to JS August 1978, JS

249 Anderson, Lindsay, ed Paul Sutton, *The Diaries*, Methuen, 2004, p452

250 *News-Press*, March 3 1978

251 author interview

252 To CB, June 16 1978, Letters 1994.95 1 B 17, PAC

253 To CB, July 22 1978, Letters 1994.95 1 B 17, PAC

254 To CB, August 1 1978, Letters 1994.95 1 B 17, PAC

255 JS/65/4 to JS August 1978, JS

256 LH to CB, January 20 1979, Letters 1994.95 1 B 17, PAC

257 May 10 1978, *Westchester Rockland Newspapers*

258 FBP Box 51.2 April 25 1977, FBP

'Unless a Job Comes for Coral'

1 author interview

2 *Evening Standard*, April 20 1984

3 letter to AG, August 1979

4 *Daily Telegraph*, August 6 2001

5 letter to AG, April 28 1980

6 Ibid

7 Tape C34, oral history collection: interview with Frank Van Straten, PAC

8 Ibid

9 C294, CB ABC and *Don Lane Show*, PAC

10 *Time Express* promotional material, Box 189, VP

11 Ibid

12 Ibid

13 *Times-Picayune*, April 29 1979

14 letter, April 26 1979, VP BOX 189, VP

15 letter, May 11 1979, VP BOX 189, VP

16 Box 154, Folder 1, VP

17 letter to AG, February 20 1981

18 letter to AG, April 28 1980

19 letter to AG, April 28 1980

20 Ibid

21 author interview

22 *Evening Standard*, April 20 1984

23 www.clivejames.com, *New Yorker*, 23 March 1987

24 Marr, David, ed, *Patrick White Letters*, Jonathan Cape, 2004, p480

25 *Evening Standard*, April 20 1984

26 C295, ABC July 28 1980, PAC

27 Box 3 Folder 5, September 1980, VP

28 Ibid

29 April 27 1977, FB Box 51, FBP

30   letter to AG, February 20 1981

31   letter to CC-T, January 2 1985

32   letter to AG, February 20 1981

33   Ibid

34   Ibid

35   Bennett, Alan, *Writing Home*, Faber & Faber, 1994, p118

36   letter to AG, December 1981

37   B.44 Folder 6, April 9 1984, VP

38   CB to FB, FBP Box 5.12 October 1979, FBP

39   letter to AG, January 7 1992

40   Price, Victoria, *Vincent Price: A Daughter's Biography*, Sidgwick & Jackson, 2000, p412

41   letter to AG, January 7 1982

42   letter to Caroline Cornish Trestrail c/o JS: March 1982, JS/65/4, JS

43   author interview

44   author interview

45   *Radio Times*, November 26 1983

46   BFI, JRS/22/5, JS

47   BFI, JRS/22/5, JS

48   BFI, JRS/22/5, letter to Charles Gray, December 23 1982, JS

49   *Radio Times*, November 26 1983

50   letter to AG, February 14 1982

51   Mann, William J, *Edge of Midnight: The Life of John Schlesinger*, Hutchinson 2004

52   *Radio Times*, November 26 1983

53   Box 3 Folder 5, August 28 1982, VP

54   Ibid

55   Ibid

56   Box 3 Folder 5, September 1 1982, VP

57   *Caviar for the General*, Channel 4, December 23 1990

58   Box 3 Folder 6, January 7 1983, VP

59   Ibid

60   JRS/22/5, letter to JS October 1982, JS

61   undated letter, Box 3, Folder 5, VP

62   Ibid

63   January 18 1983, Box 3 Folder 6, VP

64   author interview

65   author interview

66   letter to VP, January 31 1983, Box 2 Folder 7 VP

67   undated letter Box 3 Folder 6, VP

68   Ibid

69   Box 3 Folder 6, January 7 1983, VP

70   Card Box 3 Folder 6, February 2 1983, VP

71   Bennett, Alan, *Writing Home*, Faber & Faber, 1994, p212

72   Ibid, p213

73   AB to AG, undated

74   AB to AG, undated, 1983

75   Box 3 Folder 6, undated 1983, VP

76   To RMcD, *Double Exposure*, 10 May 1988 by JS

77   Box 3 Folder 6, undated 1983, VP

78   Ibid

79   1994/95/505, 1 B 17 PAC

80   Box 42 Folder 6, February 1 1983, VP

81   Box 3 Folder 6, February 25, 1983, VP

82   *Observer*, March 6 1983

83   box 44 Folder 2: card from AB to CB at Fitzroy-Nuffield Hospital, Bryanston Sq, 3 March 1983, VP

84   author interview

85   JS/65/4 28 June 1973, JS

86   BFI, JRS/22/5, letter August 1983, JS

87   Ibid

88   *Glasgow Herald*, November 28 1983

89   card, October 28 1983, to CC-T

90   *Glasgow Herald*, November 28 1983

91   *Variety*, October 10 1984

92   *Glasgow Herald*, November 28 1983

93   *New York Times*, October 26 1984

94   *The Times*, December 1 1983

95   *Daily Telegraph* December 4 1983

96   *Observer*, December 4 1983

97   *Guardian*, November 30 1983

98   Bergan, Ronald, *Beyond the Fringe...and Beyond*, Virgin Books, 1989, p182

99   Anderson, Lindsay, ed Paul Sutton, *The Diaries*, Methuen, 2004, p423

100 author interview

101 *The Times*, November 25 1983

102 author interview

103 author interview

104 *Caviar for the General*, Channel 4, December 23 1990

Curtain Calls

1   letter to AG, February 25 1984

2   Williams, Lucy Chase, *The Complete Films of Vincent Price*, Citadel Press Book, New Jersey, 1998, p50

3   author interview

4   letter to AG, March 29 1984

5   letter to AG, April 30 1984

6   letter to AG, April 30 1984

7   JS/65/4 TO CCT, 24 February 1985, JS

8   *Hollywood Reporter*, October 6 1983

9   JRS/22/5, letter to JS November 4 1984, JS

10 *New York Times*, November 2 1984

11 JRS/22/5, letter to JS November 4 1984, JS

12   author interview

13   *New York Times*, October 4 1985

14   *New York Times*, May 8 1932

15   author interview

16   undated cutting, unknown

17   author interview

18   author interview

19   *Evening Standard*, April 10 1984

20   *New York Times*, April 30 1932

21   *Women's Wear Daily*, February 19 1986

22   author interview

23   letter to AG, March 29 1984

24   letter to AG, February 20 1981

25   *Evening Standard*, July 20 1984

26   *Evening Standard*, July 20 1984

27   undated cutting

28   author interview

29   author interview

30   author interview

31   author interview

32   author interview

33   Box 1 B 11, PAC, from Dennis Potter, August 10 1984

34   BOX 151, Folder 4, letter to George Koch, Bahama Cruise Line, September 1985, VP

35   letter to AG, January 17 1978

36   *New York Times*, October 4 1985

37   *Boston Globe*, January 31 1986

38   *Pacific Sun*, January 3-9 1986

39   *New Yorker*, October 21 1985

40   *LA Herald-Examiner*, November 29 1985

41   author interview

42   *Women's Wear Daily*, February 19 1986

43   *Saturday Review*, Aug/Sep 1986

44   undated cutting, publication unknown

45   Box 1 B 11, PAC, Thorn EMI memo, January 10 1986

46   *LA Reader*, undated

47   *Photoplay*, February 1986

48   *Sunday Telegraph*, January 26 1986

49   *The Times* January 24 1986

50   *Daily Mail*, January 24 1986

51   *New York Times*, November 25 1985

52   *People Weekly*, February 3 1986

53   *LA Herald-Examiner*, undated

54   *Women's Wear Daily*, February 19 1986

55   author interview

56   *New York Times*, January 24 1986

57   Box 3 Folder 6, undated, VP

58   www.alanbates.com

59   Billington, Michael, *Peggy Ashcroft*, John Murray Ltd, 1988, p277

60   correspondence with author

61   Mann, William J, *Edge of Midnight: The Life of John Schlesinger*, Hutchinson 2004, p346/7

62   *LA Times*, June 8 1991

63   Box 46, F2, JA to CB January 9 1985, VP

64   *Women's Wear Daily*, February 19 1986

65   author interview

66   undated note, Box 35, File 4 VP

67   JS/65/4 26 June 1986, JS

68   Anderson, Lindsay, ed Paul Sutton, *The Diaries*, Methuen, 2004, p452

69   *Parade Magazine* interview, May 1 1988

70   Anderson, Lindsay, ed Paul Sutton, *The Diaries*, Methuen, 2004, p452

71   *Variety*, January 1 1987

72   *Movie Magazine*, November 20 1987

73   *Chicago Sun-Times*, November 13 1987

74   correspondence with author

75   correspondence with author

76   letter to CCT, July 3 1987

77   *LA Times*, June 8 1991

78   letter to CCT, February 13 1987

79   letter to CCT, July 3 1987

80   author interview

81   JS/65/4 August 4 1987, JS

82   *LA Times*, August 20 1987

83   *The Widow's Tale*, BBC2, May 15 2007

84   Rivers, Joan, *Still Talking*, www.coralbrowne.com

85   JS/65/4 March 1988, JS

86   JS/65/4, June 14 1988, JS

87   JS/65/4, June 14 1988, JS

88   JS/65/4 undated card, JS

89   JS/65/4 November 1 1988, JS

90   *Pacific Sun*, October 28 1988

91   author interview

92   author interview/*The Times*, June 10 1989

93   *Evening Standard*, December 9, 1988

94   *Caviar for the General*, Channel 4, December 23 1990

95   author interview

96   Bennett, Alan, *Untold Stories*, Faber & Faber/Profile Books, 2005, p267

97   *Observer*, December 4 1989

98   *Standard*, December 2 1988

99   *Daily Telegraph*, December 3 1988

100 author interview

101 Bennett, Alan, *Writing Home*, Faber & Faber, 1994, p185

102 *Daily Telegraph*, November 13 1989

103 letter to AG, January 18 1990

104 card to AG, August 26 1990

105 letter from AG to Coral, Xmas Eve, Letters 1994.95, 1 B 17, PAC

106 letter to AG, January 18 1990
107 Ibid
108 Ibid
109 JS/65/4 8 Mar 1990, JS
110 letter to AG, January 18 1990
111 *Daily Mail*, 31 October 1996
112 April 30 1991, Letters 1994.95, 1 B 17, PAC
113 Marr, David, ed, *Patrick White Letters*, Jonathan Cape, 2004, p622
114 card to AG, August 26 1990
115 letter to AG, July 16 1990
116 1990 Diary, 1994.95 PAC
117 CB to VP, November 11 90 1994.95.276, 1 B 10, PAC
118 letter to AG, July 15 1990
119 note to AG, September 8 1990
120 author interview
121 VP to Alec & Merula Guinness, undated, 1991
122 *LA Times*, May 30 1991

123 May 17 1991, Letters 1994.95 1 B 17 PAC
124 *LA Times*, June 8 1991
125 *The Times*, May 31 1991
126 *Daily Telegraph*, May 31 1991
127 www.alanbates.com
128 Letters 1994.95.171 May 29 1991 1 B 17 PAC
129 *Mail/Advertiser*, August 7 1991
130 *The Age*, November 23 1991
131 correspondence with author
132 Price, Victoria, *Vincent Price: A Daughter's Biography*, Sidgwick & Jackson, 2000, p438
133 Masek, Mark J, *Hollywood Remains To Be Seen*, Cumberland House, Tennessee, 2001, p106
134 JS/65/4/ undated, JS
135 author interview
136 author interview
137 *Woman's Journal*, November 1973

138 author interview
139 correspondence with author
140 www.tv.com
141 VP to JS, undated, 1991, JS
142 JS/65/4/ undated, 1991, JS
143 author interview
144 author interview
145 letter to AG, April 30 1984
146 letter to AG, July 15 1990
147 Box 54 Folder 8: card from RMcD: 30 Sep 1991, VP
148 author interview
149 www.ffolio.com/abarchive/tv/coral.html

Epilogue

1 *The Advocate*, November 9 1999
2 undated cutting, VP Box 213, VP
3 *Daily Telegraph*, October 27 1993
4 JS/65/4, JS

Performance History

STAGE
(Play, venue, opening date and role)

Australia

You Never Can Tell, Garrick, Melbourne, September 3 1930, Gloria

The Roof, Comedy, Melbourne, March 24 1931, Nell

Loyalties, Comedy, May 2–22 1931, Margaret Orme

The Calendar, Comedy, May 23 – June 4 1931, Wenda Panniford

The Calendar, Theatre Royal, Sydney, June 13 to July 10 1931

My Lady's Dress, Theatre Royal, Sydney, July 11–24 1931, Lize

A Warm Corner, Her Majesty's Sydney, July 25 – August 7 1931, Mimi

A Warm Corner, Royal Adelaide, August 15–21 1931

Hay Fever, Theatre Royal Adelaide, August 22–26 1931, Myra Arundel

A Warm Corner, Comedy, August 29 – September 11 1931

My Lady's Dress, Comedy, September 12–25 1931

Cape Forlorn, Comedy, September 26 to October 7 1931, Eileen Kell

Let Us Be Gay, Criterion Sydney December 5-19 1931, Madge

Let Us Be Gay, His Majesty's Brisbane, February 27 – March 4 1932

The First Mrs Fraser, His Majesty's Brisbane, Mar 5–12 1932, Murdo Fraser

Take Two From One, Comedy, December 7–11 1932, Diana

Topaze, Comedy, December 24 1932 – January 1 1933, Suzy

Autumn Crocus, Criterion, January 10–17 1933, Jenny Gray

The Command to Love, Criterion, February 4–11 1933, Manuela

The Command to Love, Royal, Mar 25 – April 8 1933

The Quaker Girl, Royal, July 22 – September 13 1933, Diane

The Apple Cart, Garrick, October 9–13 1933, Orinthia

Children in Uniform, Garrick, October 14 – November 10 1933, Fraulein von Bernberg

Hedda Gabler, Garrick, December 2–6 1933, Hedda

Dear Brutus, Garrick, December 26 1933 – 19 January 1934, Mrs Dearth

Musical Chairs, Garrick January 20 – February 3 1934, Irene Baumer

Out of the Sea, Garrick, April 14–18 1934, Isobel

Children in Uniform, Palace, Melbourne, April 28 – May 4 1934, Fraulein von Bernberg

England

Lover's Leap, Vaudeville, October 15 1934 Helen Storer (as understudy to Nora Swinburne and Ursula Jeans)

Mated, Arts, February 7 1935, Concordia

Basalik, Arts, April 7 1935, Lady Amerdine

This Desirable Residence, Embassy Swiss Cottage, May 27 1935, Mary Penshott

The Golden Gander, Embassy January 6 1936, Victoria

The Happy Medium, Savoy, May 3 1936, Freda Westerham

Heroes Don't Care, Vaudeville, June 10 1936, Connie Crawford

Death Asks a Verdict, Royalty, December 13 1936, Lydia Latimer

The Taming of the Shrew, New, March 23 1937, The Widow (and understudy to Edith Evans)

The Great Romancer, Strand, May 9 1937, then New, June 15 1937, Ida Ferrier

The Gusher, Princes, July 31 1937, Jacqueline

Emperor of the World, Strand, March 19 1939, Poppaea

Believe it or Not, New, January 23 1940, Madeleine

The Man Who Came to Dinner, Savoy, December 4 1941, Maggie Cutler

My Sister Eileen, Savoy, September 22 1943, Ruth Sherwood,

The Last of Mrs Cheyney, Savoy, June 15 1944, Mrs Cheyney

Lady Frederick, Savoy, November 21 1946, Lady Frederick Berolles

Canaries Sometimes Sing, Garrick, November 18 1947, Elma Melton

Jonathan, Aldwych, July 29 1947, Bathsheba

Castle in the Air, Adelphi, December 7 1949, then Savoy May 28 1950, "Boss" Trent

Othello, Old Vic, October 31 1951, Emilia

King Lear, Old Vic, March 3 1952, Regan

Affairs of State, Cambridge, August 21 1952, Constance Russell

Simon and Laura, Strand, November 25 1954, then Apollo February 14 1955, Laura Foster

Nina, Haymarket, July 27 1955, Nina Tessier

Macbeth, Old Vic, May 22 1956, Lady Macbeth

Hamlet, Old Vic, September 18 1957, Gertrude

A Midsummer Night's Dream, Old Vic, December 23 1957, Helena

King Lear, Old Vic, February 19 1958, Goneril

The Pleasure of His Company, Haymarket, April 23 1959, Katherine Dougherty

Toys in the Attic, Piccadilly Theatre, November 10 1960, Albertine Prine

Bonne Soupe, Comedy, October 23 1961, Marie Paule

The Rehearsal, Theatre Royal Brighton, August 1963, The Countess

The Right Honourable Gentleman, Her Majesty's, May 28 1964, Mrs Rossiter

Lady Windermere's Fan, Phoenix Theatre, October 13 1966, Mrs Erlynne

What the Butler Saw, Queen's, March 5 1969, Mrs Prentice

My Darling Daisy, Lyric Theatre, June 22 1970, Lady Warwick

Mrs Warren's Profession, Old Vic, December 30 1970, Kitty Warren

The Sea, Royal Court, May 22 1973, Louise Rafi

Waltz of the Toreadors, Haymarket, February 14 1974, Madame St Pé

Ardèle, Queen's, June 18 1975, The Countess

USA

Tamburlaine the Great, Winter Garden, New York, January 19 1956, Zabina

Macbeth, Winter Garden, New York, October 29 1956, Lady Macbeth

Troilus and Cressida, Winter Garden, New York, December 26 1956, Helen Of Troy

The Rehearsal, Royale Theater New York, September 23 1963, The Countess

The Right Honourable Gentleman, Billy Rose Theater New York, October 19 1965, Mrs Rossiter

Charley's Aunt, Cirque Dinner Theater, Seattle, August 12 1975/Granny's Dinner Theater, Dallas, March 16 1976, then tour starting in Ann Arbor May 5 1976, ending in Milwaukee, June 26 1976, Donna Lucia d'Alvadorez

The Importance of Being Earnest/Travesties, Mark Taper Forum, Los Angeles January 27 1977, Lady Bracknell/Nadya Lenin

FILM
(Title, year, character)

Waltzing Matilda, 1933, uncredited, Australia

Charing Cross Road, 1935, Lady Ruston

Line Engaged, 1935, Doreen

Guilty Melody, 1936, Cecile

The Amateur Gentleman, 1936, Pauline Darville

Black Limelight, 1938, Lily James

Yellow Sands, 1938, Emma Copplestone

Alert in the Mediterranean/On Guard in the Mediterranean, 1938, uncredited

We're Going to Be Rich, 1938, Pearl

The Nursemaid Who Disappeared, 1939, Mabel Barnes

21 Days aka *The First and the Last*, 1940, uncredited

Let George Do It, 1940, Iris

They Came By Night, 1940, uncredited

Piccadilly Incident, 1946, Virginia Pearson

The Courtneys of Curzon Street, 1947, Valerie

Beautiful Stranger, 1954, Helen

Auntie Mame, 1958, Vera Charles

The Roman Spring of Mrs Stone, 1961, Meg

Dr Crippen, 1962, Belle Elmore Crippen

Go to Blazes, 1962, Colette

Tamahine, 1963, Mme. Becque

The Night of the Generals, 1967, Eleanore von Seidlitz-Gabler

The Legend of Lylah Clare, 1968, Molly Luther

The Killing of Sister George, 1969, Mercy Croft

The Ruling Class, 1972, Lady Claire Gurney

Theater of Blood, 1973, Chloe Moon

The Drowning Pool, 1975, Olivia Devereaux

Xanadu, 1980, Female Heavenly Voice

American Dreamer, 1984, Margaret McMann

Dreamchild, 1985, Alice Hargreaves

Sparky's Magic Piano, 1987, Voice

TELEVISION
(Title, broadcast date, producer/channel, character)

Television Playhouse: The Guv'nor, BBC, January 19 1956, Amanda Pinkerton

Television Playhouse: Castle in the Air, ITA, June 15 1956, 'Boss' Trent

Close Up On: Comedy, ITV April 2 1959, self

That Was The Week That Was, March 30 1963, self

Charley's Aunt, November 23 1969, BBC1, Donna Lucia

On Reflection: Coral Browne on Mrs Patrick Campbell, February 13 1971, LWT (herself)

Stage 2: Mrs Warren's Profession, October 3 1972, BBC2, Kitty Warren

Lady Windermere's Fan, May 14 1972, BBC1, Mrs Erlynne

The Importance of Being Earnest, February 17 1974, BBC1, Lady Bracknell

Time Express, April 26 1979, CBS, Margaret

Eleanor, First Lady of the World, released May 12 1982, Lady Stella Reading

Harty, October 12 1983, self

An Englishman Abroad, November 29 1983, Coral Browne (character)

Wogan, January 27 1986, BBC1, self

Caviar for the General, Channel 4 December 23 1990, self

RADIO
(Selected: title, broadcast date, producer/ channel, character)

Dinner At Eight, date unknown

Bringing Home the Bacon, 19 Oct 1945, BBC Light Service

Man About Town, June-August 1955, BBC Home Service

Othello, February 27 1956, BBC Home Service

The Infernal Machine, November 23 1960, BBC Third

Hamlet, October 23 1960, BBC Third

Captain Brassbound's Conversion, December 17 1961, BBC Third

Carrington VC, June 11 1962, BBC Third

Oedipus the King, March 28 1968, Radio 3

The Cat Game, July 31 1973, Radio 3

Night of the Wolf, August 11 1975, Radio 4

The Price of Fear, 6 September 1975, Radio 4

Bibliography

All books published in London, unless otherwise stated.

Agate, James, *Ego 3*, George G Harrap Ltd, 1938

Agate, James, *Ego 5*, George G Harrap Ltd, 1942

Agate, James, *Ego 6*, George G Harrap Ltd, 1944

Agate, James, *Ego 7*, George G Harrap Ltd, 1945

Agate, James, *Ego 8*, George G Harrap Ltd, 1946

Agate, James, *Ego 9*, George G Harrap Ltd, 1948

Anderson, Lindsay, ed Paul Sutton, *The Diaries*, Methuen, 2004

Bate, Jonathan and Jackson, Russell, eds, *Shakespeare: An Illustrated Stage History*, Oxford University Press, 1996

Barrow, Andrew, *Gossip: A History of Society from 1920 to 1970*, Hamish Hamilton, 1978

Beaton, Cecil, *Beaton in the Sixties*, Weidenfeld & Nicolson, 2003

Behr, Edward, *Thank Heaven for Little Girls*, Hutchinson, 1993

Bennett, Alan, *Writing Home*, Faber & Faber, 1994

Bennett, Alan, *Untold Stories*, Faber & Faber/Profile Books, 2005

Bennett, Jill & Goodwin, Suzanne, *Godfrey: A Special Time Remembered*, Hodder & Stoughton, 1983

Beresford, Jack Fowler, *Stars in my Backyard*, Arthur H Stockwell, Ilfracombe, 1962

Bergan, Ronald, *Beyond the Fringe…and Beyond*, Virgin Books, 1989

Billington, Michael, *Peggy Ashcroft*, John Murray Ltd, 1988

Blundell, Graeme, *Australian Theatre*, Oxford University Press, 1997

Bourne, Stephen, *Brief Encounters*, Cassell, 1996

Boyle, Andrew, *The Climate of Treason*, Hutchinson, 1979

Boyle, Sheila Tully and Bunie, Andrew, *Paul Robeson: The Years of Promise and Achievement*, University of Massachusetts Press, 2001

Brandreth, Gyles, *Brief Encounters*, Politico's Publishing, 2001

Bryan, Dora, *According to Dora*, Bodley Head, 1987

Burton, Peter, *Parallel Lives*, GMP, 1985

Burton, Peter, *Talking to…* Third House, Exeter, 1991

Buruma, Ian, *Conversations with John Schlesinger*, Randon House, NY, 2006

Caldwell, Zoe, *I Will Be Cleopatra*, WW Norton, 2001

Callow, Simon, *The National*, Nick Hern Books, 1997

Capua, Michaelangelo, *Vivien Leigh*, McFarland & Co, North Carolina, 2003

Carpenter, Humphrey, *The Angry Young Men*, Allen Lane, 2002

Carter-Ruck, Peter, *Memoirs of a Libel Lawyer*, Weidenfeld & Nicolson, 1990

Chambers, Colin, *Peggy: The Life of Margaret Ramsay, Play Agent*, Nick Hern Books, 1997

Clark, Anne, *The Real Alice: Lewis Carroll's Dream Child*, Michael Joseph, 1981

Connon, Bryan, *Somerset Maugham & the Maugham Dynasty*, Sinclair-Stevenson, 1997

Consodine, Shaun, *Bette & Joan: The Divine Feud*, Sphere Books, 1990

Costello, John, *Mask of Treachery*, Pan, 1989

Coveney, Michael, *Maggie Smith, A Bright Particular Star*, Gollancz 1992

Crisp, Quentin, *How to Have A Lifestyle*, Cecil Woolf, 1975

Davies, Russell, ed, *The Kenneth Williams Diaries*, HarperCollins, 1994

Davies, Russell, ed, *The Kenneth Williams Letters*, HarperCollins, 1995

Dorril, Stephen & Summers, Anthony, *Honeytrap: The Scandal*, Weidenfeld and Nicolson, 1987

Driberg, Tom, *Guy Burgess: A Portrait with Background*, Weidenfeld and Nicolson, 1956

Driberg, Tom, *Ruling Passions*, Quartet Books, 1978

Duberman, Martin Bauml, *Paul Robeson*, Ballantine Books, NY, 1989

Edwards, Anne, *Vivien Leigh*, WH Allen, 1977

Elsom, John, *Post-War British Theatre*, Routledge & Kegan Paul, 1976

Evans, David & Michaels, Scott, *Rocky Horror: From Concept to Cult*, Sanctuary Publishing, 2002

Everett, Rupert, *Red Carpets and Other Banana Skins*, Little, Brown, 2006

Fairbanks Jr, Douglas, *The Salad Days*, Collins 1988

Fitton, Doris, *Not Without Heat and Dust*, Harper & Row, 1981

Forbes, Bryan, *Ned's Girl: The Life of Edith Evans*, Elm Tree Books, 1977

Gallati, Mario, *Mario of the Caprice*, Hutchinson, 1960

Gale, Maggie B, *West End Women*, Routledge, 1996

Gardiner, Jill, *From the Closet to the Screen*, Pandora Press, 2003

Garland, Patrick, *The Incomparable Rex*, Macmillan, 1998

Guinness, Alec, *Blessings in Disguise*, Penguin 1997

Guinness, Alec, *My Name Escapes Me*, Viking, 1996

Guinness, Alec, *A Positively Final Appearance*, Penguin Books, 2000

Guthrie, Tyrone, *A Life in the Theatre*, Readers' Union, 1959

Hadleigh, Boze, *Hollywood Lesbians*, Barricade Books NY, 1994

Harris, Radie, *Radie's World*, WH Allen, 1975

Harrison, Rex, *Rex: An Autobiography*, William Morrow & Company, NY, 1974

Harryhausen, Ray and Dalton, Tony, *Ray Harryhausen: An Animated Life*, Billboard Books, 2004

Harwood, Ronald, ed, *Dear Alec: Guinness at 75*, Hodder & Stoughton, 1989

Hastings, Selina, *Rosamond Lehmann*, Chatto & Windus, 2002

Hayward, Anthony, *Julie Christie*, Robert Hale, 2000

Heilpern, John, *John Osborne: A Patriot for Us*, Chatto & Windus, 2006

Herbert, Ian, ed, *Dramatic List — Who's Who in the Theatre 1939–77*, Pitman, 1984

Heston, Charlton, *In the Arena*, HarperCollins, 1995

Hoare, Philip, *Noël Coward*, Mandarin 1995

Holm, Ian, *Acting my Life*, Transworld 2004

Hordern, Michael, *A World Elsewhere*, Michael O'Mara Books Ltd, 1993

Hout, Edwin P, *Paul Robeson*, Cassell, 1968

Huggett, Richard, *Binkie Beaumont*, Hodder & Stoughton, 1989

Humphries, Barry, *More Please*, Viking, 1992

Humphries, Barry, *My Life as Me*, Michael Joseph 2002

Huth, Angela, ed, *Well-Remembered Friends*, John Murray, 2004

Jackson, Stanley, *The Savoy*, Frederick Muller Ltd, 1964

Johns, Eric, ed, *British Theatre Review 1974*, Vance-Offord Publications Ltd, Eastbourne 1975

Kael, Pauline, *Going Steady*, Temple Smith 1970

Kempson, Rachel, *A Family & Its Fortunes*, Duckworth, 1986

Korzelinski, Seweryn, *Memoirs of Gold-Digging in Melbourne*, University of Queensland Press, St Lucia, 1979

Kustow, Michael, *Peter Brook: a Biography*, Bloomsbury, 2005

Lahr, John, *Prick Up Your Ears*, Allen Lane, 1978

Lahr, John, ed, *The Orton Diaries*, Minerva, 1989

Lambert, Gavin, *Mainly About Lindsay Anderson*, Faber & Faber, 2000

Larson, Erik, *Thunderstruck*, Doubleday, 2006

Lees-Milne, Alvida and Moore, Derry, *The Englishwoman's Home*, Collins, 1984

Lewenstein, Oscar, *Kicking Against the Pricks*, Nick Hern Books, 1994

Lobenthal, Joel, *Tallulah! The Life and Times of a Leading Lady*, Aurum Press Ltd, 2004

Love, Harold, ed, *The Australian Stage*, NSW University Press, 1984

McCann, Graham, *Frankie Howerd: Stand Up Comic*, Harper Perennial, 2005

McCrindle, Joseph F, ed, *Behind the Scenes: Theater and Film Interviews from the Transatlantic Review*, Holt, Rinehart & Winston, NY, 1971

Macintyre, Stuart, *Concise History of Australia*, Cambridge University Press, 2004

Mangan, Richard, ed, *Gielgud's Letters*, Phoenix, 2005

Mann, William J, *Edge of Midnight: The Life of John Schlesinger*, Hutchinson 2004

Marr, David, ed, *Patrick White Letters*, Jonathan Cape, 2004

Marshall, Arthur, *Life's Rich Pageant*, Hamish Hamilton, 1984

Marshall, Michael, *Top Hat and Tails*, Elm Tree Books, 1978

Marshall, Peter and Adrienne Armstrong, *Backstage With The Original Hollywood Square*, Rutledge Hill Press, Tennessee, 2002

Masek, Mark J, *Hollywood Remains to Be Seen*, Cumberland House, Tennessee, 2001

Massey, Anna, *Telling Some Tales*, Hutchinson, 2006

Melville, Alan, *Merely Melville*, Hodder & Stoughton, 1970

Miller, Eugene L Jnr and Arnold, Edwin T, *The Films and Career of Robert Aldrich Interviews*, University Press of Mississippi, 1986

Miller, Eugene L Jnr and Arnold, Edwin T, *Robert Aldrich Interviews*, University Press of Mississippi, 2004

Miller, John, *Judi Dench: With a Crack in Her Voice*, Orion, 1999

Miller, John, *Darling Judi Dench*, Orion, 2004

Mitchell, Leslie, *Leslie Mitchell Reporting*, Hutchinson, 1981

Morley, Sheridan, *Review Copies*, Robson Books, 1974

Morley, Sheridan, *Asking for Trouble*, Hodder & Stoughton, 2002

Morley, Sheridan, *Robert My Father*, Weidenfeld & Nicolson, 1993

Noble, Peter, *Profiles and Personalities*, Brownlee, 1946

Noble, Peter, *British Theatre*, British Yearbooks, 1946

Norman, Barry, *The Movie Greats*, Arrow, 1981

Norman, Barry, *The Film Greats*, Futura, 1985

O'Connor, Garry, *The Secret Woman: A Life of Peggy Ashcroft*, Weidenfeld and Nicolson, 1997

O'Connor, Garry, *Alec Guinness The Unknown*, Sidgwick & Jackson, 2002

Parker, Peter, *Isherwood*, Picador, 2004

Penrose Barrie and Simon Freeman, *Conspiracy of Silence*, Grafton, 1987

Plumb, Gwen, *Plumb Crazy*, Pan Macmillan Australia, 1994

Porter, Hal, *Stars of Australian Stage & Screen*, Angus & Robertson, 1965

Price, Victoria, *Vincent Price: A Daughter's Biography*, Sidgwick & Jackson, 2000

Quayle, Anthony, *A Time to Speak*, Barrie & Jenkins, 1990

Randall, Alan and Ray Seaton, *George Formby*, W H Allen, 1974

Read, Piers Paul, *Alec Guinness*, Pocket Books, 2004

Redgrave, Michael, *In My Mind's Eye*, Weidenfeld & Nicolson, 1983

Redgrave, Vanessa, *An Autobiography*, Hutchinson, 1991

Reeve, Ada, *Take it for a Fact*, William Heinemann Ltd, 1954

Reid, Beryl and Eric Braun, *So Much Love*, Hutchinson, 1984

Richards, Dick, ed, *The Curtain Rises...*, Leslie Frewin, 1966

Robeson, Jr, Paul, *The Undiscovered Paul Robeson*, John Wiley & Sons Inc, 2001

Roberts, Peter, ed, *The Best of Plays and Players Volume One 1953–68*, Methuen, 1988

Roberts, Peter, ed, *The Best of Plays and Players Volume Two 1969–83*, Methuen, 1989

Rossi, Alfred, *Astonish Us in the Morning: Tyrone Guthrie Remembered*, Hutchinson, 1981

Rowell, George, *The Old Vic Theatre — A History*, Cambridge University Press, 1993

Russo, Vito, *The Celluloid Closet*, Harper & Row, 1981

Rutledge, Leigh W, *The Gay Decades*, Plume NY, 1992

Rutledge, Leigh W, *Unnatural Quotations*, Alyson Publications Boston, 1988

Salter, Elizabeth, *Helpmann*, Angus & Robertson, Brighton, 1978

Schanke, Robert A and Marra, Kim, eds, *Passing Performances*, University of Michigan Press, 1998

Shellard, Dominic, *British Theatre Since the War*, Yale University Press, 2000

Sherrin, Ned, *A Small Thing Like an Earthquake*, Weidefeld & Nicolson 1983

Sherrin Ned, *Ned Sherrin's Theatrical Anecdotes*, Virgin Books, 1992

Sherrin Ned, *The Autobiography*, Little, Brown, 2005

Silver, Alain, *Robert Aldrich*, George Prior Publications, 1979

Silver, Alain and Ursini, James, *Whatever Happened to Robert Aldrich? His Life and Films*, Limelight Editions, New York, 1995

Silvester, Christopher, *The Penguin Book of Interviews*, Viking, 1993

Sims, Joan, *High Spirits*, Partridge 2000

Souhami, Diana, *The Trials of Radclyffe Hall*, Weidenfeld & Nicolson, 1998

Souhami, Diana, *Greta & Cecil*, Phoenix Press, 2000

Spanier, Ginette, *It Isn't All Mink*, Collins, 1959

Spoto, Donald, *Lenya: A Life*, Viking, 1989

Spoto, Donald, *Otherwise Engaged: The Life of Alan Bates*, Hutchinson, 2007

Stephens, F, ed, *Theatre World Annual*, 1950

Strachan, Alan, *Secret Dreams*, Weidenfeld & Nicolson, 2004

Terrill, Ross, *The Australians*, Transworld, 1987

Tynan, Kenneth, *Curtains*, Longmans, 1961

Tynan, Kenneth, *A View of the English Stage 1944-63*, Davis-Poynter, 1975

Vickers, Hugo, *Cecil Beaton*, Little, Brown, 1985

Vickers, Hugo, *Loving Garbo*, Pimlico, 1995

Walker, Alexander, *Vivien*, Weidenfeld & Nicolson, 1987

Walker, Alexander, *Fatal Charm: The Life of Rex Harrison*, Orion, 1992

Walker, Alexander, *Hollywood England*, Orion Books, 2005

Wheen, Francis, *Tom Driberg, His Life and Discretions*, Chatto & Windus Ltd, 1990

White, Patrick, *Flaws in the Glass*, Vintage, 1998

Williams, Lucy Chase, *The Complete Films of Vincent Price*, Citadel Press Book, New Jersey, 1998

Williamson, Audrey, *Paul Rogers*, Rockcliff, 1956

Woddis, Carole, ed, *Sheer Bloody Magic: Conversations with Actresses*, Virago, 1991

Woodhouse, Adrian, *Angus McBean, Face-Maker*, Alma Books Ltd, 2006

Wright, Adrian, *John Lehmann: A Pagan Adventure*, Duckworth, 1998

York, Michael, *Travelling Player*, Headline, 1991

Ziegler, Philip, *London At War*, Sinclair Stevenson, 1995

Archives and Collections

The Vincent Price Papers, Manuscripts Division, Library of Congress, Washington DC

The Coral Browne Collection, The Arts Centre, Performing Arts Collection, Melbourne, Victoria

The Frith Banbury Papers, Harry Ransom Humanities Center, University of Texas at Austin, Texas

The John Schlesinger Collection, Special Collections, BFI, London

The Michael Redgrave Collection, Theatre Museum, Victoria & Albert Museum, London

Footscray Historical Society Archives, Footscray, Melbourne

Selected Online Sources

Australian Dictionary of Biography
www.adb.online.anu.edu.au

Oxford Dictionary Of National Biography online
www.oxforddnb.com

garrygillard.net/CoralBrowne/

www.coralbrowne.com

www.roguesandvagabonds.com

Paul Bentley, *Australian Culture 1789–2000*, 1999
www.twf.org.au

www.youtube.com

The Theatre Archive Project, British Library, University of Sheffield and AHRB
www.bl.uk/theatrearchive

National Archives of Australia
www.naa.gov.au/

www.tv.com

Times Digital Archive
infotrac.galegroup.com/itweb

www.seeing-stars.com

www.findagrave.com

International Film Database
www.imdb.com

International Broadway Database
www.ibdb.com

www.open.bbc.co.uk/catalogue

www.screenonline.org.uk

www.nytimes.com

www.alanbates.com/abarchive/tv/coral.html

www.ebay.com

www.thestage.co.uk/stage125

www.screenonline.org.uk

www.museum.vic.gov.au

Sunshine & District Historical Society
www.jeack.com.au/~treaclbk/relatively/shs.htm

www.ancestry.co.uk

Index